KU-468-598

Land Rover Discovery Diesel
Owners Workshop Manual

Martynn Randall

Models covered

Discovery 'Series 2' models with 2.5 litre (2495cc) 5-cylinder TD5 turbo-diesel engine, including special/limited editions

Does NOT cover petrol engine models
Does NOT cover 'Discovery 3' range introduced August 2004

(4606 - 1AR1 - 256)

ABCDE
FGHIJ

© Haynes Publishing 2012

A book in the **Haynes Owners Workshop Manual Series**

ISBN: 978 0 85733 951 5

British Library Cataloguing in Publication Data
A catalogue record for this book is available from the British Library.

Printed in the USA

Haynes Publishing
Sparkford, Yeovil, Somerset BA22 7JJ, England

Haynes North America, Inc
859 Lawrence Drive, Newbury Park, California 91320, USA

Printed using 33-lb Resolute Book 65 4.0 from Resolute Forest Products Calhoun, TN mill. Resolute is a member of World Wildlife Fund's Climate Savers programme committed to significantly reducing GHG emissions. This paper uses 50% less wood fibre than traditional offset. The Calhoun Mill is certified to the following sustainable forest management and chain of custody standards: SFI, PEFC and FSC Controlled Wood.

Contents

LIVING WITH YOUR LAND ROVER DISCOVERY

Introduction	Page	0•4
Safety first!	Page	0•6

Roadside repairs

Introduction	Page	0•7
If your car won't start	Page	0•7
Jump starting	Page	0•8
Identifying leaks	Page	0•9
Wheel changing	Page	0•10
Towing	Page	0•11

Weekly checks

Introduction	Page	0•12
Underbonnet check points	Page	0•12
Engine oil level	Page	0•13
Brake and clutch fluid level	Page	0•14
Screen washer fluid level	Page	0•14
Coolant level	Page	0•15
Power steering/ACE fluid level	Page	0•15
Tyre condition and pressure	Page	0•16
Battery	Page	0•17
Electrical systems	Page	0•18
Wiper blades	Page	0•18

Lubricants and fluids

	Page	0•19

Tyre pressures

	Page	0•19

MAINTENANCE

Routine Maintenance and Servicing	Page	1•1
Maintenance schedule	Page	1•3
Maintenance procedures	Page	1•5

Contents

REPAIRS & OVERHAUL

Engine and Associated Systems

Engine in-car procedures   Page   2A•1
General engine overhaul procedures   Page   2B•1
Cooling, heating and ventilation systems   Page   3•1
Fuel and exhaust systems   Page   4A•1
Emission control systems   Page   4B•1
Engine electrical systems   Page   5•1

Transmission

Clutch   Page   6•1
Manual transmission   Page   7A•1
Automatic transmission   Page   7B•1
Transfer gearbox   Page   7C•1
Propeller shafts   Page   8•1
Front and rear axles   Page   9•1

Brakes and Suspension

Braking system   Page   10•1
Suspension and steering   Page   11•1

Body Equipment

Bodywork and fittings   Page   12•1
Body electrical systems   Page   13•1

Wiring Diagrams

                                                             Page   13•21

REFERENCE

Dimensions and weights   Page   REF•1
Conversion factors   Page   REF•2
Buying spare parts   Page   REF•3
Vehicle identification   Page   REF•4
General repair procedures   Page   REF•5
Jacking and vehicle support   Page   REF•6
Radio/cassette anti-theft system - precautions   Page   REF•6
Tools and working facilities   Page   REF•7
MOT test checks   Page   REF•9
Fault finding   Page   REF•13
Glossary of technical terms   Page   REF•24

Index

                                                             Page   REF•29

The Discovery models covered by this manual were introduced in November 1998. Although a continuation of the existing Discovery range, they were completely redesigned; all aspects of the vehicle have been enhanced, the most significant change was the fitment of Land Rover's own TD5 direct injection turbo diesel engine.

These 5-cylinder engines, incorporated a single overhead camshaft, electronic unit injectors, turbocharger, intercooler and exhaust gas recirculation system, to give the engine class-leading ouput with reduced exhaust emissions, and enhanced refinement. 5-speed manual or 4-speed automatic transmissions were available, with a transfer gearbox to distribute the power to the front and rear axles.

All models have fully-independent front and rear suspension, with anti-roll bars fitted both to the front and rear assemblies. Self-levelling air suspension was available on some models, as was Active Cornering Enhancement (ACE). This system uses hydraulic actuators to limit the amount of body roll during cornering on the road, greatly improving roadholding.

A wide range of standard and optional equipment was available within the Discovery range to suit most tastes, including central locking, electric windows, air conditioning, electric sunroof, anti-lock braking system, electronic brake force distribution, traction control system, hill descent control, and numerous airbags. The models were available with 3 or 5 doors, and 5 or 7 seats.

Provided that regular servicing is carried out in accordance with the manufacturer's recommendations, the Discovery should prove reliable and economical. The engine compartment is well-designed, and most of the items requiring frequent attention are easily accessible.

Your Discovery manual

The aim of this manual is to help you get the best value from your vehicle. It can do so in several ways. It can help you decide what work must be done (even should you choose to get it done by a garage). It will also provide information on routine maintenance and servicing, and give a logical course of action and diagnosis when random faults occur. However, it is hoped that you will use the manual by tackling the work yourself. On simpler jobs it may even be quicker than booking the car into a garage and going there twice, to leave and collect it. Perhaps most important, a lot of money can be saved by avoiding the costs a garage must charge to cover its labour and overheads.

The manual has drawings and descriptions to show the function of the various components so that their layout can be understood. Tasks are described and photographed in a clear step-by-step sequence.

References to the 'left' and 'right' of the vehicle are in the sense of a person in the driver's seat facing forward.

Acknowledgements

Thanks are due to Draper Tools Limited, who provided some of the workshop tools, and to all those people at Sparkford who helped in the production of this manual.

We take great pride in the accuracy of information given in this manual, but vehicle manufacturers make alterations and design changes during the production run of a particular vehicle of which they do not inform us. No liability can be accepted by the authors or publishers for loss, damage or injury caused by any errors in, or omissions from, the information given.

Working on your car can be dangerous. This page shows just some of the potential risks and hazards, with the aim of creating a safety-conscious attitude.

General hazards

Scalding

• Don't remove the radiator or expansion tank cap while the engine is hot.
• Engine oil, automatic transmission fluid or power steering fluid may also be dangerously hot if the engine has recently been running.

Burning

• Beware of burns from the exhaust system and from any part of the engine. Brake discs and drums can also be extremely hot immediately after use.

Crushing

• When working under or near a raised vehicle, always supplement the jack with axle stands, or use drive-on ramps. *Never venture under a car which is only supported by a jack.*
• Take care if loosening or tightening high-torque nuts when the vehicle is on stands. Initial loosening and final tightening should be done with the wheels on the ground.

Fire

• Fuel is highly flammable; fuel vapour is explosive.
• Don't let fuel spill onto a hot engine.
• Do not smoke or allow naked lights (including pilot lights) anywhere near a vehicle being worked on. Also beware of creating sparks (electrically or by use of tools).
• Fuel vapour is heavier than air, so don't work on the fuel system with the vehicle over an inspection pit.
• Another cause of fire is an electrical overload or short-circuit. Take care when repairing or modifying the vehicle wiring.
• Keep a fire extinguisher handy, of a type suitable for use on fuel and electrical fires.

Electric shock

• Ignition HT voltage can be dangerous, especially to people with heart problems or a pacemaker. Don't work on or near the ignition system with the engine running or the ignition switched on.

• Mains voltage is also dangerous. Make sure that any mains-operated equipment is correctly earthed. Mains power points should be protected by a residual current device (RCD) circuit breaker.

Fume or gas intoxication

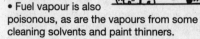

• Exhaust fumes are poisonous; they often contain carbon monoxide, which is rapidly fatal if inhaled. Never run the engine in a confined space such as a garage with the doors shut.
• Fuel vapour is also poisonous, as are the vapours from some cleaning solvents and paint thinners.

Poisonous or irritant substances

• Avoid skin contact with battery acid and with any fuel, fluid or lubricant, especially antifreeze, brake hydraulic fluid and Diesel fuel. Don't syphon them by mouth. If such a substance is swallowed or gets into the eyes, seek medical advice.
• Prolonged contact with used engine oil can cause skin cancer. Wear gloves or use a barrier cream if necessary. Change out of oil-soaked clothes and do not keep oily rags in your pocket.
• Air conditioning refrigerant forms a poisonous gas if exposed to a naked flame (including a cigarette). It can also cause skin burns on contact.

Asbestos

• Asbestos dust can cause cancer if inhaled or swallowed. Asbestos may be found in gaskets and in brake and clutch linings. When dealing with such components it is safest to assume that they contain asbestos.

Special hazards

Hydrofluoric acid

• This extremely corrosive acid is formed when certain types of synthetic rubber, found in some O-rings, oil seals, fuel hoses etc, are exposed to temperatures above 400°C. The rubber changes into a charred or sticky substance containing the acid. *Once formed, the acid remains dangerous for years. If it gets onto the skin, it may be necessary to amputate the limb concerned.*
• When dealing with a vehicle which has suffered a fire, or with components salvaged from such a vehicle, wear protective gloves and discard them after use.

The battery

• Batteries contain sulphuric acid, which attacks clothing, eyes and skin. Take care when topping-up or carrying the battery.
• The hydrogen gas given off by the battery is highly explosive. Never cause a spark or allow a naked light nearby. Be careful when connecting and disconnecting battery chargers or jump leads.

Air bags

• Air bags can cause injury if they go off accidentally. Take care when removing the steering wheel and/or facia. Special storage instructions may apply.

Diesel injection equipment

• Diesel injection pumps supply fuel at very high pressure. Take care when working on the fuel injectors and fuel pipes.

⚠️ *Warning: Never expose the hands, face or any other part of the body to injector spray; the fuel can penetrate the skin with potentially fatal results.*

Remember...

DO

• Do use eye protection when using power tools, and when working under the vehicle.

• Do wear gloves or use barrier cream to protect your hands when necessary.

• Do get someone to check periodically that all is well when working alone on the vehicle.

• Do keep loose clothing and long hair well out of the way of moving mechanical parts.

• Do remove rings, wristwatch etc, before working on the vehicle – especially the electrical system.

• Do ensure that any lifting or jacking equipment has a safe working load rating adequate for the job.

DON'T

• Don't attempt to lift a heavy component which may be beyond your capability – get assistance.

• Don't rush to finish a job, or take unverified short cuts.

• Don't use ill-fitting tools which may slip and cause injury.

• Don't leave tools or parts lying around where someone can trip over them. Mop up oil and fuel spills at once.

• Don't allow children or pets to play in or near a vehicle being worked on.

The following pages are intended to help in dealing with common roadside emergencies and breakdowns. You will find more detailed fault finding information at the back of the manual, and repair information in the main chapters.

If your car won't start and the starter motor doesn't turn

☐ Lift the bonnet, rotate the fasteners anti-clockwise and remove the battery cover. Make sure that the battery terminals are clean and tight.

☐ Switch on the headlights and try to start the engine. If the headlights go very dim when you're trying to start, the battery is probably flat. Get out of trouble by jump starting (see next page) using a friend's car.

If your car won't start even though the starter motor turns as normal

☐ Is there fuel in the tank?

☐ Is there moisture on electrical components under the bonnet? Switch off the ignition, then wipe off any obvious dampness with a dry cloth. Spray a water-repellent aerosol product (WD-40 or equivalent) on fuel system electrical connectors like those shown in the photos.

A Check the security of the injector wiring harness connector.

B Check the airflow meter wiring connector with the ignition switched off.

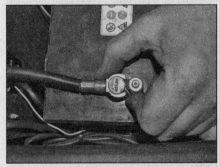

C Check the security and condition of the battery terminals.

D Check the glow plug connectors

Check that electrical connections are secure (with the ignition switched off) and spray them with a water dispersant spray like WD40 if you suspect a problem due to damp.

Jump starting

When jump-starting a car using a booster battery, observe the following precautions:

✔ Before connecting the booster battery, make sure that the ignition is switched off.

✔ Ensure that all electrical equipment (lights, heater, wipers, etc) is switched off.

✔ Take note of any special precautions printed on the battery case.

✔ Make sure that the booster battery is the same voltage as the discharged one in the vehicle.

✔ If the battery is being jump-started from the battery in another vehicle, the two vehicles MUST NOT TOUCH each other.

✔ Make sure that the transmission is in neutral (or PARK, in the case of automatic transmission).

 Jump starting will get you out of trouble, but you must correct whatever made the battery go flat in the first place. There are three possibilities:

1 *The battery has been drained by repeated attempts to start, or by leaving the lights on.*

2 *The charging system is not working properly (alternator drivebelt slack or broken, alternator wiring fault or alternator itself faulty).*

3 *The battery itself is at fault (electrolyte low, or battery worn out).*

1 Rotate the fastener anti-clockwise and remove the plastic cover from the battery, and connect the red jump lead to the positive terminal. Ensure all electrical consumers are switched off.

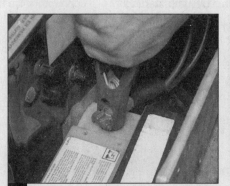

2 Connect the other end of the red lead to the positive (+) terminal of the booster battery.

3 Connect the other end of the black jump lead to the battery negative terminal.

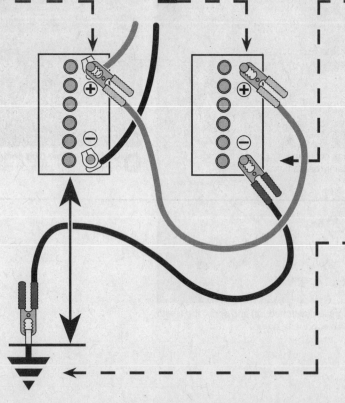

4 Connect one end of the black jump lead to the negative (-) terminal of the booster battery or a bolt or bracket on the engine block.

5 Make sure that the jump leads will not come into contact with the cooling fan drivebelts or other moving parts on the engine.

6 Start the engine, then with the engine running at fast idle speed, disconnect the jump leads strictly in the reverse order of connection, ie, negative (black) lead on the booster battery first. Securely refit the plastic cover over the battery.

Identifying leaks

Puddles on the garage floor or drive, or obvious wetness under the bonnet or underneath the car, suggest a leak that needs investigating. It can sometimes be difficult to decide where the leak is coming from, especially if the engine bay is very dirty already. Leaking oil or fluid can also be blown rearwards by the passage of air under the car, giving a false impression of where the problem lies.

 Warning: Most automotive oils and fluids are poisonous. Wash them off skin, and change out of contaminated clothing, without delay.

 HAYNES HINT *The smell of a fluid leaking from the car may provide a clue to what's leaking. Some fluids are distinctively coloured. It may help to clean the car carefully and to park it over some clean paper overnight as an aid to locating the source of the leak.*
Remember that some leaks may only occur while the engine is running.

Sump oil

Engine oil may leak from the drain plug...

Oil from filter

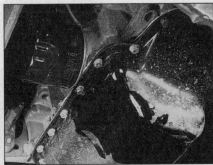

...or from the base of the oil filter.

Gearbox oil

Gearbox oil can leak from the seals at the inboard ends of the driveshafts.

Antifreeze

Leaking antifreeze often leaves a crystalline deposit like this.

Brake fluid

A leak occurring at a wheel is almost certainly brake fluid.

Power steering fluid

Power steering fluid may leak from the pipe connectors on the steering rack.

Wheel changing

 Warning: Do not change a wheel in a situation where you risk being hit by another vehicle. On busy roads, try to stop in a lay-by or a gateway. Be wary of passing traffic while changing the wheel – it is easy to become distracted by the job in hand.

Preparation

☐ When a puncture occurs, stop as soon as it is safe to do so.

☐ Park on firm level ground, if possible, and well out of the way of other traffic.

☐ Use hazard warning lights if necessary.

☐ If you have one, use a warning triangle to alert other drivers of your presence.

☐ Apply the handbrake and engage first or reverse gear. On automatic transmissions, ensure the selector lever is in position P (park). On all models, select position L for the transfer box.

☐ Chock both sides of the wheel diagonally opposite the one being removed – chocks are located with the tools in the tool bag.

 Warning: As the handbrake acts on the transmission, it is essential that the wheels are chocked securely.

☐ If the ground is soft, use a flat piece of wood to spread the load under the foot of the jack.

Changing the wheel

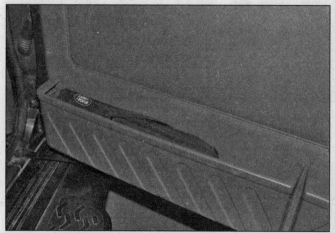

1 The spare wheel is bolted to the tailgate. The tools are stored in the tailgate storage pocket.

2 The jack is located in the front of the engine compartment, adjacent to the battery. Remove the jack.

3 Place the chocks behind and in front of the wheel diagonally opposite to the one to be removed.

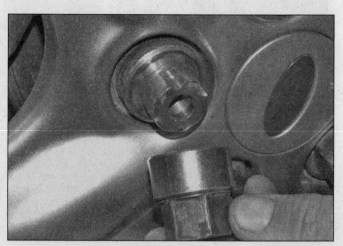

4 Remove the cover from the spare wheel (where applicable), then use the wheelbrace to unscrew the spare wheel retaining nuts, and remove the spare wheel. Note that where alloy wheels are fitted, use the locking nut adapter in the tool bag to unscrew the nut.

5 Assemble the jack handle, then use the slotted end to close the valve on the jack by turning it fully clockwise.

6 Pulling by hand or using a screwdriver, remove any wheel trim/hub cap (as applicable) then, using the wheelbrace from the toolkit, slacken each wheel nut by a half turn. If anti-theft wheel nuts are fitted, pull the cover from the nut using the tool provided, then slacken them using the adapter supplied in the tool kit.

7 Position the jack under the front or rear jacking point as appropriate. The jacking points are indicated by a notch in the front or rear suspension links. As the jack is raised, the head must enter the notched recess in the jacking point.

8 Make sure the jack is located on firm ground then insert the handle, and operate the jack until the wheel is raised clear of the ground. Unscrew the wheel nuts and remove the wheel. Fit the spare wheel and screw on the wheel nuts. Lightly tighten the nuts with the wheelbrace then slowly rotate the jack valve anti-clockwise and lower the vehicle to the ground.

9 Securely tighten the wheel nuts then refit the wheel trim/hub cap (as applicable). Stow the punctured wheel and tools, and secure them. Note that the wheel nuts should be slackened and retightened to the correct torque (140 Nm) at the earliest possible opportunity.

Finally . . .

☐ Remove the wheel chocks.

☐ Stow the jack, chocks and tools in the correct locations in the car.

☐ Check the tyre pressure on the wheel just fitted. If it is low, or if you don't have a pressure gauge with you, drive slowly to the next garage and inflate the tyre to the correct pressure.

☐ Change the transmission to H (High-range) before driving off.

☐ Have the damaged tyre or wheel repaired as soon as possible, or another puncture will leave you stranded.

Towing

When all else fails, you may find yourself having to get a tow home – or of course you may be helping somebody else. Long-distance recovery should only be done by a garage or breakdown service. For shorter distances, DIY towing using another car is easy enough, but observe the following points:

☐ Use a proper tow-rope – they are not expensive. The vehicle being towed must display an ON TOW sign in its rear window.

☐ Always turn the ignition key to the 'on' position when the vehicle is being towed, so that the steering lock is released, and that the direction indicator and brake lights work.

☐ Only attach the tow-rope to the towing eyes provided. The front towing eye is located behind a removable panel in the front spoiler, whilst two towing eyes are provided at the rear of the vehicle.

☐ Before being towed, release the handbrake and select neutral on the main transmission, or P on automatic transmissions. Set the transfer gearbox in neutral.

☐ Note that greater-than-usual pedal pressure will be required to operate the brakes, since the vacuum servo unit is only operational with the engine running. Greater-than-usual steering effort will also be required.

☐ The driver of the car being towed must keep the tow-rope taut at all times to avoid snatching.

☐ Make sure that both drivers know the route before setting off.

☐ Only drive at moderate speeds and keep the distance towed to a minimum. Drive smoothly and allow plenty of time for slowing down at junctions.

Introduction

There are some very simple checks which need only take a few minutes to carry out, but which could save you a lot of inconvenience and expense.

These *Weekly checks* require no great skill or special tools, and the small amount of time they take to perform could prove to be very well spent, for example;

☐ Keeping an eye on tyre condition and pressures, will not only help to stop them wearing out prematurely, but could also save your life.

☐ Many breakdowns are caused by electrical problems. Battery-related faults are particularly common, and a quick check on a regular basis will often prevent the majority of these.

☐ If your car develops a brake fluid leak, the first time you might know about it is when your brakes don't work properly. Checking the level regularly will give advance warning of this kind of problem.

☐ If the oil or coolant levels run low, the cost of repairing any engine damage will be far greater than fixing the leak, for example.

Underbonnet check points

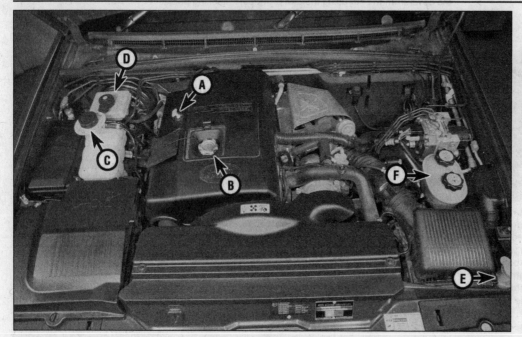

◄ Discovery TD5

A *Engine oil level dipstick*

B *Engine oil filler cap*

C *Coolant expansion tank*

D *Brake and clutch fluid reservoir*

E *Screen washer fluid reservoir*

F *Power steering/ACE (where applicable) fluid reservoir*

Engine oil level

Before you start
✔ Make sure that your car is on level ground.
✔ Check the oil level before the car is driven, or at least 5 minutes after the engine has been switched off.

The correct oil
Modern engines place great demands on their oil. It is very important that the correct oil for your car is used (See *Lubricants and fluids*).

Car care
● If you have to add oil frequently, you should check whether you have any oil leaks. Place some clean paper under the car overnight, and check for stains in the morning. If there are no leaks, the engine may be burning oil, or the oil may only be leaking when the engine is running.
● Always maintain the level between the upper and lower dipstick marks (see photo 3). If the level is too low severe engine damage may occur. Oil seal failure may result if the engine is overfilled by adding too much oil.

 HAYNES HINT *If the oil is checked immediately after driving the vehicle, some of the oil will remain in the upper engine components, resulting in an inaccurate reading on the dipstick.*

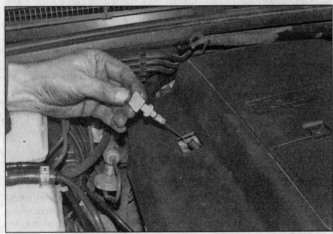

1 The dipstick top is often brightly coloured for easy identification (see *Underbonnet check points* for exact location). Withdraw the dipstick.

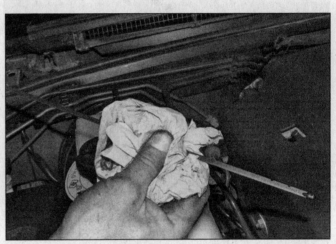

2 Using a clean rag or paper towel remove all oil from the dipstick. Insert the clean dipstick into the tube as far as it will go, then withdraw it again.

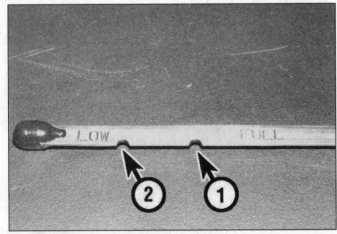

3 Note the oil level on the end of the dipstick, which should be between the upper full mark (1) and low minimum mark (2). Approximately 1.0 litre of oil will raise the level from the lower mark to the upper mark.

4 Oil is added through the filler cap. Lift up the access flap, unscrew the cap and top-up the level; a funnel may help to reduce spillage. Add the oil slowly, checking the level on the dipstick often. Don't overfill (see *Car care*).

Brake and clutch fluid level

Warning:

● *Brake fluid can harm your eyes and damage painted surfaces, so use extreme caution when handling and pouring it.*

● *Do not use fluid that has been standing open for some time, as it absorbs moisture from the air, which can cause a dangerous loss of braking effectiveness.*

● *The fluid level in the reservoir will drop slightly as the brake pads wear down, but the fluid level must never be allowed to drop below the MIN mark.*

Before you start

✔ Make sure that your car is on level ground.

Safety first!

● If the reservoir requires repeated topping-up this is an indication of a fluid leak somewhere in the system, which should be investigated immediately.

● If a leak is suspected, the car should not be driven until the braking system has been checked. Never take any risks where brakes are concerned.

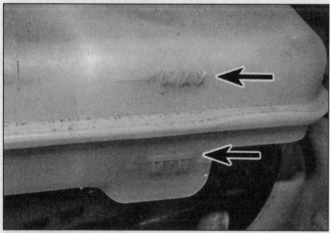

1 The MAX and MIN marks are indicated on the side of the reservoir. The fluid level must be kept between the marks at all times. If topping-up is necessary, first wipe clean the area around the filler cap to prevent dirt entering the hydraulic system.

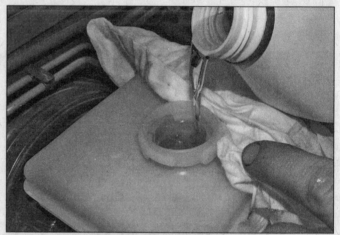

2 Unscrew the reservoir cap and carefully lift it out of position, taking care not to damage the level switch float. Carefully add fluid taking care not to spill it onto the surrounding components. Use only the specified fluid; mixing different types can cause damage to the system. After topping-up to the correct level, securely refit the cap and wipe off any spilt fluid.

Screen washer fluid level

● Screenwash additives not only keep the windscreen clean during foul weather, they also prevent the washer system freezing in cold weather – which is when you are likely to need it most. Don't top-up using plain water as the screenwash will become too diluted, and will freeze during cold weather.

Warning: On no account use coolant antifreeze in the washer system – this could discolour or damage paintwork.

1 The screen washer fluid reservoir is located in the front- left-hand corner of the engine compartment. If necessary, remove the cap.

2 When topping-up, add a screenwash additive in the quantities recommended by the manufacturer.

Coolant level

 Warning: DO NOT attempt to remove the expansion tank pressure cap when the engine is hot, as there is a very great risk of scalding. Do not leave open containers of coolant about, as it is poisonous.

Car Care

● With a sealed-type cooling system, adding coolant should not be necessary on a regular basis. If frequent topping-up is required, it is likely there is a leak. Check the radiator, all hoses and joint faces for signs of staining or wetness, and rectify as necessary.

● It is important that antifreeze is used in the cooling system all year round, not just during the winter months. Don't top-up with water alone, as the antifreeze will become too diluted.

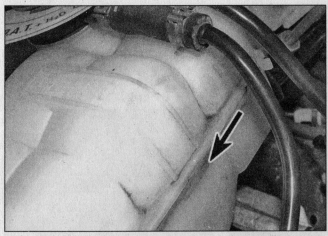

1 The coolant level is indicated by a minimum mark on the side of the expansion tank on the right-hand side of the engine compartment. If topping-up is necessary, **wait until the engine is cold**. Slowly remove the expansion tank cap, to release any pressure present in the cooling system, and remove it.

2 Add a mixture of water and antifreeze to the expansion tank until the surface of the coolant is level with the mark on the expansion tank. Refit the cap securely.

Power steering/ACE fluid level

Note: *On models equipped with Active Cornering Enhancement (ACE), the fluid reservoir is shared between the two systems. However, the reservoir is divided, and separate filler caps are provided.*

Before you start

✔ Park the vehicle on level ground.
✔ Set the steering wheel straight-ahead. For the check to be accurate, the steering must not be turned while the level is being checked.
✔ The engine should be turned off, and the fluid cool.

Safety first!

● The need for frequent topping-up indicates a leak, which should be investigated immediately.

1 The reservoir is located on the left-hand side of the engine compartment. The minimum and maximum levels are indicated by marks on the side of the reservoir. The fluid level should be between MIN and MAX.

2 If topping up is required, wipe clean the area around the reservoir filler neck(s) and unscrew the filler cap(s) from the reservoir (engine stopped).

3 When topping-up, use the specified type of fluid and do not overfill the reservoir. When the level is correct, securely refit the cap(s).

Tyre condition and pressure

 Warning: Land Rover state that if new tyres are to be fitted, ensure they are fitted to the rear axle only or both front and rear axles. New tyres should not be fitted to the front axle only.

It is very important that tyres are in good condition, and at the correct pressure - having a tyre failure at any speed is highly dangerous. Tyre wear is influenced by driving style - harsh braking and acceleration, or fast cornering, will all produce more rapid tyre wear. As a general rule, the front tyres wear out faster than the rears. Interchanging the tyres from front to rear ("rotating" the tyres) may result in more even wear. However, if this is completely effective, you may have the expense of replacing all four tyres at once! Remove any nails or stones embedded in the tread before they penetrate the tyre to cause deflation. If removal of a nail does reveal that the tyre has been punctured, refit the nail so that its point of penetration is marked. Then immediately change the wheel, and have the tyre repaired by a tyre dealer.

Regularly check the tyres for damage in the form of cuts or bulges, especially in the sidewalls. Periodically remove the wheels, and clean any dirt or mud from the inside and outside surfaces. Examine the wheel rims for signs of rusting, corrosion or other damage. Light alloy wheels are easily damaged by "kerbing" whilst parking; steel wheels may also become dented or buckled. A new wheel is very often the only way to overcome severe damage.

New tyres should be balanced when they are fitted, but it may become necessary to re-balance them as they wear, or if the balance weights fitted to the wheel rim should fall off. Unbalanced tyres will wear more quickly, as will the steering and suspension components. Wheel imbalance is normally signified by vibration, particularly at a certain speed (typically around 50 mph). If this vibration is felt only through the steering, then it is likely that just the front wheels need balancing. If, however, the vibration is felt through the whole car, the rear wheels could be out of balance. Wheel balancing should be carried out by a tyre dealer or garage.

1 Tread Depth - visual check
The original tyres have tread wear safety bands (B), which will appear when the tread depth reaches approximately 1.6 mm. The band positions are indicated by a triangular mark on the tyre sidewall (A).

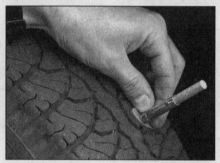

2 Tread Depth - manual check
Alternatively, tread wear can be monitored with a simple, inexpensive device known as a tread depth indicator gauge.

3 Tyre Pressure Check
Check the tyre pressures regularly with the tyres cold. Do not adjust the tyre pressures immediately after the vehicle has been used, or an inaccurate setting will result.

Tyre tread wear patterns

Shoulder Wear

Underinflation (wear on both sides)
Under-inflation will cause overheating of the tyre, because the tyre will flex too much, and the tread will not sit correctly on the road surface. This will cause a loss of grip and excessive wear, not to mention the danger of sudden tyre failure due to heat build-up.
Check and adjust pressures
Incorrect wheel camber (wear on one side)
Repair or renew suspension parts
Hard cornering
Reduce speed!

Centre Wear

Overinflation
Over-inflation will cause rapid wear of the centre part of the tyre tread, coupled with reduced grip, harsher ride, and the danger of shock damage occurring in the tyre casing.
Check and adjust pressures

If you sometimes have to inflate your car's tyres to the higher pressures specified for maximum load or sustained high speed, don't forget to reduce the pressures to normal afterwards.

Uneven Wear

Front tyres may wear unevenly as a result of wheel misalignment. Most tyre dealers and garages can check and adjust the wheel alignment (or "tracking") for a modest charge.
Incorrect camber or castor
Repair or renew suspension parts
Malfunctioning suspension
Repair or renew suspension parts
Unbalanced wheel
Balance tyres
Incorrect toe setting
Adjust front wheel alignment
Note: *The feathered edge of the tread which typifies toe wear is best checked by feel.*

Battery

Caution: Before carrying out any work on the vehicle battery, read the precautions given in 'Safety first!' at the start of this manual.

✔ Make sure that the battery tray is in good condition, and that the clamp is tight. Corrosion on the tray, retaining clamp and the battery itself can be removed with a solution of water and baking soda. Thoroughly rinse all cleaned areas with water. Any metal parts damaged by corrosion should be covered with a zinc-based primer, then painted.

✔ Periodically (approximately every three months), check the charge condition of the battery, as described in Chapter 5A.

✔ If the battery is flat, and you need to jump start your vehicle, see *Roadside repairs*.

1 The battery is located under a cover in the front- right-hand corner of the engine compartment. Rotate the fastener anti-clockwise and release the clip at the rear of the cover.

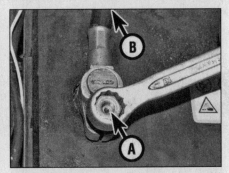

2 Check the tightness of battery clamps (A) to ensure good electrical connections. You should not be able to move them. Also check each cable (B) for cracks and frayed conductors.

Battery corrosion can be kept to a minimum by applying a layer of petroleum jelly to the clamps and terminals after they are reconnected.

3 If corrosion (white, fluffy deposits) is evident, remove the cables from the battery terminals, clean them with a small wire brush, then refit them. Automotive stores sell a tool for cleaning the battery post . . .

4 . . . as well as the battery cable clamps

Electrical systems

✔ Check all external lights and the horn. Refer to the appropriate Sections of Chapter 13 for details if any of the circuits are found to be inoperative.

✔ Visually check all accessible wiring connectors, harnesses and retaining clips for security, and for signs of chafing or damage.

 If you need to check your brake lights and indicators unaided, back up to a wall or garage door and operate the lights. The reflected light should show if they are working properly.

1 If a single indicator light, stop-light or headlight has failed, it is likely that a bulb has blown and will need to be renewed. Refer to Chapter 13 for details. If both stop-lights have failed, it is possible that the switch has failed (see Chapter 10).

2 If more than one indicator light or tail light has failed check that a fuse has not blown or that there is a fault in the circuit (see Chapter 13). The main fuses are located behind a panel under the steering column, and in the engine compartment adjacent to the coolant reservoir on the right-hand side of the engine compartment. Details of the circuits protected by the fuses are shown on the card in the fusebox, and in Chapter 13 of this manual.

3 To renew a blown fuse, using the tweezers provided, simply pull it out and fit a new fuse of the correct rating (see Chapter 13). If the fuse blows again, it is important that you find out why – a complete checking procedure is given in Chapter 13.

Wiper blades

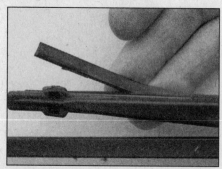

1 Check the condition of the wiper blades; if they are cracked or show any signs of deterioration, or if the glass swept area is smeared, renew them. Wiper blades should be renewed annually.

2 To remove a front wiper blade, pull the arm away from the screen, slide the locking tab to the 'unlock' position, and detach it from the arm.

3 To remove a rear wiper blade, pull the arm away from the screen, and press the blade pivot pin out from the recess in the arm.

Lubricants and fluids

Engine . . . . Multigrade engine oil, viscosity SAE 5W/40 or 5W50, to ACEA A1, B1

Cooling system . . . . Ethylene glycol based antifreeze with OATS corrosion inhibitors*

Manual transmission . . . . Texaco MTF94 transmission oil

Automatic transmission . . . . ATF Dexron IID or III

Transfer gearbox . . . . 75W/90R API GL5

Front and rear axles . . . . 75W/90R API GL5

Braking/clutch system . . . . Hydraulic fluid to DOT 4

Power steering/ACE

Ambient temperature below -20°C . . . . Texaco Cold Climate PAS fluid 14315

Ambient temperature above -20°C . . . . Use the above or Dexron II or III

Refer to your Land Rover dealer for brand name and type recommendations

Tyre pressures

	Front	Rear
Up to 4 passengers and luggage		
Up to 2003 model year	1.9 bar	2.6 bar
From 2003 model year	2.1 bar	2.6 bar
Fully-loaded		
Up to 2003 model year	1.9 bar	3.2 bar
From 2003 model year	2.6 bar	3.2 bar

Chapter 1
Routine maintenance & servicing

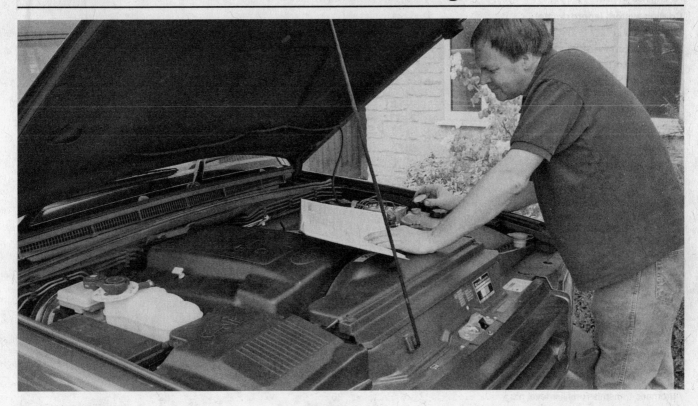

Contents

Section number

ABS wheel speed sensor harness check..................... 17
ACE actuator gaiter check and debris removal 23
ACE system filter renewal................................. 37
Air cleaner element renewal and dump valve cleaning 31
Air suspension intake filter renewal 35
Alarm handset battery renewal............................ 30
Automatic transmission oil renewal 27
Auxiliary drivebelt check and renewal 11
Axle oil level check..................................... 15
Axle oil renewal.. 38
Brake fluid renewal..................................... 25
Brake pads, discs and calipers check 4
Braking system seal, vacuum servo filter and hose renewal 36
Coolant renewal 32
Crankcase breather hose check........................... 9
Engine oil, filter and centrifugal rotor renewal 3
Fuel filter element renewal 29
Fuel sedimenter cleaning 14
Exhaust system check................................... 19
General information 1

Section number

Handbrake check and adjustment........................... 6
Hinge and lock check and lubrication 7
Hose and fluid leak check 5
Intercooler element cleaning 34
Main manual gearbox oil level check........................ 12
Main manual gearbox oil renewal.......................... 26
Propeller shaft joint lubrication............................ 18
Propeller shaft securing bolt check 20
Radiator and intercooler check 16
Regular maintenance 2
Ride height sensor harness check.......................... 24
Road test 10
Seat belt check.. 22
Seat belt pretensioners and airbag renewal................... 39
Steering and suspension component check 8
Steering box backlash adjustment.......................... 33
Towing bracket check 21
Transfer gearbox oil level check 13
Transfer gearbox oil renewal 28

Degrees of difficulty

| Easy, suitable for novice with little experience | 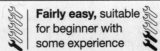 | Fairly easy, suitable for beginner with some experience | | Fairly difficult, suitable for competent DIY mechanic | | Difficult, suitable for experienced DIY mechanic | | Very difficult, suitable for expert DIY or professional | 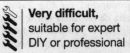 |

Specifications

Lubricants and fluids.	Refer to end of *Weekly checks*

Capacities

Engine oil (including filter)
All engines . . . . 7.2 litres

Cooling system (approximate)
All models. . . . . 8.0 litres

Transmission
Manual transmission (approximately):
   With oil cooler. . . . . 2.3 litres
   without oil cooler . . . . 1.9 litres
Automatic transmission (approximately) . . . . 9.7 litres
Transfer gearbox. . . . . 2.0 litres

Front and rear axles
All models. . . . . 1.6 litres

Washer fluid reservoir

Windscreen/rear window washer . . . . 6.0 litres

Fuel tank
All models. . . . . 95.0 litres

Cooling system

Antifreeze mixture:
   50% antifreeze . . . . Protection down to -48°C
Note: *Refer to antifreeze manufacturer for latest recommendations.*

Brakes

Friction material minimum thickness:
   Front and rear brake pads . . . . 2.0 mm

Torque wrench settings

	Nm	lbf ft
ACE filter cap	35	26
Automatic transmission drain plug.	15	11
Automatic transmission filler/level plug	30	22
Axle oil drain plug.	64	47
Axle oil filler/level plug	10	7
Drag link balljoint nut	80	59
Engine oil drain plug.	23	17
Manual transmission oil drain plug.	50	37
Manual transmission oil filler/level plug	30	22
Roadwheel nuts	140	103
Transfer gearbox oil drain plug.	30	22
Transfer gearbox oil filler/level plug	25	18

Land Rover Discovery maintenance schedule

The maintenance intervals in this manual are provided with the assumption that you, not the dealer, will be carrying out the work. These are the minimum maintenance intervals recommended by the manufacturers for vehicles driven daily under normal operating conditions. If you wish to keep your vehicle in peak condition at all times, you may wish to perform some of these procedures more often. This applies especially if the vehicle is used in particularly hot or dusty climates, or if the vehicle is regularly used for towing. We encourage frequent maintenance because it enhances the efficiency, performance and resale value of your vehicle.

When the vehicle is new, it should be serviced by a dealer service department (or other workshop recognised by the vehicle manufacturer as providing the same standard of service) in order to preserve the warranty. The vehicle manufacturer may reject warranty claims if you are unable to prove that servicing has been carried out as and when specified, using only original equipment parts or parts certified to be of equivalent quality.

Every 250 miles or weekly
☐ Refer to Weekly checks

Every 6000 miles or 6 months, whichever occurs first
☐ Renew the engine oil (Section 3)
☐ Check the condition of the brake pads and discs (Section 4)
☐ Check the brake calipers for leaks (where applicable) (Section 4)
☐ Check the cooling and heater system hoses for security and leaks (Section 5)
☐ Check all underbody brake, fuel and clutch pipes and hoses for leaks and condition (Section 5)
☐ Check the handbrake adjustment (Section 6)
☐ Check the operation of all door, bonnet and tailgate locks (Section 7)
☐ Lubricate all hinges and locks (including the fuel filler) (Section 7)
☐ Check the steering and suspension components, including all hydraulic pipes and hoses for leaks and condition (Section 8)
☐ Check the condition of the crankcase breather system hoses (Section 9)
☐ Carry out a road test (Section 10)

Every 12 000 miles or 12 months, whichever occurs first
In addition to all the items listed above, carry out the following:
☐ Renew the oil centrifuge rotor (Section 3)
☐ Check the condition of the auxiliary drivebelt (Section 11)
☐ Check the main manual gearbox oil level (Section 12)
☐ Check the transfer gearbox oil level (Section 13)
☐ Drain the fuel sedimenter (Section 14)
☐ Check the front and rear axle oil levels (Section 15)
☐ Check the radiator and intercooler for obstructions, and clean if necessary (Section 16)
☐ Check ABS wheel speed sensor harness (Section 17)
☐ Lubricate the propeller shaft universal joints and sliding joints (Section 18)
☐ Check the exhaust system for security and condition (Section 19)
☐ Check the tightness of the propeller shaft coupling bolts (Section 20)
☐ Check the security of the towing bracket (Section 21)
☐ Check the condition and operation of all seat belts (Section 22)
☐ Check the condition of the ACE actuator gaiters and remove and debris between the ACE valve block and vehicle chassis (Section 23)
☐ Check the ride height sensor harnesses for damage (models with self-levelling suspension) (Section 24)

Every 24 000 miles or 2 years, whichever occurs first
In addition to all the items listed above, carry out the following:
☐ Renew the brake fluid (Section 25)
☐ Renew the main gearbox oil (Section 26)
☐ Renew the automatic transmission oil (Section 27)
☐ Renew the transfer gearbox oil (Section 28)
☐ Renew the fuel filter element (Section 29)
☐ Renew alarm handset batteries (Section 30)

Every 36 000 miles or 3 years, whichever occurs first
In addition to all the items listed above, carry out the following:
☐ Renew the oil filter cartridge (Section 3)
☐ Renew the air cleaner element and clean the dump valve (Section 31)
☐ Renew the coolant (Section 32)

Every 48 000 miles or 4 years, whichever occurs first
In addition to all the items listed above, carry out the following:
☐ Adjust the steering box backlash (Section 33)
☐ Clean the intercooler element (Section 34)

Every 60 000 miles
☐ Renew the air suspension intake filter (where fitted) (Section 35)

Every 72 000 miles
☐ Renew all braking system hydraulic fluid seals, the vacuum servo filter, and all flexible brake fluid hoses (Section 36)
☐ Renew the ACE (Active Cornering Enhancement) system filter (Section 37)

Every 96 000 miles
☐ Renew the auxiliary drivebelt (Section 11)
☐ Renew the front and rear axle oil (Section 38)

Every 15 years
☐ Renew the seat belt pretensioners and airbags Section 39)

Underbonnet view

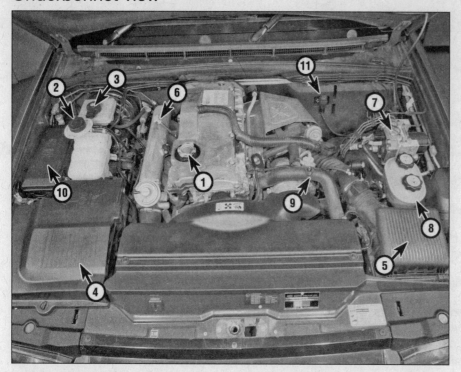

1 Oil filler cap
2 Coolant expansion tank filler cap
3 Brake fluid reservoir cap
4 Battery cover
5 Air filter cover
6 Oil level dipstick
7 ABS modulator
8 ACE and power steering fluid reservoir
9 Radiator top hose bleed screw
10 Fuse/relay box
11 Engine inertia cut-off switch

Front underbody view

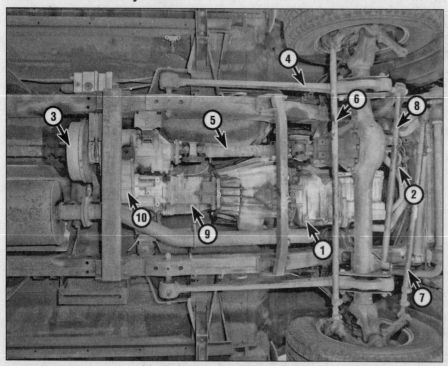

1 Engine oil drain plug
2 Coolant drain plug
3 Handbrake drum
4 Radius arm
5 Front propeller shaft
6 Track rod
7 Drag link
8 Panhard rod
9 Main gearbox
10 Transfer gearbox

Rear underbody view

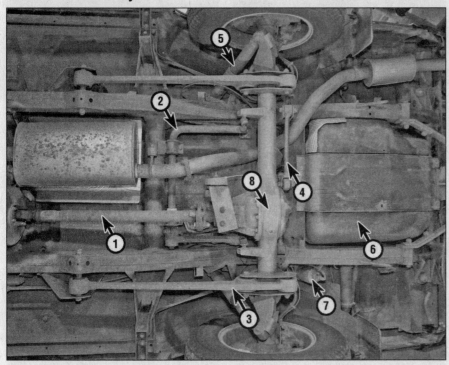

1 Rear propeller shaft
2 Rear anti-roll bar
3 Radius arm
4 Watts linkage
5 Shock absorber
6 Fuel tank
7 Fuel filter
8 Rear axle

1 General information

1 This Chapter is designed to help the home mechanic maintain his/her vehicle for safety, economy, long life and peak performance.

2 The Chapter contains a master maintenance schedule, followed by Sections dealing specifically with each task in the schedule. Visual checks, adjustments, component renewal and other helpful items are included. Refer to the accompanying illustrations of the engine compartment and the underside of the vehicle for the locations of the various components.

3 Servicing your vehicle in accordance with the Schedule and the following Sections will provide a planned maintenance programme, which should result in a long and reliable service life. This is a comprehensive plan, so maintaining some items but not others at the specified service intervals will not produce the same results.

4 As you service your vehicle, you will discover that many of the procedures can – and should – be grouped together, because of the particular procedure being performed, or because of the proximity of two otherwise-unrelated components to one another. For example, if the vehicle is raised for any reason, the exhaust can be inspected at the same time

as the suspension and steering components.

5 The first step in this maintenance programme is to prepare yourself before the actual work begins. Read through all the Sections relevant to the work to be carried out, then make a list and gather all the parts and tools required. If a problem is encountered, seek advice from a parts specialist, or a dealer service department.

2 Regular maintenance

1 If, from the time the vehicle is new, the routine maintenance schedule is followed closely, and frequent checks are made of fluid levels and high-wear items, as suggested throughout this manual, the engine will be kept in relatively good running condition, and the need for additional work will be minimised.

2 It is possible that there will be times when the engine is running poorly due to the lack of regular maintenance. This is even more likely if a used vehicle, which has not received regular and frequent maintenance checks, is purchased. In such cases, additional work may need to be carried out, outside of the regular maintenance intervals.

3 If engine wear is suspected, a compression test (refer to Part A of Chapter 2) will provide valuable information regarding the overall

performance of the main internal components. Such a test can be used as a basis to decide on the extent of the work to be carried out. If, for example, a compression test indicates serious internal engine wear, conventional maintenance as described in this Chapter will not greatly improve the performance of the engine, and may prove a waste of time and money, unless extensive overhaul work is carried out first.

4 The following series of operations are those most often required to improve the performance of a generally poor-running engine:

Primary operations

a) Clean, inspect and test the battery (See 'Weekly checks').
b) Check all the engine-related fluids (See 'Weekly checks').
c) Check the condition of the air filter, and renew if necessary (Section 31).
d) Check the condition of all hoses, and check for fluid leaks (Section 5).

5 If the above operations do not prove fully effective, carry out the following secondary operations:

Secondary operations

6 All items listed under *Primary operations*, plus the following:
a) Check the charging system (see Chapter 5).
b) Check the fuel system (see relevant Part of Chapter 4).

3.3 Rotate the drain plug access cover (arrowed) anti-clockwise

3.4 Engine oil drain plug (arrowed)

3.6 Fit a new sealing washer to the drain plug

3 Engine oil, filter and centrifugal rotor renewal

HAYNES HiNT *Frequent oil and filter changes are the most important preventative maintenance procedures that can be undertaken by the DIY owner. As engine oil ages, it becomes diluted and contaminated, which leads to premature engine wear.*

Note: *Not all these items are renewed at this interval (see 'Maintenance schedule').*

Oil renewal

1 Before starting this procedure, gather together all the necessary tools and materials. Also make sure that you have plenty of clean rags and newspapers handy, to mop-up any spills. Ideally, the engine oil should be warm, as it will drain better, and more built-up sludge will be removed with it. Take care, however, not to touch the exhaust or any other hot parts of the engine when working under the vehicle. To avoid any possibility of scalding, and to protect yourself from possible skin irritants and other harmful contaminants in used engine oils, it is advisable to wear rubber gloves when carrying out this work.
2 Access to the underside of the vehicle will be greatly improved if it can be raised on a lift, driven onto ramps, or jacked up and supported on axle stands (see *Jacking and vehicle support*). Whichever method is chosen, make sure that the vehicle remains as level as possible, to enable the oil to drain fully.
3 Lift the flap in the engine cover, and unscrew the oil filler cap from the valve cover, then twist the access cover in the engine undershield anti-clockwise to reveal the sump drain plug **(see illustration)**. Position a suitable container beneath the sump.

4 Clean the drain plug and the area around it, then slacken it using a suitable socket or spanner **(see illustration)**. If possible, try to keep the plug pressed into the sump while unscrewing it by hand the last couple of turns. As the plug releases from the threads, move it away sharply, so that the stream of oil issuing from the sump runs into the container, not up your sleeve.
5 Allow some time for the old oil to drain, noting that it may be necessary to reposition the container as the oil flow slows to a trickle.
6 After all the oil has drained, wipe off the drain plug with a clean rag, and discard the sealing washer – a new sealing washer must be fitted. Clean the area around the drain plug opening, then fit the washer and tighten the plug to the specified torque setting **(see illustration)**.
7 Remove the old oil and all tools from under the vehicle, then (if applicable) lower the vehicle to the ground.
8 Fill the engine with the specified quantity and grade of oil. Pour the oil in slowly, otherwise it may overflow from the top of the valve cover. Check that the oil level is up to the correct level on the dipstick (see *Weekly checks*), then refit and tighten the oil filler cap.
9 Run the engine for a few minutes, and check that there are no leaks around the sump drain plug. Switch off the engine, and wait a few minutes for the oil to settle in the sump once more. With the new oil circulated and the filter now completely full, recheck the level on the dipstick, and add more oil

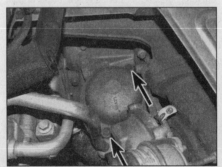

3.12 Oil centrifuge rotor housing bolts (arrowed)

if necessary. Refit the engine undershield access cover.
10 Dispose of the used engine oil responsibly, with reference to *General repair procedures* in the reference Sections of this manual.

Oil centrifuge rotor

Note: *This procedure must be accompanied by changing the engine oil as described earlier in this Section.*

11 The centrifugal oil cleaner is fitted on the left-hand side of the engine block. Oil enters the centrifuge from the side under pressure, and spins the rotor within at up to 15 000 rpm. Any dirt/particles within the oil are captured on the inner surface of the rotor as the oil is thrown outwards, forming a sludge inside the rotor. The rotor is able to trap very fine impurities that would normally pass through a paper element type normal filter.
12 Undo the two bolts and remove the centrifuge cover **(see illustration)**. Discard the cover O-ring seal – a new one must be fitted.
13 Lift out the rotor and discard it – a new one must be fitted **(see illustration)**.
14 Use shop rag to clean the centrifuge body and cover.
15 Fit the new rotor into the body, then refit the cover with a new O-ring seal. Tighten the cover bolts securely.

Oil filter cartridge

Note: *This procedure must be accompanied by changing the engine oil as described earlier in this Section.*

16 Undo the three bolts and remove the

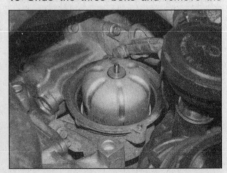

3.13 Lift out the oil filter rotor

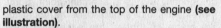

3.16 The plastic cover is fastened at 3 places (arrowed)

3.18 The oil filter cartridge (arrowed) is located under the exhaust manifold, on the left-hand side of the engine

3.20 Apply a little clean engine oil to the seal at the top of the filter cartridge

plastic cover from the top of the engine (**see illustration**).

17 Clean the area around the filter housing, and place a container under the engine beneath the filter.

18 Using an oil filter removal tool if necessary, slacken the filter initially (**see illustration**). Loosely wrap some rags around the oil filter, then unscrew it. Remove the oil filter from the engine compartment, and empty the oil into the container used to drain the sump.

19 Use a clean rag to remove all oil, dirt and sludge from the filter sealing area on the engine. Check the old filter, to make sure that the rubber sealing ring hasn't stuck to the engine. If it has, carefully remove it.

20 Apply a light coating of clean oil to the sealing ring on the new filter, then screw it into position on the engine (**see illustration**). Tighten the filter firmly by hand only – do not use any tools. Wipe clean the exterior of the oil filter.

21 Refitting is a reversal of removal.

4 Brake pads, discs and calipers check

1 Jack up the vehicle, support securely on axle stands, then remove the roadwheels (see *Jacking and vehicle support*).

2 For a quick check, the thickness of friction material remaining on each pad can be measured through the slot in the caliper body. If any pad is worn to the specified minimum thickness or less, **all four** pads must be renewed (see Chapter 10).

3 For a comprehensive check, the brake pads should be removed and cleaned. This will allow the operation of the caliper to be checked, and the condition of the brake disc itself to be fully examined on both sides (see Chapter 10).

4 With the pads removed, check the area around the caliper piston for any signs of fluid leakage. Use a large screwdriver to gently move the pistons back into the caliper body a little. If it is impossible to move the pistons, the caliper may need overhauling/renewing as described in Chapter 10.

5 Hose and fluid leak check

1 Visually inspect the engine joint faces, gaskets and seals for any signs of water or oil leaks. Pay particular attention to the areas around the camshaft cover, cylinder head, oil filter and sump joint faces. Bear in mind that, over a period of time, some very slight seepage from these areas is to be expected – what you are really looking for is any indication of a serious leak. Should a leak be found, renew the offending gasket or oil seal by referring to the appropriate Chapters in this manual.

2 Also check the security and condition of all the engine-related pipes and hoses. Ensure that all cable-ties or securing clips are in place and in good condition. Clips which are broken or missing can lead to chafing of the hoses, pipes or wiring, which could cause more serious problems in the future.

3 Carefully check the radiator hoses and heater hoses along their entire length. Renew any hose which is cracked, swollen or deteriorated. Cracks will show up better if the hose is squeezed. Pay close attention to the hose clips that secure the hoses to the cooling system components. Hose clips can pinch and puncture hoses, resulting in cooling system leaks.

A leak in the cooling system will usually show up as white- or antifreeze-coloured deposits on the areas adjoining the leak.

4 Inspect all the cooling system components (hoses, joint faces, etc) for leaks (**see Haynes Hint**). Where any problems of this nature are found on system components, renew the component or gasket with reference to Chapter 3.

5 Where applicable, inspect the automatic transmission fluid cooler hoses for leaks or deterioration.

6 With the car raised, inspect the fuel tank and filler neck for punctures, cracks and other damage. The connection between the filler neck and tank is especially critical. Sometimes a rubber filler neck or connecting hose will leak due to loose retaining clamps or deteriorated rubber.

7 Carefully check all rubber hoses and metal fuel lines leading away from the fuel tank. Check for loose connections, deteriorated hoses, crimped lines, and other damage. Pay particular attention to the vent pipes and hoses, which often loop up around the filler neck and can become blocked or crimped. Follow the lines to the front of the car, carefully inspecting them all the way. Renew damaged sections as necessary.

8 Closely inspect the metal brake pipes which run along the car underbody. If they show signs of excessive corrosion or damage they must be renewed.

9 From within the engine compartment, check the security of all fuel hose attachments and pipe unions, and inspect the fuel hoses and vacuum hoses for kinks, chafing and deterioration.

10 Check the condition of the power steering/ACE fluid hoses and pipes.

6 Handbrake check and adjustment

1 The handbrake mechanism is mounted onto the rear of the transfer box assembly.

2 To check the handbrake, pull the lever up. After 3 'clicks' the handbrake should be fully applied.

3 If it isn't, select a gear, then release the handbrake lever and chock the front wheels.

4 Jack up the rear of the vehicle and support

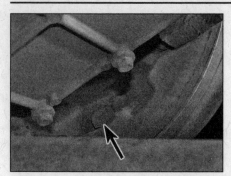

6.5 Handbrake adjusting bolt (arrowed)

it on axle stands so that the wheels are clear of the ground.

5 From underneath the vehicle, using a suitable spanner, rotate the adjuster on the rear of the handbrake assembly clockwise, until both shoes are fully expanded and the drum is locked **(see illustration)**.

6 With the shoes in full contact with the drum, rotate the handbrake adjuster one and a half turns in an anti-clockwise direction. Check that the handbrake drum is free to rotate easily.

7 Applying normal, moderate pressure, pull the handbrake lever to the fully-applied position, counting the number of clicks emitted from the handbrake ratchet mechanism as described in Paragraph 2. If the handbrake action is still unsatisfactory, adjust the cable as follows.

Vehicles up to VIN XA222819

8 Remove the electric window switch pack from the centre console, as described in Chapter 13, Section 4.

9 Prise the handbrake lever gaiter from the console.

10 Rotate the cable adjuster anti-clockwise to increase the tension (reduce the number of notches), or clockwise to reduce tension (increase the number of notches) **(see illustration)**.

11 Refit the switch pack.

Vehicles from VIN XA222820

12 The outer cable is fitted with an in-line adjuster where it enters the vehicle body, on

6.10 On earlier models, the cable adjusting nut (arrowed) can be accessed by remove the centre console switch pack

the underside of the transmission tunnel.

13 Rotate the cable adjuster clockwise to increase cable tension and reduce the number of 'clicks', or anti-clockwise to reduce the tension and increase the number of 'clicks' **(see illustration)**.

All vehicles

14 When adjustment is correct, release the handbrake lever, and check the drum is free to rotate easily. If all is well, lower the vehicle to the ground.

7 Hinge and lock check and lubrication

1 Lubricate the hinges of the bonnet, doors and tailgate with a light general-purpose oil. Similarly, lubricate all latches, locks and lock strikers. At the same time, check the security and operation of all the locks, adjusting them if necessary (see Chapter 12).

2 Lightly lubricate the bonnet release mechanism and cable with a suitable grease.

8 Steering and suspension component check

1 Apply the handbrake, then raise the front of the vehicle and securely support it on axle stands.

2 Visually inspect the balljoint dust covers for splits, chafing or deterioration. Any damage will cause loss of lubricant, together with dirt and water entry, resulting in rapid deterioration of the balljoints.

3 Where applicable, check the power steering fluid hoses for chafing or deterioration, and the pipe and hose unions for fluid leaks. Also check for signs of fluid leakage under pressure from the steering box, which would indicate failed fluid seals within the steering box assembly.

4 Grasp the roadwheel at the 12 o'clock and 6 o'clock positions, and try to rock it. Very slight freeplay may be felt, but if the movement is appreciable, further investigation is necessary to determine the source. Continue rocking

6.13 In-line adjuster and locknut – later models

the wheel while an assistant depresses the footbrake. If the movement is now eliminated or significantly reduced, it is likely that the hub bearings are at fault. If the freeplay is still evident with the footbrake depressed, then there is wear in the suspension joints or mountings.

5 Now grasp the wheel at the 9 o'clock and 3 o'clock positions, and try to rock it as before. Any movement felt now may again be caused by wear in the hub bearings, or the steering track rod and drag link balljoints. If a balljoint is worn, the visual movement will be obvious.

6 Using a large screwdriver or flat bar, check for wear in the suspension mounting bushes by levering between the relevant suspension component and its attachment point. Some movement is to be expected, as the mountings are made of rubber, but excessive wear should be obvious. Also check the condition of any visible rubber bushes, looking for splits, cracks or contamination of the rubber.

7 With the vehicle standing on its wheels, have an assistant turn the steering wheel back-and-forth. There should be very little, if any, lost movement between the steering wheel and roadwheels. If this is not the case, closely observe the joints and mountings previously described, but in addition, check the steering column universal joints for wear. The steering box backlash is adjustable (see Section 33).

9 Crankcase breather hose check

1 Check all the engine breather hoses for signs of cracking, leaks, and general deterioration.

2 It is advisable to loosen the hose clips, and remove each hose to check for a build-up of deposits, which may cause restrictions or even a blockage. If necessary, clean the hose using paraffin, but ensure that the hose is completely dry before refitting.

10 Road test

Instruments and electrical equipment

1 Check the operation of all instruments and electrical equipment, including the washers and wipers.

2 Make sure that all instruments read correctly, and switch on all electrical equipment in turn, to check that it functions properly.

Steering and suspension

3 Check for any abnormalities in the steering, suspension, handling or road 'feel'.

4 Drive the vehicle, and check that there are no unusual vibrations or noises.

5 Check that the steering feels positive, with

no excessive 'sloppiness', or roughness, and check for any suspension noises when cornering and driving over bumps.

Drivetrain

6 Check the performance of the engine, clutch and propeller shafts.

7 Listen for any unusual noises from the engine, clutch and transmission.

8 Make sure that the engine runs smoothly when idling, and that there is no hesitation when accelerating.

9 Check that the clutch action is smooth and progressive, that the drive is taken up smoothly, and that the pedal travel is not excessive. Also listen for any noises when the clutch pedal is depressed.

10 Check that all gears can be engaged smoothly without noise, and that the gear lever action is smooth and not abnormally vague or 'notchy'. This check applies to both the main gearbox and the transfer gearbox.

Braking system

11 Make sure that the vehicle does not pull to one side when braking, and that the wheels do not lock when braking hard.

12 Check that there is no vibration through the steering when braking.

13 Check that the handbrake operates correctly without excessive movement of the lever, and that it holds the vehicle stationary on a slope.

14 Test the operation of the brake servo unit as follows. With the engine switched off, depress the footbrake four or five times to exhaust the vacuum. Start the engine, keeping the footbrake depressed. As the engine starts, there should be a noticeable 'give' in the brake pedal as vacuum builds-up. Allow the engine to run for at least two minutes, and then switch it off. If the brake pedal is depressed again, it should be possible to detect a hiss from the servo. After about four or five applications, no further hissing should be heard, and the pedal should feel considerably firmer.

Every 12 000 miles or 12 months

11 Auxiliary drivebelt check and renewal

Check

1 An automatic drivebelt tensioner is fitted, and no checking of the tension is necessary.

11.4 Rotate the auxiliary belt tensioner pulley bolt clockwise to relieve the tension

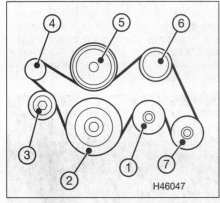

11.7 Auxiliary belt routing

1	Power steering pump
2	Crankshaft
3	Tensioner
4	Alternator
5	Cooling fan viscous coupling
6	Air conditioning compressor
7	ACE pump

However, the belt should be inspected for wear and damage and the recommended intervals.

2 The belt should be inspected along its entire length, and if it is found to be worn, frayed or cracked, it should be renewed as a precaution against breakage in service. It is advisable to carry a spare drivebelt of the correct type in the vehicle at all times.

Renewal

3 Remove the viscous cooling fan coupling as described in Chapter 3.

4 Using a suitable ring spanner, rotate the belt tensioner pulley retaining bolt clockwise to move the tensioner and relieve the tension in the belt **(see illustration)**.

5 Take note of the routing, then slide the belt from the pulleys.

6 If the original belt is to be refitted, mark the running direction to ensure correct refitting.

7 Refitting is a reversal of removal, but ensure that the belt is correctly routed **(see illustration)**.

12 Main manual gearbox oil level check

1 Ensure that the vehicle is level.

2 Locate the oil filler/level plug in the side of the gearbox casing, and place a suitable

12.3 Unscrew the main gearbox filler/level plug

container beneath the hole to catch any escaping oil. Note that a Torx 55 bit may be required to undo the plug.

3 Unscrew the filler/level plug, and check the oil level. The level should be up to the lower edge of the filler/level plug hole **(see illustration)**.

4 If necessary, add oil of the specified type (see *Lubricants and fluids*) until the oil overflows from the filler/level hole.

5 Clean and refit the filler/level plug, and tighten to the specified torque. **Do not** overtighten the plug, as it has tapered threads.

6 Wipe any spilt oil from the gearbox casing.

13 Transfer gearbox oil level check

Proceed as described for the main gearbox in Section 12, noting that the filler/level plug is located in the rear of the transfer gearbox casing **(see illustration)**.

14 Fuel sedimenter cleaning

1 The sedimenter is fitted to the base of the fuel filter, and is designed to remove the larger droplets of water and dirt from the fuel.

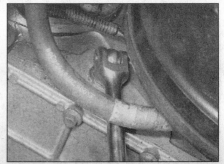

13.1 The transfer gearbox filler plug is on the rear of the unit

14.3 Disconnect the wiring plug, then unscrew the sedimenter (arrowed)

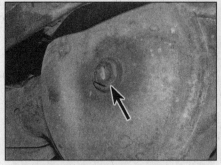

15.4 Unscrew the filler/level plug from the axle (arrowed)

18.1 Rear propeller shaft grease nipples (arrowed)

2 Position a container under the fuel filter, located on the chassis longitudinal member, below the right-hand rear wheel arch.
3 Disconnect the wiring plug, then rotate the sedimenter and allow any water to run out from the drain tube. When clean, uncontaminated fuel runs from the drain, tighten the sedimenter **(see illustration)**.
4 Reconnect the wiring plug then start the engine and check for fuel leaks around the sedimenter.

15 Axle oil level check

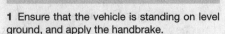

1 Ensure that the vehicle is standing on level ground, and apply the handbrake.
2 Working underneath the vehicle, unscrew the front axle oil filler/level plug, which is located in the differential housing.
3 The oil level should be up to the lower edge of the filler/level plug hole.
4 If necessary, top-up with the specified grade of oil, until oil just begins to run from the plug hole. Do not overfill – if too much oil is added, wait until the excess has run out of the plug hole **(see illustration)**.
5 Once the level is correct, refit the filler/level plug and tighten it to the specified torque.
6 Repeat the procedure for the rear axle.

16 Radiator and intercooler check

1 Check that the radiator and intercooler matrixes are clean, and free from obstructions which would reduce the airflow through them. Remove any debris, taking great care not to damage either component.

17 ABS wheel speed sensor harness check

1 Working underneath the vehicle, check each sensor harness for chafing and damage, and that they are correctly routed.

18 Propeller shaft joint lubrication

Note: *A low-pressure grease gun and 1/4" UNF grease nipple will be required for this operation.*
1 Working under the vehicle, locate the grease nipples on the rear propeller shaft **(see illustration)**.
2 Thoroughly clean the around each nipple.

3 Fill a grease gun with a suitable type of greas, then apply the grease gun to each of the nipples in turn, and pump grease into the joints **(see illustration)**. Apply grease until it emerges from the end of the nipple, then wipe away the excess.
4 Working on the front shaft, remove the blanking plug from the sliding joint, and screw in a 1/4" UNF grease nipple **(see illustrations)**.
5 Pump grease into the nipple, then wipe away the excess.
6 Unscrew the nipple and refit the blanking plug, tightening it securely.

19 Exhaust system check

1 With the engine cold (at least an hour after the vehicle has been driven), check the complete exhaust system from the engine to the end of the tailpipe. Ideally, the inspection should be carried out with the vehicle raised (see *Jacking and vehicle support*).
2 Check the exhaust pipes and connections for evidence of leaks, severe corrosion and damage. Make sure that all brackets and mountings are in good condition, and tight. Leakage at any of the joints or in other parts of the system will usually show

18.3 Use a grease gun attached to the grease nipples

18.4a Unscrew the blanking plug . . .

18.4b . . . and screw-in a 1/4" UNF grease nipple

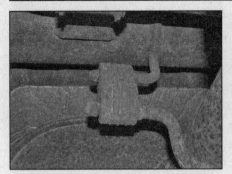

19.3 Check the exhaust rubber mountings

23.1 Check the rubber gaiters on the ACE actuator

23.2 Clear any debris between the ACE valve block and the chassis

up as a black sooty stain in the vicinity of the leak.

3 Rattles and other noises can often be traced to the exhaust system, especially the brackets and mountings **(see illustration)**. Try to move the pipes and silencers. If the components can come into contact with the body or suspension parts, secure the system with new mountings. If possible, separate the joints, and twist the pipes as necessary to provide additional clearance.

4 Run the engine at idle speed, then temporarily place a cloth rag over the rear end of the exhaust pipe, and listen for any escape of exhaust gases that would indicate a leak.

5 On completion, where applicable, lower the vehicle to the ground.

20 Propeller shaft securing bolt check

1 Working under the vehicle, use a torque wrench to check the tightness of the bolts securing the propeller shafts to the transfer gearbox and axle drive flanges (see Chapter 8).

21 Towing bracket check

1 Where applicable, check the security of the towbar bracket mountings. Also check that all wiring is intact, and that the trailer electrical systems function correctly.

22 Seat belt check

1 Carefully examine the seat belt webbing for cuts, or any signs of serious fraying or deterioration. If the seat belt is of the retractable type, pull the belt all the way out, and examine the full extent of the webbing.

2 Fasten and unfasten the belt, ensuring that the locking mechanism holds securely, and releases properly when intended. If the belt is of the retractable type, check also that the retracting mechanism operates correctly when the belt is released.

3 Check the security of all seat belt mountings

and attachments which are accessible (without removing any trim or other components) from inside the vehicle.

4 Renew any worn components as described in Chapter 12.

23 ACE actuator gaiter check and debris removal

1 Working underneath the vehicle, check the condition and security of the rubber gaiters fitted to the ACE (Active Cornering Enhancement) actuators **(see illustration)**.

2 Remove any debris between the ACE valve block (located under the right-hand side of the vehicle, below the passenger doors) and the chassis **(see illustration)**.

24 Ride height sensor harness check

1 Working underneath the rear of the vehicle, check each sensor harness for chafing and damage, and that they are correctly routed.

Every 24 000 miles or 2 years

25 Brake fluid renewal

1 The procedure is similar to that for the bleeding of the hydraulic system as described in Chapter 10, except that the brake fluid reservoir should be emptied before starting. Either syphon off the fluid, using a (clean) old battery hydrometer or similar, or open the first bleed screw in the sequence, and pump the fluid from the reservoir. Allowance should be made for all the old fluid to be expelled from the circuit when bleeding each section of the circuit. Used brake fluid is usually much darker in colour than fresh fluid, making it easy to distinguish the two.

26 Main manual gearbox oil renewal

1 Ideally, the oil should be drained shortly after the vehicle has been driven, when the oil will be warm (allow time for the exhaust system to cool, however). Park the vehicle on level ground.

2 Unscrew the oil filler/level plug from the side of the main gearbox casing. Note that a Torx 55 bit may be required to unscrew the plug **(see illustration 12.3)**.

3 Locate the main gearbox casing drain plug, and place a suitable container beneath the plug to catch the escaping oil.

4 Unscrew the drain plug, and allow the oil to

drain. If the oil is hot, take precautions against scalding. Allow at least ten minutes for all the oil to drain **(see illustration)**. Discard the sealing washer, a new one must be fitted.

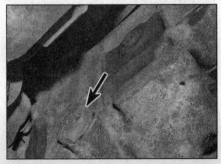

26.4 Main gearbox oil drain plug (arrowed)

27.1 Undo the automatic transmission drain plug (arrowed)

27.3 Automatic transmission oil filler/level plug (arrowed)

28.3 Unscrew the transfer gearbox oil drain plug (arrowed)

5 The drain plug is fitted with a magnet to attach any ferrous debris in the gearbox oil. Examine the plug, then clean any debris from it.

6 When all the oil has drained from the gearbox, clean, refit and tighten the drain plug, using a new washer. Tighten the plugs to the specified torque.

7 Fill the gearbox with the specified grade of oil (see *Lubricants and fluids*), until the oil flows from the filler/level plug hole. It is advisable to fill the gearbox slowly, to avoid a sudden spillage.

8 On completion, refit the filler/level plug, and tighten to the specified torque. **Do not** overtighten the plug, as it has a tapered thread.

9 Wipe any split oil from the gearbox casing.

27 Automatic transmission oil renewal

1 Place a suitable container under the transmission casing, then clean the area around the filler and drain plugs, and undo the drain plug **(see illustration)**. Discard the plug sealing washer, a new one must be fitted.

2 When all the oil has drained from the transmission, clean and refit the drain plug with a new washer. Tighten the plug to the specified torque.

3 Unscrew the filler/level plug and discard the sealing washer, a new one must be fitted **(see illustration)**.

4 Fill the transmission with the correct grade of oil (see *Lubricants and fluids*), until the oil flows from the filler/level plug.

5 Ensure the selector lever is in the Park position, and the handbrake is fully applied. Start the engine and allow it to idle.

6 Apply the footbrake, then move the selector lever through all of the positions, while as assistant continues to fill the transmission. Select Park position.

7 With the engine still at idle speed, continue to fill the transmission until oil flows from the filler/level plug.

8 Refit the level plug and tighten it to the specified torque.

9 Stop the engine, and wipe away any excess oil.

28 Transfer gearbox oil renewal

1 Park the vehicle on level ground.

2 Locate the filler/level plug in the side of the transfer gearbox casing, then unscrew the plug (see Section 13).

3 Place a container beneath the drain plug in the bottom of the gearbox casing, then unscrew the drain plug and allow the oil to drain **(see illustration)**. Recover the sealing washer.

4 When the oil has finished draining, refit and tighten the drain plug, using a new sealing washer if necessary.

5 Refill the gearbox with oil of the specified

type through the filler/level hole, until the oil level reaches the lower edge of the hole (place a container beneath the hole, to catch any escaping oil).

6 Clean and refit the filler/level plug, and tighten to the specified torque. **Do not** overtighten the plug, as it has tapered threads.

7 Wipe any split oil from the gearbox casing.

29 Fuel filter element renewal

1 The fuel filter is mounted on the longitudinal chassis member below the right-hand rear wheel arch. Jack up the rear of the vehicle and support it securely on axle stands (see *Jacking and vehicle support*).

2 Clean the area around the filter head, and place a container beneath the filter.

3 Undo the plug at the base of the filter, then unscrew the filter cartridge from the filter head **(see illustration)**.

4 Unscrew the sedimenter from old filter, and transfer it to the new one, using the new rubber seal included with the new filter **(see illustrations)**.

5 Thoroughly clean the mating face of the filter head, then screw the new filter cartridge into place by hand.

6 Reconnect the wiring plug and lower the vehicle to the ground.

7 Start the engine and check for leaks around the filter. There is no need to prime or bleed the fuel system following filter renewal.

29.3 Unscrew the old fuel filter

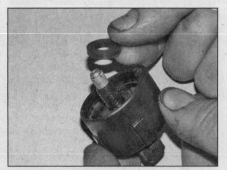

29.4a Fit a new seal to the sedimenter . . .

29.4b . . .then screw it onto the base of the new filter

30.2 Prise the cover from the handset . . .

30.3 . . . and slide the battery from the holder

30.5 Ensure the battery is fitted with the positive side (+) upwards

30 Alarm handset battery renewal

⚠ **Warning: Do not remove the battery until you are ready to install a new one. The engine will immobilise 5 minutes after the ignition key is removed from the switch (or 30 seconds**

after the engine has been switched off and the driver's door opened).

1 Unlock the vehicle/disable the alarm system using the unlock button on the remote handset.
2 Remove the key from the ignition, and using a small flat-bladed screwdriver, prise the cover from the handset **(see illustration)**.
3 Note its fitted location, then slide the battery from the retaining clip **(see illustration)**. Do not touch the circuit board or contact surfaces of the clip with bare skin.

4 Press and hold any one of the handset buttons for at least 5 seconds to drain any residual electrical energy.
5 Fit the new battery (type CR2032), into the clip with the positive (+) side facing upwards **(see illustration)**. Avoid touching the flat surfaces of the battery with bare skin as this may reduce the life of the battery.
6 Clip the two halves of the handset back together, and check for correct operation.

Every 36 000 miles or 3 years

31 Air cleaner element renewal and dump valve cleaning

1 Release the clips and disconnect the airflow meter from the air cleaner cover **(see illustration)**.
2 Release the two clips and lift the air cleaner cover from the housing **(see illustration)**.
3 Lift the old element from place, then remove any debris and clean the inside of the housing and cover **(see illustration)**.
4 Fit the new element into the housing.
5 Refit the cover and secure it in place with the clips.
6 Refit the airflow meter and secure the retaining clips.

7 Reach under the wheel arch, and squeeze together the sides of the dump valve on the underside of the air cleaner housing, and remove any debris within it.

32 Coolant renewal

⚠ **Warning: Wait until the engine is cold before starting this procedure. Do not allow antifreeze to come in contact with your skin, or with the painted surfaces of the vehicle. Rinse off spills immediately with plenty of water. Never leave antifreeze lying around in an open container, or in a puddle in the**

driveway or garage floor. Children and pets are attracted by its sweet smell, but antifreeze is fatal if ingested. Refer to the 'Antifreeze mixture' sub-Section below before proceeding.

Cooling system draining

1 To drain the cooling system, first cover the expansion tank cap with a wad of rag, and slowly turn the cap anti-clockwise to relieve the pressure in the cooling system (a hissing sound will normally be heard). Wait until any pressure remaining in the system is released, then continue to turn the cap until it can be removed.
2 Position a suitable container beneath the radiator. Open the drain plug access cover

31.1 Release the airflow meter clips (arrowed)

31.2 Release the air filter cover clips (arrowed)

31.3 Note how it's fitted, and lift the old element from the housing

32.2a Rotate the drain plug access cover in the undershield anti-clockwise . . .

32.2b . . . then unscrew the drain plug (arrowed)

in the engine undershield, then unscrew the drain plug and allow the coolant to drain into the container (see illustrations). Discard the drain plug sealing washer, a new one must be fitted.

3 To fully drain the system, remove the alternator as described in Chapter 5, then slacken and remove the coolant drain plug from the left-hand side of the cylinder block, and allow any residual coolant to drain from the block. When the flow of coolant has stopped, wipe clean the threads of the drain plug and block. Where the plug was fitted with a sealing washer, fit a new sealing washer. Where no washer was fitted, apply a smear of suitable sealant to the drain plug threads. Refit the drain plug to the block, and tighten it securely.

4 If the coolant has been drained for a reason other than renewal, then provided it is clean and less than two years old, it can be re-used.

Cooling system flushing

5 If coolant renewal has been neglected, or if the antifreeze mixture has become diluted, then in time, the cooling system may gradually lose efficiency, as the coolant passages become restricted due to rust, scale deposits, and other sediment. The cooling system efficiency can be restored by flushing the system clean.

32.12 Undo the bleed screw in the top hose

6 The radiator should be flushed independently of the engine, to avoid unnecessary contamination.

7 To flush the radiator, disconnect the top hose at the radiator, then insert a garden hose into the radiator top inlet. Direct a flow of clean water through the radiator, and continue flushing until clean water emerges from the radiator bottom outlet (the bottom radiator hose should have been disconnected to drain the system). If after a reasonable period, the water still does not run clear, the radiator can be flushed with a good proprietary cleaning agent. It is important that the cleaning agent manufacturer's instructions are followed carefully. If the contamination is particularly bad, insert the hose in the radiator bottom outlet, and flush the radiator in reverse ('reverse-flushing').

8 Remove the thermostat as described in Chapter 3.

9 With the radiator top hose disconnected from the radiator, insert a hose into the thermostat hose. Direct a clean flow of water through the engine, and continue flushing until clean water emerges from the radiator top hose.

10 On completion of flushing, refit the thermostat with reference to Chapter 3, and reconnect the hoses.

Cooling system filling

11 Before attempting to fill the cooling system, make sure that all hoses and clips are in good condition, and that the clips are tight. Note that an antifreeze mixture must be used all year round, to prevent corrosion of the alloy engine components.

12 Slacken the bleed screw in the radiator top hose (see illustration).

13 Release the upper bleed hose from the battery box, then remove the coolant expansion tank from the mounting bracket, and lift it approximately 20 cm.

14 Fill the system by slowly pouring the coolant into the expansion tank to prevent airlocks from forming.

15 If the coolant is being renewed, begin by

pouring in a couple of litres of water, followed by the correct quantity of antifreeze, then top-up with more water.

16 When air-free coolant emerges, tighten the bleed screw in the radiator top hose.

17 Top-up the expansion tank to the correct level, then refit the expansion tank cap.

18 Refit the expansion tank to its mounting bracket, and clip the bleed hose into place.

19 Start the engine, run it until it reaches normal operating temperature, then stop the engine and allow it to cool.

20 Check for leaks, particularly around disturbed components. Check the coolant level in the expansion tank, and top-up if necessary. Note that the system must be cold before an accurate level is indicated in the expansion tank. If the expansion tank cap is removed while the engine is still warm, cover the cap with a thick cloth. Unscrew the cap slowly, to gradually relieve the system pressure (a hissing sound will normally be heard). Wait until any pressure remaining in the system is released, then continue to turn the cap until it can be removed.

Antifreeze mixture

21 Always use an ethylene-glycol based antifreeze with OAT (Organic Acid Technology) corrosion inhibitors. Note: Do not mix this with any other type of antifreeze.

22 Before adding antifreeze, the cooling system should be completely drained, preferably flushed, and all hoses and clips checked for condition and security.

23 After filling with antifreeze, a label should be attached to the radiator or expansion tank, stating the type and concentration of antifreeze used, and the date installed. Any subsequent topping-up should be made with the same type and concentration of antifreeze.

24 Do not use engine antifreeze in the windscreen/tailgate washer system, as it will cause damage to the vehicle paintwork. A screenwash should be added to the washer system, in the quantities recommended on the bottle.

33.2 Separate the steering box drop arm from the drag link

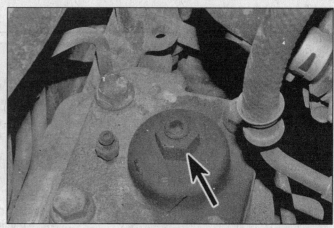

33.5 Steering box adjustment locknut and screw (arrowed)

Every 48 000 miles or 4 years

33 Steering box backlash adjustment

1 Raise the front of the vehicle and support it securely on axle stands (see *Jacking and vehicle support*).
2 Undo the balljoint nut, then use a universal balljoint separator tool to detach the drag link from the drop arm – refer to Chapter 11 **(see illustration)**.
3 Ensure the steering is centralised, then hold the drop arm and attempt to rotate the steering column lower shaft at the universal joint. If any movement exists, adjust the steering box backlash as follows.

4 Remove the cooling fan and lower cowling as described in Chapter 3.
5 Slacken the lock nut, and tighten the adjuster screw only as much as is necessary to eliminate the movement at the universal joint. Take care not to overtighten the adjuster – any free play should only just be eliminated **(see illustration)**.
6 With the adjustment correct, hold the adjuster and tighten the locknut securely.
7 Rotate the steering wheel and check that the steering operates smoothly with no binding. If binding does exist, it's probable that the steering box is excessively worn, consult a Land Rover dealer or specialist.
8 Reconnect the drag link to the drop arm and tighten the balljoint nut to the specified torque.
9 Lower the vehicle to the ground.

34 Intercooler element cleaning

1 Remove the intercooler as described in Chapter 4A.
2 Check the element for damage and deterioration, and renew if necessary.
3 If the original element is to be refitted, flush the element with solvent cleaner Land Rover part No STC 9713 or a suitable alternative (check with your Land Rover dealer or specialist, following the instructions supplied with the cleaner).
4 Dry the element thoroughly, then refit as described in Chapter 4.

Every 60 000 miles

35 Air suspension intake filter renewal

1 On models fitted with air suspension, remove the left-hand rear tail light as described in Chapter 13, Section 7.
2 Release the filter from its retaining clip **(see illustration)**.
3 Working underneath the left-hand rear of the vehicle, squeeze together the sides, and disconnect the filter hose quick-release connector **(see illustration)**.
4 Note its fitted location, and pull the filter upwards from place.
5 Feed the new filter hose down through the vehicle body, and reconnect the quick-release connector.
6 Secure the filter with the retaining clip.

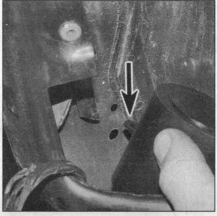

35.2 Release the air suspension filter from the clip (arrowed)

35.3 Disconnect the quick-release connector by depressing the release button (arrowed)

Every 72 000 miles

36 Braking system seal, vacuum servo filter and hose renewal

1 At this interval, Land Rover recommend that all the brake system rubber seals and flexible rubber hoses are renewed, and the hydraulic system filled with fresh fluid. Refer to the relevant Sections of Chapter 10 for renewal information.

37 ACE system filter renewal

1 Raise the front and rear of the vehicle and support it securely on axle stands (see *Jacking and vehicle support*).
2 Position a suitable container underneath the ACE valve block, located on the chassis rail on the right-hand side of the vehicle, below the passenger doors.
3 Thoroughly clean the area around the valve block, and the valve block itself.
4 Unscrew the filter cap and discard the O-ring seal – a new one must be fitted **(see illustration)**.

⚠ *Warning: It is absolutely vital the no dirt is allowed to enter the ACE system. All openings must be*

37.4 Unscrew the ACE filter cap from the valve block (arrowed)

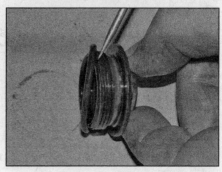

37.5 Screw in a 6 mm bolt and pull (don't twist) the filter from place

covered/plugged. Use only new fluid from a sealed container.
5 Screw a 6 mm bolt into the base of the filter **(see illustration)**. Do not allow the filter to rotate with the bolt, then pull the bolt and filter from the valve block.
6 Ensure the new filter has an O-ring fitted, then insert the new filter into the valve block.
7 Fit a new O-ring seal to the filter cap, then refit and tighten it to the specified torque **(see illustration)**.
8 Lower the vehicle to the ground, and check the ACE fluid level (see *Weekly checks*).
9 Start the engine and allow it to idle for approximately 2 minutes, then recheck and if necessary, top-up the fluid level.

37.7 Renew the filter cap O-ring seal

Every 96 000 miles

38 Axle oil renewal

Note: *A 13 mm square-section wrench will be required to undo the axle drain plug. These wrenches can be obtained from most motor factors, or from your Land Rover dealer.*
1 This operation is much quicker and more efficient if the car is first taken on a journey of sufficient length to warm the axle oil up to normal operating temperature. Allow time, however, for the exhaust system to cool.
2 Park the car on level ground, switch off the 'ignition', and apply the handbrake firmly.
3 Wipe clean the area around the front axle

filler/level plug, which is on the differential housing. Unscrew the plug, and clean it. Discard the O-ring seal if it shows any sign of deterioration.
4 Position a suitable container under the drain plug situated on the base of the differential housing.
5 Unscrew the drain plug, and allow the oil to drain completely into the container. If the oil is hot, take precautions against scalding. Clean both the filler/level and the drain plugs.
6 When the oil has finished draining, clean the drain plug threads and those of the differential casing, then refit the drain plug and washer, tightening it to the specified torque.
7 Refilling the axle is an extremely awkward operation. Above all, allow plenty of time for

the oil level to settle properly before checking it. Note that the car must be parked on level ground when checking the oil level.
8 Refill the axle with the exact amount of the specified type of oil (see *Lubricants and fluids*), then check the oil level as described in Section 15. If the correct amount was poured into the transmission, and a large amount flows out on checking the level, refit the filler/level plug; take the car on a short journey so that the new oil is distributed fully around the axle components, then check the level again on your return.
9 When the level is correct, refit the filler/level plug, tightening it to the specified torque, and wash off any spilt oil.
10 Repeat the procedure for the rear axle.

Every 15 years

39 Seat belt pretensioners and airbag renewal

Refer to Chapters 12 and 13.

Chapter 2 Part A:
Engine in-car repair procedures

Contents

	Section number
Camshaft, rocker arms and hydraulic adjusters – removal, inspection and refitting	8
Compression and leakdown tests – description and interpretation	2
Crankshaft pulley – removal and refitting	5
Crankshaft spigot bush – renewal	15
Cylinder head – removal, inspection and refitting	10
Cylinder head cover – removal and refitting	4
Engine mountings – removal and refitting	18
Engine oil, filter and centrifuge rotor renewal	See Chapter 1
Engine oil level check	See Weekly checks
Flywheel/driveplate – removal, inspection and refitting	14

	Section number
General information	1
Injector rocker shaft – removal refitting	9
Oil cooler – removal and refitting	16
Oil pressure switch – renewal	17
Oil pump/stiffener plate – removal and refitting	12
Oil seals – renewal	13
Sump – removal and refitting	11
Timing chain, sprockets and guides – removal, inspection and refitting	7
Timing chain cover – removal and refitting	6
Top dead centre (TDC) for No 1 piston – locating	3

Degrees of difficulty

Easy, suitable for novice with little experience 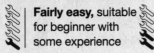	**Fairly easy,** suitable for beginner with some experience	**Fairly difficult,** suitable for competent DIY mechanic	**Difficult,** suitable for experienced DIY mechanic	**Very difficult,** suitable for expert DIY or professional

Specifications

General

Engine type	Five-cylinder, in-line, water-cooled. Double (duplex) chain-driven camshaft, operating valves via roller-rockers arms and hydraulic clearance adjusters
Bore	84.45 mm
Stroke	88.95 mm
Capacity	2495 cc
Firing order	1-2-4-5-3 (No 1 at timing chain end)
Direction of crankshaft rotation	Clockwise (viewed from timing chain end of engine)
Compression ratio	19.5:1
Maximum power (DIN)	101 kW @ 4200 rpm
Maximum torque	315 Nm @ 1950 rpm
Maximum compression pressure difference between cylinders (typical value)	5.0 bar
Maximum engine speed:	
Governed	4850 rpm
Overrun	5460 rpm
Idle speed (not adjustable):	
Manual transmission	740 ± 50 rpm
Automatic transmission	760 ± 50 rpm
Emission standard:	
Engine Serial No prefixes 10P to 14P	EU2
Engine Serial No prefixes 15P to 19P	EU3

Lubrication system

Normal oil pressure:	
At idle speed (cold)	3.0 bar
At 3500 rpm (hot)	1.5 to 3.0 bar
Oil pump type	Eccentric rotor, chain driven from crankshaft
Relief valve opening pressure	4.0 bar
Relief valve spring free length (minimum)	42.00 mm
Pressure switch opening pressure	0.2 to 0.6 bar
Oil pump clearances:	
Outer rotor-to-body	0.295 to 0.375 mm
Inner rotor-to-outer rotor (maximum)	0.13 mm
Outer rotor endfloat	0.038 to 0.075 mm

Camshaft

Endfloat . . . . 0.16 to 0.60 mm
Drive . . . . Duplex chain

Torque wrench settings

	Nm	lbf ft
Auxiliary drivebelt tensioner bolt	50	37
Big-end cap bolts*:		
Stage 1	20	15
Stage 2	Angle-tighten a further 80°	
Camshaft carrier bolts	25	18
Camshaft sprocket bolts*	36	27
Centrifugal oil filter drain hose bolts	10	7
Crankshaft damper bolt	80	59
Crankshaft pulley bolt*	460	339
Crankshaft rear oil seal housing bolts	10	7
Cylinder head bolts:*		
Stage 1	30	22
Stage 2	65	48
Stage 3	Angle-tighten a further 90°	
Stage 4	Angle-tighten a further 180°	
Stage 5	Angle-tighten a further 45°	
Cylinder head cover bolts	10	7
Cylinder head nut and bolt to engine block (see text)	25	18
EGR valve pipe to cylinder head	25	18
Engine mountings:		
Mounting bracket to cylinder block	48	35
Mounting to chassis	85	63
Mounting to mounting bracket	85	63
Exhaust manifold heat shield:		
M6	10	7
M8	25	18
Flywheel/driveplate securing bolts:*		
Stage 1	40	30
Stage 2	Angle-tighten a further 90°	
Injector rocker shaft adjusting screw locknut*	16	12
Injector rocker shaft bolts*	32	24
Main bearing cap bolts:*		
Stage 1	33	24
Stage 2	Angle-tighten a further 90°	
Oil cooler bolts	25	18
Oil filter cartridge adapter bolts	25	18
Oil pressure relief valve plug	23	17
Oil pressure warning light switch	15	11
Oil pump sprocket bolt	25	18
Oil pump strainer bolts	10	7
Piston cooling/lubrication jets	8	6
Stiffener plate retaining bolts*	23	17
Sump drain plug	23	17
Sump-to-engine block bolts:		
All except bolts 11, 14, 15 and 18 (see text)	25	18
Bolts 11, 14, 15 and 18 (see text)	28	21
Sump-to-transmission casing bolts	45	33
Timing chain cover bolts	27	20
Timing chain fixed guide bolts:		
Allen screw	25	18
M6	10	7
M10	45	33
Timing chain lubrication jet bolt	10	7
Timing chain tensioner blade bolt	25	18
Timing chain tensioner retaining bolt	55	41
Torque converter bolts*	50	37
Transmission-to-engine bolts	50	37
Turbocharger-to-exhaust manifold nuts	30	22
Turbocharger oil feed banjo bolt	25	18

* Do not re-use

1 General information

How to use this Chapter

This Part of Chapter 2 describes the repair procedures which can reasonably be carried out on the engine while it remains in the vehicle. If the engine has been removed from the vehicle and is being dismantled as described in Chapter 2B, any preliminary dismantling procedures can be ignored.

Note that, while it may be *possible* physically to overhaul items such as the piston/connecting rod assemblies while the engine is in the vehicle, this is not recommended. Such tasks are not usually carried out as separate operations, and usually require the execution of several additional procedures (not to mention the cleaning of components and of oilways); for this reason, all such tasks are classed as major overhaul procedures, and are described in Chapter 2B.

Chapter 2B describes the removal of the engine from the vehicle, and the full overhaul procedures which can then be carried out.

Engine description

The TD5 is a new engine from Land Rover, not based on any previous design. The engine is a 5-cylinder single overhead camshaft, 2 valves per cylinder, with direct injection, turbocharger and intercooler. The engine block is made from cast iron, with an aluminium stiffener plate fitted to its base. The cylinder head and sump are aluminium – no refacing/skimming or the cylinder head is permitted. The cylinders are 'direct' bored into the engine block, then plateau honed – no reboring of the cylinders is possible. Lubrication and cooling of the pistons/gudgeon pins is provided by jets bolted to the base of the cylinder bores.

The single camshaft runs directly in the cylinder head, and is retained by an aluminium camshaft carrier assembly. The valves are operated by roller-rocker arms fitted directly below the camshaft lobes. The roller-rocker arms pivot on hydraulic lash adjusters – no checking or maintenance of the valve clearances is required.

'Unit' fuel injectors are fitted into the cylinder head. With this design, a second set of lobes on the camshaft operate a second set of rocker arms located on a rocker shaft fitted to the camshaft carrier assembly. The rocker arms operate directly on the top of the injectors, forcing the injector pistons down, and highly pressurising (1500 to 1750 bar approximately) the fuel within as the camshaft rotates. When the pressure within the injectors is sufficient to overcome the resistance of the pintle spring, fuel is injected into the combustion chambers. The injectors are fitted with solenoids which control the release of the pressure back into the return system, effectively controlling the injection period. The solenoids are actuated by an ECM (Electronic Control Module), which receives information from the various engine/system sensors.

The camshaft is driven from the crankshaft by a duplex (twin-row) timing chain. The chain is tensioned automatically by a hydraulic tensioner assembly. A single row chain from a separate sprocket on the crankshaft drives the eccentric-rotor oil pump, which is integral with the aluminium stiffener plate fitted to the base of the engine block.

The hardened cast iron crankshaft is supported on 6 plain bearing shells, with endfloat controlled by thrustwashers fitted either side of the No 3 main bearing shell.

The connecting rods are attached to the crankshaft by fracture-split big end caps. With this design, the connecting rods are made as one casting, then fractured and split to form the removable big-end cap. This ensures a unique fit between the two components, resulting in greater rigidity and strength. The aluminium pistons have graphite coated skirts to reduce friction, and swirl chambers located in the piston crown. The pistons are attached to the connecting rods by gudgeon pins, which are a push-fit in the connecting rod small-end bores. The gudgeon pins are retained by circlips. The pistons are fitted with three piston rings – two compression rings and an oil control ring.

The coolant pump is located in a casting behind the power steering pump, and is driven by the steering pump, which itself is crankshaft driven via a rubber auxiliary drivebelt.

Operations with engine in vehicle

The following operations can be carried out without having to remove the engine from the vehicle.

a) Removal and refitting of the camshaft/rocker shaft/hydraulic lash adjusters.
b) Removal and refitting of the cylinder head.
c) Removal and refitting of the timing chain and sprockets.
d) Removal and refitting of the sump.
e) Removal and refitting of the big-end bearings, connecting rods, and pistons*.
f) Removal and refitting of the oil pump/stiffener plate.
g) Renewal of the engine mountings.
h) Removal and refitting of the flywheel.

* Although the operation marked with an asterisk can be carried out with the engine in the vehicle (after removal of the sump), it is preferable for the engine to be removed, in the interests of cleanliness and improved access. For this reason, the procedure is described in Chapter 2B.

2 Compression and leakdown tests – description and interpretation

Compression test

Note: *A compression tester specifically designed for diesel engines must be used for this test.*

1 When engine performance is down, or if misfiring occurs which cannot be attributed to the fuel system, a compression test can provide diagnostic clues as to the engine's condition. If the test is performed regularly, it can give warning of trouble before any other symptoms become apparent.

2 A compression tester specifically intended for diesel engines must be used, because of the higher pressures involved. The tester is connected to an adapter which screws into the glow plug hole. It is unlikely to be worthwhile buying such a tester for occasional use, but it may be possible to borrow or hire one – if not, have the test performed by a garage.

3 Unless specific instructions to the contrary are supplied with the tester, observe the following points:

a) The battery must be in a good state of charge, the air filter must be clean, and the engine should be at normal operating temperature.
b) All the glow plugs should be removed before starting the test.

4 There is no need to hold the accelerator pedal down during the test, because the diesel engine air inlet is not throttled.

5 The actual compression pressures measured are not so important as the balance between cylinders. Land Rover do not specify compression pressures, but a typical value for the maximum difference between cylinders is given in the Specifications.

6 The cause of poor compression is less easy to establish on a diesel engine than on a petrol one. The effect of introducing oil into the cylinders ('wet' testing) is not conclusive, because there is a risk that the oil will sit in the recess on the piston crown, instead of passing to the rings. However, the following can be used as a rough guide to diagnosis.

7 All cylinders should produce very similar pressures; any difference greater than that specified indicates the existence of a fault. Note that the compression should build-up quickly in a healthy engine; low compression on the first stroke, followed by gradually-increasing pressure on successive strokes, indicates worn piston rings. A low compression reading on the first stroke, which does not build-up during successive strokes, indicates leaking valves or a blown head gasket (a cracked head could also be the cause). Deposits on the undersides of the valve heads can also cause low compression.

8 A low reading from two adjacent cylinders is almost certainly due to the head gasket having blown between them; the presence of coolant in the engine oil will confirm this.

9 If the compression reading is unusually high, the cylinder head surfaces, valves and pistons are probably coated with carbon deposits. If this is the case, the cylinder head should be removed and decarbonised (see Chapter 2B).

Leakdown test

10 A leakdown test measures the rate at which compressed air fed into the cylinder

3.3 The mark on the camshaft sprocket (arrowed) must align between the bronze (pre EU3 models) or blue (post EU3 models) coloured links on the chain

3.4 Insert a 17/64" diameter drill bit through the hole in the cam carrier (arrowed) into the slot in the camshaft drive flange

3.5a Remove the plug (arrowed) from the transmission bellhousing

is lost. It is an alternative to a compression test, and in many ways it is better, since the escaping air provides easy identification of where pressure loss is occurring (piston rings, valves or head gasket).

11 The equipment needed for leakdown testing is unlikely to be available to the home mechanic. If poor compression is suspected, have the test performed by a suitably-equipped garage.

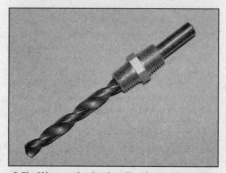

3.5b We used a hydraulic pipe union with a 14 x 1.5 mm thread, and drilled out the centre to accept a 5/16" in drill bit

3.5c Screw in the union and insert the drill bit into the slot in the flywheel perimeter

3 Top dead centre (TDC) for No 1 piston – locating

Note: *Suitable tools will be required to lock the flywheel and the camshaft in position during this operation. The Land Rover special tool available to lock the flywheel is LRT-12-158, and the camshaft tool is LRT-12-058. It is possible to fabricate home-made equivalents, details are given in the text.*

1 Top dead centre (TDC) is the highest point in the cylinder that each piston reaches as the crankshaft turns. Each piston reaches TDC at the end of the compression stoke, and again at the end of the exhaust stroke.

2 Remove the cylinder head cover as described in Section 4.

3 Using a spanner/socket on the crankshaft pulley, rotate the crankshaft until the mark

on the camshaft sprocket aligns between the coloured links on the timing chain **(see illustration)**.

4 Insert LRT-12-058 through the hole in the camshaft carrier and into the camshaft. Note that it may be necessary to turn the crankshaft forwards or backwards a few degrees in order to fully insert the tool. In the absence of the special Land Rover tool, a 17/64" drill bit will suffice **(see illustration)**.

5 With the camshaft locked in position, it should now be possible to insert LRT-12-158 through the bellhousing to lock the flywheel/ crankshaft in position **(see illustration)**. In the absence of the special Land Rover tools,

a home-made equivalent may be fabricated using the dimensions given **(see illustration)**.

6 The engine is now locked at TDC for No 1 cylinder.

4 Cylinder head cover – removal and refitting

Removal

1 Undo the three bolts and remove the acoustic cover from the top of the engine **(see illustrations)**.

4.1a The acoustic cover is retained by two bolts on the exhaust manifold side (arrowed) . . .

4.1b . . . and one (arrowed) on the intake side

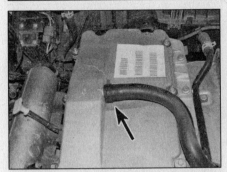

4.2 Release the clip and disconnect the breather hose from the cylinder head cover (arrowed)

4.3a Undo the cylinder head cover bolts

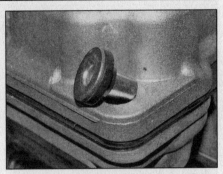

4.3b Check the condition of the sealing washers and spacers

2 Release the clip and disconnect the breather hose from the cover **(see illustration)**.
3 Undo the 13 bolts, recover the sealing washers and spacers, then remove the cylinder head cover **(see illustration)**. Discard the gasket – a new one must be fitted. Check the condition of the sealing washers and spacers and renew as necessary **(see illustration)**.

Refitting

4 Commence refitting by thoroughly cleaning the gasket faces of the cover and the cylinder head.
5 On engines manufactured before July 1999, apply a 3 mm diameter bead of sealant (Land Rover No STC 50550 or equivalent) to the top corners of the semi-circular cut-out on the camshaft carrier.
6 Position the new gasket on the cylinder head cover, then refit the spacers and sealing washers, and tighten the retaining bolts to the specified torque **(see illustration)**.
7 Reconnect the breather hose and secure it with the clip.
8 Refit the acoustic cover and tighten the bolts securely.

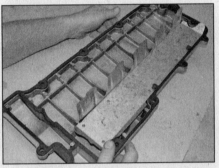

4.6 Fit a new gasket to the cylinder head cover

Note: *If it is required to completely remove the undershield, the front propeller shaft must be disconnected from the axle as described in Chapter 8.*
2 Remove the radiator as described in Chapter 3.
3 Use a 15 mm spanner to relieve the tension on the auxiliary drivebelt, then manoeuvre the belt from the pulleys (see Chapter 1).
4 Undo the three bolts securing the damper to the crankshaft pulley **(see illustration)**.
5 The crankshaft pulley bolt must now be slackened. To prevent the crankshaft from rotating, a special Land Rover tool LRT-51-003, is available which attaches to the bolt holes in the pulley. Alternatively, a home-made tool may be used **(see Tool Tip)**.

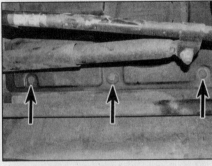

5.1 Engine undershield front fasteners (arrowed)

6 With the crankshaft held using the tool previously described, slacken the retaining bolt and slide the pulley from the crankshaft **(see illustration)**. Note that the pulley bolt is extremely tight – an assistant will be required. Discard the pulley bolt – a new one must be fitted.

Refitting

7 Refitting is a reversal of removal, bearing in mind the following points:
a) Tighten the new pulley retaining bolt and damper screws to the recommended torque.
b) Refit and tension the auxiliary drivebelt as described in Chapter 1.
c) Refit the radiator as described in Chapter 3.
d) On completion, refill the cooling system as described in Chapter 1.

5 Crankshaft pulley – removal and refitting

Removal

1 Undo the fasteners, and move the engine undershield rearwards **(see illustration)**.

5.4 Undo the 3 bolts securing the damper to the crankshaft pulley

To counterhold the crankshaft pulley, use two lengths of steel strip bolted together, and fixed to the crankshaft pulley using two of the damper bolts.

5.6 With the pulley held, slacken the centre bolt

6.4 Undo the auxiliary belt tensioner bolt (arrowed)

6.5 Release the clip (arrowed) and disconnect the vacuum pump oil drain hose from the timing chain cover

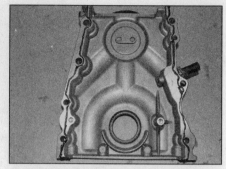
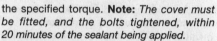

6.9 Apply a bead of sealant to the timing cover

6 Timing chain cover – removal and refitting

Removal

1 Remove the crankshaft pulley as described in Section 5.

2 Remove the cylinder head as described in Section 10.

3 Remove the oil sump as described in Section 11.

4 Undo the bolt and remove the auxiliary belt tensioner assembly **(see illustration)**.

5 Release the clip and disconnect the vacuum pump drain hose from the timing chain cover **(see illustration)**.

6 Undo the 8 bolts and carefully pull the timing chain cover from place.

Refitting

7 Commence refitting by cleaning all traces of old gasket from the mating faces of the timing chain cover and the cylinder block.

8 It is advisable to fit a new crankshaft front oil seal to the cover as follows:
a) Prise the old seal from the aperture in the cover using a suitable screwdriver.
b) Clean the seal seat in the cover.
c) Press a new seal into position using a suitable socket or tube. The seal lips should face the crankshaft. Take care not to damage the seal lips.

9 Apply a thin and even film of sealant (STC-50550 from Land Rover dealers, or equivalent) to the timing chain cover **(see illustration)**.

10 Refit the cover to the cylinder block, then refit the securing bolts, and tighten them to the specified torque. **Note:** *The cover must be fitted, and the bolts tightened, within 20 minutes of the sealant being applied.*

11 Reconnect the vacuum pump drain hose and secure the retaining clip.

12 Refit the auxiliary drivebelt tensioner assembly and tighten the bolt to the specified torque.

13 Refit the sump as described in Section 11.

14 Refit the cylinder head as described in Section 10.

15 Refit the crankshaft pulley as described in Section 5.

7 Timing chain, sprockets and guides – removal, inspection and refitting

Removal

1 Remove the timing chain cover as described in Section 6.

2 Withdraw the camshaft sprocket from the timing chain, then manoeuvre the chain over the end of the crankshaft.

3 Undo the two bolts and remove the timing chain fixed guide **(see illustration)**.

4 Undo the bolt and remove the timing chain tensioner blade **(see illustration)**.

5 If required, undo the bolt and remove the timing chain lubrication jet from the front face of the engine block **(see illustration)**.

6 Undo the bolt and slide the oil pump sprocket, chain and crankshaft sprocket from place **(see illustration)**. If loose, recover the Woodruff (half-moon) key from the crankshaft.

Inspection

7 Examine the timing chain. If there are any obvious signs of wear or damage, renew the chain. Hold the chain horizontally (link plates facing downwards) – if the chain takes on a deeply-bowed appearance, this indicates that the links are worn, and the chain should be renewed.

8 Examine the teeth on the camshaft and crankshaft sprockets.

9 If the teeth are worn or significantly hooked in appearance, the relevant sprocket should be renewed.

10 Examine the chain guides and tensioner

7.3 Timing chain fixed guide bolts (arrowed)

7.4 Timing chain tensioner blade bolt (arrowed)

7.5 Undo the bolt and remove the chain lubrication jet

7.6 Undo the oil pump sprocket bolt and slide the chain and sprockets from place

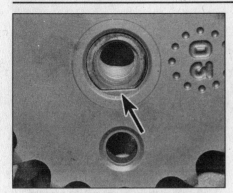

7.13 The flat on the drive sprocket must align with the flat on the oil pump shaft (arrowed)

blade. If there is any signs of excessive wear or damage, renew them. **Note:** *Different timing chains, tensioner bodies and blades are fitted depending on engine number. The timing chains and sprockets fitted to engine number prefixes 15P to 19P may be fitted to early engines as an assembly only. Early engines timing chains have blue-coloured timing links, and later ones (with thicker chain links), have bronze-coloured timing links. If the tensioner body is to be renewed, note that there are two different tensioners available: On engines with number prefixes 10P to 14P the tensioner body is colour coded black, and on engines 15P to 19P the tensioner body is coded yellow. It is permissible to fit the later (yellow) tensioner to the earlier engines only if the later tensioner blade is also fitted.*

Refitting

11 If removed, refit the timing chain lubrication jet to the engine block and tighten the retaining bolt to the specified torque.

12 Ensure the crankshaft is still set to TDC on No 1 cylinder as described in Section 3.

13 Fit the oil pump drive chain around the crankshaft and oil pump sprockets, ensure the Woodruff key is in place on the crankshaft, then side the sprocket/chain over the end of

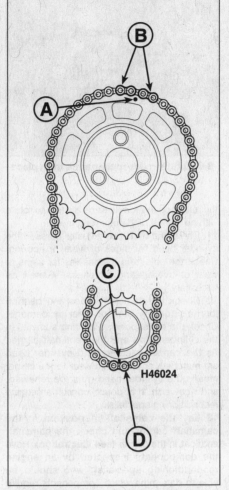

7.17 Align the camshaft sprocket timing mark (A) between the coloured links (B), and the crankshaft sprocket timing mark (C) with the coloured link (D)

the crankshaft. The locating slot in the inside diameter of the crankshaft sprocket must align with the Woodruff key, and the flat on the oil pump driveshaft must align with the corresponding flat in the sprocket bore **(see illustration)**.

14 Refit the sprocket to the oil pump, then apply a little thread-locking compound to the sprocket retaining bolt and tighten it to the specified torque.

15 Refit the timing chain fixed guide to the engine block and tighten the retaining bolts to the specified torque. Note the are two different torque setting for the two different diameter bolts.

16 Refit the timing chain tensioner blade, and tighten the retaining bolt to the specified torque.

17 Fit the camshaft sprocket into the timing chain, ensuring the timing mark on the sprocket is between the two coloured links **(see illustration)**.

18 Fit the timing chain around the crankshaft sprocket aligning the coloured link of the chain with the timing mark on the sprocket **(see illustration 7.17)**.

19 Refit the timing chain cover as described in Section 6.

8 Camshaft, rocker arms and hydraulic adjusters – removal, inspection and refitting

Removal

1 Remove the cylinder head as described in Section 10.

2 Disconnect the wiring plugs from each of the injectors, and remove the wiring harness from the camshaft carrier. Discard the multiplug O-ring, a new one must be fitted **(see illustrations)**

3 Slacken the locknuts, and fully undo the injector rocker arms adjusting screws, so that there is maximum clearance between the base of the screws and the top of the injectors **(see illustration)**. **Note:** *Land Rover recommend that the adjusting screws and locknuts are discarded – new ones must be fitted.*

4 Gradually and evenly, slacken and remove

8.2a Depress the clip (arrowed) and pull the wiring plug from each injector

8.2b Pull the harness and plug (arrowed) upwards from the cylinder head

8.3 Slacken the locknuts, then fully unscrew the adjusting screws. Note that the screws will not come up and out through the top of the rocker arms due to the ball at the base of the screw

8.4 Injector rocker shaft bolts (front 3 arrowed)

8.8 Lift the roller-rocker arms from place

8.9 Pull the hydraulic adjusters from place, and store them in an upright position

the 6 rocker shaft retaining bolts, and lift the shaft from position **(see illustration)**. Discard the bolts, new ones must be fitted.

5 Working in the **reverse** of the sequence shown **(see illustration 8.19)**, gradually and evenly slacken and remove the 13 bolts securing the camshaft carrier to the cylinder head.

6 Using a soft-faced hammer, carefully tap the camshaft carrier upwards to release it from the cylinder head. Note that the carrier is located on the cylinder head by two dowels.

7 Lift the camshaft from position. Discard the camshaft rear oil seal – a new one must be fitted.

8 Note their fitted locations, and lift the roller-rocker arms from place. Mark or label them to ensure they are fitted to their original locations **(see illustration)**.

9 Carefully pull the hydraulic adjusters from their locations in the cylinder head, and store them in their fitted order to ensure they are refitted to their original locations. It's essential the hydraulic adjusters are stored upright **(see illustration)**.

Inspection

10 Thoroughly clean all components, and check them for obvious signs of wear or damage. Absolute cleanliness is essential – ensure all oil ways and fuel galleries in the cylinder head are free of dirt/debris. Any contamination could cause severe damage to the cylinder head and/or injectors. Check

the rollers on the rocker arms are free to rotate with no sign of binding or roughness.

11 Check the hydraulic adjuster bores in the cylinder head for signs of wear or scoring. Check the adjusters themselves for signs of wear or overheating (blueness). Renew as necessary.

12 Check the camshaft lobes and bearing journals for any sign of wear or damage. Check the corresponding bearing surfaces in the cylinder head and the camshaft carrier. As the camshaft carrier and cylinder head are matched, any damage/wear to the carrier means the cylinder head must be renewed, and *vice-versa*. If in doubt, consult an engine reconditioning specialist.

13 Lay the camshaft in position in the camshaft carrier and check the camshaft endfloat in the carrier **(see illustration)**. Have the components inspected by an engine reconditioning specialist, who should be able to determine which components require renewal.

Refitting

14 Refit the hydraulic adjusters into their original locations in the cylinder head.

15 Refit the roller-rockers arms to their original locations above the hydraulic adjusters and the valve stems.

16 Ensure the bearing surfaces in the cylinder head are clean, then lubricate the surfaces and the camshaft journals with clean engine oil. Carefully lay the camshaft in the cylinder

head, with the locking hole at the timing chain end in the vertical position.

17 Using a short-haired roller, apply a thin film of sealant (Land Rover No STC-4600 or equivalent) to the camshaft carrier mating surface. Ensure the sealant does not block any oilways, or contaminate the bearing surfaces **(see illustration)**. Note that the carrier must be refitted, and the bolts tightened, within 20 minutes of applying the sealant.

18 Position the carrier over the cylinder head/camshaft, and engage the locating dowels. Refit the bolts and finger-tighten them only at this stage.

19 Progressively tighten the camshaft carrier bolts to the specified torque in sequence **(see illustration)**.

20 Lubricate the lips of the new camshaft rear seal, and use a socket or tubular spacer to drive the new seal into location at the rear of the cylinder head. Ensure the seal lips face inwards.

21 Locate the injector rocker shaft on the dowels in the camshaft carrier, fit the new bolts and starting from the centre working outwards, tighten them progressively to the specified torque.

22 Fit the new O-ring seal to the injector harness multiplug, then refit the harness and reconnect the wiring plugs to the injectors.

23 Refit the cylinder head as described in Section 10.

24 Prior to fitting the cylinder head cover, rotate the crankshaft clockwise until the

8.13 Attach a DTI gauge to the camshaft carrier, then pull the camshaft forwards and backwards to measure the endfloat

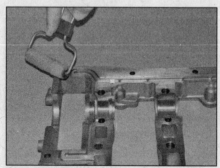

8.17 Use a roller to apply sealant to the camshaft carrier

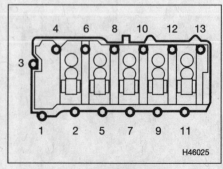

8.19 Camshaft carrier bolt tightening sequence

8.24 Rotate the crankshaft clockwise until the injector lobe on the camshaft (arrowed) is in the full lift position

8.25 When the adjuster screw is felt to 'bottom out', rotate it one complete turn anti-clockwise

injector lobe for No 1 cylinder is at full lift **(see illustration)**.

25 Fit a new adjusting screw to the No 1 injector rocker arm and tighten the screw, compressing the injector piston until it is felt to 'bottom out'. Now rotate the screw 1 complete turn anti-clockwise to give the required clearance, then fit and tighten the locknut without allowing the screw to rotate **(see illustration)**. Repeat this procedure on the remaining 4 rocker arms.

26 After completing the adjustment procedure, rotate the crankshaft 2 complete revolutions to ensure that no injectors are 'bottoming out'.

27 Refit the cylinder head cover as described in Section 4.

9 Injector rocker shaft
– removal and refitting

Removal

1 Remove the cooling fan as described in Chapter 3.

2 Remove the cylinder head cover as described in Section 4.

3 Slacken the injector rocker arm adjusting screws locknuts, then completely unscrew each of the adjusting screws **(see illustration 8.3)**.

4 Rotate the crankshaft clockwise until the timing mark on the camshaft sprocket aligns between the coloured links on the timing chain **(see illustration 7.17)**.

5 Insert LRT-12-058 through the hole in the camshaft carrier and into the camshaft. Note that it may be necessary to turn the crankshaft forwards or backwards a few degrees in order to fully insert the tool. In the absence of the special Land Rover tools, a 17/64" drill bit will suffice **(see illustration 3.4)**.

6 Gradually and evenly slacken and remove the rocker shaft retaining bolts. Discard the bolts, and the adjusting screws/locknuts – new ones must be fitted. Lift the rocker shaft from place.

Refitting

7 Two different types of rocker shafts may

be fitted. On engines with a serial No prefix 10P to 14P, type A rocker shaft is fitted, and on engine serial No prefix 15P to 19P, type B rocker shaft is fitted **(see illustration)**. Note that it is possible to substitute type A shafts with type B, but not the other way around.

8 Fit new adjusting screws and locknuts to the rocker arms, but do not tighten the locknuts yet. Ensure the screws are fully retracted **(see illustration)**.

9 Locate the rocker shaft assembly on the dowels, then fit the new retaining bolts, and tighten them progressively to the specified torque working from the centre outwards **(see illustration 8.4)**.

10 Remove the locking tool from the camshaft carrier/camshaft, then rotate the crankshaft clockwise until the camshaft injector lobe for No 1 injector is at the full lift position **(see illustration 8.24)**.

11 Rotate the adjusting screw in No 1 rocker arm clockwise, compressing the injector piston until it can be felt to 'bottom out'. Now rotate the screw 1 complete turn anti-

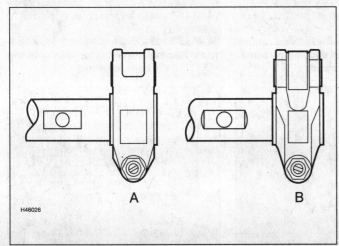

9.7 Injector rocker shaft type A is fitted to engine serial No prefix 10P to 14P, and type B to serial No prefix 15P to 19P

9.8 Ensure the adjusting screws are fully retracted

clockwise to give the required clearance, then fit and tighten the locknut without allowing the screw to rotate **(see illustration 8.25)**. Repeat this procedure on the remaining 4 rocker arms.

12 After completing the adjustment procedure, rotate the crankshaft 2 complete revolutions to ensure that no injectors are 'bottoming out'.

13 Refit the cylinder head cover as described in Section 4.

14 Refit the cooling fan as described in Chapter 3.

10 Cylinder head – removal, inspection and refitting

Removal

1 Disconnect the battery negative lead as described in Chapter 5, then remove the bonnet as described in Chapter 12.

2 Undo the fasteners and remove the engine undershield. Note that to completely remove the engine undershield, the front propeller shaft must be disconnected from the axle (see Chapter 8).

3 Drain the cooling system as described in Chapter 1.

4 Remove the cylinder head cover as described in Section 4.

5 Remove the cooling fan viscous coupling as described in Chapter 3.

6 Disconnect the wiring plug from the airflow

10.6 Disconnect the airflow meter wiring plug

meter, then release the clip and disconnect the meter from the air filter **(see illustration)**.

7 Release the clip and disconnect the intake hose from the turbocharger **(see illustration)**.

8 Undo the three bolts and remove the heat shield from the top of the exhaust manifold **(see illustration)**.

9 Undo the turbocharger oil feed banjo bolt – discard the sealing washers, new ones must be fitted **(see illustration)**.

10 Undo the 3 nuts, pull the turbocharger from the exhaust manifold and position it to one side. Discard the gasket – a new one must be fitted.

11 Undo the two bolts securing the wiring harness to the front of the camshaft carrier **(see illustration)**.

12 Note their fitted positions, then disconnect the injector multiplug **(see illustration)**, followed by the wiring plugs from the

10.7 Release the clip (arrowed) and disconnect the turbo intake hose

coolant sensor, and glow plugs. Check that all electrical connectors/harnesses that will prevent the cylinder heads removal have been disconnected/moved to one side.

13 Disconnect the wiring plug from the MAP (manifold absolute pressure) sensor located on the intake manifold.

14 Note its fitted position/routing, and disconnect the vacuum hose from the EGR valve **(see illustration)**.

15 Release the clip and disconnect the air intake hose from the EGR valve.

16 Release the clips and disconnect the coolant hoses from the fuel cooler, located under the intake manifold.

17 Disconnect the fuel hose from the fuel tank to the cooler, then plug the opening in the cooler and plug the end of the pipe. It is essential that the fuel system is protected from dirt ingress **(see illustration)**.

10.8 The heat shield is secured by 3 bolts (arrowed)

10.9 Undo the turbo oil supply pipe banjo bolt (arrowed)

10.11 Remove the wiring harness retaining bolts (arrowed)

10.12 Squeeze at the sides to disconnect the injector multiplug

10.14 Disconnect the vacuum hose from the EGR valve

10.17 Depress the locking release button to disconnect the fuel hoses

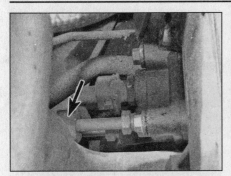

10.18 Pull back the collar (arrowed) and disconnect the fuel hose from the cylinder head

10.19 Slacken the union (arrowed) and disconnect the vacuum pump pipe

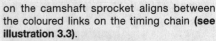

18 Disconnect the fuel hose from the connector on the right-hand rear corner of the cylinder head **(see illustration)**. Again, plug the open fuel connections to prevent ingress of dirt, etc. Any contamination of the fuel system could wreck the cylinder head/injectors.

19 Disconnect the vacuum pump pipe union from the cylinder head, and discard the O-ring seal **(see illustration)**.

20 Undo the 2 retaining bolts and disconnect the alternator support bracket from the cylinder head.

Models without an EGR cooler

21 Undo the bolts securing the EGR valve pipe to the cylinder head.

Models with and EGR cooler

22 Release the clips and disconnect the coolant hoses from the EGR cooler, then undo the bolts/nut and detach the cooler from the cylinder head and EGR pipes **(see illustrations)**.

All models

23 Release the clips and disconnect the top hose, and heater hoses from the cylinder head.

24 Undo the nut and bolt securing the cylinder head to the timing chain cover **(see illustration)**.

25 Using a spanner/socket on the crankshaft pulley, rotate the crankshaft until the mark

on the camshaft sprocket aligns between the coloured links on the timing chain **(see illustration 3.3)**.

26 Insert LRT-12-058 through the hole in the camshaft carrier and into the camshaft **(see illustration 3.4)**. Note that it may be necessary to turn the crankshaft forwards or backwards a few degrees in order to fully insert the tool. In the absence of the special Land Rover tools, a 17/64" drill bit will suffice.

27 With the camshaft locked in position, it should now be possible to insert LRT-12-158 through the bellhousing to lock the flywheel/crankshaft in position **(see illustration 3.5a)**. In the absence of the special Land Rover tools, a home-made equivalent may be fabricated using the dimensions given **(see illustration 3.5b)**.

28 Undo the timing chain tensioner from the right-hand side of the cylinder head. Discard the sealing washer, a new one must be fitted **(see illustration)**.

29 Remove the Allen screw securing the top of the timing chain fixed guide to the cylinder head **(see illustration)**.

30 Carefully lever out the camshaft sprocket access plug from the front of the cylinder head **(see illustration)**. Discard the O-ring seal, a new one must be fitted.

31 Undo the 3 bolts securing the sprocket to the camshaft, and allow the sprocket to rest on

10.22a Using a spring clip release tool on the EGR cooler coolant hoses

10.22b Disconnect the EGR hoses and remove the EGR cooler (arrowed)

10.24 Undo the nut and bolt (arrowed) securing the cylinder head to the timing cover

10.28 Unscrew the timing chain tensioner

10.29 Undo the Allen screw (arrowed) securing the top of the timing chain fixed guide to the cylinder head

10.30 Lever out the rubber plug in front of the camshaft sprocket

10.31 Undo the 3 bolts securing the sprocket to the camshaft

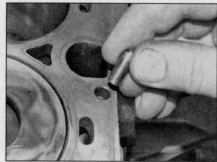

10.35 If plastic dowels are fitted, update them with steel ones

> ⚠️ **Warning: Make sure that all oil is removed, otherwise there is a possibility of the block being cracked by hydraulic pressure when the bolts are tightened.**

40 Examine the bolt threads and the threads in the cylinder block for damage. If necessary, use the correct-size tap to chase out the threads in the block, and use a die to clean the threads on the bolts.

Gasket selection

Note: *This procedure is only necessary if the pistons, connecting rods or crankshaft have be renewed. If none of these components have been changed, use a new head gasket with the same thickness indicator (number of holes) as the original.*

41 When the pistons are at the top dead centre (TDC) position, they protrude above the top face of the cylinder block. The amount of protrusion determines the thickness of the cylinder head gasket required. The protrusion of all the pistons above the cylinder block must be measured, and the thickness of the gasket to be used is determined by the largest protrusion measured.

42 Turn the crankshaft to bring piston No 1 to just below the TDC position (just below the top face of the cylinder block). Position a dial test indicator (DTI) on the cylinder block, and zero it on the block face. Transfer the probe to the crown of No 1 piston (as close as possible to the centre, avoiding the combustion chamber), then slowly turn the crankshaft back-and-forth past TDC, noting the highest reading produced on the indicator. Record this reading.

43 Repeat this measurement procedure on the remaining pistons **(see illustration)**. Ensure that all measurements are taken along the longitudinal centreline of the crankshaft (this will eliminate errors due to piston slant).

44 If a dial test indicator is not available, piston protrusion may be measured using a straight-edge and feeler blades or vernier calipers. However, these methods are inevitably less accurate, and cannot be recommended.

45 Ascertain the greatest piston protrusion measurement, and use this to determine the correct cylinder head gasket from the following table. The gasket identification holes are located at the front right-hand side of the gasket **(see illustration)**.

the top of the chain guides **(see illustration)**. Discard the sprocket retaining bolts, new ones must be fitted.

32 Working in the **reverse** of the sequence shown **(see illustration 10.49a)**, gradually slacken and remove the 12 cylinder head bolts, together with their captive washers.

33 With the help of an assistant, carefully lift the cylinder head from the cylinder block. If necessary, tap the cylinder head gently with a soft-faced mallet to free it from the block, but **do not** lever at the mating faces. Note that the cylinder head is located on dowels. Lift the cylinder head from the vehicle.

34 Recover the cylinder head gasket. The thickness of the cylinder head gasket is indicated by a series of holes at the front left hand edge. Take a note of the number or holes before discarding the gasket.

Caution: As the injector nozzles and valves project below the surface of the cylinder head, do not place the head on any work surface without positioning a block at each end to prevent damage.

35 If plastic dowels are fitted to the top of the engine block, discard them. On vehicles up to VIN 2A 736339 new plastic dowels must be fitted. On vehicles from VIN 2A 736340 to 3A 793894, discard the plastic dowels and update them with steel ones. If steel dowels are already fitted, leave them in place **(see illustration)**.

Inspection

36 The mating faces of the cylinder head and block must be perfectly clean before

refitting the head. Use a scraper to remove all traces of gasket and carbon, and also clean the tops of the pistons. Take particular care with the aluminium cylinder head, as the soft metal is damaged easily. Also, make sure that debris is not allowed to enter the oil and water channels – this is particularly important for the oil circuit, as carbon could block the oil supply to the camshaft or crankshaft bearings. Using adhesive tape and paper, seal the water, oil and bolt holes in the cylinder block. Clean the piston crowns in the same way.

> **HAYNES HiNT**
>
> *To prevent carbon entering the gap between the pistons and bores, smear a little grease in the gap. After cleaning the piston, rotate the crankshaft so that the piston moves down the bore, then wipe out the grease and carbon with a cloth rag.*

37 Check the block and head for nicks, deep scratches and other damage. If slight, they may be removed carefully with a file. Note that if the scratches are deep, the head may need to be renewed. Refacing or skimming of the cylinder head is not permitted. If in doubt have the cylinder head inspected by an engine reconditioning specialist.

38 If warpage of the cylinder head is suspected, use a straight-edge to check it for distortion. Refer to Part B of this Chapter if necessary.

39 Clean out the bolt holes in the block using a pipe cleaner, or a rag and screwdriver.

Piston protrusion	Gasket identification
0.351 to 0.500 mm	2 holes
0.501 to 0.570 mm	1 hole
0.571 to 0.650 mm	3 holes

Refitting

46 Clean out the holes in the engine block, then fit the two new locating dowels to the gasket face (refer to paragraph 35).

47 Fit the correct gasket with the word

10.43 Measure the piston protrusion using a DTI gauge

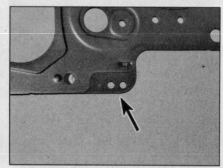

10.45 The holes (arrowed) identify the cylinder head gasket – see text

10.47 Fit the cylinder head gasket with the word TOP uppermost

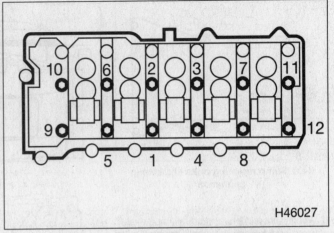

H46027

10.49a Cylinder head bolt tightening sequence

TOP uppermost on the cylinder block **(see illustration).**

48 Lower the cylinder head onto the block, and position the head over the two dowels in the engine block.

49 Fit the new cylinder head bolts and washers, then tighten the bolts in sequence to the Stage 1 torque setting, then in sequence to the Stage 2 setting, then angle-tighten them in turn to the Stage 3, 4 and 5 settings as given in the Specifications at the start of this Chapter **(see illustrations).**

50 Fit the nut and bolt securing the cylinder head to the engine block and tighten them to the specified torque.

51 Check then crankshaft and camshaft locking tools are still in place, then clean the camshaft and sprocket mating faces.

52 Check the chain is still correctly positioned on the camshaft sprocket (timing mark between the two coloured links), then position the sprocket on the camshaft. Finger tighten the new sprocket retaining bolts, then undo each one 180°.

53 Apply a little thread-locking compound to the threads, then refit the Allen screw securing

the top of the timing chain fixed guide. Tighten the bolt to the specified torque.

54 Position a new sealing washer, then refit the timing chain tensioner to the engine block – tighten the retaining bolt to the specified torque.

55 Now tighten the camshaft sprocket retaining bolts to the specified torque.

56 Remove the camshaft and crankshaft locking tools.

57 Refit the camshaft sprocket bolts access plug to the cylinder head with a new O-ring seal.

58 The remainder of refitting is a reversal of removal, noting the following points:

a) *Tighten all fasteners to their specified torque where given.*

b) *Refill the cooling system as described in Chapter 1.*

c) *No bleeding of the fuel system should be necessary. Turn the ignition switch to position II, and wait 10 seconds before attempting to start the engine. This should allow sufficient time for the fuel pump to prime the system.*

11 Sump – removal and refitting

Removal

1 Disconnect the battery negative lead as described in Chapter 5. Disconnect the front propeller shaft from the axle as described in Chapter 8, then undo the fasteners and remove the engine undershield.

2 Remove the front exhaust pipe as described in Chapter 4A.

3 Drain the engine oil as described in Chapter 1.

4 Remove the two bolts securing the ACE pipes (where fitted) to the front crossmember.

5 Undo the bolts securing the coolant pipe and automatic transmission oil cooler pipe (where fitted) to the front crossmember.

6 Undo the 4 bolts securing the sump to the transmission casing.

7 Undo the two bolts securing the centrifugal oil filter drain tube to the sump casing **(see illustration).** Discard the gasket a new one must be fitted.

10.49b Use an angle-measuring gauge to correctly tighten the new cylinder head bolts

11.7 Centrifugal oil filter drain tube nuts

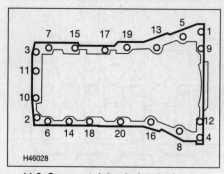

11.8 Sump retaining bolts slackening sequence

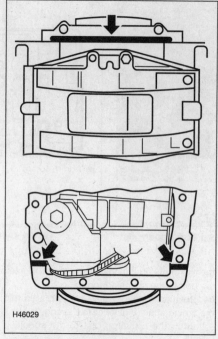

11.12 Apply a bead of sealant to the areas arrowed

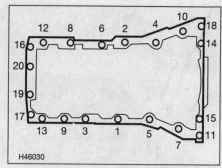

11.15 Sump bolt tightening sequence

8 Working in sequence, gradually and evenly slacken and remove the sump retaining bolts **(see illustration)**. Note their fitted locations – the bolts are different lengths.
9 Lower the sump from the engine, and discard the gasket.

Refitting

10 Clean all traces of gasket (or sealant) and oil from the mating faces of the engine and the sump, taking care not to allow debris to enter the engine.
11 Examine the sump for damage or distortion. Check the condition of the drain plug threads.
12 Apply a thin bead of sealant (Land Rover STC 50550 or equivalent) to the underside of the engine block as shown **(see illustration)**. Note that the sump must be refitted within 20 minutes of applying the sealant.
13 Position the new gasket, lift the sump into place, then loosely fit the securing bolts sufficiently to locate the sump securely on the engine.
14 Refit the sump-to-transmission casing bolts and tighten them to the specified torque.
15 Refit the sump-to-engine block bolts and tighten them in sequence to the specified torque **(see illustration)**.
16 Using a new gasket, refit the centrifugal oil filter drain hose to the sump casing. Tighten the bolts to the specified torque.

17 The remainder of refitting is a reversal of removal, noting the following points:
a) Refit the sump drain plug with a new sealing washer.
b) Refill the engine with new oil as described in Chapter 1.
c) Reconnect the battery negative lead as described in Chapter 5.

12 Oil pump/stiffener plate – removal, inspection and refitting

Removal

1 Remove the sump as described in Section 11.
2 Undo the bolt securing the oil pump sprocket

to the pump driveshaft **(see illustration 7.6)**. Pull the sprocket from the pump.
3 Undo the 3 Torx screws and remove the oil pump pick-up strainer **(see illustration)**. Discard the O-ring seal, a new one must be fitted.
4 In the **reverse** of the sequence shown **(see illustration 12.20)**, gradually slacken and remove the oil pump/stiffener plate retaining bolts. Discard the bolts, new ones must be fitted.
5 Lower the oil pump/stiffener plate, noting that it is located on dowels. Discard the pump outlet gasket.

Inspection

6 With the pump removed from the engine, thoroughly clean the external surfaces.
7 Undo the 5 screws securing the oil pump cover **(see illustration)**.
8 Using permanent marker pen, make alignment marks between the pump inner rotor, outer rotor and pump body **(see illustration)**.
9 Remove the rotors and check all components for signs of wear or damage. If damaged/worn the complete oil pump and stiffener plate must be renewed.
10 Refit the rotors to the pump body, ensuring the marks align.
11 Using feeler gauges, check the clearance between the pump outer rotor and body, and the inner-to-outer rotor clearance. Compare

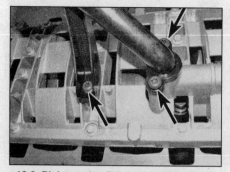

12.3 Pick-up pipe Torx screws (arrowed)

12.7 The oil pump cover is secured by 5 Torx screws

12.8 Alignment marks (arrowed) on the inner and outer rotors

12.11a Check the clearance between the outer rotor and body . . .

12.11b . . . and the inner and outer rotor

12.12 Check the rotor endfloat with a straight-edge

the clearances with those specified at the start of this Chapter. If the clearances are excessive, the complete oil pump and stiffener plate must be renewed (see illustrations).

12 Place a straight-edge along the end of the pump body and use feeler gauges to check the outer rotor endfloat (see illustration). Compare the endfloat with that specified. Again, if the endfloat is excessive, renew the pump and stiffener plate.

13 If the pump is usable, lubricate the rotors with clean engine oil, refit the cover and tighten the Torx screws securely. Rotate the pump shaft to ensure the rotor are free to revolve.

14 Undo the oil pressure relief valve plug, then remove the spring and valve plunger

(see illustrations). Discard the plug, a new one must be fitted.

15 Clean the spring and valve plunger, then check them for signs of wear, damage or corrosion.

16 Use a ruler to measure the spring free length and compare that dimension with the one specified (see illustration). If any of the relief valve components are damaged or worn, it is possible to renew them separately from the oil pump.

17 Lubricate the pump bore, and refit the relieve valve plunger and spring, then apply a little thread-sealing compound to the threads of the new plug and tighten it to the specified torque.

Refitting

18 Clean the mating faces of the stiffener plate and engine block.

19 Fit a new gasket to the pump outlet, and position the oil pump/stiffener plate on the underside of the engine block, ensuring it locates over the two dowels (see illustration).

20 Fit the new stiffener plate retaining bolts and tighten them in sequence to the specified torque (see illustration).

21 Lubricate the new O-ring seal with clean engine oil, then refit the oil pump strainer. Apply a little sealing compound to the retaining screws and tighten them to the specified torque.

12.14a Unscrew the oil pressure relief valve plug . . .

12.14b . . . then withdraw the spring . . .

12.14c . . . followed by the plunger

12.16 Measure the spring free length

12.19 Pump outlet gasket

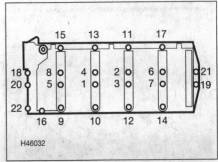

12.20 Stiffener plate retaining bolts tightening sequence

22 Refit the drive sprocket to the oil pump shaft, ensuring the flat machined on the shaft aligns with the flat on the sprocket internal diameter **(see illustration 7.13)**.
23 Apply a little thread-locking compound to the threads, then refit the sprocket retaining bolts and tighten it to the specified torque.
24 Refit the sump as described in Section 11.

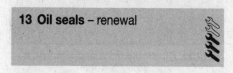

13 Oil seals – renewal

Crankshaft front oil seal

1 Remove the crankshaft pulley as described in Section 5.
2 Use a flat-bladed screwdriver to prise the seal from the timing chain cover. Take great care not to mark the crankshaft **(see illustration)**.
3 Ensure the seal bore in the timing chain cover is clean, then drive the new seal into place using a socket or tubular spacer which fits over the end of the crankshaft, and bears only on the outer edge of the seal **(see illustration)**.
4 Refit the crankshaft pulley as described in Section 5.

Crankshaft rear oil seal

5 Remove the flywheel/driveplate as described in Section 14.
6 Remove the sump as described in Section 11.
7 Undo the bolts and prise the oil seal housing from the rear of the engine block **(see illustration)**. Discard the seal and housing, they must be renewed as an assembly.
8 Ensure the seal housing mating face on the engine block is clean, then position Land Rover tool LRT-12-061 (seal protector) over the end of the crankshaft. If the tool is not available, wrap a length of insulating tape around the shoulder of the crankshaft to protect the seal lips as it is installed **(see illustration)**.
9 Carefully manoeuvre the new seal and housing over the end of the crankshaft, then remove the seal protector/insulating tape.
10 Refit the housing retaining bolts and

13.2 Lever the oil seal from the timing cover

tighten them evenly to the specified torque.
11 The remainder of refitting is a reversal of removal.

Camshaft oil seal

12 Undo the bolts and remove the cover from the rear of the cylinder head (where fitted).
13 Note its fitted depth then, using a large, sharp screwdriver (or similar), pierce the centre of the rear camshaft oil seal and lever it from position **(see illustration)**.
14 Ensure the bore in the camshaft carrier/cylinder head is clean, then lubricate the outer lips of the new seal and drive it into position using a suitable tubular spacer or socket.
15 Refit the cover (where applicable).

14 Flywheel/driveplate – removal, inspection and refitting

Removal

1 On manual transmission models, remove the clutch as described in Chapter 6. On models with automatic transmission, remove the transmission as described in Chapter 7B.
2 Undo the 8 bolts and remove the flywheel/driveplate from the end of the crankshaft. Discard the bolts, new ones must be fitted. Note the flywheel/driveplate locates on a dowel.

⚠️ **Warning: The flywheel is heavy – take care not to drop it.**

13.3 Drive the oil seal into place using a socket or tube

Inspection

3 If the clutch friction disc contact surface of the flywheel is scored or, on close inspection, shows signs of small hairline cracks (caused by overheating), it may be possible to have the flywheel surface-ground. Consult a Land Rover dealer or a specialist engine repairer, and if grinding is not possible, renew the flywheel complete.
4 A dual-mass type flywheel is fitted, to insulate the transmission from the torsional and transient vibrations produced by the engine. The flywheel is made up of two halves – a primary and secondary flywheel, with drive between the two transmitted by a torsional damper consisting or four coil springs. A roller bearing is fitted to the centre boss of the primary flywheel, which provides the mounting for the secondary flywheel. This arrangement allows up to 70° of torsional rotation between the two flywheels. No aspect of the dual mass flywheel is serviceable – if faulty it must be renewed.
5 If the teeth on the flywheel/driveplate starter ring are badly worn, or if some are missing, then it will be necessary to remove the ring gear and fit a new one.
6 To renew the ring gear, firstly drill a 3.0 mm hole in the side of the ring gear between the roots of any two gear teeth, and the inner diameter of the ring gear. The hole should be just deep enough to weaken the gear – *take great care not to allow the drill to touch the flywheel.*
7 Clamp the flywheel/driveplate securely in a

13.7 Rear oil seal housing bolts

13.8 With the inside the seal, fit the assembly over the end of the crankshaft

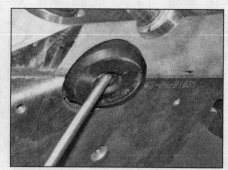

13.13 Lever the rear camshaft oil seal from position

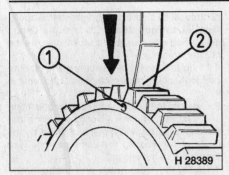

14.8 Removing the ring gear from the flywheel

1 Drill a 3.0 mm hole
2 Split the gear using a cold chisel

vice, and cover it with a large cloth to reduce the possibility of personal injury.

⚠ *Warning: Wear eye protection during the following procedure.*

8 Place a cold chisel between the gear teeth above the drilled hole, then split the gear with the chisel. Take great care not to damage the flywheel during this operation., and wear eye protection at all times. Once the ring has been split, it will spread apart, and can be lifted from the flywheel/driveplate **(see illustration)**.
9 The new ring gear must be heated to 350ºC, and unless facilities for heating by oven or flame are available, leave the fitting to a Land Rover dealer or engineering works. The new ring gear must not be overheated during this work, or the temper of the metal will be affected.
10 The ring should be tapped gently down onto its register, and left to cool naturally – the contraction of the metal on cooling will ensure that it is a secure and permanent fit.

Refitting
11 Commence refitting by thoroughly cleaning the mating faces of the flywheel/driveplate and the crankshaft.
12 Align the dowel hole in the flywheel/driveplate with the crankshaft dowel, then lift the flywheel/driveplate onto the end of the crankshaft **(see illustration)**.
13 Fit the new flywheel/driveplate bolts, and tighten them to the Stage 1 torque setting, then angle-tighten them to the Stage 2 setting, as given in the Specifications.

16.6 Centrifugal oil filter housing bolts (arrowed)

14.12 Align the hole in the flywheel with the dowel in the crankshaft (arrowed)

14 Refit the clutch as described in Chapter 6, or the automatic transmission as described in Chapter 7B (as applicable).

15 Crankshaft spigot bush – renewal

1 On manual transmission models, remove the clutch as described in Chapter 6. On automatic transmission models, remove the transmission as described in Chapter 7B.
2 The bush can be removed as follows:
a) Obtain a short length of metal rod, with a diameter which provides a firm sliding fit in the bore of the bush.
b) Pack the bore of the bush with grease.
c) Insert the metal rod into the bush, and cover the rod and bush with a cloth or rag (to prevent the possibility of injury due to grease splashes or the ejection of the bush).
d) Give the rod a sharp tap with a hammer – the grease should force the bush from the crankshaft **(see illustration)**.
3 Thoroughly clean the bush location in the end of the crankshaft, and make sure that the new bush is absolutely clean.
4 Tap the bush into position in the end of the crankshaft, using a suitable drift. Take care not to produce any burrs on the edge of the bush. The bush should be fitted flush with the end of the crankshaft.
5 Refit the clutch or automatic transmission as applicable.

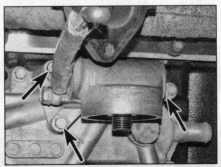

16.10 Oil filter adapter bolts (arrowed)

15.2 Give the rod a sharp tap, and the grease should force the bush out

16 Oil cooler – removal and refitting

Removal
1 Drain the cooling system as described in Chapter 1.
2 Undo the two bolts securing the centrifugal oil filter drain tube to the sump. Discard the gasket.
3 Remove the turbocharger as described in Chapter 4A.
4 On air conditioned models, remove the auxiliary drivebelt as described in Chapter 1, then undo the bolts and move the compressor to one side. There is no need to disconnect the refrigerant hoses.
5 Unscrew the oil filter cartridge from the oil cooler. Be prepared for oil spillage.
6 Undo the 3 retaining bolts and remove the centrifugal oil filter housing from the oil cooler **(see illustration)**. Discard the O-ring seal, a new one must be fitted. Manoeuvre the oil filter from place.
7 Undo the bolt securing the coolant pipe to the rear of the engine.
8 Release the clip and disconnect the coolant hose from the oil cooler.
9 Disconnect the oil pressure switch wiring plug.
10 Undo the three bolts and remove the oil filter cartridge adapter from the cooler **(see illustration)**.
11 Undo the 7 bolts and remove the oil cooler **(see illustration)**.

16.11 Oil cooler bolts (arrowed)

Refitting

12 Ensure the mating faces of the cooler and engine block are clean. Position a new gasket and refit the oil cooler. Tighten the retaining bolts to the specified torque.

13 Fit the oil cartridge adapter to the oil cooler with a new gasket, and tighten the bolts to the specified torque.

14 The remainder of refitting is a reversal of removal, noting the following:
  a) Fit a new oil filter cartridge and top-up the engine oil as described in Chapter 1.
  b) Refill the cooling system as described in Chapter 1.
  c) Tighten all fasteners to the specified torque where given.

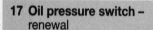

17 Oil pressure switch – renewal

1 The switch is located on the left-hand side of the engine, just behind the oil filter cartridge. Disconnect the wiring plug from the oil pressure switch, then unscrew the switch from the oil cooler housing **(see illustration)**. Be prepared for oil spillage.

2 Ensure the switch threads are clean then refit it to the oil cooler, and tighten it to the specified torque.

3 The remainder of refitting is a reversal of removal, remembering to top-up the engine oil as described in Chapter 1.

17.1 Oil pressure switch (arrowed)

18 Engine mountings – removal and refitting

Removal

Front left-hand mounting

1 Undo the fasteners and move the engine undershield rearwards.

2 Undo the two bolts securing the centrifugal oil filter drain tube to the sump. Discard the gasket.

3 Remove the turbocharger as described in Chapter 4A.

4 On air conditioned models, remove the auxiliary drivebelt as described in Chapter 1, then undo the bolts and move the compressor to one side. There is no need to disconnect the refrigerant hoses.

5 Undo the 3 retaining bolts and remove the

centrifugal oil filter housing from the oil cooler **(see illustration 16.6)**. Discard the O-ring seal, a new one must be fitted. Manoeuvre the oil filter from place.

6 Undo the three bolts securing the oil filter cartridge adapter to the oil cooler, and remove it.

7 Suspend the engine using a hoist and lifting chains/straps, or place a workshop jack under the engine sump with a piece of wood on the jack head to protect the sump casing. Take the weight of the engine.

8 Undo the nuts/bolts and remove the mounting. If required, undo the nut and separate the mounting from the bracket.

Front right-hand mounting

9 Undo the fasteners and remove the plastic cover from the top of the engine.

10 Disconnect the battery negative lead as described in Chapter 5.

11 Raise the front of the vehicle and support it securely on axle stands (see *Jacking and vehicle support*).

12 Undo the four retaining bolts and move the fuel cooler to one side.

13 Suspend the engine using a hoist and lifting chains/straps, or place a workshop jack under the engine sump with a piece of wood on the jack head to protect the sump casing. Take the weight of the engine.

14 Undo the nuts/bolts and remove the mounting. If required, undo the nut and separate the mounting from the bracket.

Refitting

15 Refitting is a reversal of removal, but tighten all fixings to the specified torque.

Chapter 2 Part B:
General engine overhaul procedures

Contents

Section number

Crankshaft – inspection 13
Crankshaft – refitting 16
Crankshaft – removal 10
Cylinder block/crankcase – cleaning and inspection 11
Cylinder head – dismantling 6
Cylinder head – reassembly 8
Cylinder head and valve components – cleaning and inspection . . . 7
Engine – initial start-up after overhaul 18
Engine – removal and refitting 4

Section number

Engine overhaul – dismantling sequence 5
Engine overhaul – general information 2
Engine overhaul – reassembly sequence 15
Engine removal – methods and precautions 3
General information 1
Main and big-end bearings – inspection 14
Piston/connecting rod assembly – inspection 12
Piston/connecting rod assembly – refitting 17
Piston/connecting rod assembly – removal 9

Degrees of difficulty

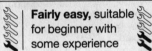

Easy, suitable for novice with little experience	**Fairly easy,** suitable for beginner with some experience	**Fairly difficult,** suitable for competent DIY mechanic	**Difficult,** suitable for experienced DIY mechanic	**Very difficult,** suitable for expert DIY or professional

Specifications

Cylinder head
Maximum permissible distortion of sealing face (typical value) . . . .   0.10 mm
Valve seat angle:
   Intake . . . .   30°
   Exhaust . . . .   45°
Note: *It is not permissible to recut or renew the valve seats on TD5 engines.*

Valves
Valve clearance (intake and exhaust) . . . .   Hydraulic adjusters
Valve stem diameter:
   Intake . . . .   6.907 to 6.923 mm
   Exhaust . . . .   6.897 to 6.913 mm
Maximum valve head deflection (valve head 10 mm out of seat):
   Intake valve . . . .   0.025 to 0.059 mm
   Exhaust valve . . . .   0.035 to 0.069 mm

Valve springs
Free length . . . .   47.00 ± 0.025 mm

Cylinder block
Cylinder rebore oversizes . . . .   No oversizes available

Crankshaft and bearings
Main bearing journal diameter:
   Production standard . . . .   62.000 ± 0.013 mm
   No oversizes available
Big-end bearing journal diameter:
   Production standard . . . .   54.00 ± 0.01 mm
   No oversizes available
Crankshaft endfloat . . . .   0.02 to 0.25 mm

Piston rings

Ring end gaps:

Top compression	0.300 to 0.400 mm
Middle compression	0.400 to 0.600 mm
Oil control	0.250 to 0.500 mm

Clearance in piston groove:

Top compression	Not available
Middle compression	0.050 to 0.082 mm
Oil control	0.050 to 0.082 mm

Torque wrench settings

Refer to Chapter 2A Specifications.

1 General information

This Part of Chapter 2 includes details of engine removal and refitting, and general overhaul procedures for the cylinder head, cylinder block/crankcase and internal engine components.

The information ranges from advice concerning preparation for an overhaul and the purchase of new parts, to detailed step-by-step procedures covering removal, inspection, renovation and refitting of internal engine components.

The following Sections have been compiled based on the assumption that the engine has been removed from the vehicle. For information concerning in-vehicle engine repair, as well as information on the removal and refitting of the external components necessary to facilitate overhaul, refer to Chapter 2A, and to Section 5 of this Part.

2 Engine overhaul – general information

It is not always easy to determine when, or if, an engine should be completely overhauled, as a number of factors must be considered.

High mileage is not necessarily an indication that an overhaul is needed, while low mileage does not preclude the need for an overhaul. Frequency of servicing is probably the most important consideration. An engine which has had regular and frequent oil and filter changes, as well as other required maintenance, will most likely give many thousands of miles of reliable service. Conversely, a neglected engine may require an overhaul very early in its life.

Excessive oil consumption is an indication that piston rings, valve seals and/or valve guides are in need of attention. Make sure that oil leaks are not responsible before deciding that the rings and/or guides are worn. Perform a cylinder compression check or a leakdown test to determine the extent of the work required.

Check the oil pressure with a gauge fitted in place of the oil pressure sender, and compare it with the Specifications (Chapter 2A). If it is extremely low, the main and big-end bearings and/or the oil pump are probably worn out.

Loss of power, rough running, knocking or metallic engine noises, excessive valve gear noise and high fuel consumption may also point to the need for an overhaul, especially if they are all present at the same time. If a complete tune-up does not remedy the situation, major mechanical work is the only solution.

An engine overhaul involves restoring the internal parts to the specifications of a new engine. During an overhaul, the pistons and rings are renewed, and the cylinder bores are reconditioned (where possible). New main bearings, connecting rod (big-end) bearings and camshaft bearings are generally fitted, and if necessary/possible, the crankshaft may be reground, to restore the journals. The valves are also serviced as well, since they are usually in less-than-perfect condition at this point. While the engine is being overhauled, other components, such as the starter and alternator, can be overhauled as well. The end result should be a like-new engine that will give many trouble-free miles. **Note:** *Critical cooling system components such as the hoses, drivebelts, thermostat and water pump MUST be renewed when an engine is overhauled. The radiator should be checked carefully, to ensure that it is not clogged or leaking. Also it is a good idea to renew the oil pump whenever the engine is overhauled.*

Before beginning the engine overhaul, read through the entire procedure to familiarise yourself with the scope and requirements of the job. Overhauling an engine is not difficult if you follow all of the instructions carefully, have the necessary tools and equipment, and pay close attention to all specifications; however, it can be time-consuming. Plan on the vehicle being tied up for a minimum of two weeks, especially if parts must be taken to an engineering works for repair or reconditioning. Check on the availability of parts, and make sure that any necessary special tools and equipment are obtained in advance. Most work can be done with typical hand tools, although a number of precision measuring tools are required for inspecting parts to determine if they must be renewed. Often, the engineering works will handle the inspection of parts and offer advice concerning reconditioning and renewal. **Note:** *Always wait until the engine has been completely dismantled, and all* *components (especially the engine block) have been inspected, before deciding what service and repair operations must be performed by an engineering works. Since the condition of the block will be the major factor to consider when determining whether to overhaul the original engine or buy a reconditioned unit, do not purchase parts or have overhaul work done on other components until the block has been thoroughly inspected. As a general rule, time is the primary cost of an overhaul, so it does not pay to fit worn or substandard parts.*

As a final note, to ensure maximum life and minimum trouble from a reconditioned engine, everything must be assembled with care in a spotlessly-clean environment.

3 Engine removal – methods and precautions

If you have decided that an engine must be removed for overhaul or major repair work, several preliminary steps should be taken.

Locating a suitable place to work is extremely important. Adequate work space, along with storage space for the vehicle, will be needed. If a garage is not available, at the very least a flat, level, clean work surface is required.

Cleaning the engine compartment and engine before beginning the removal procedure will help keep tools clean and organised.

An engine hoist or A-frame will also be necessary. Make sure that the equipment is rated in excess of the weight of the engine. Safety is of primary importance, considering the potential hazards involved in lifting the engine out of the vehicle.

If this is the first time you have removed an engine, an assistant should be available. Advice and aid from someone more experienced would also be helpful. There are many instances when one person cannot simultaneously perform all of the operations required when lifting the engine out of the vehicle.

Plan the operation ahead of time. Arrange for, or obtain, all of the tools and equipment you will need, prior to beginning the job. Some of the equipment necessary to perform engine removal and installation safely and with relative ease are (in addition to an engine hoist) a heavy-duty floor (trolley) jack, complete sets of spanners and sockets as described at the rear of this manual, wooden blocks, and plenty of rags and cleaning solvent for mopping-up spilled oil, coolant and fuel. If the hoist must be hired, make sure that you arrange for it in advance, and perform all of the operations possible without it beforehand. This will save you money and time.

Plan for the vehicle to be out of use for quite a while. An engineering works will be required to perform some of the work which the do-it-yourselfer cannot accomplish without special equipment. These places often have a busy schedule, so it would be a good idea to consult them before removing the engine, in order to accurately estimate the amount of time required to rebuild or repair components that may need work.

Always be extremely careful when removing and refitting the engine. Serious injury can result from careless actions. Plan ahead, take your time, and you will find that a job of this nature, although major, can be accomplished successfully.

The engine is most easily removed by separating it from the transmission, and lifting the engine upwards from the engine compartment.

4.10 Disconnect the coolant hoses from the fuel cooler (arrowed) – located beneath the intake manifold

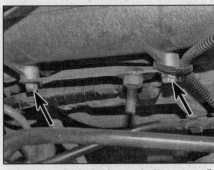

4.12 Undo the bolts (upper bolts arrowed) and remove the fuel cooler

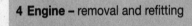

4 Engine – removal and refitting

Note: *An engine hoist and suitable lifting tackle will be required for this operation..*

Removal

1 Ensure that the vehicle is parked on level ground, and apply the handbrake. Where applicable, disconnect the front propeller shaft from the axle, then undo the fasteners and remove the engine undershield.

2 Disconnect the battery negative lead (see Chapter 5).

3 Drain the engine oil with reference to Chapter 1.

4 Drain the cooling system as described in Chapter 1.

5 Remove the bonnet as described in Chapter 12.

6 Undo the screws and remove the plastic cover from the top of the engine.

7 Remove the radiator as described in Chapter 3.

8 Remove the turbocharger and air cleaner housing as described in Chapter 4A.

9 Remove the starter motor as described in Chapter 5.

10 Release the clips and disconnect the coolant hoses from the fuel cooler and coolant rail **(see illustration)**.

11 Disconnect the fuel hoses from the fuel cooler. Plugs the openings to prevent dirt ingress.

12 Disconnect the servo vacuum hose, then undo the four bolts and remove the fuel cooler **(see illustration)**.

13 Unclip the coolant expansion tank and disconnect the hose as the tank is withdrawn **(see illustration)**.

14 Unclip the engine compartment fusebox cover, then undo the bolts securing the alternator, battery and glow plug leads, and unplug the 2 engine harness multiplugs **(see illustration)**.

15 Undo the screw and lift the engine management ECM. Disconnect the 2 multiplugs from the engine management ECM, and unbolt the earth lead from the battery negative cable **(see illustration)**.

16 Release the servo vacuum hose from the retaining clips along its length, then disconnect it from the servo and remove it from the engine compartment.

17 Undo the 3 bolts and remove the power

steering pump pulley, then undo the 4 bolts and move the pump to one side without disconnecting the hoses – refer to Chapter 11 if necessary.

18 Disconnect all relevant wiring from the engine ancillary components. Note that on most models, wiring harness connectors are provided, which eliminates the need to disconnect all the wiring from the individual components – the engine wiring harness can then be removed with the engine. Note the routing of all wiring, to ensure correct refitting. Make a check to ensure that all relevant wiring has been disconnected, to enable the engine to be removed. Undo the bolts/clips and move the harnesses away from the engine.

19 On automatic transmission models, working through the starter motor aperture, undo the three bolts securing the torque converter to the driveplate. Use a spanner to rotate the crankshaft and access the bolts as the driveplate rotates.

20 Undo the 2 bolts securing the transmission oil cooler pipes to the sump and alternator bracket, then note their fitted positions, remove the pipe clamps nuts, and move the pipes to one side. If necessary, slacken the right-hand cooler pipe union to allow it to move.

21 Slacken the hose clips, and remove the intercooler air trunking from the engine compartment.

22 Unbolt the compressor and move it to one side without disconnecting the refrigerant pipes/discharging the refrigerant.

4.13 Unclip the expansion tank and disconnect the hose

4.14 Disconnect the alternator, battery, and glow plug leads, then unplug the two wiring connectors (arrowed)

4.15 Disconnect the earth lead from the battery negative cable (arrowed)

4.25 Release the clips and disconnect the coolant hoses from the engine

4.26 Undo the bolts (4 right-hand ones arrowed) and remove the crossmember from beneath the transmission

 Warning: DO NOT open the refrigerant lines.

23 Undo the 3 bolts and move the ACE pump to one side (where applicable).

24 Note their fitted positions, then disconnect all vacuum pipes from the engine.

25 Release the clips and disconnect all coolant hoses from the engine **(see illustration)**.

26 Undo the 8 bolts and remove the crossmember beneath the transmission bellhousing **(see illustration)**.

27 Working underneath the vehicle, undo the 6 bolts securing the transmission casing to the engine block.

28 Undo the 4 bolts and nuts securing the right- and left-hand engine mountings to the chassis rails.

29 Undo the remaining transmission-to-engine block bolts.

30 Place a trolley jack under the transmission, with an interposed block of wood to spread the load. Raise the jack to support the transmission.

31 Connect a suitable hoist and lifting tackle to the front and rear engine lifting brackets.

32 Raise the hoist sufficiently to just take the weight of the engine.

33 Undo the nuts securing the left- and right-hand engine mounting brackets to the mountings.

34 Carefully raise the hoist, and lift the engine from the transmission. It will be necessary to pull the engine forwards to disengage the transmission input shaft – take care not to allow the weight of the engine or transmission to hang on the input shaft. If necessary, alter the position of the jack supporting the transmission, and the hoist supporting the engine, until the engine is free. On models with automatic transmission, ensure the torque converter remains within the transmission casing.

35 Make a final check to ensure that all hoses, pipes and wires have been disconnected from the engine, and released from any brackets, to facilitate engine removal.

36 With the aid of an assistant, carefully raise the hoist to lift the engine from the vehicle, taking care not to damage surrounding components in the engine compartment.

 Fasten a suitable hose clip around the transmission input shaft to prevent the release bearing from being inadvertently pushed forwards on the shaft whilst the engine is removed from the vehicle.

Refitting

37 Ensure that the clutch friction disc has been centralised (where applicable), as described in Chapter 6.

38 Where applicable, remove the hose clip from the transmission input shaft.

39 On manual transmission models, apply a little clutch assembly grease to the splines of the transmission input shaft. Do not apply too much grease, as it may contaminate the clutch.

40 Attach the hoist and lifting tackle to the engine, as during the removal procedure, and lift the engine into position over the vehicle engine compartment.

41 Lower the engine into position, taking care not to damage the surrounding components.

42 Manipulate the engine and transmission as necessary to enable the two assemblies to be mated together. Alter the position of the jack supporting the transmission, and the hoist supporting the engine, until the two assemblies are correctly aligned. Ensure that the weight of the engine or transmission is not allowed to hang on the transmission input shaft, and ensure that the transmission input shaft engages with the splines of the clutch friction disc (where applicable).

43 Fit the transmission housing-to-engine block bolts, and tighten them to the specified torque.

44 Ensure the engine mounting brackets locate over the mountings, then refit the nuts and tighten them to the specified torque.

45 Disconnect the hoist and lifting tackle from the engine lifting brackets.

46 Further refitting is a reversal of removal, bearing in mind the following points:

a) *Reconnect all relevant engine harness wiring, and clip the harness into position, ensuring that it is routed as noted before removal.*

b) *Reconnect the exhaust front section to the turbocharger, with reference to Chapter 4A.*

c) *Refit the turbocharger as described in Chapter 4A, and the starter motor as in Chapter 5.*

d) *Use new bolts to secure the torque converter to the driveplate (where applicable) and tighten the bolts to the specified torque.*

e) *Where applicable, reconnect the fluid hoses to the power steering pump, using new O-ring seals.*

f) *Reconnect the oil cooler pipes to the oil filter adapter and the oil cooler, using new O-ring seals (where applicable).*

g) *Refit the radiator, cooling fan and cowl with reference to Chapter 3.*

h) *Refit the bonnet with reference to Chapter 12.*

i) *Check the power steering fluid level, and top-up as necessary as described in 'Weekly checks'.*

j) *Refill the cooling system as described in Chapter 1.*

k) *Refill the engine with oil as described in Chapter 1.*

5 Engine overhaul – dismantling sequence

1 It is far easier to dismantle and work on the engine if it is mounted on a portable engine stand. These stands can often be hired from a tool hire shop. Depending on the type of stand used, the flywheel may have to be removed from the engine, to allow the engine stand bolts to be tightened into the end of the cylinder block.

2 If a stand is not available, it is possible to dismantle the engine while supported on blocks on a sturdy workbench, or on the floor. Be extra careful not to tip or drop the engine when working without a stand.

3 Before starting the overhaul procedure, the external engine ancillary components must be removed (this is the case even if a reconditioned engine is to be fitted, in which case, the components from the old engine must be transferred to the reconditioned unit). These components include the following (check with the supplier of a reconditioned unit to see which components are included):

a) *Wiring looms (note all connections and routing).*

b) *Glow plugs.*

c) *Fuel injectors.*

d) *Coolant pump.*

e) *Alternator.*

f) *Starter motor.*

g) *Power steering pump.*

h) *Manifolds and turbocharger.*

i) *Thermostat and housing.*

j) *Clutch (where applicable)*

k) *Oil pressure switch.*

l) *Temperature gauge sender.*

6.2 Fuel connector block bolts (arrowed)

6.3 Valve spring compressor tool in position on No 8 valve

6.7 Place the valve components in a labelled polythene bag

m) Oil filter adapter.
n) Crankcase breather and oil separator components.
o) Dipstick and tube.
p) Auxiliary component mounting bracket(s).

6 Cylinder head – dismantling

Note: *New and reconditioned cylinder heads may be available from the manufacturers, and from engine overhaul specialists. Due to the fact that some specialist tools are required for the dismantling and inspection procedures, and new components may not be readily available, it may be more practical and economical for the home mechanic to purchase a reconditioned head, rather than to dismantle, inspect and recondition the original head. A valve spring compressor tool will be required for this operation.*

1 With the cylinder head removed as described in Chapter 2A, clean away all external dirt and, if desired, remove any ancillaries such as engine lifting brackets, thermostat housing, etc, which are still attached to the cylinder head.
2 Remove the camshaft, rocker arms and hydraulic adjusters as described in Chapter 2A, and the injectors as described in Chapter 4A. If required, undo the bolts and remove the fuel connector block from the cylinder head. Discard the gasket and O-rings, new ones must be fitted **(see illustration)**.
3 To remove a valve, fit a valve spring compressor tool. Ensure that the arms of the compressor tool are securely positioned on the head of the valve and the spring cap **(see illustration)**.
4 Compress the valve spring to relieve the pressure of the spring cap acting on the collets.

 HAYNES HINT *If the spring cap sticks to the valve stem, support the compressor tool, and give the end a light tap with a soft-faced mallet to help free the spring cap.*

5 Extract the two split collets, then slowly release the compressor tool.
6 Remove the spring cap, spring and valve stem oil seal (using long-nosed pliers if necessary). Withdraw the valve from the cylinder head.
7 Repeat the procedure for the remaining valves, keeping all components in strict order, so that they can be refitted in their original positions, unless all the components are to be renewed. If the components are to be kept and used again, place each valve assembly in a labelled polythene bag or a similar small container. Note that as with cylinder numbering, the valves are normally numbered from the timing chain end of the engine **(see illustration)**.

7 Cylinder head and valve components – cleaning and inspection

1 Thorough cleaning of the cylinder head and valve components, followed by a detailed inspection, will enable a decision to be made on whether further work is necessary before reassembling the components.

Cleaning

2 Scrape away all traces of old gasket material and sealing compound from the cylinder head surfaces. Take care not to damage the cylinder head surfaces. It is advisable not to use a metal scraper on aluminium heads.
3 Scrape away the carbon from the surface of the cylinder head, then wash the cylinder head thoroughly with paraffin or a suitable solvent.

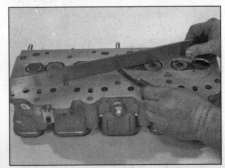

7.6 Checking the cylinder head surface for distortion

4 Scrape off any heavy carbon deposits that may have formed on the valves, then use a power-operated wire brush to remove deposits from the valve heads and stems.

Inspection

Note: *Be sure to perform all the following inspection procedures before concluding that the services of a machine shop or engine overhaul specialist are required. Make a list of all items that require attention.*

Cylinder head

5 Inspect the head very carefully for cracks, evidence of coolant leakage, and other damage. If cracks are found, a new cylinder head should be obtained.
6 Use a straight-edge and feeler blade to check that the cylinder head surface is not distorted **(see illustration)**. If the specified distortion limit is exceeded, the cylinder head must be renewed – consult a Land Rover dealer for further information. **Note:** *Cylinder head refacing/machining is not permissible on TD5 engines.*
7 Examine the valve seats in the cylinder head. If the seats are severely pitted, cracked or burned, then the cylinder head may need to be renewed – valve seat recutting or renewal is not permissible on TD5 engines. If only slight pitting is evident, this can be removed by grinding the valve heads and seats together with coarse then fine grinding paste, as described later in this Section.
8 If the valve guides are worn, indicated by a side-to-side motion of the valve, the guides cannot be renewed. To measure the valve stem play in the guide, insert the valve into the relevant guide, with the valve head positioned approximately 10.0 mm from the seat. A square and feeler blade may be used to determine whether the amount of side play of the valve exceeds the specified maximum.
9 Check the camshaft bearing surfaces for wear or damage. If evident, then the cylinder head and camshaft carrier must be renewed, as they are a matched pair.

Valves

Note: *A micrometer will be required for this operation.*

10 Examine the head of each valve for pitting,

7.10 Measuring a valve stem diameter

7.13 Grinding-in a valve

 Warning: Wear eye protection when using compressed air.

Valve springs

14 Check that all the valve springs are intact. If any one is broken, all should be renewed.

15 Stand each spring on a flat surface, and check it for squareness. If possible, check the free length of each spring against the value given in the Specifications. If a spring is found to be too short, or damaged in any way, renew all the springs as a set. Springs suffer from fatigue, and it is a good idea to renew them, even if they look serviceable.

Valve stem oil seals

16 All valve stem oil seals should be renewed as a matter of course.

burning, cracks and general wear, and check the valve stem for scoring and wear ridges. Rotate the valve, and check for any obvious indication that it is bent. Look for pitting and excessive wear on the end of each valve stem. If the valve appears satisfactory at this stage, measure the valve stem diameter at several points, using a micrometer. Any significant difference in the readings obtained indicates wear of the valve stem **(see illustration)**. Should any of these conditions be apparent, the valve(s) must be renewed.

11 If the valves are in satisfactory condition, they should be ground (lapped) onto their respective seats, to ensure a smooth gas-tight seal.

12 Valve grinding is carried out as follows. Place the cylinder head upside down on a bench, with a block of wood at each end to give clearance for the valve stems.

13 Smear a trace of coarse carborundum

paste on the seat face in the cylinder head, and press a suction grinding tool onto the relevant valve head. With a semi-rotary action, grind the valve head to its seat, lifting the valve occasionally to redistribute the grinding paste **(see illustration)**. When a dull, matt, even surface is produced on the faces of both the valve seat and the valve, wipe off the paste and repeat the process with fine carborundum paste. A light spring placed under the valve head will greatly ease this operation. When a smooth unbroken ring of light grey matt finish is produced on both the valve and seat faces, the grinding operation is complete. Carefully clean away every trace of grinding paste, taking great care to leave none in the ports or in the valve guides. Clean the valves and valve seats with a paraffin-soaked rag, then with a clean rag, and finally, if an air line is available, blow the valves, valve guides and cylinder head ports clean.

8 Cylinder head – reassembly

Note: *A valve spring compressor will be required for this operation. New valve stem oil seals should be fitted on reassembly.*

1 With all the components cleaned, starting at one end of the cylinder head, fit the valve components as follows. If the original components are being refitted, all components must be refitted in their original positions.

2 Lubricate the valve stem oil seal with clean engine oil, then fit the oil seal by pushing it into position on the cylinder head using a suitable socket **(see illustrations)**. Ensure that the seal engages correctly over the valve guide.

3 Insert the appropriate valve into its guide (if new valves are being fitted, insert each valve into the location to which it has been ground), ensuring that the valve stem is well-lubricated with clean engine oil. Take care not to damage the valve stem oil seal as the valve is fitted.

4 Fit the valve spring (either way up) and the spring cap **(see illustration)**. Make sure that the spring cap is correctly located on the top of the spring.

5 Fit the spring compressor tool, and compress the valve spring until the spring cap passes beyond the collet groove in the valve stem.

6 Apply a little grease to the collet groove, then fit the split collets into the grooves, with the narrow ends nearest the valve head **(see illustration)**. The grease should hold them in the grooves.

7 Slowly release the compressor tool, ensuring that the collets are not dislodged from the groove. When the compressor is fully released, give the top of the valve assembly a tap with a soft-faced mallet to settle the components.

8 Repeat the procedure for the remaining valves, ensuring that if the original components are being used, they are all refitted in their original positions.

9 Where applicable, refit any brackets, etc, which were removed before dismantling the cylinder head.

8.2a Position the oil seal on the valve stem . . .

8.2b . . . and push it into place using a socket

8.4 Fit the valve spring and cap

8.6 Compress the valve spring and fit the collet to the grooves (arrowed)

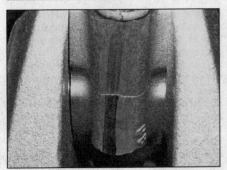

9.2 The big-end caps are 'split fractured'

11.1 Piston oil spray jet

11.7 Using a tap to clean an cylinder block bolt thread

9 Piston/connecting rod assembly – removal

1 Before proceeding, the following components must be removed as described in Chapter 2A:
  a) *Cylinder head.*
  b) *Oil pump/stiffener plate.*
2 Rotate the crankshaft so that No 1 big-end cap (nearest the timing chain end of the engine) is at the lowest point of its travel. If the big-end cap and connecting rod are not already numbered, mark them with a permanent marker. Also make alignment marks between the cap and connecting rod – as these caps are 'split fractured' it is absolutely essential that they are refitted into their original positions **(see illustration)**.
3 Unscrew and remove the big-end bearing cap bolts. Withdraw the cap, complete with bearing shell, from the connecting rod. Strike the cap with a wooden or copper mallet if it is stuck. **Note:** *Land Rover insist that the bearing shells should be renewed whenever the bearing caps are removed.*
4 If only the bearing shells are being attended to, push the connecting rod up and off the crankpin, and remove the upper bearing shell.
5 If desired, push the connecting rod up, and remove the piston and rod assembly from the bore. Note that if there is a pronounced wear ridge at the top of the bore, there is a risk of damaging the piston as the rings foul the ridge. However, it is reasonable to assume that a rebore and new pistons will be required in any case if the ridge is so pronounced.
6 Repeat the procedure for the remaining piston/connecting rod assemblies. Ensure that the caps and rods are marked before removal, as described previously, and keep all components in order.

10 Crankshaft – removal

1 Before proceeding, the following components must be removed:
  a) *Flywheel/driveplate (Chapter 2A).*

  b) *Piston/connecting rod assemblies (Section 9).*
  c) *Timing chain and rear oil seal (Chapter 2A)*
2 Unscrew the securing bolts, and remove the rear crankshaft oil seal housing from the rear of the cylinder block. Discard the housing, and recover the gasket, and the sealing ring if it is loose (where applicable).
3 Before the crankshaft is removed, check the endfloat, using a dial gauge in contact with the end of the crankshaft. Push the crankshaft fully one way, and then zero the gauge. Push the crankshaft fully the other way, and check the endfloat. The result can be compared with the specified amount, and will give an indication as to whether new thrustwashers are required.
4 If a dial gauge is not available, feeler blades can be used. First push the crankshaft fully towards the flywheel end of the engine. Slip the feeler blade between the web of No 3 crankpin and the thrustwasher of the centre main bearing (located in the crankcase).
5 Check the main bearing caps for identification marks, and if none are present, number them so that the numbers can be read from the timing chain end of the engine, using a centre-punch. Again note that No 1 cylinder is at the timing chain end of the engine.
6 Unscrew and remove the main bearing cap securing bolts.
7 Withdraw the caps, complete with bearing shells. Tap the caps with a wooden or copper mallet if they are stuck.
8 Carefully lift the crankshaft from the crankcase.
9 Remove the thrustwashers, then remove the bearing shell upper halves from the crankcase. Place each shell with its respective bearing cap.

11 Cylinder block/crankcase – cleaning and inspection

Cleaning

1 For complete cleaning, the core plugs should be removed. Drill a small hole in them, then insert a self-tapping screw and pull out the plugs using a pair of grips or a slide-hammer. Also remove all external components,

brackets and senders (if not already done), noting their locations. Where applicable, remove the securing bolts, and withdraw the piston oil spray jets from the bottom of the cylinder block. Also recover the sealing washers, where applicable **(see illustration)**.
2 Remove all oil gallery plugs and, where applicable, recover the sealing washers. Note that the plugs may be fitted using sealant.
3 Scrape all traces of gasket and sealant from the cylinder block, taking care not to damage the mating faces of the head and sump.
4 If the block is extremely dirty, it should be steam-cleaned.
5 After the block has been steam-cleaned, clean all oil holes and oil galleries one more time. Flush all internal passages with warm water until the water runs clear, then dry the block thoroughly and wipe all machined surfaces with a light rust-preventative oil. If you have access to compressed air, use it to speed up the drying process, and to blow out all the oil holes and galleries.

⚠ *Warning: Wear eye protection when using compressed air.*

6 If the block is not very dirty, you can do an adequate cleaning job with hot soapy water and a stiff brush. Take plenty of time, and do a thorough job. Regardless of the cleaning method used, be sure to clean all oil holes and galleries very thoroughly, dry the block completely, and coat all machined surfaces with light oil.
7 The threaded holes in the block must be clean, to ensure accurate torque wrench readings during reassembly. Run the proper-size tap into each of the holes to remove rust, corrosion, thread sealant or sludge, and to restore damaged threads **(see illustration)**. If possible, use compressed air to clear the holes of debris produced by this operation, noting the warning given in paragraph 5. Now is a good time to clean the threads on the head bolts and the main bearing cap bolts as well.
8 After coating the mating surfaces of the new core plugs with suitable sealant, refit them in the cylinder block. Make sure that they are driven in straight and seated properly, or leakage could result. Special tools are available for this purpose, but a large socket,

with an outside diameter that will just slip into the core plug, will work just as well.

9 Refit the oil gallery plugs, using new sealing washers or sealant where applicable.

10 Check the oil holes in the jets for blockage. Clean if necessary, then refit the jets and tighten the securing bolts. Ensure that the locating pegs on the jets engage with the corresponding holes in the cylinder block.

11 If the engine is not going to be reassembled right away, cover it with a large plastic bag, to keep it clean and prevent it rusting.

Inspection

12 Visually check the block for cracks, rust and corrosion. Look for stripped threads in the threaded holes. If there has been any history of internal water leakage, it may be worthwhile having an engine overhaul specialist check the block with special equipment. If defects are found, have the block repaired, if possible, or renewed.

13 Check the cylinder bores for scuffing and scoring. Normally, bore wear will be evident in the form of a wear ridge at the top of the bore. This ridge marks the limit of piston travel.

14 If in doubt, or there is any sign of wear, have the cylinder bores inspected and measured by an engine reconditioning specialist. **Note:** *On TD5 engines, it is not permissible to rebore the cylinders, consequently no oversize pistons are available. If worn or damaged, the engine block must be renewed.*

15 If the cylinders are in reasonably good condition, then it may only be necessary to renew the piston rings.

16 If this is the case, the bores should be honed, in order to allow the new rings to bed-in correctly and provide the best possible seal. The conventional type of hone has spring-loaded stones, and is used with a power drill. You will also need some paraffin or honing oil and rags. The hone should be moved up-and-down the cylinder to produce a crosshatch pattern, and plenty of honing oil should be used. Ideally, the crosshatch lines should intersect at approximately a 60° angle. Do not take off more material than is necessary to produce the required finish. If new pistons are being fitted, the piston manufacturers may specify a finish with a different angle, so their instructions should be followed. Do not

withdraw the hone from the cylinder while it is still being turned – stop it first. After honing a cylinder, wipe out all traces of the honing oil. If equipment of this type is not available, or if you are not sure whether you are competent to undertake the task yourself, an engine overhaul specialist will carry out the work at a moderate cost.

17 Where applicable, refit all external components and senders in their correct locations, as noted before removal.

12 Piston/connecting rod assembly – inspection

1 Before the inspection process can begin, the piston/connecting rod assemblies must be cleaned, and the original piston rings removed from the pistons.

2 Carefully expand the old rings over the top of the pistons. The use of two or three old feeler blades will be helpful in preventing the rings dropping into empty grooves **(see illustration)**. Note that the oil control ring has two sections.

3 Scrape away all traces of carbon from the top of the piston. A hand-held wire brush or a piece of fine emery cloth can be used, once the majority of the deposits have been scraped away.

4 Remove the carbon from the ring grooves in the piston by cleaning them using an old ring. Break the ring in half to do this. Be very careful to remove only the carbon deposits; do not remove any metal, nor nick or scratch the sides of the ring grooves. Protect your fingers – piston rings are sharp.

5 Once the deposits have been removed, clean the piston/connecting rod assembly with paraffin or a suitable solvent, and dry thoroughly. Make sure that the oil return holes in the back sides of the ring grooves are clear.

6 If the pistons and cylinder bores are not damaged or worn excessively, the original pistons can be re-used. Normal piston wear appears as even vertical wear on the piston thrust surfaces, and slight looseness of the top ring in its groove. New piston rings, however, should always be used when the engine is reassembled.

7 Carefully inspect each piston for cracks around the skirt, at the gudgeon pin bosses, and at the piston ring lands (between the piston ring grooves).

8 Look for scoring and scuffing on the sides of the skirt, holes in the piston crown, and burned areas at the edge of the crown. If the skirt is scored or scuffed, the engine may have been suffering from overheating and/or abnormal combustion, which caused excessively-high operating temperatures. The cooling and lubricating systems should be checked thoroughly. Scorch marks on the sides of the pistons show that blow-by has occurred. A hole in the piston crown, or burned areas at the edge of the piston crown indicates that abnormal combustion has been occurring. If any of the above problems exist, the causes must be investigated and corrected, or the damage will occur again. The causes may include incorrect injection pump timing, or a faulty injector.

9 Corrosion of the piston, in the form of small pits, indicates that coolant is leaking into the combustion chamber and/or the crankcase. Again, the cause must be corrected, or the problem may persist in the rebuilt engine.

10 If new rings are being fitted to old pistons, measure the piston ring-to-groove clearance by placing a new piston ring in each ring groove, and measuring the clearance with a feeler blade. Check the clearance at three or four places around each groove. If the measured clearance is outside the specified limits, new pistons will be required. If the new ring is excessively tight, the most likely cause is dirt remaining in the groove.

11 Check the fit of the gudgeon pin by twisting the piston and connecting rod in opposite directions. Any noticeable play indicates excessive wear, which must be corrected.

12 To separate a piston from its connecting rod, prise out the circlips and push out the gudgeon pin **(see illustrations)**. Hand pressure is sufficient to remove the pin. Identify the piston and rod, to ensure correct reassembly.

13 The connecting rods themselves should not be in need of renewal, unless seizure or some other major mechanical failure has occurred. Check the alignment of the

12.2 Using a feeler blade to aid removal of a piston ring

12.12a Prise out the circlip . . .

12.12b . . . and push out the gudgeon pin

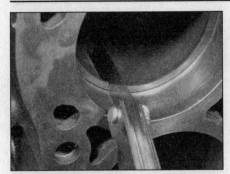

12.16 Measuring a piston ring end gap

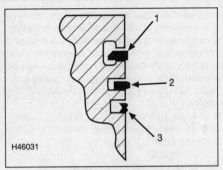

12.18 Piston ring identification – TD5 engines

1 *Top compression ring*
2 *Middle compression ring*
3 *Oil control ring*

connecting rods visually – if the rods are not straight, take them to an engine overhaul specialist for a more detailed check.

14 Reassemble the pistons and rods. Make sure that the pistons are fitted the right way round: the arrow on the piston crown must be on the same side as the cast boss on the connecting rod.

15 Oil the gudgeon pins before fitting them. When assembled, the piston should pivot freely on the rod.

16 Before refitting the rings to the pistons, check their end gaps by inserting each of them in their cylinder bores. Use the piston to make sure that they are square. Check that the gaps are within the specified limits **(see illustration)**. Land Rover rings are supplied pregapped; no attempt should be made to adjust the gaps by filing.

17 Once the ring end gaps have been checked, the rings can be fitted to the pistons.

18 Fit the piston rings using the same technique as for removal. Fit the bottom (oil control) ring first, and work up. When fitting the oil control ring, first insert the expander, then fit the ring. Where applicable, ensure that the TOP marking on the face of the piston ring faces the piston crown. Also note that, where applicable, the polished chrome compression ring fits in the top piston ring groove – do

not mix up the compression rings, as they have different cross-sections. Identify the top and middle compression rings from their cross-sectional profile **(see illustration)**. Note that the piston ring end gaps must be correctly positioned before refitting the piston/ connecting rod assemblies to the engine – see Section 17.

13 Crankshaft – inspection

1 Clean the crankshaft using paraffin or a suitable solvent, and dry it, preferably with compressed air if available. Be sure to clean the oil holes with a pipe cleaner or similar probe, to ensure that they are not obstructed.

⚠ *Warning: Wear eye protection when using compressed air.*

2 Check the main and big-end bearing journals for uneven wear, scoring, pitting and cracking.

3 Big-end bearing wear is accompanied by distinct metallic knocking when the engine is running, particularly noticeable when the

engine is pulling from low revs, and some loss of oil pressure.

4 Main bearing wear is accompanied by severe engine vibration and rumble – getting progressively worse as engine revs increase – and again by loss of oil pressure.

5 Check the bearing journal for roughness by running a finger lightly over the bearing surface. Any roughness (which will be accompanied by obvious bearing wear) indicates that the crankshaft may have to be renewed.

6 If the crankshaft has been reground, check for burrs around the crankshaft oil holes (the holes are usually chamfered, so burrs should not be a problem, unless regrinding has been carried out carelessly). Remove any burrs with a fine file or scraper, and thoroughly clean the oil holes as described previously.

7 Take the crankshaft to an engine reconditioning specialist for inspection. If the crankshaft journals are worn or damaged, the crankshaft may have to be renewed. **Note:** *It is not possible to regrind the journals on TD5 engines. If damaged or worn, the crankshaft must be renewed.*

8 Check the oil seal contact surfaces at each end of the crankshaft for wear and damage. If the seal has worn an excessive groove in the surface of the crankshaft, consult an engine overhaul specialist, who will be able to advise whether a repair is possible or whether a new crankshaft is necessary.

14 Main and big-end bearings – inspection

1 Even though the main and big-end bearings should be renewed during engine overhaul, the old bearings should be retained for close examination, as they may reveal valuable information about the condition of the engine. The bearing shells carry identification marks to denote their size, in the form of a code marked on the back of the shell. If the shells are to be renewed, without carrying out any crankshaft regrinding, the old shells should be taken along when obtaining new shells, to ensure that the correct shells are obtained.

2 Bearing failure occurs because of lack of lubrication, the presence of dirt or other foreign particles, overloading the engine, or corrosion **(see illustration)**. If a bearing fails, the cause must be found and eliminated before the engine is reassembled, to prevent the failure from happening again.

3 To examine the bearing shells, remove them from the cylinder block, the main bearing caps, the connecting rods and the big-end bearing caps, and lay them out on a clean surface, in the same order as they were fitted to the engine. This will enable any bearing problems to be matched with the corresponding crankshaft journal.

4 Dirt and other foreign particles can enter the engine in a variety of ways. Contamination may be left in the engine during assembly, or

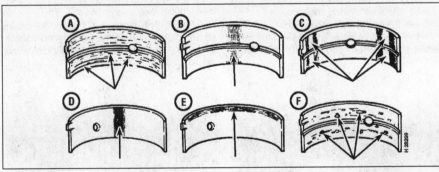

14.2 Typical bearing failures

A *Scratched by dirt; dirt embedded into bearing material*
B *Lack of oil; overlay wiped out*
C *Improper seating; bright (polished) sections*
D *Tapered journal; overlay gone from entire surface*
E *Radius ride*
F *Fatigue failure; craters or pockets*

it may pass through filters or the crankcase ventilation system. Normal engine wear produces small particles of metal, which can eventually cause problems. If particles find their way into the lubrication system, it is likely that they will eventually be carried to the bearings. Whatever the source, these foreign particles often end up embedded in the soft bearing material, and are easily recognised. Large particles will not embed in the bearing, and will score or gouge the bearing and journal. To prevent possible contamination, clean all parts thoroughly and keep everything spotlessly-clean during engine assembly. Once the engine has been installed in the vehicle, ensure that regular engine oil and filter changes are carried out at the recommended intervals.

5 Lack of lubrication (or lubrication breakdown) has a number of interrelated causes. Excessive heat (which thins the oil), overloading (which squeezes the oil from the bearing face) and oil leakage (from excessive bearing clearances, worn oil pump or high engine speeds) all contribute to lubrication breakdown. Blocked oil passages, which may be the result of misaligned oil holes in a bearing shell, will also starve a bearing of oil, and destroy it. When lack of lubrication is the cause of bearing failure, the bearing material is wiped or extruded from the steel backing of the bearing. Temperatures may increase to the point where the steel backing turns blue from overheating.

6 Driving habits can have a definite effect on bearing life. Full-throttle, low-speed operation (labouring the engine) puts very high loads on bearings, which tends to squeeze out the oil film. These loads cause the bearings to flex, which produces fine cracks in the bearing face (fatigue failure). Eventually the bearing material will loosen in pieces, and tear away from the steel backing. Regular short journeys can lead to corrosion of bearings, because insufficient engine heat is produced to drive off the condensed water and corrosive gases which form inside the engine. These products collect in the engine oil, forming acid and sludge. As the oil is carried to the bearings, the acid attacks and corrodes the bearing material.

7 Incorrect bearing installation during engine assembly will also lead to bearing failure. Tight-fitting bearings leave insufficient bearing lubrication clearance, and will result in oil starvation. Dirt or foreign particles trapped behind a bearing shell results in high spots on the bearing, which can lead to failure.

15 Engine overhaul – reassembly sequence

1 Before reassembly begins, ensure that all new parts have been obtained, and that all necessary tools are available. Read through the entire procedure, to familiarise yourself with the work involved, and to ensure that all items necessary for reassembly of the engine are at hand. In addition to all normal tools and materials, a thread-locking compound will be needed. Note also that certain nuts and bolts must be renewed when reassembling the engine.

2 In order to save time and avoid problems, engine reassembly can be carried out in the following order:
  a) *Crankshaft.*
  b) *Pistons/connecting rod assemblies.*
  c) *Flywheel/driveplate.*
  d) *Oil pump/stiffener plate.*
  e) *Camshaft.*
  f) *Camshaft carrier.*
  g) *Timing chain.*
  h) *Timing chain cover.*
  i) *Sump.*
  j) *Cylinder head.*
  k) *Engine external components (use appropriate new gaskets and seals where necessary).*

16 Crankshaft – refitting

1 Refit the piston cooling/lubrication jets to the engine block at the base of the cylinder bores. Tighten the retaining bolts to the specified torque.

2 Clean the backs of the bearing shells, and the bearing recesses in both the cylinder block and main bearing caps. If new shells are being fitted, ensure that all traces of the protective grease are cleaned off, using paraffin. **Note:** *Land Rover insist that new shells are fitted whenever the bearing caps are removed.*

3 Locate the new, grooved bearing shells in their locations in the engine block, and locate the new thrustwashers either side of No 3 main bearing. Ensure the grooves on the thrustwashers face outwards.

4 Lubricate the bearing surfaces and thrustwashers with clean engine oil.

5 Lower the crankshaft into position.

6 Fit the new plain bearing shells into the main bearing caps, then lubricate the crankshaft journals, and refit the bearing caps. Ensure the caps are refitted to their original positions, aligning the previously-made marks.

7 Fit the new main bearing cap bolts and, starting with No. 3 cap and working outwards, tighten all of the bolts to the Stage 1 torque setting. Working in the same sequence, tighten the bolts to the Stage 2 angle-tightening setting. **Note:** *Do not lubricate the main bearing cap retaining bolt threads prior to fitting.*

8 Check that the crankshaft is free to rotate, and fit a new rear crankshaft oil seal as described in Chapter 2A.

17 Piston/connecting rod assembly – refitting

Note: *A piston ring compressor tool will be required for this operation. New big-end bolts nuts must be used on refitting.*

1 Clean the backs of the big-end bearing shells and the recesses in the connecting rods and big-end caps. If new shells are being fitted, ensure that all traces of the protective grease are cleaned off, using paraffin. Wipe the shells and connecting rods dry with a lint-free cloth.

2 Press the big-end bearing shells into the connecting rods and caps, in their correct locations if original shells are to be re-used. **Note:** *'Sputter' type bearing shells are fitted to the connecting rod. These are easily identified as they are darker in colour than the shells fitted into the connecting rod caps. No locating tabs are fitted to TD5 engines.*

3 Lubricate No 1 piston and piston rings, and check that the piston ring end gaps are correctly positioned. Position the ring end gaps at 120° to each other, and away from the thrust- (left-hand side) of the piston. **Note:** *Always follow the instructions supplied with the new piston ring sets – different manufacturers may specify different procedures.*

4 Fit a ring compressor to No 1 piston, then insert the piston and connecting rod into No 1 cylinder. The arrow on the piston crown should point towards the front of the engine. With No 1 crankpin at its lowest point, drive

17.4a Insert the piston and connecting rod into the cylinder with a piston ring compressor fitted . . .

17.4b . . . then drive the piston into the cylinder

the piston carefully into the cylinder with the wooden handle of a hammer, at the same time guiding the connecting rod onto the crankpin **(see illustrations)**. Take great care not to damage the piston cooling/lubrication jets.

5 Liberally lubricate the crankpin journals and big-end bearing shells. Fit the bearing caps, ensuring the previously made marks align. Lightly oil the threads, then tighten the new bearing cap bolts to the specified torque, and turn the crankshaft each time to make sure that it is free before moving on to the next assembly.

6 Refit the oil pump/stiffener plate, the sump and the cylinder head, as described in Chapter 2A.

18 Engine – initial start-up after overhaul

1 With the engine refitted to the vehicle, check the engine oil and coolant levels, and check that the battery is well-charged.

2 Start the engine using the recommended cold-starting procedure. Additional cranking may be necessary to bleed the fuel system before the engine starts.

3 Once started, keep the engine running at fast tickover. Check that the oil pressure light goes out, then check that there are no leaks of oil, fuel or coolant. Where applicable, check the power steering pipe/hose unions for leakage. Do not be alarmed if there are some odd smells and smoke from parts getting hot and burning off oil deposits.

4 Keep the engine idling until hot coolant is felt circulating through the radiator top hose, indicating that the engine is at normal operating temperature, then stop the engine and allow it to cool.

5 Recheck the oil and coolant levels, and top-up if necessary.

6 If new pistons, rings or bearings have been fitted, the engine must be run-in at reduced speeds and loads for the first 500 miles or so. Do not operate the engine at full throttle, or allow it to labour in any gear during this period. It is beneficial to change the engine oil and filter at the end of this period.

Chapter 3
Cooling, heating and ventilation systems

Contents

Section number

Air conditioning compressor drivebelt – check and
renewal ....See Chapter 1
Air conditioning system – general information and precautions 10
Air conditioning system components – removal and refitting 11
Antifreeze mixture...............................See Chapter 1
Coolant level check ....See *Weekly checks*
Coolant pump – removal and refitting 7
Coolant temperature gauge sender – testing, removal and refitting . 6

Section number

Cooling fan and cowling – removal and refitting 5
Cooling system – draining, flushing and refilling ....See Chapter 1
Cooling system hoses – disconnection and renewal 2
General information and precautions......................... 1
Heater/ventilation components – removal and refitting 9
Heating and ventilation system – general information 8
Radiator – removal, inspection and refitting.................. 3
Thermostat – removal and refitting......................... 4

Degrees of difficulty

| Easy, suitable for novice with little experience | | Fairly easy, suitable for beginner with some experience | | Fairly difficult, suitable for competent DIY mechanic | | Difficult, suitable for experienced DIY mechanic | | Very difficult, suitable for expert DIY or professional | |

Specifications

General
Expansion tank cap opening pressure......................... 1.4 bar

Thermostat
Opening temperature .... 82°C

Torque wrench setting	Nm	lbf ft
Compressor mounting bolts................................	25	18
Coolant pump nut/bolts	10	7
Coolant temperature sensor..............................	15	11

1 General information and precautions

General information

The cooling system is of pressurised type, comprising of a belt-driven coolant pump, an aluminium crossflow radiator, the cooling fan, and a thermostat. The coolant pump is attached to, and driven by, the power steering pump, which in turn is driven by the auxiliary drivebelt. The system functions as follows. Cold coolant from the radiator passes through the hose to the coolant pump, where it is pumped around the cylinder block and head passages. After cooling the cylinder bores, combustion surfaces and valve seats, the coolant reaches the underside of the thermostat, which is initially closed. The coolant passes through the heater, and is returned via the cylinder block to the coolant pump.

When the engine is cold, the coolant circulates only through the cylinder block, cylinder head, expansion tank and heater. When the coolant reaches a predetermined temperature, the thermostat opens and the coolant passes through to the radiator. As the coolant circulates through the radiator, it is cooled by the inrush of air when the car is in forward motion. Upon reaching the radiator, the coolant is now cooled, and the cycle is repeated.

The cooling fan is driven via a viscous coupling. The viscous coupling varies the fan speed, according to engine temperature. At low temperatures, the coupling provides very little resistance between the fan and pump pulley, so only a slight amount of drive is transmitted to the cooling fan. As the temperature of the coupling increases, so does its internal resistance, therefore increasing drive to the cooling fan.

Refer to Section 10 for information on the air conditioning system.

Precautions

⚠️ **Warning: Do not attempt to remove the expansion tank filler cap, nor disturb any part of the cooling** system, while the engine is hot, as there is a high risk of scalding. If the expansion tank filler cap must be removed before the engine and radiator have fully cooled (even though this is not recommended) the pressure in the cooling system must first be relieved. Cover the cap with a thick layer of cloth, to avoid scalding, and slowly unscrew the filler cap until a hissing sound can be heard. When the hissing has stopped, indicating that the pressure has reduced, slowly unscrew the filler cap until it can be removed; if more hissing sounds are heard, wait until they have stopped before unscrewing the cap completely. At all times keep well away from the filler cap opening.

⚠️ **Warning: Do not allow antifreeze to come into contact with skin, or with the painted surfaces of the vehicle. Rinse off spills immediately with plenty of water. Never leave antifreeze lying around in an open container, or in a puddle in the driveway or on the garage floor. Children and pets are attracted by its sweet smell, but antifreeze can be fatal if ingested.**

⚠️ **Warning: Refer to Section 10 for precautions to be observed when working on models with air conditioning.**

2 Cooling system hoses – disconnection and renewal

Note: *Refer to the warnings given in Section 1 of this Chapter before proceeding.*

1 If the checks described in Chapter 1 reveal a faulty hose, it must be renewed as follows.
2 First drain the cooling system (see Chapter 1). If the coolant is not due for renewal, it may be re-used if it is collected in a clean container.
3 To disconnect a hose, use a screwdriver to slacken the clips, then move them along the hose, clear of the relevant inlet/outlet union. On some applications, the clips are released by squeezing together the tangs at the ends of the clips. This can be achieved using pliers/ pipe grips, or using a tool specifically for this purpose (see illustration). Carefully work the hose free. The hoses can be removed with relative ease when new – on an older vehicle, they may have stuck.
4 If a hose proves stubborn, try to release it by rotating it on its unions before attempting to work it off. Gently prise the end of the hose with a blunt instrument (such as a flat-bladed screwdriver), but do not apply too much force, and take care not to damage the pipe stubs or hoses. Note in particular that the radiator hose unions are fragile; do not use excessive force when attempting to remove the hoses.

HAYNES HiNT *If all else fails, cut the hose with a sharp knife, then slit it so that it can be peeled off in two pieces. While expensive, this is preferable to buying a new radiator. Check first, however, that a new hose is readily available.*

5 When fitting a hose, first slide the clips onto the hose, then work the hose into position. If clamp-type clips were originally fitted, it is a good idea to update them with screw-type clips when refitting the hose. If the hose is stiff, use a little soapy water as a lubricant, or soften the hose by soaking it in hot water.
6 Work the hose into position, checking that it is correctly routed, then slide each clip along the hose until it passes over the flared end of the relevant inlet/outlet union, before tightening the clips securely.
7 Refill the cooling system with reference to Chapter 1.
8 Check thoroughly for leaks as soon as possible after disturbing any part of the cooling system.

3 Radiator – removal, inspection and refitting

HAYNES HiNT *If leakage is the reason for wanting to remove the radiator, bear in mind that minor leaks can be often be cured using a radiator sealant, with the radiator in situ.*

Removal

1 Drain the cooling system as described in Chapter 1.
2 Remove the intercooler as described in Chapter 4A.
3 Release the clips and disconnect the bleed hose and top hose from the radiator (see illustration).
4 Release the clip and disconnect the bottom hose from the radiator.
5 Release the clip and disconnect the fuel

2.3 A special tool is available to release the hose clips

3.3 Disconnect the bleed hose and top hose from the radiator

3.5 Disconnect the fuel cooler hose from the radiator (arrowed)

3.7 Undo the automatic transmission oil cooler screw (arrowed)

cooler hose from the base of the radiator **(see illustration)**.

6 Release the clip and disconnect the coolant hose from the oil cooler.

7 On automatic transmission models, undo the screw securing the transmission cooler to the cooling pack, and move the transmission cooler to one side **(see illustration)**.

8 Lift the radiator upwards and manoeuvre it from the engine compartment. Recover the rubber mountings at the base of the radiator.

Refitting

9 Refitting is the reverse of the removal procedure, noting the following points:
  a) *Ensure that the radiator is correctly engaged with its lower mounting rubbers.*
  b) *Securely tighten all hose retaining clips.*
  c) *On completion, refill the cooling system as described in Chapter 1.*

4 Thermostat – removal and refitting

Removal

1 Drain the cooling system as described in Chapter 1.

2 Remove the cooling fan viscous coupling as described in Section 5.

3 Undo the two screws and lift out the cooling fan lower cowling.

4 Slacken the clip and disconnect the air intake hose from the EGR valve. Move the air intake hose to one side.

5 Release the three clips and disconnect the hoses from the thermostat housing **(see illustration)**. No further dismantling of the thermostat housing is possible.

Refitting

6 Refitting is the reverse of the relevant removal procedure. On completion, refill the cooling system as described in Chapter 1.

5 Cooling fan and cowling – removal and refitting

Note: *A special narrow open-ended spanner will be required to unscrew the coupling assembly.*

Removal

1 Disconnect the battery negative lead, as described in Chapter 5.

2 Undo the bolts and remove the plastic cover over the top of the engine.

3 Undo the 4 fasteners, and remove the cooling fan upper shroud **(see illustration)**.

4 Using the special 36 mm open-ended spanner (Land Rover part No LRT-12-94 and LRT-12-93 or equivalent), unscrew the viscous coupling from the idler pulley **(see**

illustration). Note: *The viscous coupling has a normal* **right-hand thread** *– ie, it unscrews* **anti-clockwise**.

Refitting

5 Refitting is the reverse of removal, making sure that the cooling fan is fitted the correct way around.

6 Coolant temperature gauge sender – testing, removal and refitting

Testing

1 The coolant temperature sensor, located in the coolant outlet housing at the front left-hand corner of the cylinder head, provides data to the engine management ECM, which uses the data to adjust the fuelling of the engine, glow plug operation, and control the operation of the temperature gauge/warning system. The sensor is an NTC (Negative Temperature Co-efficient) sensor, meaning that as the temperature rises, the resistance of the sensor decreases. Although no specific values are given by Land Rover, it should be possible to check that the resistance of the sensor changes as the temperature changes using a digital multimeter. Should the sensor fail, a fault code should be stored in the ECM memory by the self-diagnosis system, which can be interrogated using a suitable fault code reader.

Removal

2 Either partially drain the cooling system to just below the level of the sender (as described in Chapter 1), or have ready a suitable plug which can be used to plug the sender aperture whilst it is removed. If a plug is used, take great care not to damage the sender unit threads, and do not use anything which will allow foreign matter to enter the cooling system.

3 Undo the fasteners and remove the plastic cover from the top of the engine.

4 Release the fixings and remove the cooling fan upper cowling.

5 Disconnect the wiring from the sender, then

4.5 Release the clips and disconnect the hoses from the thermostat housing

5.3 Cooling fan upper shroud (right-hand fasteners arrowed)

5.4 The viscous coupling has a normal right-hand thread

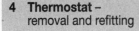

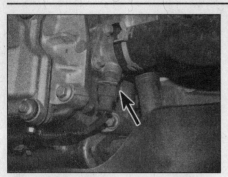

6.5 Disconnect the coolant temperature sensor wiring plug (arrowed)

7.5 Centrifugal oil filter housing bolts (arrowed)

unscrew the unit from the coolant outlet and discard the sealing washer (see illustration).

Refitting

6 Ensure the sensor and coolant outlet mating faces are clean, then using a new washer, fit the sensor to the outlet and tighten it to the specified torque.

7 Refit the cowling and engine cover, then top-up the coolant as described in Chapter 1.

7 Coolant pump – removal and refitting

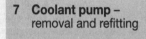

Removal

1 Drain the cooling system as described in Chapter 1.

2 Undo the two bolts securing the centrifugal oil filter drain tube to the sump. Discard the gasket.

3 Remove the turbocharger as described in Chapter 4A.

4 On air conditioned models, remove the auxiliary drivebelt as described in Chapter 1, then undo the bolts and move the compressor to one side. There is no need to disconnect the refrigerant hoses.

5 Undo the 3 retaining bolts and remove the centrifugal oil filter housing from the oil cooler (see illustration). Discard the O-ring seal, a new one must be fitted. Manoeuvre the oil filter from place.

6 Release the clip and disconnect the coolant hose from the coolant pump cover.

7 Undo the 5 bolts and remove the coolant pump cover. Withdrawn the cover, pump and 3 O-rings from the housing (see illustrations). Discard the O-rings, new ones must be fitted.

Refitting

8 Ensure that the pump and housing mating surfaces are clean and dry, then refit the pump and cover using new O-ring seals. Tighten the cover retaining bolts to the specified torque.

9 Reconnect the hose to the pump cover, and secure it in place with the clip.

10 The remainder of refitting is a reversal of removal, remembering to top-up the cooling system as described in Chapter 1.

8 Heating and ventilation system – general information

1 The heating/ventilation system consists of a multi-speed blower motor, face-level vents in the centre and at each end of the facia, and air ducts to the front and rear footwells.

2 The control unit is located in the facia, and the controls operate flap valves to deflect and mix the air flowing through the various parts of the heating/ventilation system. The flap valves are contained in the air distribution housing, which acts as a central distribution unit,

passing air to the various ducts and vents.

3 Cold air enters the system through the grille at the side of the engine compartment.

4 The airflow, which can be boosted by the blower, then flows through the various ducts, according to the settings of the controls. Stale air is expelled through ducts at the rear of the vehicle. If warm air is required, the cold air is passed through the heater matrix, which is heated by the engine coolant.

5 A recirculation lever enables the outside air supply to be closed off, while the air inside the vehicle is recirculated. This can be useful to prevent unpleasant odours entering from outside the vehicle, but should only be used briefly, as the recirculated air inside the vehicle will soon deteriorate.

6 On some models, a Fuel Burning Heater (FBH) is fitted to supplement the heating system, and compensate for the slow warm-up characteristics of the diesel engine. This unit is fully automatic, and consists of a pump, air temperature sensor, and a fuel burning unit with integral ECU.

9 Heater/ventilation components – removal and refitting

Heater unit assembly

Models without air conditioning

1 Drain the cooling system as described in Chapter 1.

2 Undo the 3 bolts and remove the plastic cover at the rear of the cylinder head.

3 Release the retaining clips, and disconnect the coolant hoses from the heater matrix unions (see illustration).

4 Remove the complete facia assembly as described in Chapter 12.

5 Note their fitted locations, disconnect the heater unit wiring connector(s), and free the wiring from any necessary retaining clips.

6 Undo the retaining bolt and 2 nuts, and remove the blower motor housing assembly (see illustrations 9.19a, 9.19b and 9.19c).

7 Disconnect the drain tubes from the base of the heater unit.

7.7a Undo the coolant pump cover bolts

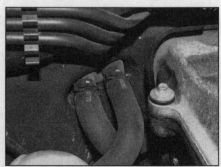

7.7b Renew the 3 O-rings

9.3 Disconnect the heater hoses at the engine compartment bulkhead

9.8 Remove the centre console bracket (arrowed)

9.10 The heater unit is secured by 4 nuts and 1 central bolt (arrowed)

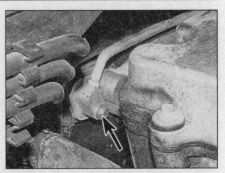

9.15 Access to the refrigerant pipe unions (arrowed) behind the cylinder head is restricted

8 Undo the 2 screws and remove the console bracket from the centre tunnel **(see illustration)**.

9 Release the radio coaxial cable from behind the heater pipes.

10 Undo the 4 nuts and 1 bolt, then remove the heater unit from the vehicle **(see illustration)**.

 Be prepared for some coolant spillage as the heater is removed; wash off any spilt coolant immediately with cold water.

11 Refitting is the reverse of removal, ensuring that an airtight seal is made between the heater unit and bulkhead.

Models with air conditioning

12 Have the air conditioning system

refrigerant discharged by a Land Rover dealer of specialist.

13 Drain the cooling system as described in Chapter 1.

14 Release the retaining clips, and disconnect the coolant hoses from the heater matrix unions **(see illustration 9.3)**.

15 Undo the two bolts securing the air conditioning refrigerant pipes at the engine compartment bulkhead. Discard the O-ring seals, and plug/cover the openings in the ends of the pipes **(see illustration)**. Note: *Where applicable, remove the plastic cover from the rear of the cylinder head – the cover is retained by two bolts.*

16 Remove the complete facia as described in Chapter 12.

17 Undo the retaining screws, and remove the passenger cabin rear heating ducts from either side of the centre tunnel **(see illustration)**.

18 Note their fitted locations, disconnect the heater unit wiring connector(s), and free the wiring from any necessary retaining clips.

19 Undo the retaining bolt and 2 nuts, and remove the blower motor housing assembly **(see illustrations)**.

20 Undo the 2 screws and remove the console bracket from the centre tunnel **(see illustration 9.8)**.

21 Undo the 2 retaining nuts and remove the right-hand facia support bracket **(see illustration)**.

22 Disconnect the drain hoses from the base of the heater/evaporator housing.

23 Undo the screw and remove the heater ducting from the left-hand side of the heater housing.

24 Undo the 4 nuts and 1 bolts, and manoeuvre the heater unit from the passenger cabin **(see illustration)**.

9.17 Undo the two screws (arrowed) and remove the rear heating ducts

9.19a Undo the lower nuts (arrowed) . . .

9.19b . . . upper bolt (arrowed) . . .

9.19c . . . and remove the blower motor housing

9.21 Remove the right-hand facia support bracket

9.24 Heater unit left-hand mounting bolts (arrowed)

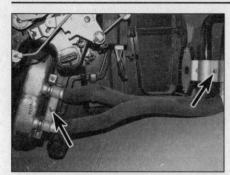

9.27a Undo the pipe clamp screws (arrowed) . . .

9.27b . . . then undo the pipe-to-matrix clamp screws (arrowed)

9.28 Slide the matrix from the housing

HAYNES HINT

Be prepared for some coolant spillage as the heater is removed; wash off any spilt coolant immediately with cold water.

25 Refitting is the reverse of removal, ensuring that an airtight seal is made between the heater unit and bulkhead.

Heater matrix

26 Remove the heater unit assembly as described above.
27 Undo the two screws securing the heater pipe clamps, then slacken the retaining screws, release the clamps and disconnect the heater pipes from the matrix (see illustrations). Discard the O-ring seals.
28 Slide the heater matrix out from the housing (see illustration).
29 On refitting, slide the matrix into the

housing, making sure the temperature sensor (where fitted) is in place.
30 Ensure that the matrix is correctly seated, then refit the pipes using new O-ring seals.
31 The remainder of refitting is a reversal of removal.

Heater blower motor

32 Prise out the 4 studs and remove the passenger's side lower facia panel.
33 Undo the 4 screws and remove the passenger's side glovebox (see illustration).
34 Disconnect the wiring connector from the blower motor, undo the screw securing the wiring harness.
35 Slacken and remove the 3 retaining screws, and lower the blower motor from the housing (see illustration).
36 Refitting is the reverse of removal.

Heater blower motor resistor

37 Prise out the 4 studs and remove the passenger's side lower facia panel.

38 Undo the 4 screws and remove the passenger's side glovebox (see illustration 9.33).
39 Disconnect the resistor wiring plug, then undo the screw and pull the resistor from the housing (see illustration).
40 Refitting is a reversal of removal.

Heater control panel and cables

Control panel without air conditioning

41 Remove the facia audio unit as described in Chapter 13.
42 Carefully release and remove the audio unit bracket from the centre panel.
43 Prise off the screw cover from the audio unit aperture.
44 Remove the coin tray and ashtray from the centre panel, then undo the 6 retaining screws, and remove the drinks holder from the panel (see illustrations).
45 Carefully prise the clock/door lock switch

9.33 Undo the 4 screws (arrowed) and remove the passenger's glovebox

9.35 Heater blower motor retaining screws (arrowed)

9.39 Undo the resistor screw (arrowed)

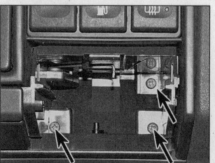

9.44a Open the coin tray, depress the clip and pull the tray from the facia

9.44b Drinks holder right-hand screws (arrowed)

9.44c Pull the drinks tray from position

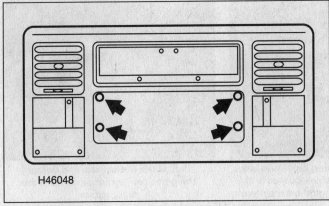

9.48 Heater control panel-to-centre panel screws (arrowed)

9.49 Facia centre panel screws (arrowed)

from the panel, and disconnect the wiring plugs.

46 Prise the switch pack from the centre panel, note their fitted positions, and disconnect the wiring plugs.

47 Pull the blower speed and heater control knobs from place, then undo the 2 screws in the knob recesses, and carefully prise the knob surround trim from place.

48 Undo the 4 screws securing the heater control panel to the centre panel **(see illustration)**.

49 Undo the 4 retaining screws and pull the facia centre panel from position **(see illustration)**.

50 Note their fitted locations, then release the inner and outer cables from the heater control panel. Disconnect the wiring plugs and remove the control panel.

51 Refitting is a reversal of removal.

Cables

52 Remove the heater control panel as previously described.

53 Undo the fasteners and remove the panel below the steering column on the driver's side.

54 Undo the 4 screws and remove the passenger's side glovebox **(see illustration 9.33)**.

55 Release the clips securing the relevant outer cable to the heater housing, and disconnect the inner cable from the flap lever.

56 Note its fitted routing, and pull the relevant cable from position.

57 To refit a cable, first attach the inner and outer cable to the control panel.

58 Connect the other end of the inner cable to the flap lever.

59 Turn the control knob to the maximum temperature or windscreen demist (as applicable), hold the flap lever in the fully closed position, and secure the outer cable in place on the heater unit with the retaining clip.

60 The remainder of refitting is a reversal of removal.

Control panel with air conditioning

61 Remove the facia mounted audio unit as described in Chapter 13.

62 Reach through the audio unit aperture, depress the spring clip each side and push the air conditioning control panel from the centre panel, and disconnect the wiring plugs **(see illustration)**.

63 Refitting is a reversal of removal.

Fuel burning heater (FBH)

64 Disconnect the battery negative lead as described in Chapter 5. The FBH is located in the engine compartment, at the bulkhead.

65 Use suitable clamps to clamp the coolant hoses to and from the heater unit, then release the clips and disconnect the hoses.

66 Disconnect the wiring plugs from the FBH.

67 Clean the area around the fuel supply

pipe, then disconnect the pipe at the quick-release coupling **(see illustration)**. Be prepare for fuel spillage, and plug the ends of the pipe to prevent contamination.

68 Undo the Torx bolt securing the FBH to the mounting bracket and remove it from the engine compartment. No dismantling of the unit is recommended.

69 Refitting is a reversal of removal, remembering to top-up the coolant as described in Chapter 1.

10 Air conditioning system
– general information and precautions

General information

An air conditioning system was offered as an optional extra on some models. It enables the temperature of incoming air to be lowered, and also dehumidifies the air, which makes for rapid demisting and increased comfort.

The cooling side of the system works in the same way as a domestic refrigerator. Refrigerant gas is drawn into a belt-driven compressor, and passes into a condenser mounted in front of the radiator, where it loses heat and becomes liquid. The liquid passes through an expansion valve to an evaporator, where it changes from liquid under high pressure to gas under low pressure. This change is accompanied by a drop in temperature, which cools the evaporator. The refrigerant returns to the compressor, and the cycle begins again.

Air blown through the evaporator passes to the air distribution unit, where it is mixed with hot air blown through the heater matrix, to achieve the desired temperature in the passenger compartment.

The heating side of the system works in the same way as on models without air conditioning (see Section 8).

The operation of the system is controlled electronically by a unit mounted in the facia centre panel. Any problems with the system should be referred to a Land Rover dealer or specialist.

9.62 Depress the spring clips either side of the control panel, and push it from the facia

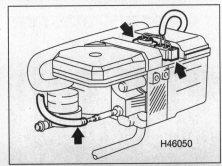

9.67 Fuel burning heater fuel pipe quick-release coupling and wiring plugs (arrowed)

The high- and low-pressure service ports are located in the left-hand rear corner of the engine compartment **(see illustration)**.

Precautions

When an air conditioning system is fitted, it is necessary to observe special precautions whenever dealing with any part of the system, its associated components and any items which necessitate disconnection of the system. If for any reason the system must be discharged, entrust this task to your Land Rover dealer or a refrigeration engineer.

⚠️ **Warning: The refrigeration circuit contains a liquid refrigerant (R134a) under pressure, and it is dangerous to disconnect any part of the system without specialised knowledge and equipment. The refrigerant should only be handled by qualified persons. If it is splashed onto the skin, it can cause frostbite. It is not itself poisonous, but in the presence of a naked flame (including a lighted cigarette) it forms a poisonous gas. Uncontrolled discharging of the refrigerant is dangerous and potentially damaging to the environment.**

Do not operate the air conditioning system if it is known to be short of refrigerant, as this may damage the compressor.

11 Air conditioning system components – removal and refitting

⚠️ **Warning: Before opening any part of the refrigerant circuit, have the system discharged by a Land Rover dealer or suitably-equipped specialist.**

Compressor

1 Have the system refrigerant discharged by a suitably-equipped specialist or Land Rover dealer.
2 Undo the 3 bolts and remove the plastic cover from the top of the engine.
3 Drain the cooling system and remove the auxiliary drivebelt as described in Chapter 1.
4 Disconnect the compressor wiring plug.
5 Undo the screws and detach the refrigerant pipes from the compressor **(see illustration)**.

10.6 The air conditioning high- and low-pressure service ports are located in the left-hand rear of the engine compartment

Plug or cover the ends of the pipes to prevent contamination. Discard the pipe O-ring seals, new ones must be fitted.
6 Release the clips and remove the top hose from the coolant outlet to the heater pipe.
7 Undo the 4 retaining bolts and remove the compressor.
8 Refitting is a reversal of removal, noting the following points:
a) Tighten the compressor mounting bolts to the specified torque.
b) Lubricate the new pipe O-ring seals with refrigerant oil prior to fitting.
c) Top-up the cooling system as described in Chapter 1.
d) Have the refrigerant oil replenished, and the system recharged by a suitably-equipped specialist or Land Rover dealer.

Condenser

9 Have the system refrigerant discharged by a suitably-equipped specialist or Land Rover dealer.
10 Remove the radiator as described in Chapter 3.
11 Working in the radiator aperture, disconnect the dual-pressure switch wiring plug **(see illustration)**.
12 Undo the bolt securing the refrigerant pipe from the evaporator to the condenser, then disconnect the pipe and discard the O-ring seal – a new one must be fitted **(see illustration)**. Plug the pipe openings to prevent contamination.
13 Undo the bolt and detach the refrigerant

11.5 Undo the screws and detach the pipes refrigerant pipes from the compressor

pipe from the evaporator to the receiver/drier **(see illustration)**. Discard the O-ring seal, a new one must be fitted. Plug the pipe openings to prevent contamination.
14 Undo the three remaining bolts securing the cooling fan support rails to the condenser, then remove the condenser with the receiver/drier.
15 Undo the bolt and detach the refrigerant pipe from the condenser to the receiver drier. Discard the O-ring seal, a new one must be fitted. Plug the pipe openings to prevent contamination.
16 Undo the mounting bracket bolts and detach the receiver/drier assembly from the condenser.
17 Refitting is a reversal of removal, noting the following points:
a) Lubricate the new pipe O-ring seals with refrigerant oil prior to fitting.
b) Tighten the refrigerant pipe bolts securely.
c) Top-up the cooling system as described in Chapter 1.
d) Have the refrigerant oil replenished, and the system recharged by a suitably-equipped specialist or Land Rover dealer.

Receiver/drier

18 Have the system refrigerant discharged by a suitably-equipped specialist or Land Rover dealer.
19 Remove the front grille as described in Chapter 12.
20 Disconnect the wiring plug from the dual pressure switch on top of the receiver/drier.

11.11 Disconnect the dual-pressure switch wiring plug

11.12 Disconnect the evaporator-to-condenser pipe . . .

11.13 . . . and the pipe on the receiver/drier (arrowed)

11.21 Undo the bolt and disconnect the pipe from the condenser (arrowed)

11.22 Remove the switch block from the top of the receiver/drier (screw arrowed)

11.23 Slacken the bolt and remove the clamp from the receiver/drier

21 Undo the retaining bolt, securing the refrigerant pipe from the condenser to the receiver/drier **(see illustration)**. Discard the O-ring seal, a new one must be fitted. Plug the pipe openings to prevent contamination.

22 Undo the retaining bolt, then detach the switch block/connector from top of the receiver/drier **(see illustration)**. Discard the O-ring seal, a new one must be fitted. Plug the pipe openings to prevent contamination.

23 Undo the bolts securing the receiver/drier mounting bracket to the condenser, then manoeuvre it from the vehicle. If required, slacken the bolt and pull the receiver/drier from the clamp **(see illustration)**.

24 Refitting is a reversal of removal, noting the following points:

a) *Lubricate the new pipe O-ring seals with refrigerant oil prior to fitting.*

b) *Tighten the refrigerant pipe bolts securely.*

c) *Top-up the cooling system as described in Chapter 1.*

d) *Have the refrigerant oil replenished, and the system recharged by a suitably-equipped specialist or Land Rover dealer.*

Condenser cooling fan

25 Remove the front grille as described in Chapter 12.

26 Undo the 2 retaining bolts and remove the bonnet slam panel right-hand support stay.

27 Disconnect the cooling fan motor wiring plug, then undo the 4 screws and remove the cooling fan **(see illustration)**. Recover the spacers.

28 Refitting is a reversal of removal.

Front evaporator, thermistor and expansion valve

29 Remove the heater matrix as described in Section 9.

30 Remove the seals from the refrigerant pipes where they exit the heater assembly to enter the bulkhead.

31 Disconnect the thermistor wiring plug.

32 Undo the screw(s) each side securing the control servo motors to the heater housing **(see illustration)**.

33 Undo the five retaining screws, release the 12 spring clips and remove the evaporator casing and insulation **(see illustrations)**.

34 Remove the evaporator from the casing, and pull the thermistor from the evaporator cooling fins **(see illustration)**.

35 If required, remove the cover from the

11.27 Condenser cooling fan lower mounting screws (arrowed)

11.32 Undo the screws securing the servo motor to the housing

11.33a Undo the screws (arrowed) . . .

11.33b . . . and prise off the clips (arrowed) . . .

11.33c . . . then lift off the top of the evaporator casing

11.34 Pull the thermistor from the evaporator fins

11.35 Undo the unions and remove the expansion valve

expansion valve, release the clips, undo the unions, and remove the valve **(see illustration)**. Plug or cove the pipe openings to prevent contamination. Discard the sealing O-rings, new ones must be fitted.

36 Refitting is a reversal of removal.

Rear evaporator

37 Have the system refrigerant discharged by a suitably-equipped specialist or Land Rover dealer.

38 Working underneath the rear of the vehicle, undo the retaining bolts and detach the refrigerant pipes from the underside of the evaporator housing. Plug the pipe openings to prevent contamination. Discard the pipes' O-ring seals, new ones must be fitted.

39 Undo the two bolts securing the pipes' grommet flange to the vehicle body.

40 Remove the left-hand luggage compartment side panel as described in Chapter 12, Section 26.

41 Undo the 5 retaining bolts and remove the

seat support bracket to access the evaporator housing.

42 Disconnect the evaporator housing wiring harness plug.

43 Release the spring clips securing the housing to the air ducting, then undo the 4 bolts and remove the housing from the luggage compartment.

44 Remove the insulation from the expansion valve, and detach the relay from the support bracket.

45 Undo the 4 screws securing the lower section of the housing, then remove the 6 screws and 4 clips, and remove the top half of the casing.

46 Undo the refrigerant pipes unions, and lift the evaporator from position. Plug the pipes openings to prevent contamination. Discard the pipes O-rings seals, new ones must be fitted.

47 Refitting is a reversal of removal.

Rear expansion valve

48 Remove the evaporator housing as previously described.

49 Remove the insulation from the valve and sensor, then unclip the sensor from the refrigerant pipe.

50 Undo the pipe unions and remove the expansion valve. Plug the pipes openings to prevent contamination. Discard the pipes O-rings seals, new ones must be fitted.

51 Refitting is a reversal of removal.

Rear blower motor

52 Remove the luggage compartment left-hand side panel as described in Chapter 12, Section 26.

53 Disconnect the motor wiring plug.

54 Release the hose from the motor casing.

55 Undo the 3 screws and remove the blower motor from the casing.

56 Refitting is a reversal of removal.

Rear blower motor resistor

57 Remove the luggage compartment left-hand side panel as described in Chapter 12, Section 26.

58 Disconnect the resistor wiring plug, then undo the 2 screws and pull the resistor from the casing.

59 Refitting is a reversal of removal.

Ambient temperature sensor

60 Remove the front grille as described in Chapter 12.

61 Unclip the sensor from the support bracket, and disconnect the wiring plug **(see illustration)**.

62 Refitting is a reversal of removal.

Passenger cabin air temperature sensor

63 Undo the fasteners and remove the facia lower trim panel above the driver's pedals.

64 Working underneath the facia, disconnect the wiring plug, then undo the two screws and remove the sensor from the facia **(see illustration)**.

65 Refitting is a reversal of removal.

Sunlight sensor

66 Carefully prise the sensor up from the centre of the facia **(see illustration)**. Disconnect the wiring plug as the sensor is removed.

67 Refitting is a reversal of removal.

11.61 Ambient air temperature sensor (arrowed)

11.64 Cabin air temperature sensor (arrowed)

11.66 Carefully prise the sunlight sensor from the facia

Chapter 4 Part A:
Fuel and exhaust systems

Contents

Section number

Accelerator pedal – removal and refitting. 3
Air cleaner assembly – removal and refitting 2
Air cleaner element renewal . . . . See Chapter 1
Engine management electronic components –
   removal and refitting 10
Exhaust system – general information and component renewal 16
Fuel cooler – removal and refitting. 4
Fuel filter element renewal . . . . See Chapter 1
Fuel gauge sender unit and pump – removal and refitting. 6
Fuel injectors – testing, removal and refitting. 8
Fuel pressure regulator – removal and refitting 9

Section number

Fuel sedimenter cleaning . . . . See Chapter 1
Fuel system – priming and bleeding. 5
Fuel tank – removal and refitting 7
General information and precautions. 1
Intercooler – removal and refitting 14
Intercooler element cleaning . . . . See Chapter 1
Manifolds – removal and refitting. 15
Turbocharger – description and precautions 11
Turbocharger – examination and overhaul. 13
Turbocharger – removal and refitting 12

Degrees of difficulty

Easy, suitable for novice with little experience	**Fairly easy,** suitable for beginner with some experience	**Fairly difficult,** suitable for competent DIY mechanic	**Difficult,** suitable for experienced DIY mechanic	**Very difficult,** suitable for expert DIY or professional

Specifications

General

System type	Direct injection, with unit injectors, two-stage tank-mounted lift pump, fuel cooler and regulator. Injector timing controlled by ECM (Electronic Control Module)
Firing order.	1-2-4-5-3 (No 1 at timing chain end)

Maximum engine speed (not adjustable):

Governed	4850 rpm
Overrun	5460 rpm

Idle speed (not adjustable):

Manual trasnmission.	740 ± 50 rpm
Automatic transmission	760 ± 50 rpm

Emission standard:

Engine Serial No prefixes 10P to 14P.	EU2
Engine Serial No prefixes 15P to 19P.	EU3

Injection timing

All TD5 engines	ECM controlled (not adjustable)

Injectors

Type	Lucas EV1 Dual Stage Unit injectors, solenoid controlled
Maximum pressure.	1750 bar

Turbocharger

Type	Garrett GT20
Maximum boost pressure.	Not available

Fuel pump

Low pressure output	30 litre/hour @ 0.5 bar
High pressure output	180 litre/hour @ 4.0 bar

Fuel level sender unit

Resistance:

Full tank	15 ohms
3/4 full	36 ohms
1/2 full	64 ohms
1/4 full	110 ohms
Reserve light on at	158 ohms
Empty	245 ohms

Torque wrench settings

	Nm	lbf ft
Accelerator pedal retaining nuts.	13	10
Alternator support bracket	45	33
Crankshaft speed and position sensor bolt	10	7
Crossmember bolts	25	18
EGR delivery pipe bolts	10	7
EGR valve securing bolts	10	7
Exhaust front pipe to turbocharger	30	22
Exhaust manifold securing nuts	25	18
Fuel cooler bolts:		
Upper bolts	18	13
Lower bolts	25	18
Fuel injector clamp Torx screw	32	24
Fuel pressure regulator bolts	25	18
Fuel temperature sensor	13	10
Intake manifold securing nuts/bolts	25	18
Manifold absolute pressure/intake air temperature sensor bolts	10	7
Turbocharger oil drain pipe to turbocharger	10	7
Turbocharger oil feed pipe banjo bolt	25	18
Turbocharger to manifold	30	22

1 General information and precautions

General information

The fuel system consists of a moulded fuel tank containing a two-stage fuel lift pump combined with a level sender unit, a fuel filter with sedimenter/water sensor, a pressure regulator, five unit injectors, and a fuel cooler for the fuel returning to the tank (see illustration). A turbocharger, intercooler, and EGR system (Exhaust Gas Recirculation) is fitted to all models.

The engine management ECM (Electronic Control Module) energises a relay which causes the low-pressure side (0.75 bar) of the pump to draw fuel through a coarse filter and into the main fuel filter. A proportion of the low-pressure fuel passes through a restrictor to the jet pump in the swirl pot at the base of the pump, to keep the fuel there circulating. The high-pressure stage (4.0 bar) of the pump draws fuel from the main filter and feeds it to the pressure regulator at the rear of the

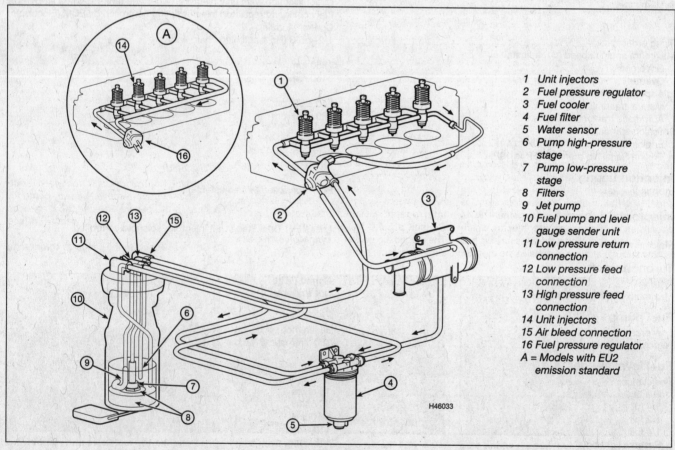

1 Unit injectors
2 Fuel pressure regulator
3 Fuel cooler
4 Fuel filter
5 Water sensor
6 Pump high-pressure stage
7 Pump low-pressure stage
8 Filters
9 Jet pump
10 Fuel pump and level gauge sender unit
11 Low pressure return connection
12 Low pressure feed connection
13 High pressure feed connection
14 Unit injectors
15 Air bleed connection
16 Fuel pressure regulator
A = Models with EU2 emission standard

1.1 Fuel system

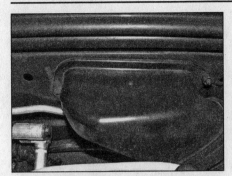

2.1 The air intake duct is located on the left-hand inner wing

2.2 Release the airflow meter retaining clips (arrowed)

cylinder head. The pressurised fuel passes through channels in the cylinder head to feed the five injectors. Any fuel not used by the injectors passes through further channels in the cylinder head, back to the regulator, on to the fuel cooler, then through the filter before passing to the fuel tank. The fuel cooler is essential, as the hot fuel from the cylinder head may otherwise cause damage to the moulded fuel tank.

The TD5 engine is not equipped with a fuel injection pump. Instead the fuel from the tank-mounted pump is fed to the injectors through channels in the cylinder head, where it is then compressed to very high pressure (up to 1700 bar) by a piston arrangement on the top of each injector. The piston is operated by a rocker arm which in turn is operated by a second set of lobes on the camshaft. This arrangement results in high engine power and torque output, with reduced exhaust emissions and noise. As the camshaft rotates, the lobes begin to lift the injector rocker arms, the injector pistons begin to depress, compressing the fuel within the injectors. When the pressure of the fuel inside the injector reaches a predetermined limit (depending on emission standard) the pintle spring at the base of the injectors is overcome and the pintle is forced off its seat, allowing the highly pressurised fuel to inject into the combustion chamber. The injection period is controlled by the engine management ECM energising a solenoid on the injector which opens a port and allows the pressurised fuel to flow through another channel in the cylinder

head, on to the pressure regulator and fuel cooler. When the pressure within the injector collapses, the spring forces the pintle back down, terminating the injection of fuel. The length of the injection period is determined by the ECM based on data concerning engine speed, intake manifold pressure, ambient air pressure, accelerator pedal position/rate of change, coolant temperature, fuel temperature, and airflow volume into the intake manifold.

No accelerator cable is fitted to TD5 models. Instead, a position sensor is attached to the accelerator pedal which informs the engine management ECM of the pedal position and rate of change.

A turbocharger is fitted to the exhaust manifold on all TD5 models, which uses the energy from the exhaust gases to spin a turbine on a shaft. The other end of the shaft is attached to another turbine which, when spinning, pressurises the air entering the intake manifold. This results in much improved engine torque and power output, whilst at the same time reducing fuel consumption and noise generation. The intake air leaving the turbocharger passes through an intercooler mounted in front of the coolant radiator. This cools the intake air, increasing its density, which further enhances the efficiency of the combustion process.

Should a fault develop, have the engine management systems self-diagnosis facility interrogated using a fault code reader. Consult a Land Rover dealer or specialist. The diagnostic socket is located in the driver's side lower facia panel.

Precautions

⚠️ **Warning: It is necessary to take certain precautions when working on the fuel system components, particularly the fuel injectors. Before carrying out any operations on the fuel system, refer to the precautions given in 'Safety first!' at the beginning of this manual, and to any additional warning notes at the start of the relevant Sections. Absolute cleanliness is essential when working on the fuel system – do not allow dirt to enter when any part of the system is disconnected.**

2 Air cleaner assembly – removal and refitting

Removal

1 Undo the two nuts and remove the air intake duct (see illustration).
2 Release the two clips and position the airflow sensor to one side (see illustration). Recover the O-ring seal.
3 Disconnect the wiring plug from the ambient air pressure (AAP) sensor on the side of the air cleaner assembly (see illustration).
4 Pull the air cleaner assembly upwards, releasing it from the three mounting grommets (see illustration).

Refitting

5 Refitting is a reversal of removal, but inspect the O-ring seals for damage/wear, and renew as necessary.

3 Accelerator pedal – removal and refitting

Removal

1 Working in the driver's footwell, undo the fasteners and remove the trim panel for access to the pedals. Release the diagnostic socket from the panel as it is withdrawn (see illustration).
2 Squeeze together the tangs of the orange

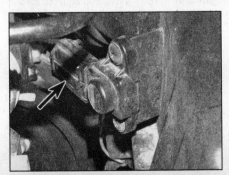

2.3 Disconnect the AAP sensor wiring plug (arrowed)

2.4 Pull the air cleaner housing from the 3 grommets (arrowed)

3.1 Prise out the fasteners and remove the facia panel above the pedals (arrowed)

3.2 Squeeze together the side of the orange clip, and lever away the wiring loom support bracket

retaining clip, and carefully lever the wiring loom support bracket from the pedal bracket **(see illustration)**.

3 Undo the two nuts and manoeuvre the accelerator pedal assembly from position. Recover the spacer block from the pedal assembly.

4 Disconnect the accelerator pedal position sensor wiring plug as the pedal is withdrawn. Note that the position sensor is integral with the pedal assembly and no attempt should be made to dismantle it.

Refitting

5 Refitting is a reversal of removal, tightening the retaining nuts to the specified torque.

---

4 Fuel cooler – removal and refitting

Note: *Refer to the precautions given in Section 1 of this Chapter before proceeding.*

Removal

1 Undo the bolts and remove the plastic cover from the top of the engine. The fuel cooler is located on the underside of the intake manifold.

2 Disconnect the battery negative lead as described in Chapter 5.

6.4 Prise up the plastic strip to remove the carpet fixing strip screws

4.4 Disconnect the coolant hoses from the fuel cooler

3 Drain the cooling system as described in Chapter 1.

4 Release the clips, then note their fitted locations and disconnect the coolant hoses from the cooler **(see illustration)**.

5 Disconnect the two fuel hoses from the cooler. Be prepared for fuel spillage. Plug all fuel cooler/hose openings, it is essential that the fuel system is not contaminated by dirt, etc.

6 Release the vacuum pipe clip, undo the four bolts and remove the cooler from the intake manifold.

Refitting

7 Position the fuel cooler on the intake manifold, then apply a little locking compound to the threads, and tighten the retaining bolts to the specified torque.

8 Ensure the connections are clean, then reconnect the fuel hoses to the cooler.

9 Reconnect the coolant hoses to the cooler, and secure them with the retaining clips.

10 The remainder of refitting is a reversal of removal, remembering to refill the cooling system as described in Chapter 1.

---

5 Fuel system – priming and bleeding

Note: *Refer to the precautions given in Section 1 before proceeding.*

6.5 The sender unit/pump access panel is retained by 6 screws

1 If the vehicle runs out of fuel, or fails to start due to air in the system, it is necessary to purge the air from the system as follows:

2 Switch off the ignition and wait for 15 seconds.

3 Turn the ignition switch to position II, and wait for 30 seconds. This allows the fuel system to purge any air from the cylinder head fuel channels.

4 Repeat steps 2 and 3 six times.

5 Fully depress the accelerator pedal, and turn the ignition switch to the start position whilst holding the pedal down. Note that this procedure is controlled by the engine management ECM, and should not be performed on a vehicle that has not run out of fuel/become starved of fuel, as it can lead to flooding the engine with unburnt fuel.

 Warning: Do not crank the engine for more than 20 seconds at a time. Allow the starter motor/battery to rest for a few minutes.

6 The ECM will cancel the purging operation as soon the engine speed exceeds 600 rpm, the driver lifts the accelerator pedal to less than 90% of its travel, or the ignition switch is released from the start position.

7 There should be no need to bleed/purge the system after renewing the fuel filter or pump assembly.

---

6 Fuel gauge sender unit and pump – removal and refitting

Note: *Refer to the precautions given in Section 1 before proceeding.*

Removal

1 Disconnect the battery negative lead as described in Chapter 5.

Models with third row of seats

2 Remove the third row of seats, then undo the bolts and remove the seat latch brackets from the floor panel.

All models

3 Remove the right-hand side luggage compartment side trim panel as described in Chapter 12, Section 26.

4 Prise up the plastic covering strip, undo the 6 retaining screws, and remove the luggage compartment carpet fixing strip, then move the carpet aside **(see illustration)**.

5 Undo the 6 screws and remove the sender unit/pump access panel **(see illustration)**.

6 Clean the area around the fuel pipe connections, and position absorbent cloth to catch any spilled fuel.

7 Disconnect the wiring plug, then note their fitted positions (colour-coded left-to-right: white, green, blue and unmarked) and squeeze together the sides of the collars to disconnect the 4 fuel pipes from the sender/pump unit

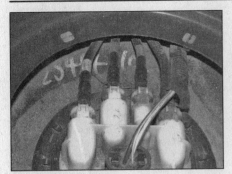

6.7a The fuel pipes are colour-coded. Left-to-right: white, green, blue and unmarked

6.7b Push-in the sides of the collars, and pull each hose from place

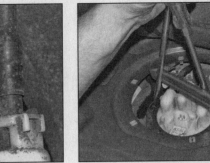

6.8 Use 2 crossed screwdrivers to undo the retaining collar

6.9a Lift the sender unit/pump assembly from the tank

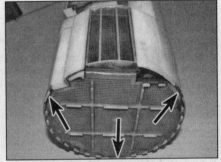

6.9b Release the clips (arrowed) and slide off the filter

(see illustrations). Plug the pipe openings to prevent contamination.

8 Unscrew the sender unit retaining collar using a pair of large, crossed-screwdrivers, or improvise a tool (see illustration). Make alignment marks between the collar and the tank to aid refitting.

9 Withdraw the sender unit from the fuel tank, and discard the sealing ring (see illustration). A new sealing ring must be fitted. At the time of writing, it would appear that the sender unit is not available separately from the pump. If necessary, the coarse filter can be removed from the base of the pump by releasing the clips, and sliding the filter away (see illustration).

Refitting

10 Refitting is a reversal of removal, but use a new sealing ring, and ensure that the lug on the sender unit engages with the cut-out in the tank aperture.

7 Fuel tank – removal and refitting

Note: Refer to the precautions given in Section 1 before proceeding.

Removal

1 As no drain plug is fitted to the base of the moulded tank, this procedure is best performed when the tank is almost empty. If this is not possible, use a syphoning device

to remove as much fuel from the tank as possible.

2 Disconnect the tank pump/sender unit wiring plug and hoses as described in Section 6.

3 Raise the rear of the vehicle and support it securely on axle stands (see Jacking and vehicle support).

4 Release the clips and disconnect the filler hose and breather hose from the filler neck and tank (see illustration).

5 Position a workshop jack under the fuel tank, with a length of wood on the jack head to prevent any damage to the tank. Take the weight of the tank.

6 Undo the 2 bolts and 2 nuts securing the fuel tank cradle to the chassis (see illustrations).

7 With the help of an assistant, lower the cradle and tank from position, and manoeuvre it from under the vehicle.

Refitting

8 Refitting is a reversal of removal.

8 Fuel injectors – testing, removal and refitting

⚠ Warning: Exercise extreme caution when working on the fuel injectors. Never expose the hands, or any part of the body, to injector spray, as the high working pressure can cause the fuel to penetrate the skin, with possibly fatal results. You are strongly advised to have any work which involves testing the injectors under pressure carried out by a Land Rover dealer or fuel injection specialist. Refer to the precautions given in Section 1 of this Chapter before proceeding.

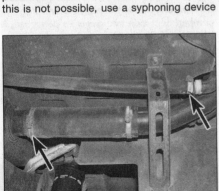

7.4 Slacken the clamps (arrowed) and disconnect the fuel filler and breather hoses

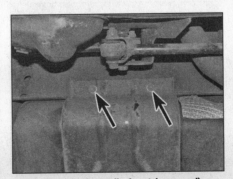

7.6a Fuel tank cradle front (arrowed) ...

7.6b ... and rear fasteners (arrowed)

8.3a Slide off the green plastic cover, and pull the collar towards the hose (arrowed) to disconnect it from the connector block/regulator . . .

8.3b . . . and pull the black collar towards the hose to disconnect it from the cooler (arrowed)

8.4 Depress the clip (arrowed) and disconnect the wiring plugs from the injectors

Testing

1 Injectors do deteriorate with prolonged use, and it is reasonable to expect them to need reconditioning or renewal after 100 000 miles, or so. Accurate testing, overhaul and calibration of the injectors must be left to a specialist.

Removal

2 Remove the injector rocker shaft as described in Chapter 2A.
3 Carefully clean around the area, then disconnect the fuel feed and return connections to the pressure regulator at the rear of the cylinder head, and the black-collared hose from the fuel cooler to drain the cylinder head of fuel **(see illustrations)**. Be prepared for fuel spillage. Immediately plug or cover the openings to prevent dirt ingress.

8.5 Undo the injector clamp bolt (arrowed)

4 Press in the wire clips and disconnect the injector wiring plugs **(see illustration)**.
5 Undo the bolt securing each injector clamp to the cylinder head **(see illustration)**. Recover the clamps.
6 In order to remove the injectors, they must be pulled straight upwards sharply. Land Rover special tool LRT-12-154/1 is intended for this task, and may be available from Land Rover dealers. This is a slide hammer which engages in the sides of the injector. A generic slide hammer, available from good automotive tool shops, will do the same job. Hook the end of the slide hammer under the injector body (not the solenoid body), and pull the injector out using a few gentle taps **(see illustration)**. Pull each injector from the cylinder head **(see illustration)**.
Note: *In order to fit the tool to the injector body, it*

8.6a Hook the slide hammer hook under the injector body, not the solenoid . . .

will be necessary to rotate the crankshaft to align the camshaft lobes for access. If the injectors are to be re-used, store them in their fitted order, so they can be refitted to their original positions.
7 With the injectors removed, rotate the crankshaft to TDC for each cylinder in turn, and use a syringe to remove any fuel from the crown in the top of the pistons.
8 Carefully remove the sealing washer and O-ring seal from each injector. No further dismantling of the injectors is recommended. If the injectors are not to be refitted for some time, cover the holes in the cylinder head to prevent dirt ingress.

Refitting

9 Prior to refitting the injectors, the O-ring and sealing washer on each injector must be renewed. Due to the high injection pressures, it is essential that the O-rings are fitted without being twisted. Land Rover recommend the use of two special assembly sleeves (LRT-12-154/2 and LRT-12-154/3) to install the O-rings/washers squarely. It may be prudent to entrusted O-ring/sealing washer renewal to a Land Rover dealer or suitably-equipped injection specialist, rather than risk subsequent leaks **(see illustration)**.
10 With the O-ring and sealing washer in place, position the clamp on the injector and fit it into the cylinder head, ensuring it locates on its dowel **(see illustration)**. Tighten the clamp Torx screw to the specified torque. Repeat this procedure on the remaining injectors.

8.6b . . . and pull the injector from the head

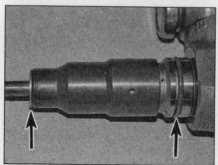

8.9 Renew the sealing washer and O-ring seal (arrowed). The seal must be installed without twisting it

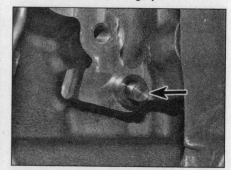

8.10 The injector clamp must located over the dowel (arrowed)

9.4 Pull back the black collar to disconnect the hose from the regulator body (arrowed)

9.7 Withdraw the O-ring and pull the gauze filter from the cylinder head

9.8 The regulator is retained by a circlip

11 The remainder of refitting is a reversal of removal, noting that if new injectors have been fitted, the engine management ECM must be programmed using Land Rover's dedicated test equipment.

9 Fuel pressure regulator – removal and refitting

Note: *Refer to the precautions given in Section 1 of this Chapter before proceeding.*

Removal

1 Disconnect the battery negative lead, as described in Chapter 5.
2 Undo the bolts and remove the plastic cover from the top of the engine.
3 Undo the two bolts and remove the engine lifting eye from the rear left-hand corner of the cylinder head.
4 Disconnect the fuel hoses/pipe from the regulator **(see illustration)**. Be prepared for fuel spillage, and plug/cover all fuel openings to prevent dirt ingress. Note that on EU3 emission standard models, it is necessary to undo the union and pull the pipe from the regulator – discard the O-ring, a new one must be fitted.
5 Disconnect the fuel temperature sensor wiring plug.
6 Undo the 3 retaining bolts, and remove the regulator.
7 Note that a small gauze filter is fitted in to the fuel channel in the cylinder head **(see illustration)**. If required, pull the filter from the

channel and discard the O-ring – a new one must be fitted.
8 Although it is possible to remove the circlip and withdraw the regulator from the connector block, at the time of writing, the regulator and O-rings were not available as separate parts, and must be renewed as an assembly with the connector block **(see illustration)**.

Refitting

9 Ensure the regulator and cylinder head mating surfaces are clean.
10 Where removed, refit the filter into the cylinder head channel, and fit a new O-ring.
11 Using a new gasket, position the pressure regulator and tighten the bolts to the specified torque.
12 Reconnect the hoses to the regulator. Where applicable, reconnect the return pipe to the regulator with a new O-ring and tighten the union securely.
13 The remainder of refitting is a reversal of removal.

10 Engine management electronic components – removal and refitting

ECM (Electronic Control Module)

1 Disconnect the battery negative lead, as described in Chapter 5, then wait at least 10 minutes for any residual electrical energy in the ECM to dissipate.

2 Release the retaining strap and remove the vehicle jack from the engine compartment.
3 Undo the screw, lift the ECM from position, and disconnect the wiring plugs **(see illustration)**.
4 Refitting is a reversal of removal. Note that if a new ECM is fitted, it may have to be reprogrammed using Land Rover test equipment (Testbook) – refer to a Land Rover dealer or specialist.

Fuel temperature sensor

5 Undo the 3 bolts and remove the plastic cover from the top of the engine.
6 Disconnect the battery negative lead as described in Chapter 5.
7 The sensor is fitted to the fuel pressure regulator located at the right-hand rear of the cylinder head. Disconnect the sensor wiring plug **(see illustration)**.
8 Thoroughly clean the area around the sensor, then unscrew it from the regulator. Discard the sealing washer, a new one must be fitted. Plug the open fuel port to prevent dirt ingress.
9 Refitting is a reversal of removal, remembering to fit a new sealing washer and tighten it to the specified torque.

Inertia fuel cut-off switch

10 The inertial fuel cut-off switch is located on the engine compartment bulkhead. In the event of a collision, the switch cuts electrical power to the fuel pump. Disconnect the switch wiring plug **(see illustration)**.

10.3 Undo the screw (arrowed) and lift up the ECM

10.7 The fuel temperature sensor (arrowed) is located at the right-hand rear of the cylinder head

10.10 The inertia fuel cut-off switch (arrowed) is located on the left-hand side engine compartment bulkhead

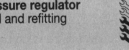
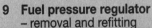

10.13 Disconnect the mass airflow sensor wiring plug

10.15 Release the mass airflow sensor retaining clips

10.18 The MAP/IAT sensor is fitted to the intake manifold (arrowed)

11 Undo the two retaining screws and remove the switch.
12 Refitting is a reversal of removal. To reset the switch, depress the top of the switch.

Mass airflow sensor

13 Disconnect the wiring plug from the sensor **(see illustration)**.
14 Slacken the clip and disconnect intake hose from the sensor.
15 Release the 2 clips and detach the sensor from the air cleaner cover **(see illustration)**.
16 Refitting is a reversal of removal.

Manifold absolute pressure/ intake air temperature sensor

17 Undo the bolts and remove the plastic cover from the top of the engine.
18 Disconnect the sensor wiring plug **(see illustration)**.
19 Undo the two retaining bolts and remove the sensor from the intake manifold. Discard the O-ring seal, a new one must be fitted.
20 Refitting is a reversal of removal. Tighten the retaining bolts to the specified torque.

Ambient air pressure sensor

21 The AAP sensor is fitted to the side of the air cleaner cover. Disconnect the sensor wiring plug **(see illustration)**.
22 Undo the two screws and remove the sensor. Discard the O-ring, a new one must be fitted.
23 Refitting is a reversal of removal. Tighten the retaining screws securely.

10.21 Disconnect the AAP sensor wiring plug (arrowed)

Accelerator pedal position sensor

24 The accelerator pedal position sensor is integral with the accelerator pedal. Refer to Section 3.

Fuel filter water sensor

25 Refer to *'Fuel filter renewal'* in Chapter 1.

Crankshaft speed and position sensor

26 The crankshaft speed and position sensor is located on the right-hand side of the transmission bellhousing, with the tip of the sensor adjacent to the circumference of the flywheel. The outer circumference of the flywheel is divided into 36 segments. 31 of the segments have drilled holes, whilst the remaining 5 do not. These undrilled segments corresponds to TDC on each of the five cylinders. As each undrilled segment passes the sensor tip, the magnetic field produced by the sensor is cut. The ECM measures this fluctuation in the magnetic field as an AC voltage. From the level of the voltage and the position of the voltage peaks, the ECM can determine crankshaft position and speed.
27 Disconnect the sensor wiring plug **(see illustration)**.
28 Undo the retaining bolt and remove the sensor. Discard the O-ring seal, a new one must be fitted. Recover the spacer (if fitted).
29 Ensure the mating faces or the sensor and bellhousing are clean.

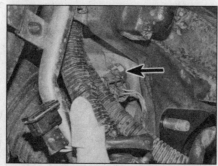

10.27 The crankshaft position/speed sensor is bolted to the right-hand side of the transmission bellhousing, directly behind the starter motor (arrowed)

30 Refit the spacer (where applicable), then refit the sensor with a new O-ring seal. Tighten the retaining bolt to the specified torque.
31 Reconnect the sensor wiring plug.

Coolant temperature sensor

32 Refer to Chapter 3.

11 Turbocharger – description and precautions

Description

1 The turbocharger increases engine efficiency by raising the pressure in the intake manifold above atmospheric pressure. Instead of the air simply being sucked into the cylinders, it is forced in. Additional fuel is supplied by the injectors, in proportion to the increased amount of air.
2 Energy for the operation of the turbocharger comes from the exhaust gas. The gas flows through a specially-shaped housing (the turbine housing) and in so doing spins the turbine wheel. The turbine wheel is attached to a shaft, at the end of which is another vaned wheel, known as the compressor wheel. The compressor wheel spins in its own housing, and compresses the inducted air on the way to the intake manifold.
3 The compressed air passes through an intercooler, between the turbocharger and the intake manifold. The intercooler is an air-to-air heat exchanger, mounted at the front of the vehicle, next to the radiator, and supplied with air through the front grille. The purpose of the intercooler is to remove some of the heat gained in being compressed from the inducted air. Because cooler air is denser, removal of this heat further increases engine efficiency.
4 Boost pressure (the pressure in the intake manifold) is limited by a wastegate, which diverts the exhaust gas away from the turbine wheel. The position of the wastegate is controlled by a vacuum valve, which in turn is controlled by the engine management ECM.
5 The turbo shaft is pressure-lubricated by an oil feed pipe from the main oil gallery. The shaft 'floats' on a cushion of oil. A drain pipe returns the oil to the sump.

12.5 Disconnect the vacuum hose from the wastegate control (arrowed)

12.8 Undo the turbocharger oil feed pipe banjo bolt (arrowed)

Precautions

- *The turbocharger operates at extremely high speeds and temperatures. Certain precautions must be observed to avoid premature failure of the turbo, or injury to the operator.*
- *Do not operate the turbo with any parts exposed. Foreign objects falling onto the rotating vanes could cause excessive damage and (if ejected) personal injury.*
- *Do not race the engine immediately after start-up, especially if it is cold. Give the oil approximately 15 seconds to circulate.*
- *Always allow the engine to return to idle speed before switching it off – do not blip the throttle and switch off, as this will leave the turbo spinning without lubrication.*
- *Allow the engine to idle for several minutes before switching off after a high-speed run.*
- *Observe the recommended intervals for oil and filter changing, and use a reputable oil of the specified quality. Neglect of oil changing, or use of inferior oil, can cause carbon formation on the turbo shaft, and subsequent failure.*

12 Turbocharger – removal and refitting

Removal

1 Disconnect the battery negative lead, as described in Chapter 5.
2 Undo the 3 bolts and remove the plastic cover from the top of the engine.
3 Undo the 3 bolts and remove the heat shield from above the exhaust manifold.
4 Release the clip and disconnect the engine breather hose from the cylinder head cover.
5 Release the clip and disconnect the vacuum

hose from the turbocharger wastegate **(see illustration)**.
6 Slacken the clip and disconnect the air intake hose from the turbocharger.
7 Slacken the clip and disconnect the outlet hose from the turbocharger.
8 Undo the oil feed banjo bolt and discard the sealing washers **(see illustration)**.
9 Undo the 2 bolts securing the turbo drain tube to the underside of the turbocharger. Discard the gasket.
10 Undo the 3 nuts and detach the exhaust front pipe from the turbocharger. Discard the gasket, a new one must be fitted.
11 Slacken and remove the 3 nuts securing the turbocharger to the exhaust manifold **(see illustration)**.
12 Withdraw the turbocharger from the exhaust manifold. Discard the gasket.

Refitting

13 Refitting is a reversal of removal, bearing in mind the following points:
a) *Refit the turbocharger to the manifold using a new gasket, and tighten the securing nuts to the specified torque.*
b) *Tighten the drain tube union securely.*
c) *Ensure that the oil feed pipe banjo bolt is tightened to the specified torque.*
d) *Reconnect the exhaust front section to*

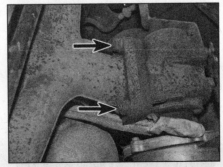

12.11 Turbocharger-to-exhaust manifold upper mounting nuts (arrowed)

the turbocharger elbow, with reference to Section 16.

13 Turbocharger – examination and overhaul

1 With the turbocharger removed, inspect the housing for cracks or other visible damage.
2 Spin the turbine or the compressor wheel, to verify that the shaft is intact, and to feel for excessive shake or roughness. Some play is normal, since in use the shaft is 'floating' on a film of oil. Check that the wheel vanes are undamaged.
3 The wastegate actuator would appear not to be available as a separate unit. If faulty, the complete turbocharger must be renewed.
4 If the exhaust or intake passages are oil-contaminated, the turbo shaft oil seals have probably failed. (On the intake side, this will also have contaminated the intercooler, which if necessary should be flushed with a suitable solvent.)
5 Check the oil feed and return pipes for contamination or blockage, and clean if necessary.
6 No DIY repair of the turbocharger is possible. A new unit may be available on an exchange basis.

14 Intercooler – removal and refitting

Removal

1 Remove the viscous cooling fan as described in Chapter 3.
2 Remove the front grille as described in Chapter 12.
3 Undo the 2 screws and remove the

14.3 Undo the fasteners (arrowed) and lift out the cooling fan lower shroud

14.4a Slacken the central screws, then prise out the scrivets (arrowed) . . .

14.4b . . . and remove the air deflector panels

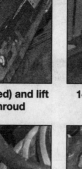

14.5a Intercooler outlet hose (arrowed) . . .

14.5b . . . and intake hose (arrowed)

sound insulation material from behind each horn.

7 Undo the bolt each side and remove the radiator right- and left-hand upper mounting brackets from the body panel **(see illustration)**.

8 Remove the 2 screws each side securing the right- and left-hand upper mounting brackets to the condenser **(see illustration)**, then remove the brackets from the intercooler complete with rubber mountings.

9 Undo the 2 bolts securing the intercooler to the radiator **(see illustration)**.

10 Carefully lift and move the radiator rearwards sufficiently to allow the intercooler to be removed **(see illustration)**.

Refitting

11 Refitting is a reversal of removal, ensuring that the hose sleeves are securely reconnected.

lower half of the cooling fan shroud **(see illustration)**.

4 Remove the 6 'scrivets' and remove the right- and left-hand air deflector panels from the front panel **(see illustrations)**.

5 Slacken the clamps and disconnect the intake and outlet hoses from the intercooler **(see illustrations)**.

6 Undo the mounting nuts and move the horns to one side. Remove the

15 Manifolds – removal and refitting

Intake manifold

Removal

1 Undo the 3 bolts and remove the plastic cover from the top of the engine.

2 Disconnect the MAP sensor, and glow plug wiring connectors.

3 Undo the 2 Allen bolts and detach the EGR pipe from the exhaust manifold or EGR cooler as applicable **(see illustration)**.

14.7 Undo the radiator upper mounting bracket bolt each side (right-hand bolt arrowed)

14.8 Undo the 2 screws (arrowed) and remove the upper mounting bracket each side

14.9 Remove the intercooler mounting bolts (right-hand bolt arrowed)

14.10 Take great care not to damage the radiator or condenser cooling fins when removing the intercooler

15.3 Undo the EGR pipe-to-exhaust manifold bolts (arrowed)

15.4 EGR valve retaining bolts (arrowed)

15.8 The intake manifold is secured by 2 nuts and 8 bolts

15.14 Undo the nuts securing the exhaust manifold

4 Undo the bolt securing the EGR pipe to the cylinder head (where applicable), and the 4 bolts securing the EGR valve to the manifold **(see illustration)**.

5 Undo the 4 bolts securing the fuel cooler to the intake manifold.

6 Undo the retaining bolt, then pull the oil level dipstick and guide tube upwards from position. Discard the O-ring seal, a new one must be fitted.

7 Slacken and remove the two bolts, and remove the alternator support bracket.

8 The manifold is secured to the cylinder head by 2 nuts and 8 bolts **(see illustration)**. Undo the nuts/bolts.

9 Detach the wiring harness from its retaining clips, and remove the manifold. Discard the gasket.

Refitting

10 Refitting is a reversal of removal, bearing in mind the following points:
a) *Renew the manifold gasket – clean all traces of old gasket from the mating faces of the cylinder head and manifold before fitting a new gasket.*
b) *Tighten all fasteners to their specified torque (where given)*

Exhaust manifold

Removal

11 Remove the turbocharger as described in Section 12.

12 On models with air conditioning, remove the auxiliary drivebelt (Chapter 1), then undo the bolts and move the compressor to one side, without disconnecting the refrigerant hoses.

13 Undo the 2 Allen bolts securing the EGR pipe to the exhaust manifold **(see illustration 15.3)**.

14 Undo the 10 nuts and remove the exhaust manifold **(see illustration)**. Discard the gasket.

Refitting

15 Refitting is a reversal of removal, bearing in mind the following points:
a) *Thoroughly clean the mating faces of the manifold and the cylinder head, and refit the manifold using a new gasket.*

b) *Tighten all fasteners to their specified torque (where given).*
c) *Refit the EGR pipe to the manifold using a new gasket.*

---

16 Exhaust system – general information and component renewal

General information

1 The exhaust system consists of a number of separate sections, the sections varying in detail depending on model. Each exhaust section can be renewed individually, leaving the remaining section(s) in place.

Component renewal

2 To remove the system or part of the system, first jack up the front or rear of the vehicle, as applicable, and support it securely on axle stands (see *Jacking and vehicle support*).

Front section

3 Undo the bolts and remove the plastic cover from the top of the engine.

4 Undo the bolts and remove the heat shield from the top of the exhaust manifold.

5 Undo the 3 nuts and detach the exhaust front pipe from the turbocharger.

6 Undo the nuts and detach the front pipe from the intermediate section.

7 The chassis crossmembers are secured by 8 bolts each. Undo the fasteners and remove the crossmembers **(see illustration)**.

16.7 Undo the retaining bolts (arrowed) and remove both front crossmembers

8 Release the front exhaust pipe from the rubber mounting and remove it from the vehicle.

9 Refitting is a reversal of removal, bearing in mind the following points:
a) *Where applicable, check the condition of the exhaust mounting rubbers, and renew if necessary.*
b) *Where applicable, use a new exhaust-to-manifold gasket. On models with a clamped joint, apply a little exhaust jointing compound to the joint before fitting.*
c) *Where applicable, check the condition of the exhaust front section-to-intermediate section sealing ring, and renew if necessary.*
d) *Do not fully tighten the mountings and clamp nuts and bolts until the completion of refitting.*

Intermediate and rear sections

10 A number of different configurations of system may be used, depending on model.

11 Generally, it should be possible to remove each individual component, leaving the remaining components in place. In some cases, it may be necessary to release the surrounding exhaust components from their mountings, in order to allow sufficient movement to withdraw the desired component.

12 Various types of mountings and clamp fixings may be encountered, and removal should be self-evident. Note the positions of any washers and spacers, so that they can be refitted in their original locations.

13 Always renew gaskets and sealing rings if they show signs of deterioration. Similarly, renew mounting rubbers and clamp bolts/U-bolts, etc, if they shown signs of damage or corrosion.

14 Where necessary, apply exhaust jointing compound to seal flanged joints where no gasket or sealing ring is used.

15 When refitting, do not fully-tighten mounting and clamp fixings until the components have been manipulated into their final positions. Similarly, ensure that the components are not under strain before tightening the fixings.

Chapter 5
Engine electrical systems

Contents

Section number

Alternator – brush renewal 7
Alternator – removal and refitting 6
Auxiliary drivebelt checking and renewal . . . . See Chapter 1
Battery – removal and refitting 4
Battery – testing and charging 3
Battery check . . . . See Weekly checks
Charging system – testing 5
Electrical fault finding – general information 2
Electrical system check . . . . See Weekly checks

Section number

General information and precautions 1
Glow plugs – removal and refitting 13
Ignition switch – removal and refitting 11
Oil pressure warning light switch – removal and
    refitting . . . . See Chapter 2A
Preheating system – description and testing 12
Starter motor – brush renewal 10
Starter motor – removal and refitting 9
Starting system – testing 8

Degrees of difficulty

Easy, suitable for novice with little experience	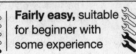	Fairly easy, suitable for beginner with some experience	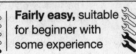	Fairly difficult, suitable for competent DIY mechanic	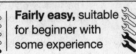	Difficult, suitable for experienced DIY mechanic	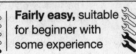	Very difficult, suitable for expert DIY or professional	

Specifications

General
Electrical system type . . . . 12 volt, negative-earth

Battery
Type . . . . Lead-acid, low-maintenance or maintenance-free

Alternator
Type . . . . Nippon Denso 120 A
Regulated voltage . . . . 13.6 to 14.4 volts at 3000 engine rpm
Minimum brush length . . . . No information available

Starter motor
Make and type . . . . Nippon Denso 2 kW

Glow plugs
Type . . . . Beru 12V

Torque wrench settings

	Nm	lbf ft
Alternator mounting bolt	45	33
Alternator support bracket	25	18
Auxiliary drivebelt tensioner bolt	50	37
Glow plugs	16	12
Starter motor nuts/bolts	27	20
Vacuum pump bolts	10	7
Vacuum pump oil feed pipe bolt	10	7

1 General information and precautions

The engine electrical system includes all charging, starting and preheating components. Because of their engine-related functions, these components are covered separately from the body electrical devices such as the lights, instruments, etc (which are covered in Chapter 13).

The electrical system is of the 12 volt, negative-earth type.

The battery is of the low-maintenance or maintenance-free type, and is charged by the alternator, which is belt-driven from a crankshaft-mounted pulley.

The starter motor is of the pre-engaged reduction gear type, incorporating an integral solenoid. On starting, the solenoid moves the drive pinion into engagement with the flywheel ring gear before the starter motor is energised. Once the engine has started, a one-way clutch prevents the motor armature being driven by the engine until the pinion disengages from the flywheel. The motor is fitted with a reduction gear mechanism, in order to achieve the high torque necessary to turn the engine against the high compression pressures encountered in a diesel engine.

Precautions

Further details of the various systems are given in the relevant Sections of this Chapter. While some repair procedures are given, the usual course of action is to renew the component concerned. The owner whose interest extends beyond mere component renewal should obtain a copy of the *Automotive Electrical & Electronic Systems Manual*, available from the publishers of this manual.

It is necessary to take extra care when working on the electrical system, to avoid damage to semi-conductor devices (diodes and transistors), and to avoid the risk of personal injury. In addition to the precautions given in *Safety first!* at the beginning of this manual, observe the following when working on the system:

- *Always remove rings, watches, etc, before working on the electrical system*. Even with the battery disconnected, capacitive discharge could occur if a component's live terminal is earthed through a metal object. This could cause a shock or nasty burn.
- *Do not reverse the battery connections*. Components such as the alternator, preheating electronic control unit, or any other components having semi-conductor circuitry could be irreparably damaged.
- If the engine is being started using jump leads and a slave battery, connect the batteries *positive-to-positive* and *negative-to-negative* (see *Jump starting*). This also applies when connecting a battery charger.
- Never disconnect the battery terminals, the alternator, any electrical wiring or any test

instruments, when the engine is running.
- Do not allow the engine to turn the alternator when the alternator is not connected.
- Never 'test' for alternator output by 'flashing' the output lead to earth.
- Never use an ohmmeter of the type incorporating a hand-cranked generator for circuit or continuity testing.
- Always ensure that the battery negative lead is disconnected when working on the electrical system.
- Before using electric-arc welding equipment on the car, disconnect the battery, alternator and components such as the preheating electronic control unit, ABS electronic control unit, etc, to protect them from the risk of damage.
- The radio/cassette unit fitted as standard equipment by Land Rover may have a built-in security code to deter thieves. If the power source to the unit is cut, the anti-theft system will activate. Even if the power source is immediately reconnected, the radio/cassette unit will not function until the correct security code has been entered. Therefore, if you do not know the correct security code for the radio/cassette unit, do not disconnect the battery negative terminal of the battery, nor remove the radio/cassette unit from the vehicle. Refer to the manufacturer's handbook supplied with the vehicle for details of how to enter the security code.

2 Electrical fault finding – general information

Refer to Chapter 13.

3 Battery – testing and charging

Note: *Refer to the precautions given in 'Safety first!' and in Section 1 of this Chapter before proceeding.*

Testing

Standard and low-maintenance battery

1 If the vehicle covers a small annual mileage, it is worthwhile checking the specific gravity of the electrolyte every three months to determine the state of charge of the battery. Use a hydrometer to make the check and compare the results with the following table. Note that the specific gravity readings assume an electrolyte temperature of 15°C; for every 10°C below 15°C subtract 0.007. For every 10°C above 15°C add 0.007.

	Ambient temperature	
	Above 25°C	Below 25°C
Fully-charged	1.210 to 1.230	1.270 to 1.290
70% charged	1.170 to 1.190	1.230 to 1.250
Discharged	1.050 to 1.070	1.110 to 1.130

2 If the battery condition is suspect, first check the specific gravity of electrolyte in each cell. A variation of 0.040 or more between any cells indicates loss of electrolyte or deterioration of the internal plates.

3 If the specific gravity variation is 0.040 or more, the battery should be renewed. If the cell variation is satisfactory but the battery is discharged, it should be charged as described later in this Section.

Maintenance-free battery

4 In cases where a 'sealed for life' maintenance-free battery is fitted, topping-up and testing of the electrolyte in each cell is not possible. The condition of the battery can therefore only be tested using a battery condition indicator or a voltmeter.

5 Certain models may be fitted with a maintenance-free battery with a built-in charge condition indicator. The indicator is located in the top of the battery casing, and indicates the condition of the battery from its colour. If the indicator shows green, then the battery is in a good state of charge. If the indicator shows black, then the battery requires charging, as described later in this Section. If the indicator shows blue, then the electrolyte level in the battery is too low to allow further use, and the battery should be renewed.
Caution: Do not attempt to charge, load or jump start a battery when the indicator shows clear/yellow.

All battery types

6 If testing the battery using a voltmeter, connect the voltmeter across the battery. The test is only accurate if the battery has not been subjected to any kind of charge for the previous six hours. If this is not the case, switch on the headlights for 30 seconds, then wait four to five minutes before testing the battery after switching off the headlights. All other electrical circuits must be switched off, so check that the doors and tailgate are fully shut when making the test.

7 If the voltage reading is less than 12.2 volts, then the battery is discharged, whilst a reading of 12.2 to 12.4 volts indicates a partially-discharged condition.

8 If the battery is to be charged, remove it from the vehicle (Section 4) and charge it as described later in this Section.

Charging

Note: *The following is intended as a guide only. Always refer to the manufacturer's recommendations (often printed on a label attached to the battery) before charging a battery.*

Standard and low-maintenance battery

9 Charge the battery at a rate of 3.5 to 4 amps and continue to charge the battery at this rate until no further rise in specific gravity is noted over a four hour period.

10 Alternatively, a trickle charger charging at the rate of 1.5 amps can safely be used overnight.

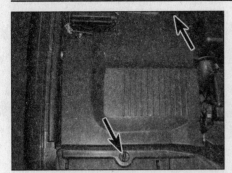

4.2 Undo the fastener and release the clip, then remove the battery cover (arrowed)

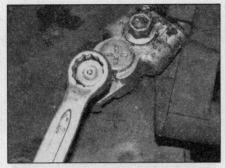

4.3 Slacken the nut and pull the positive clamp from the battery terminal

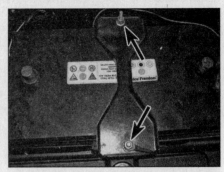

4.4 Battery clamp retaining nuts (arrowed)

11 Specially rapid 'boost' charges which are claimed to restore the power of the battery in 1 to 2 hours are not recommended, as they can cause serious damage to the battery plates through overheating.

12 While charging the battery, note that the temperature of the electrolyte should never exceed 37.8°C.

Maintenance-free battery

13 This battery type takes considerably longer to fully recharge than the standard type, the time taken being dependent on the extent of discharge, but it can take anything up to three days.

14 A constant voltage type charger is required to be set, when connected, to 13.9 to 14.9 volts with a charger current below 25 amps. Using this method, the battery should be usable within three hours, giving a voltage reading of 12.5 volts, but this is for a partially-discharged battery and, as mentioned, full charging can take considerably longer.

15 If the battery is to be charged from a fully-discharged state (condition reading less than 12.2 volts), have it recharged by your Land Rover dealer or local automotive electrician, as the charge rate is higher and constant supervision during charging is necessary.

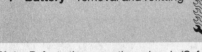

4 Battery – removal and refitting

Note: *Refer to the precautions given in 'Safety first!' and in Section 1 of this Chapter before proceeding.*

Removal

1 The battery is located in the front of the engine compartment.

2 Release the fasteners and remove the battery cover **(see illustration)**.

3 Slacken the nut and disconnect the battery negative terminal clamp, followed by the positive terminal clamp **(see illustration)**.

4 Undo the nuts and remove the battery clamp **(see illustration)**.

5 Lift the battery from position.

Refitting

6 Refitting is a reversal of removal, but always connect the positive terminal clamp first

and the negative terminal clamp last. After connecting the battery terminals, it's a good idea to apply a layer of petroleum jelly to the terminals to prevent corrosion.

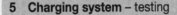

5 Charging system – testing

Note: *Refer to the warnings given in 'Safety first!' and in Section 1 of this Chapter before proceeding.*

1 If the 'ignition' (no-charge) warning light fails to illuminate when the ignition is switched on, first check the security of the alternator wiring connections. If satisfactory, check that the warning light bulb has not blown, and that the bulbholder is secure in its location in the instrument panel. If the light still fails to illuminate, check the continuity of the warning light feed wire from the alternator to the bulbholder. If all is satisfactory, the alternator is at fault. and should be renewed, or taken to an auto-electrician for testing and repair.

2 If the ignition warning light illuminates when the engine is running, stop the engine and check that the drivebelt is correctly tensioned (Chapter 1) and that the alternator connections are secure. If the fault persists, the alternator should be renewed, or taken to an auto-electrician for testing and repair.

3 If the alternator output is suspect even though the warning light functions correctly, the regulated voltage may be checked as follows.

4 Connect a voltmeter across the battery terminals, and start the engine.

6.3 Prise up the rubber boot and disconnect the wiring

5 Increase the engine speed until the voltmeter reading remains steady; as a rough guide, the reading should be between 13.6 and 14.4 volts.

6 Switch on as many electrical accessories (headlights, heater blower, cigarette lighter, etc) as possible, and check that the alternator maintains the regulated voltage between 13.6 and 14.4 volts. It may be necessary to increase engine speed slightly.

7 If the regulated voltage is not as stated, the fault may be due to worn brushes, weak brush springs, a faulty voltage regulator, a faulty diode, a severed phase winding, or worn or damaged slip-rings. The alternator should be renewed, or taken to an auto-electrician for testing and repair.

6 Alternator – removal and refitting

Note: *Refer to the precautions given in 'Safety first!' and in Section 1 of this Chapter before proceeding.*

Removal

1 Disconnect the battery negative lead as described in Section 4.

2 Remove the auxiliary drivebelt as described in Chapter 1.

3 Prise up the rubber boot, undo the nut and disconnect the lead from the alternator **(see illustration)**, then disconnect the wiring plug from the rear of the alternator.

4 Undo the bolt, and remove the auxiliary drivebelt tensioner assembly **(see illustration)**.

6.4 Undo the drivebelt tensioner retaining bolt (arrowed)

6.6 Release the oil drain hose clip

5 Remove the bolt securing the support bracket to the top of the alternator.

6 Release the clip securing the oil drain hose to the vacuum pump **(see illustration)**.

7 Slacken the union bolt and disconnect the vacuum pump oil feed pipe. Discard the sealing washers, new ones must be fitted.

8 Undo the alternator lower mounting bolt, and remove the alternator, disconnecting the vacuum pump oil drain hose as the alternator is withdrawn **(see illustration)**. Take great care not to damage the radiator cooling fins as the unit is withdrawn.

9 If necessary, undo the 4 bolts and detach the vacuum pump from the alternator **(see illustration)**.

Refitting

10 Refitting is a reversal of removal, but tighten all fasteners to their specified torque (where given).

7 Alternator – brush renewal

It would appear at the time of writing that brushes are not available. However, check with a Land Rover dealer or auto electrical specialist before dismantling the alternator or renewing it.

8 Starting system – testing

Note: *Refer to the precautions given in 'Safety first!' and in Section 1 of this Chapter before proceeding.*

1 If the starter motor fails to operate when the ignition key is turned to the appropriate position, the possible causes are as follows:
a) *The battery is faulty.*
b) *The electrical connections between the switch, solenoid, battery and starter motor are somewhere failing to pass the necessary current from the battery through the starter to earth.*
c) *The solenoid is faulty.*
d) *The starter motor is mechanically or electrically defective.*
e) *The starter motor solenoid relay is faulty.*

2 To check the battery, switch on the headlights. If they dim after a few seconds, this indicates that the battery is discharged – recharge (see Section 3) or renew the battery. If the headlights glow brightly, operate the starter switch and observe the lights. If they dim, then this indicates that current is reaching the starter motor, therefore the fault must lie in the starter motor. If the lights continue to glow brightly (and no clicking sound can be heard from the starter motor solenoid), this indicates that there is a fault in the circuit or solenoid – see the following paragraphs. If the starter motor turns slowly when operated, but the battery is in good condition, then this indicates either that the starter motor is faulty, or there is considerable resistance somewhere in the circuit.

3 If a fault in the circuit is suspected, disconnect the battery leads, the starter/solenoid wiring and the engine/transmission earth strap(s). Thoroughly clean the connections, and reconnect the leads and wiring. Use a voltmeter or test light to check that full battery voltage is available at the battery positive lead connection to the solenoid. Smear petroleum jelly around the battery terminals to prevent corrosion – corroded connections are among the most frequent causes of electrical system faults.

4 If the battery and all connections are in good condition, check the circuit by disconnecting the wire from the solenoid blade terminal. Connect a voltmeter or test light between the wire end and a good earth (such as the battery negative terminal), and check that the wire is live when the ignition switch is turned to the start position. If it is, then the circuit is sound – if not, there is a fault in the ignition/starter switch or wiring.

5 The solenoid contacts can be checked by connecting a voltmeter or test light between the battery positive feed connection on the starter side of the solenoid, and earth. When the ignition switch is turned to the start position, there should be a reading or lighted bulb, as applicable. If there is no reading or lighted bulb, the solenoid is faulty and should be renewed.

6 If the circuit and solenoid are proved sound, the fault must lie in the starter motor. The starter motor can be checked by a Land Rover dealer or an automotive electrical specialist. A specialist may be able to overhaul the unit at a cost significantly less than that of a new or exchange starter motor.

9 Starter motor – removal and refitting

Note: *Refer to the precautions given in 'Safety first!' and in Section 1 of this Chapter before proceeding.*

Removal

1 Disconnect the battery negative lead as described in Section 4.

2 Raise the front of the vehicle and support it securely on axle stands (see *Jacking and vehicle support*).

6.8 Undo the alternator lower mounting bolt (arrowed)

6.9 Vacuum pump mounting bolts (arrowed)

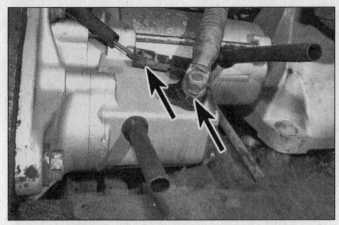

9.4 Starter motor electrical connections (arrowed)

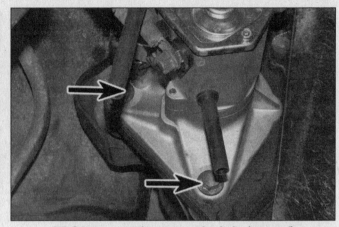

9.5 Starter motor lower mounting bolts (arrowed)

3 Undo the bolts and move the engine undershield to one side.

4 Disconnect the electrical connections from the starter motor **(see illustration)**.

5 Undo the nuts/bolts, and detach the starter from the transmission bellhousing **(see illustration)**.

Refitting

6 Refitting is a reversal of removal. Tighten the fasteners to their specified torque, where given.

10 Starter motor – brush renewal

Starter motor brush renewal is considered to be beyond the scope of the DIY mechanic, and the task should be entrusted to a Land Rover dealer, or an automotive electrical specialist.

11 Ignition switch – removal and refitting

The ignition switch is integral with the steering column lock, and can be removed as described in Chapter 11.

12 Preheating system – description and testing

Description

1 Heater (glow) plugs are only fitted to 4 of the 5 cylinders on this engine – Nos 1, 2, 3 and 4. The plugs are electrically-operated, and controlled by the engine management ECM. Using information supplied from engine coolant temperature sensors the ECM energises the plugs for a brief period before starting to aid combustion, and a brief period after starting – to reduce the warm-up period and improve exhaust emissions.

Testing

Note: *Refer to the precautions given in 'Safety first!' and in Section 1 of this Chapter before proceeding.*

2 Remove the glow plugs as described in Section 13.

3 Inspect the glow plugs for physical damage. Burnt or eroded glow plug tips can be caused by a bad injector spray pattern. Have the injectors checked if this sort of damage is found.

4 The glow plugs can be energised by applying 12 volts to them, to verify that they heat up evenly and in the required time. Observe the following precautions:

a) *Support the glow plug by clamping it carefully in a vice or self-locking pliers. Remember – it will become **red-hot**.*

b) *Make sure that the power supply or test lead incorporates a fuse or overload trip, to protect against damage from a short-circuit.*

c) *After testing, allow the glow plug to cool for several minutes before attempting to handle it.*

5 A glow plug in good condition will start to glow red at the tip after drawing current for 5 seconds or so. Any plug which takes much longer to start glowing, or which starts glowing in the middle instead of at the tip, is defective – the tip must glow first.

6 If a starting fault is still not evident, have the engine management systems self-diagnosis facility interrogated using a fault code reader.

13.3 The glow plugs (arrowed) are accessible through the intake manifold

Consult a Land Rover dealer or specialist. The vehicle's diagnostic plug is located in the driver's side lower facia panel.

13 Glow plugs – removal and refitting

Caution: If the preheating system has just been energised, or if the engine has been running, the glow plugs may be extremely hot.

Removal

1 Undo the 3 bolts and remove the plastic cover from the top of the engine.

2 Disconnect the battery negative lead as described in Section 4.

3 Make a note of the wiring routes and pull the wiring connector from each glow plug **(see illustration)**.

4 Slacken and remove the glow plugs **(see illustration)**.

Refitting

5 Refitting is a reversal of removal, bearing in mind the following points:

a) *Apply a smear of copper-based anti-seize compound to the plug threads, and tighten the glow plugs to the specified torque. Do not overtighten, as this can damage the glow plug element.*

b) *Ensure that the glow plug wiring is routed as noted before removal.*

13.4 Slacken and remove the glow plug

Chapter 6
Clutch

Contents

Section number

Clutch assembly – removal, inspection and refitting 2
Clutch fluid level check . . . . See *Weekly checks*
Clutch pedal – removal and refitting. 7
Clutch release mechanism – removal, inspection and refitting 3

Section number

General information 1
Hydraulic slave cylinder – removal, overhaul and refitting. 4
Hydraulic system – bleeding 6
Master cylinder – removal, overhaul and refitting 5

Degrees of difficulty

Easy, suitable for novice with little experience	**Fairly easy,** suitable for beginner with some experience	**Fairly difficult,** suitable for competent DIY mechanic	**Difficult,** suitable for experienced DIY mechanic	**Very difficult,** suitable for expert DIY or professional

Specifications

General

Clutch type. . . . . Single dry plate, diaphragm spring, hydraulically-operated
Adjustment. . . . . Automatic
Hydraulic fluid type. . . . . See *Lubricants and fluids*

Clutch friction disc

Diameter . . . . 267.0 mm

Torque wrench settings

	Nm	lbf ft
Clutch cover nuts.	25	18
Clutch master cylinder bolts.	25	18
Clutch slave cylinder bolts	25	18
Hydraulic fluid pipe and hose unions	15	11

1 General information

All models are fitted with a single dry plate clutch, which consists of five main components – friction disc, pressure plate, diaphragm spring, cover and release bearing.

The friction disc is free to slide along the splines of the gearbox input shaft, and is held in position between the flywheel and the pressure plate by the pressure exerted on the pressure plate by the diaphragm spring. Friction lining material is riveted to both sides of the friction disc. All TD5 models are equipped with a dual mass flywheel which incorporates torsional damping to absorb transmission shocks.

The diaphragm spring is mounted on pins, and is held in place in the cover by annular fulcrum rings.

The release bearing is located on a guide sleeve at the front of the gearbox. The bearing is free to slide on the sleeve, under the action of the release arm which pivots inside the clutch bellhousing.

The release mechanism is operated by the clutch pedal, using hydraulic pressure. The pedal acts on the hydraulic master cylinder pushrod, and a slave cylinder, mounted on the gearbox bellhousing, operates the clutch release lever via a pushrod.

When the clutch pedal is depressed, the release arm pushes the release bearing forwards, to bear against the centre of the diaphragm spring, thus pushing the centre of the diaphragm spring inwards. The diaphragm spring acts against the fulcrum rings in the cover; as the centre of the spring is pushed in, the outside of the spring is pushed out, so allowing the pressure plate to move backwards away from the friction disc.

When the clutch pedal is released, the diaphragm spring forces the pressure plate into contact with the friction linings on the friction disc, and simultaneously pushes the friction disc forwards on its splines, forcing it against the flywheel. The friction disc is now firmly sandwiched between the pressure plate and the flywheel, and drive is taken up.

The clutch is self-adjusting. As wear takes place on the friction disc over a period of time, the pressure plate automatically moves closer to the friction disc to compensate.

2 Clutch assembly – removal, inspection and refitting

Warning: Dust created by clutch wear and deposited on the clutch components may contain asbestos, which is a health hazard. DO NOT blow it out with compressed air, nor inhale any of it. DO NOT use petrol (or petroleum-based solvents) to clean off the dust. Brake system cleaner or methylated spirit should be used to flush the dust into a suitable receptacle. After the clutch components are wiped clean with rags, dispose of the contaminated rags and cleaner in a sealed, marked container.

Removal

1 Remove the gearbox, as described in Chapter 7A, or the engine, as described in Chapter 2B.
2 If the original clutch is to be refitted, make alignment marks between the clutch cover and the flywheel, so that the clutch can be refitted in its original position.
3 Progressively unscrew the nuts securing the clutch cover to the flywheel, and recover the washers. Do not disturb the three bolts located in the side of the clutch cover **(see illustration)**.
4 Withdraw the clutch cover from the flywheel. Be prepared to catch the clutch friction disc, which may drop out of the cover as it is withdrawn, and note which way round the friction disc is fitted. The greater projecting side of the hub faces the flywheel.

Inspection

5 With the clutch assembly removed, clean off all traces of dust using a dry cloth. Although most friction discs now have asbestos-free linings, some do not, and it is wise to take suitable precautions; *asbestos dust is harmful, and must not be inhaled.*
6 Examine the linings of the clutch disc for wear or loose rivets, and the disc for distortion, cracks and worn splines. The surface of the friction linings may be highly glazed, but, as long as the friction material pattern can be clearly seen, this is satisfactory. If there is any sign of oil contamination, indicated by a continuous, or patchy, shiny black discolouration, the disc must be renewed. The source of the contamination must be traced and rectified before fitting new clutch components; typically, a leaking crankshaft rear oil seal or gearbox input shaft oil seal – or both – will be to blame. The disc must also be renewed if the lining thickness has worn down to, or just above, the level of the rivet heads. Given the amount of labour involved in removing the clutch, if in any doubt, renew the assembly.
7 Check the machined faces of the flywheel and pressure plate. If either is grooved, or heavily scored, renewal is necessary. The pressure plate must also be renewed if any cracks are apparent, or if the diaphragm spring is damaged or its pressure suspect.
8 With the clutch removed, it is advisable to check the condition of the release bearing, as described in Section 3. It is considered good practice to renew the release bearing as a matter of course, whenever new clutch components are fitted, given the amount of work required to gain access to the clutch.

Refitting

9 It is important to ensure that no oil or grease gets onto the friction disc linings, or the pressure plate and flywheel faces. It is advisable to refit the clutch assembly with clean hands, and to wipe down the pressure plate and flywheel faces with a clean rag before assembly begins.
10 Apply a smear of clutch assembly grease to the splines of the friction disc hub, then offer the disc to the flywheel, with the greater projecting side of the hub facing the flywheel (most friction discs will have a 'Flywheel side' or 'FW SIDE' marking, which should face the flywheel) **(see illustration)**. Hold the friction disc against the flywheel while the cover/pressure plate assembly is offered into position.
11 Fit the clutch cover assembly, where applicable aligning the marks on the flywheel and clutch cover. Refit the securing bolts/nuts and washers, and tighten them finger-tight, so that the friction disc is gripped, but can still be moved. Note that the pressure plate assembly locates on dowels **(see illustration)**.

2.3 Undo the nuts securing the clutch cover

2.10 The greater projecting side of the disc hub (arrowed) must face the flywheel

2.11 The pressure plate assembly locates on dowels (arrowed)

2.13a Use a clutch alignment tool . . .

2.13b . . . to centre the friction disc

3.3 Slide the release bearing from the sleeve

12 The friction disc must now be centralised, so that when the engine and gearbox are mated, the gearbox input shaft splines will pass through the splines in the friction disc hub.

13 Centralisation can be carried out by inserting a round bar or a long screwdriver through the hole in the centre of the friction disc, so that the end of the bar rests in the spigot bearing in the centre of the crankshaft. Where possible, use a blunt instrument, but if a screwdriver is used, wrap tape around the blade, to prevent damage to the bearing surface. Moving the bar sideways or up-and-down as necessary, move the friction disc in whichever direction is necessary to achieve centralisation. With the bar removed, view the friction disc hub in relation to the hole in the centre of the crankshaft and the circle created by the ends of the diaphragm spring fingers. When the hub appears exactly in the centre, all is correct. Alternatively, use a clutch plate alignment tool (see illustrations).

14 Tighten the cover retaining nuts gradually in a diagonal sequence, to the specified torque. Remove the alignment tool.

15 Refit the gearbox or engine, as applicable, as described in Chapter 7A or Chapter 2B respectively.

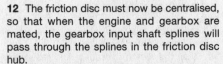

3   Clutch release mechanism – removal, inspection and refitting

Release bearing

Removal

1 Remove the gearbox, described in Chapter 7A, or the engine, as described in Chapter 2B.

2 Where applicable, remove the clip securing the release bearing assembly to the release lever.

3 Slide the bearing assembly from the guide sleeve (see illustration).

4 Note that on all TD5 models, the bearing is not available separately from the bearing carrier.

Inspection

5 Spin the release bearing, and check it for

excessive roughness. Hold the outer race, and attempt to move it laterally against the inner race. If any excessive movement or roughness is evident, renew the bearing. If a new clutch has been fitted, it is wise to renew the release bearing as a matter of course.

Refitting

6 Lightly smear the outer faces of the release bearing guide sleeve with clutch assembly grease.

7 Slide the bearing assembly onto the guide sleeve.

8 Refit the clip securing the release bearing assembly to the release lever.

9 Refit the gearbox or engine, as applicable, as described in Chapter 7A or Chapter 2B respectively.

Release lever

Removal

10 Remove the release bearing, as described previously in this Section, and the slave cylinder, as described in Section 4 (note that if the gearbox is in position in the vehicle, there is no need to disconnect the hydraulic fluid pipe from the slave cylinder – move the

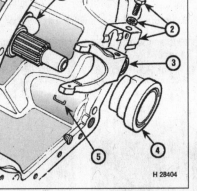

3.12 Clutch release components

1   Release lever pivot post
2   Release lever securing clip, screw and washer
3   Release lever
4   Release bearing
5   Release bearing securing clip

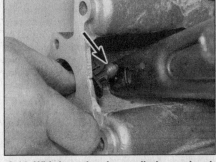

3.11 Withdraw the slave cylinder pushrod from the bellhousing

slave cylinder to one side, leaving the pipe connected).

11 Unclip the slave cylinder pushrod from the end of the release lever, and withdraw the pushrod through the bellhousing (see illustration).

12 Remove the securing screw, and prise off the clip securing the release lever to the pivot post. Note that the clip locates behind the washer on the pivot post (see illustration).

13 Withdraw the release lever from the bellhousing.

Refitting

14 Apply a little high-melting-point grease to the contact faces of the pivot post and the release lever (see illustration).

15 Manipulate the release lever into position on the pivot post, and engage the securing

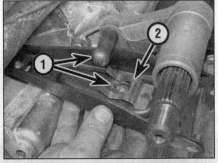

3.14 Apply a little high-melting-point grease to the contact faces (1). Note the release lever securing clip (2)

clip. Ensure that the securing clip locates behind the washer on the pivot post.

16 Refit the securing screw and washer to the release lever securing clip.

17 Refit the slave cylinder pushrod to the end of the release arm, ensuring that the securing clip is engaged.

18 Refit the release bearing as described previously in this Section, and the slave cylinder as described in Section 4.

4 Hydraulic slave cylinder – removal, overhaul and refitting

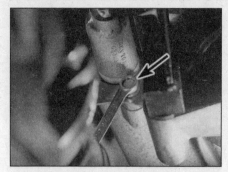

4.3 Clutch slave cylinder retaining bolts (lower bolt arrowed)

5.1 Release the clevis pin retaining clip (arrowed)

⚠️ *Warning: Hydraulic fluid is poisonous; wash off immediately and thoroughly in the case of skin contact, and seek immediate medical advice if any fluid is swallowed or gets into the eyes. Certain types of hydraulic fluid are inflammable, and may ignite when allowed into contact with hot components. When servicing any hydraulic system, it is safest to assume that the fluid IS inflammable, and to take precautions against the risk of fire as though it is petrol that is being handled. Finally, it is hygroscopic (it absorbs moisture from the air) – old fluid may be contaminated, and unfit for further use. When topping-up or renewing the fluid, always use the recommended type, and ensure that it comes from a freshly-opened sealed container.*
Caution: Hydraulic fluid is an effective paint stripper, and will attack plastics; if any is spilt, it should be washed off immediately, using copious quantities of fresh water.
Note: *Suitable jointing compound may be required to coat the mating faces of the slave cylinder mounting plate on refitting.*

Removal

1 Jack up the front of the vehicle and support it securely on axle stands (see *Jacking and vehicle support*).

2 Unscrew the union nut, and disconnect the hydraulic fluid pipe from the end of the slave cylinder, located on the left-hand side of the transmission bellhousing. Plug or cover the open ends of the pipe and the slave cylinder, to prevent dirt ingress and fluid loss. If desired, to improve access, the pipe can be removed completely, in which case, plug or cover the open end of the flexible hose-to-pipe union.

3 Unscrew the two securing bolts, and withdraw the slave cylinder and the mounting plate from the gearbox bellhousing **(see illustration)**. Recover the slave cylinder pushrod if it is loose.

Overhaul

4 At the time of writing, it appears that no overhaul kits are available for the TD5 Discovery. Check with your local dealer, motor factor or specialist.

Refitting

5 Clean the slave cylinder and transmission housing mating faces.

6 Lubricate the end of the pushrod with a little molybdenum disulphide grease.

7 Manipulate the slave cylinder into position in the bellhousing, and feed the pushrod through the slave cylinder dust cover, ensuring that the pushrod engages with the slave cylinder piston.

8 Ensure that heat shield is in position, then

refit and tighten the slave cylinder securing bolts.

9 Reconnect the fluid pipe to the slave cylinder, and tighten the union nut.

10 Refill the clutch hydraulic fluid reservoir, and bleed the hydraulic system as described in Section 6.

5 Master cylinder – removal, overhaul and refitting

⚠️ *Warning: Refer to the warning at the beginning of Section 4 before proceeding.*

Removal

1 Undo the fasteners and remove the lower facia panel above the driver's pedals.

2 Release the spring clip and remove the clevis pin securing the master cylinder pushrod to the clutch pedal **(see illustration)**.

3 Unscrew the union nut, and disconnect the hydraulic fluid pipe from the master cylinder **(see illustration)**. Plug the open ends of the pipe and master cylinder, to prevent dirt ingress. Be prepared for fluid spillage.

4 Use a clamp on the hose, then release the clip and disconnect the fluid supply hose from the master cylinder **(see illustration)**. Be prepared for fluid spillage.

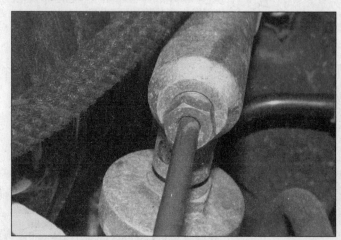

5.3 Undo the union nut from the end of the clutch master cylinder

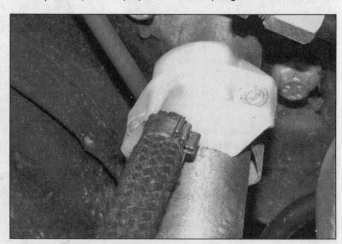

5.4 Release the clip and disconnect the fluid supply hose

5 Undo the two bolts and pull the master cylinder from the engine compartment bulkhead.

Overhaul

6 At the time of writing, it would appear that no overhaul kits are available for the Discovery TD5. Check with your local dealer, motor factor or specialist.

Refitting

7 Ensure the mating faces are clean, then refit the master cylinder, and tighten the mounting bolts to the specified torque.
8 Refit the pushrod clevis pin and securing it with the retaining clip.
9 Insert the fluid pipe and tighten the union securely.
10 Reconnect the fluid supply hose, refit the clip and remove the hose clamp.
11 Refit the facia panel.
12 Refill the reservoir with fluid of the recommended type, then bleed the hydraulic system as described in Section 6.

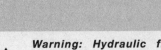

6 Hydraulic system – bleeding

> ⚠ **Warning: Hydraulic fluid is poisonous; wash off immediately and thoroughly in the case of skin contact, and seek immediate medical advice if any fluid is swallowed or gets into the eyes. Certain types of hydraulic fluid are inflammable, and may ignite when allowed into contact with hot components; when servicing any hydraulic system, it is safest to assume that the fluid is inflammable, and to take precautions against the risk of fire as though it is petrol that is being handled. Hydraulic fluid is also an effective paint stripper, and will attack plastics; if any is spilt, it should be washed off immediately, using copious quantities of fresh water. Finally, it is hygroscopic (it absorbs moisture from the air) – old fluid may be contaminated and unfit for further use. When topping-up or renewing the fluid, always use the recommended type, and ensure that it comes from a freshly-opened sealed container.**

General

1 The correct operation of any hydraulic system is only possible after removing all air from the components and circuit; and this is achieved by bleeding the system.
2 During the bleeding procedure, add only clean, unused hydraulic fluid of the recommended type; never re-use fluid that

has already been bled from the system. Ensure that sufficient fluid is available before starting work.
3 If there is any possibility of incorrect fluid being already in the system, the hydraulic components and circuit must be flushed completely with uncontaminated, correct fluid, and new seals should be fitted throughout the system.
4 If hydraulic fluid has been lost from the system, or air has entered because of a leak, ensure that the fault is cured before proceeding further.

Bleeding procedure

5 Unscrew the master cylinder reservoir cap, and top the master cylinder reservoir up to the MAX level line; refit the cap loosely, and remember to maintain the fluid level at least above the MIN level line throughout the procedure, otherwise there is a risk of further air entering the system.
6 There is a number of one-man, do-it-yourself brake/clutch bleeding kits currently available from motor accessory shops. It is recommended that one of these kits is used whenever possible, as they greatly simplify the bleeding operation, and also reduce the risk of expelled air and fluid being drawn back into the system. If such a kit is not available, the basic (two-man) method must be used, which is described in detail below.
7 If a kit is to be used, prepare the vehicle as described previously, and follow the kit manufacturer's instructions, as the procedure may vary slightly according to the type being used; generally, they are as outlined below in the relevant sub-section.

Basic (two-man) method

8 Clean the area around the bleed screw at the rear of the clutch slave cylinder (located on the gearbox bellhousing). Where applicable, remove the dust cover from the bleed screw **(see illustration)**.
9 Collect a clean glass jar, a suitable length of plastic or rubber tubing which is a tight fit over the bleed screw, and a ring spanner to fit the screw. The help of an assistant will also be required.

6.8 Remove the dust cover from the clutch slave cylinder bleed screw

10 Fit a suitable spanner and tube to the screw, place the other end of the tube in the jar, and pour in sufficient fluid to cover the end of the tube.
11 Ensure that the master cylinder reservoir fluid level is maintained at least above the MIN level line throughout the procedure.
12 Unscrew the bleed screw (approximately one turn).
13 Have the assistant fully depress the clutch pedal, then hold the pedal depressed. When the flow of fluid into the jar stops, tighten the bleed screw again, have the assistant release the pedal slowly, and recheck the reservoir fluid level.
14 Repeat the steps given in paragraphs 12 and 13 until the fluid emerging from the bleed screw is free from air bubbles. If the master cylinder has been drained and refilled, allow approximately five seconds between cycles for the master cylinder passages to refill.
15 When no more air bubbles appear, tighten the bleed screw securely, remove the tube and spanner, and refit the dust cap (where applicable). Do not overtighten the bleed screw.
16 On completion, recheck the fluid level in the reservoir, and top-up if necessary.
17 Discard any hydraulic fluid that has been bled from the system; it will not be fit for re-use.

Using a one-way valve kit

18 As their name implies, these kits consist of a length of tubing with a one-way valve fitted, to prevent expelled air and fluid being drawn back into the system; some kits include a translucent container, which can be positioned so that the air bubbles can be more easily seen flowing from the end of the tube.
19 The kit is connected to the bleed screw, which is then opened. The user returns to the driver's seat, depresses the clutch pedal with a smooth, steady stroke, and slowly releases it; this is repeated until the expelled fluid is clear of air bubbles.
20 Note that these kits simplify work so much that it is easy to forget the master cylinder reservoir fluid level; ensure that this is maintained at least above the MIN level line at all times.

7 Clutch pedal – removal and refitting

Removal

1 Prise out the fasteners and remove the lower facia panel from above the pedals.
2 Prise of the clip and remove the pin securing the clutch master cylinder pushrod to the pedal **(see illustration 5.1)**.
3 Prise off the spring clip securing the

7.3 Prise out the clip securing the servo pushrod to the brake pedal (arrowed)

7.4 Note the fitted positions of the pedal return springs

servo pushrod to the brake pedal **(see illustration)**.

4 Undo the bolt at each end of the pedal pivot shaft, and carefully lower the pedal assembly. Note the fitted positions of the pedal return springs **(see illustration)**.

5 Slide the pedal(s) from the shaft, noting the positions of any spacers, roll-pins, etc.

Refitting

6 Lightly grease the pedal pivot bushes.

7 Refit the pedal(s) to the shaft, ensuring all bushes, spacers, etc, are in their original positions.

8 Manoeuvre the assembly into place, ensure the pedal return springs are correctly located.

9 Tighten the pivot shaft bolts securely.

10 Reconnect the pushrods to the clutch and brake pedals, and secure them with the clevis pins and clips.

11 Refit the lower facia panel.

Chapter 7 Part A:
Manual transmission

Contents

Section number

General information 1
Manual transmission – removal and refitting 3
Manual transmission oil renewal . . . . See Chapter 1

Section number

Manual transmission overhaul – general information. 4
Reversing light switch – testing, removal and refitting. 2

Degrees of difficulty

Easy, suitable for novice with little experience	Fairly easy, suitable for beginner with some experience	Fairly difficult, suitable for competent DIY mechanic	Difficult, suitable for experienced DIY mechanic	Very difficult, suitable for expert DIY or professional

Specifications

General

Transmission type.	R380 type transmission; five forward speeds and reverse

Ratios:

First gear.	3.692 : 1
Second gear.	2.132 : 1
Third gear	1.397 : 1
Fourth gear	1.000 : 1
Fifth gear.	0.770 : 1
Reverse.	3.536 : 1

Torque wrench settings

	Nm	lbf ft
Clutch slave cylinder-to-bellhousing bolts.	25	18
Gearbox cooling housing bolts	25	18
Gearbox mountings:		
Bolts	85	63
Nuts	48	37
Handbrake backplate.	75	55
Reversing light switch	24	17
Transfer gearbox-to-main transmission bolts	45	33
Transmission bellhousing-to-engine bolts	45	33

1 General information

Drive from the clutch is picked up by the input shaft, which runs in parallel with the layshaft. The input shaft runs on the same axis as the mainshaft, and a bearing between the two shafts allows the shafts to rotate independently. A fixed gear at the rear of the input shaft drives the layshaft. The input shaft and mainshaft gears are in constant mesh, and selection of gears is by sliding synchromesh hubs, which lock the appropriate mainshaft gear to the mainshaft. The direct-drive fourth gear is obtained by locking the input shaft to the mainshaft.

Reverse gear is obtained by sliding an idler gear into mesh with two straight-cut gears on the mainshaft (the 1st/2nd gear synchro sleeve) and the layshaft.

All the forward gear teeth are helically-cut, to reduce noise and to improve wear characteristics.

The mainshaft provides drive to the transfer gearbox, which is described in part C of this Chapter.

Gear selection is by means of a floor-mounted gearchange lever, acting directly on the gearchange rail in the transmission.

2 Reversing light switch – testing, removal and refitting

Testing

1 The switch is located in the left-hand side of the gearbox casing (see illustration), and is accessible from under the vehicle.
2 Disconnect the wiring from the switch.
3 Connect a continuity tester or an ohmmeter across the switch terminals. There should be no continuity (infinite resistance) between the switch terminals.
4 Engage reverse gear. There should now be continuity (close to zero resistance) between the terminals.
5 If the above readings are not as expected, try cleaning the switch terminals. If the readings are still not as expected, it is likely that the switch is faulty or incorrectly positioned. The switch can be tested after it is removed.

Removal

6 Disconnect the switch wiring plug.
7 Unscrew the switch from the gearbox casing, and recover the sealing ring.
8 Examine the condition of the sealing ring, and renew if necessary.

Refitting

9 Refitting is a reversal of removal, but use a new sealing ring if necessary.

3 Manual transmission – removal and refitting

Note: *Although the following procedure is not difficult, the transmission assembly (the main transmission is removed complete with the transfer gearbox) is heavy, and awkward to handle. Read through the entire procedure before proceeding, to familiarise yourself with the steps. The help of an assistant will prove invaluable during this operation. A suitable engine lifting crane and tackle will be required.*

Removal

1 Disconnect the battery negative lead (see Chapter 5).
2 Jack up the vehicle, and support securely on axle stands placed under the axle tubes (see *Jacking and vehicle support*). Note that the vehicle must be raised sufficiently to give enough clearance for the transmission assembly to be removed from under the vehicle.
3 Remove the centre console as described in Chapter 12.
4 Lift the sound insulation from the top of the transmission tunnel (see illustration).
5 If not already done, unscrew the securing bolt, and remove the upper section of the gear lever.
6 Remove the viscous fan unit and cowl, as described in Chapter 3 (this is necessary to allow the engine to tilt during the transmission removal procedure).
7 Remove the front section of the exhaust pipe, and intermediate silencer as described in Chapter 4A.
8 Remove the starter motor as describe in Chapter 5.
9 Drain the gearbox and transfer gearbox oils as described in Chapter 1.
10 Remove the front and rear propeller shafts as described in Chapter 8.
11 Undo the bolt and remove the handbrake drum.
12 Slacken and remove the 4 retaining bolts, then detach the handbrake backplate, and position it to one side complete with shoes, etc.
13 Unscrew the bolts securing the clutch slave cylinder to the transmission bellhousing.
14 Release the clutch slave cylinder from the bellhousing. Move the slave cylinder clear of the bellhousing, but take care not to strain the hydraulic fluid pipe.
15 The main transmission/transfer gearbox assembly must now be supported. This is most easily and safely accomplished using an engine crane, as follows:

a) *Working under the vehicle, unscrew one of the top securing bolts from the power take-off cover at the rear of the transfer gearbox. Make up a lifting bracket, and bolt it to the transfer gearbox using the previously-removed bolt (see illustration).*
b) *Pass a lifting strap or chain around the main transmission casing. Pass the ends of the strap/chain up through the hole in the transmission tunnel.*
c) *Attach a second lifting strap/chain to the lifting bracket on the transfer gearbox, and again pass the end of the strap/chain up through the transmission tunnel.*
d) *Open one of the front doors, and secure the door in the fully-open position using a length of string.*
e) *Pass the engine lifting crane in through the front door aperture, and position the lifting hook over the transmission tunnel aperture. Attach the previously-positioned lifting straps to the crane. Take care not to damage the interior trim when positioning the lifting gear.*
f) *Raise the crane sufficiently to just take the weight of the transmission assembly.*

2.1 The reversing light switch is located on the left-hand side of the main gearbox casing (arrowed)

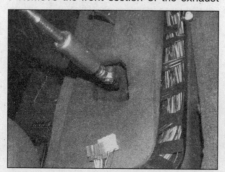

3.4 Remove the sound insulation material from the transmission tunnel

3.15 Lifting bracket bolted to the transfer gearbox (arrowed)

16 Ensure that the transmission assembly is adequately supported before proceeding.

17 Undo the nuts securing the gearbox mountings to the vehicle body.

18 Undo the 4 bolts securing the mountings to the gearbox, then raise the gearbox a little and remove the mountings.

19 Lower the gearbox to be able to access the top of the gearbox – ensure no pipes or wires are trapped as the gearbox is lowered.

20 Remove the clevis pin and slide out the retaining clip securing the low ratio selector cable to the lever and lever housing.

21 Again working under the vehicle, disconnect all electrical wiring connectors from the main transmission and the transfer gearbox, noting their locations. Release the wiring from any clips on the main transmission/ transfer gearbox casing, noting its routing.

22 Undo the banjo bolts securing the breather pipes and recover the sealing washers, then release the breather hoses from any retaining clips on the gearbox/transfer gearbox.

23 Undo the two bolts securing the cooling pipe housing to the gearbox, detach the housing and discard the O-ring seals. Be prepared for fluid spillage, and plug the openings to prevent contamination.

24 Use a workshop jack to support the engine, and undo the 8 bolts securing the transmission bellhousing to the engine. Note that the transmission assembly may move backwards from the engine once the bolts are removed – be prepared for this, and do not allow the assembly to swing uncontrolled. Slide the transmission assembly back from the engine, taking care not to strain the transmission input shaft.

25 Position a trolley jack and a large block of wood under the transmission assembly (the wood should be suitably-shaped to support the transmission when it is lowered), then lower the engine crane to position the transmission assembly on the trolley jack and support block.

26 Disconnect the lifting straps/chains from the transmission assembly and the engine crane, then carefully slide the transmission assembly out from under the vehicle, using the trolley jack. Take care when moving the transmission, and do not attempt to lift the assembly without suitable lifting tackle – the assembly is very heavy!

27 If desired, the transfer gearbox can be separated from the main gearbox as described in part C of this Chapter.

Refitting

28 Where applicable, refit the transfer gearbox to the main transmission, as described in part C of this Chapter. Ensure that the Low range is selected in the transfer gearbox.

29 Ensure the mating faces of the engine and gearbox are clean.

30 Position the transmission assembly under the vehicle using the trolley jack and support block, then fit the lifting straps/chains to the transmission (as during removal). Pass the lifting straps/chains up through the transmission tunnel, and connect them to the engine crane.

31 Using the crane, lift the transmission assembly into position, then slide the bellhousing into place. Ensure that the wiring harness and connectors, and the breather pipes, are not trapped as the transmission is moved into position. Note that it will be necessary to tilt the rear of the engine down to align the engine and transmission (the engine can easily be tilted on its mountings if an assistant pushes the assembly from above).

32 Manipulate the engine and transmission as necessary to align the transmission input shaft splines with the splines in the clutch friction disc hub (it may be necessary to turn the crankshaft using a spanner or socket on the pulley bolt.

33 Refit and tighten the engine-to-transmission bolts. Tighten the bolts to the specified torque.

34 The remainder of the refitting procedure is a reversal of removal, bearing in mind the following points:

a) *Ensure that all wiring is routed correctly, and that all plugs are reconnected to their correct locations.*

b) *Refit the propeller shafts with reference to Chapter 8.*

c) *Refit the exhaust front section and intermediate silencer with reference to Chapter 4A.*

d) *Refit the gearbox cooling housing using new O-ring seals.*

e) *Tighten all fasteners to the specified torque where given.*

f) *Before refitting the centre console, check*

the handbrake cable adjustment as described in the relevant part of Chapter 1.

g) *Where applicable, on completion, refill the main transmission and transfer gearbox with oil of the correct type, as described in Chapter 1.*

4 Manual transmission overhaul – general information

Overhauling a manual transmission is a difficult and involved job for the DIY home mechanic. In addition to dismantling and reassembling many small parts, clearances must be precisely measured and, if necessary, changed by selecting shims and spacers. Transmission internal components are also often difficult to obtain, and in many instances, extremely expensive. Because of this, if the transmission develops a fault or becomes noisy, the best course of action is to have the unit overhauled by a specialist repairer, or to obtain an exchange reconditioned unit.

Nevertheless, it is not impossible for the more experienced mechanic to overhaul a transmission, provided the special tools are available, and the job is done in a deliberate step-by-step manner so that nothing is overlooked.

The tools necessary for an overhaul include internal and external circlip pliers, bearing pullers, a slide-hammer, a set of pin punches, a dial test indicator, and possibly a hydraulic press. In addition, a large, sturdy workbench and a vice will be required.

During dismantling of the transmission, make careful notes of how each component is fitted, to make reassembly easier and more accurate.

Before dismantling the transmission, it will help if you have some idea of which area is malfunctioning. Certain problems can be closely related to specific areas in the transmission, which. can make component examination and renewal easier. Refer to the *Fault finding* Section at the end of this manual for more information.

Chapter 7 Part B:
Automatic transmission

Contents

Section number

Automatic transmission – removal and refitting 6
Automatic transmission ECU (EAT) – removal and refitting 8
Automatic transmission fluid renewal . . . . See Chapter 1
Automatic transmission overhaul – general information 7
Gear selector indicator – removal and refitting 5
General information 1

Section number

Oil cooler – removal and refitting 9
Selector assembly – removal and refitting 2
Selector cable – removal, refitting and adjustment 3
Starter inhibitor switch – description, removal and refitting 4
Transmission fluid filter – removal, cleaning and refitting 10

Degrees of difficulty

Easy, suitable for novice with little experience	Fairly easy, suitable for beginner with some experience	Fairly difficult, suitable for competent DIY mechanic	Difficult, suitable for experienced DIY mechanic	Very difficult, suitable for expert DIY or professional

Specifications

General
Type . . . . ZF 4HP22

Torque wrench settings	**Nm**	**lbf ft**
Dipstick tube-to-sump union nut	68	50
Selector lever-to-transmission bolts	25	18
Starter inhibitor switch	10	7
Sump drain plug	15	11
Sump securing bolts	8	6
Torque converter-to-driveplate bolts*	50	37
Transmission bellhousing-to-engine bolts	45	33
Transmission mountings bolts and nuts	85	63

* Do not re-use

2.3 Prise up the outer cable C-clip

2.4a Prise out the inner cable locking ring . . .

2.4b . . . and pull the inner cable from the lever, complete with plastic bush

1 General information

A 4-speed fully-automatic transmission is available as an option on certain models. The transmission consists of a torque converter, an epicyclic geartrain, and hydraulically-operated clutches and brakes. The transmission is a customised version of the ZF 4HP22 unit used in many other vehicles.

The torque converter provides a fluid coupling between the engine and transmission, acts as an automatic clutch, and also provides a degree of torque multiplication when accelerating. The torque converter incorporates a lock-up clutch which improves transmission throttle response once the converter is fully engaged.

The epicyclic geartrain provides either one of the four forward gear ratios, or reverse gear, according to which of its component parts are held stationary or allowed to turn. The components of the geartrain are held or released by brakes and clutches, which are activated by a hydraulic governor. A fluid pump within the transmission provides the necessary hydraulic pressure to operate the brakes and clutches.

First, second and third gears are reduction gears, but fourth gear is an overdrive gear for high-speed cruising. A direct-drive clutch, integral with the torque converter, operates to engage fourth gear.

Operation of the transmission is controlled by an Electronic Control Unit (ECU), which is networked to the engine management ECM, to enable the ECU to determine the optimum gearchange point, kick-down point, and to improve gearchange quality by reducing engine torque at the change points.

Due to the complexity of the automatic transmission, any repair or overhaul work must be entrusted to a Land Rover dealer, or a suitably-qualified transmission specialist, with the necessary specialist equipment and knowledge for fault diagnosis and repair. Refer to the *Fault finding* Section at the end of this manual for further information. Any faults within the transmission should generate a fault code, which will be stored in the transmission ECU. The ECU can be interrogated and the details of any stored faults extracted using dedicated test equipment (fault code reader) via the diagnostic socket located under the facia on the driver's side. Depending on the type of fault, the Sport and Manual warning lamps on the instrument panel may flash, the ECU may enter the limp-home mode, where engine performance may be reduced, kick-down disabled, and reduced transmission function (no manual shift, etc).

2 Selector assembly – removal and refitting

Removal

1 Remove the centre console as described in Chapter 12.

2 Remove the sound insulation pad from around the selector lever.

3 Prise up the C-clip securing the selector outer cable to the assembly **(see illustration)**.

4 Prise out the locking ring and release the inner cable from the lever **(see illustrations)**.

5 Undo the 3 bolts securing the selector lever assembly **(see illustration)**.

Refitting

6 Refitting is a reversal of removal, remembering to adjust the cable as described in Section 3.

3 Selector cable – removal, refitting and adjustment

Removal and refitting

1 Remove the centre console as described in Chapter 12.

2 Prise up the C-clip securing the outer cable to the selector lever assembly, then prise out the locking clip and disconnect the inner cable **(see illustrations 2.3, 2.4a and 2.4b)**.

3 Working underneath the vehicle, slacken the selector inner cable clamp nut, and prise out the C-clip securing the outer cable to the support bracket **(see illustrations)**.

4 Note the cable routing and remove it from the vehicle.

5 Refitting is a reversal of removal, but adjust the cable as follows:

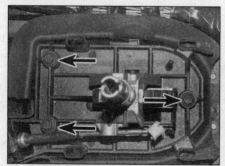

2.5 Selector lever housing retaining bolts (arrowed)

3.3a Slacken the inner cable clamp nut . . .

3.3b . . . and prise out the C-clip (arrowed)

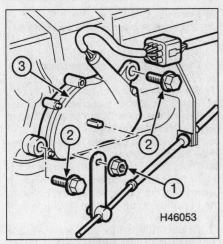

4.7 Starter inhibitor/selector position switch

1 *Lever retaining nut*
2 *Switch retaining bolts*
3 *Switch*

Adjustment

6 Working under the vehicle, slacken the selector inner cable clamp nut, and push the lever on the side of the transmission fully forward (P position).

7 Ensure the selector lever in the passenger cabin is in the P position.

8 Tighten the selector inner cable clamp nut securely.

---

4 Starter inhibitor switch
– description, removal and refitting

Description

1 The starter/inhibitor switch is fitted to the transmission casing.

2 The inhibitor function of the switch ensures that the engine can only be started with the selector lever in either the N or the P positions, therefore preventing the engine from being started with the transmission in gear. This is achieved by the switch cutting the supply to the starter motor solenoid. If at any time it is

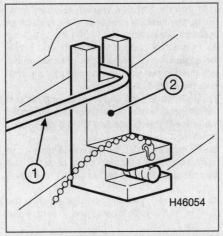

4.13 Fit tool (2) to the shaft, then rotate the switch until the setting pin (1) engages

noted that the engine can be started with the selector lever in any position other than N or P, then it is likely that the inhibitor function of the switch is faulty.

3 The reversing lights are operated by the transmission ECU as it monitors the gear selector lever position.

4 If is faulty, it must be renewed as a unit.

Removal

Note: *Refitting and adjustment of the switch requires access to Land Rover tool LRT-44-011.*

5 Remove the front section of the exhaust pipe as described in Chapter 4A.

6 Ensure the selector lever is in position P.

7 Undo the nut securing the lever to the side of the transmission, and pull the lever from the shaft **(see illustration)**.

8 Undo the two retaining bolts and pull the switch from the transmission. Disconnect the wiring plug as the switch is withdrawn.

Refitting

9 Commence refitting by cleaning the switch, and the switch housing in the transmission casing.

10 Select P position by rotating the shaft fully clockwise, then select N position by rotating the shaft 2 detents anti-clockwise.

11 Fit the switch to the shaft and reconnect

the wiring plug. Do not tighten the retaining bolts at this stage.

12 Fit LRT-44-011 to the selector shaft, then insert the setting pin into the tool.

13 Rotate the switch until the setting pin engages with the hole in the switch **(see illustration)**.

14 Tighten switch retaining bolts to the specified torque.

15 Refit the lever to the shaft, and refit the front exhaust pipe.

---

5 Gear selector indicator
– removal and refitting

1 Pull the knob upwards sharply to remove it from the lever, and recover the spacer **(see illustrations)**.

2 Carefully prise up the indicator panel from the centre console **(see illustration)**.

3 Disconnect the wiring plug as the panel is withdrawn. At the time of writing, it would appear that there are no separate parts available for the indicator – check with your dealer or specialist.

4 Refitting is a reversal of removal.

---

6 Automatic transmission
– removal and refitting

Note: *Although the following procedure is not difficult, the transmission assembly (the main transmission is removed complete with the transfer gearbox) is heavy, and awkward to handle. Read through the entire procedure before proceeding, to familiarise yourself with the steps. The help of an assistant will prove invaluable during this operation. A suitable engine lifting crane and tackle will be required.*

Removal

1 The automatic transmission is removed with the transfer gearbox as a complete unit.

2 Disconnect the battery negative lead, as described in Chapter 5.

3 Jack up the vehicle, and support securely on axle stands placed under the axle tubes (see *Jacking and vehicle support*). Note that

5.1a Pull the selector lever knob sharply upwards to release it

5.1b Recover the spacer from the lever

5.2 Carefully prise the selector panel upwards

the vehicle must be raised sufficiently to give enough clearance for the transmission assembly to be removed from under the vehicle.

4 Remove the starter motor as described in Chapter 5.

5 Undo the 2 upper bolts securing the transmission to the engine, and the bolt securing the adapter plate to the transmission casing.

6 Remove the front section of the exhaust pipe and the intermediate silencer as described in Chapter 4A.

7 Drain the automatic transmission fluid and the transfer box oil as described in Chapter 1.

8 Remove the front and rear propeller shafts as described in Chapter 8.

9 Working through the starter motor aperture in the bellhousing, make alignment marks between the torque converter and the driveplate, to ensure that the alignment is maintained on refitting.

10 Again working through the starter motor aperture, unscrew and remove the four torque converter-to-driveplate bolts. It will be necessary to turn the crankshaft to gain access to each bolt in turn, and this can be done using a suitable spanner or socket on the crankshaft pulley bolt.

11 Undo the bolt and remove the transmission brake drum, then undo the 4 bolts and remove the brake backplate, and position it to one side.

12 Note their fitted positions, and disconnect the all wiring plugs from the transmission and transfer box.

Models with high/low shift interlock solenoid

13 Remove the sleeve retaining rings, and remove the sleeve from the high/low selector cable.

Models with centre diff lock

14 Remove the clevis pin securing the diff lock selector cable to the transfer gearbox.

15 Slack the selector outer cable locknuts, and move the cable to one side.

All models

16 Remove the clevis pin securing the high/low ratio selector cable to the selector lever, then prise out the C-clip and remove the outer cable from the bracket.

17 Detach the transmission and transfer box breather pipes from the rear of the cylinder head.

18 Remove the viscous fan unit and cowl, as described in Chapter 3 (this is necessary to allow the engine to tilt during the transmission removal procedure).

19 Position a workshop jack under the transmission to take its weight. Bearing in mind that the assembly is very heavy, and will almost certainly cause damage should it slip from the jack, it is recommended that Land Rover tool LRT-99-008A is obtained. This tool bolts to the underside of the assembly, and provides a secure, positively located platform

to fit into the top of a workshop trolley jack. During the removal procedure, the help of an assistant is essential.

20 Position a second workshop jack under the engine sump. Use a block of wood on the jack head to prevent any damage to the sump. Take the weight of the engine.

21 Undo the 2 bolts and one nut, and remove the left-hand transmission mounting assembly, then repeat this procedure on the right-hand mounting.

22 Remove the bolts securing the transmission oil cooler pipe clips to the alternator support bracket and the engine sump.

23 Undo the 2 nuts and one bolt securing the clamps to the oil cooler pipes. Remove the clamps.

24 Place a suitable container under the transmission to collect escaping fluid, then unscrew the union nuts, and disconnect the transmission fluid cooler pipes from the underside of the transmission. Plug the open ends of the pipes and transmission, to prevent dirt ingress and further fluid loss. Discard the O-rings, new ones must be fitted.

25 Disconnect the selector cable from the lever on the side of the transmission (see Section 3).

26 Ensure that the transmission assembly is adequately supported before proceeding.

27 Progressively unscrew the remaining transmission-to-engine securing nuts and bolts.

Caution: The transmission assembly may move backwards from the engine once the bolts are removed – be prepared for this, and do not allow the assembly to slip from the jack head.

28 Carefully slide the transmission assembly back from the engine.

29 Fit a suitable strip of metal across the bellhousing, to retain the torque converter. **Do not** allow the torque converter to fall out of the transmission.

30 Position a trolley jack and a large block of wood under the transmission assembly (the wood should be suitably-shaped to support the transmission when it is lowered), then lower the engine crane to position the transmission assembly on the trolley jack and support block.

31 Carefully slide the transmission assembly out from under the vehicle, using the trolley jack. Take care when moving the transmission, and do not attempt to lift the assembly without suitable lifting tackle – the assembly is very heavy!

32 If desired, the transfer gearbox can be separated from the main transmission as described in part C of this Chapter.

Refitting

33 If a new transmission is to be fitted, it will be necessary to transfer the following components from the existing assembly to the new unit. Take great care to prevent dirt from entering the transmission – plug all openings to prevent dirt ingress.

a) Extension shaft spacer – this is vital!
b) Transmission breather pipe union and washers.
c) Transmission selector lever.
d) Transmission mounting assembles.
e) Fluid cooler pipe unions.
f) Starter inhibitor switch.

34 Where applicable, reconnect the transfer gearbox to the transmission as described in part C of this Chapter.

35 Ensure that the Low gear range is selected in the transfer gearbox.

36 Thoroughly clean the mating faces of the engine flywheel housing and the transmission bellhousing, then apply sealing compound to the transmission bellhousing mating face of the engine flywheel housing.

37 Fit four M10 studs (or bolts with the heads cut off) to the lower engine-to-transmission bolt holes in the engine. The studs should be approximately 100 mm long.

38 Position the transmission assembly under the vehicle using the trolley jack. Remove the torque converter retaining strap from the bellhousing.

39 Carefully lift the transmission assembly into position, then slide the bellhousing onto the studs previously fitted. Ensure that the wiring harness and connectors, and the breather pipes, are not trapped as the transmission is moved into position. Note that it will be necessary to tilt the rear of the engine down to align the engine and transmission (the engine can easily be tilted on its mountings if an assistant pushes the assembly from above). Push the transmission bellhousing onto the studs sufficiently to enable nuts to be fitted to the studs.

40 Progressively tighten the nuts fitted to the four studs in the flywheel housing, to draw the transmission bellhousing flush against the engine.

41 Refit and tighten the engine-to-transmission upper nuts, then unscrew the nuts and studs from the lower bolt holes, and refit the four lower bolts. Tighten the bolts.

42 Secure the wiring harness and breather pipes, as noted during removal, using new cable-ties where necessary.

43 Raise the transmission assembly sufficiently to enable the left- and right-hand mountings to be refitted. Tighten the nuts and bolts to the specified torque.

44 The remainder of the refitting procedure is a reversal of removal, bearing in mind the following points:

a) Ensure that all wiring is routed correctly, and that all plugs are reconnected to their correct locations.
b) Refit the propeller shafts with reference to Chapter 8.
c) Refit the exhaust front section with reference to Chapter 4A.
d) Use new torque converter-to-driveplate bolts.
e) If the original torque converter and driveplate components are being refitted, ensure that the marks made on the torque

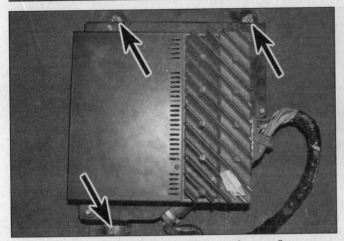

8.3 Undo the power amplifier nuts (arrowed)

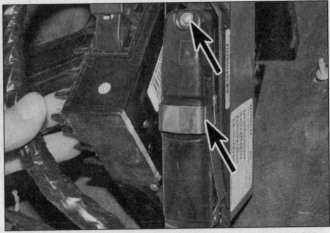

8.4 Undo the screw and lift the catch to disconnect the ECM wiring plug (arrowed)

converter and the driveplate before removal are aligned. Tighten the new bolts to the specified torque.

f) Where applicable, on completion, refill the main transmission and transfer gearbox with fluid and oil of the correct type, as described in the relevant part of Chapter 1.

7 Automatic transmission overhaul – general information

In the event of a fault occurring on the transmission, it is first necessary to determine whether it is of an electrical, mechanical or hydraulic nature, and to achieve this, special test equipment is required. It is therefore essential to have the work carried out by a Land Rover dealer, or a suitably-equipped specialist, if a transmission fault is suspected.

Do not remove the transmission from the vehicle for possible repair before professional fault diagnosis has been carried out, since most tests require the transmission to be in the vehicle.

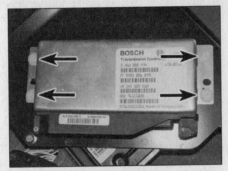

8.5 The transmission ECM is secured by 4 'scrivets' (arrowed)

8 Automatic transmission ECU (EAT) – removal and refitting

1 Disconnect the battery negative lead as described in Chapter 5.
2 Remove the passenger's front seat as described in Chapter 12.
3 Undo the 3 nuts securing the power amplifier bracket to the vehicle body **(see illustration)**.

4 Disconnect the transmission ECU multiplug (under the amplifier mounting bracket) **(see illustration)**.
5 Slacken the screws, prise out the plastic rivets, and remove the ECU from the mounting bracket **(see illustration)**.
6 Refitting is a reversal of removal. **Note:** *If a new ECU is fitted, it must be reprogrammed using Land Rover's Testbook diagnostic tool (or equivalent). Entrust this task to a Land Rover dealer or suitably-equipped specialist.*

9 Oil cooler – removal and refitting

1 Remove the intercooler as described in Chapter 4A.
2 Disconnect the fluid temperature sensor wiring plug.
3 Press the coupling release collar towards the hose, and disconnect the cooler hoses from the cooler **(see illustration)**. Be prepared for fluid spillage.
4 Undo the screw on the right-hand side, and manoeuvre the cooler from position **(see illustration)**.

9.3 Pull back the collar (arrowed) and disconnect the cooler hose

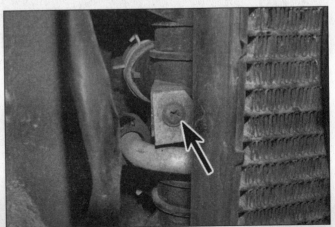

9.4 Undo the screw (arrowed) and withdraw the cooler

5 If required, unscrew the temperature sensor, and discard the sealing washer – a new one must be fitted.

6 Refitting is a reversal of removal.

10 Transmission fluid filter – removal, cleaning and refitting

1 Drain the transmission fluid as described in Chapter 1.

2 Undo the 6 bolts, remove the spacers and lower the transmission fluid sump **(see illustration)**. Discard the gasket, a new one must be fitted.

3 Undo the Torx screw and remove the fluid pick-up tube.

4 Undo the two bolts and remove the filter from the valve body **(see illustration)**. Discard the O-ring seals, new ones must be fitted.

10.2 To access the filter, remove the transmission fluid sump

5 Clean the filter and the pick-up tube using lint-free cloth.

6 Fit new O-ring seals, then refit the filter and tighten the retaining screws securely.

7 The remainder of refitting is a reversal of removal, remembering to top-up the transmission fluid as described in Chapter 1.

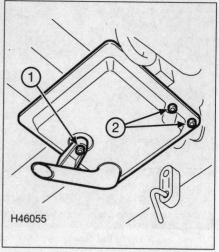

H46055

10.4 Pick-up pipe screw (1) and filter screws (2)

Chapter 7 Part C:
Transfer gearbox

Contents

	Section number		Section number
General information	1	Transfer gearbox oil level check	See Chapter 1
Range selector cable – removal, refitting and adjustment	4	Transfer gearbox oil renewal	See Chapter 1
Transfer gearbox – removal and refitting	2	Transfer gearbox overhaul – general information	3

Degrees of difficulty

Easy, suitable for novice with little experience	**Fairly easy,** suitable for beginner with some experience	**Fairly difficult,** suitable for competent DIY mechanic	**Difficult,** suitable for experienced DIY mechanic	**Very difficult,** suitable for expert DIY or professional

Specifications

Gear ratios (final drive to axles)
High range	1.211 : 1
Low range	3.320 : 1

Torque wrench settings
	Nm	lbf ft
Breather pipe union bolt	15	11
Transfer gearbox-to-main gearbox/transmission bolts and nuts	45	33

1 General information

The transfer gearbox is mounted in-line with the main manual gearbox/automatic transmission. The transfer gearbox is a two-speed ratio-reducing gearbox, and provides drive to the front and rear axles via the propeller shafts.

Permanent four-wheel-drive is provided, and the unit incorporates a differential assembly to allow for any difference in the rotational speed of the front and rear wheels (and a resulting difference in speed between the front and rear propeller shafts). This centre differential (the axles also incorporate differentials, to allow for the difference in rotational speed between left- and right-hand wheels on the same axle) can be locked by mechanical means, to provide increased traction in particularly slippery conditions.

Selection of the High/Low ranges and the differential lock is made using a selector lever mounted forward of the main gear lever.

2 Transfer gearbox – removal and refitting

Removal

1 The transfer gearbox is most easily removed complete with the manual gearbox/automatic transmission as an assembly. This procedure is described in part A or B of this Chapter, as applicable.

2 To separate the transfer gearbox from the manual gearbox/automatic transmission, proceed as follows.

3 Position the transmission assembly securely on a bench or a suitable stand, or rest the assembly on wooden blocks on the workshop floor.

4 Where applicable, unbolt the bracing bar connecting the transfer box to the main gearbox/transmission.

5 Unscrew the union bolt, and disconnect the breather pipe from the top of the transfer gearbox casing **(see illustration)**. Recover the sealing washers.

6 Remove the split-pin, or the spring clip (as applicable), securing the differential lock connecting rod/cable to the lever on the transfer gearbox, and disconnect the rod from the lever **(see illustration)**. Where applicable, recover the washers.

7 Ensure that the main gearbox/transmission and the transfer gearbox are adequately supported, then remove the transfer gearbox-to-main gearbox/transmission securing bolts, and slide the transfer gearbox rearwards from the main gearbox/transmission **(see illustration)**.

2.5 Unscrew the breather pipe union bolt (arrowed)

2.6 Disconnect the differential lock connecting rod (1) from the lever (2)

2.7 Three of the transfer gearbox-to-main gearbox bolts and nuts (arrowed)

Refitting

8 Refitting is a reversal of removal, bearing in mind the following points:

a) *Thoroughly clean the mating faces of the transfer gearbox and the main gearbox/ transmission.*

b) *On models with automatic transmission, before attempting to mate the main transmission and transfer gearbox together, select P in the main transmission.*

c) *Before attempting to mate the main gearbox and the transfer gearbox together, select the Low range, and engage the differential lock in the transfer gearbox.*

d) *As the two assemblies are mated together, engage the transfer gear selector rod with the yoke.*

e) *Refit the complete transmission assembly as described in Chapter 7A or 7B, as applicable.*

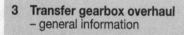

3 Transfer gearbox overhaul – general information

Overhauling a transfer gearbox is a difficult and involved job for the DIY home mechanic. In addition to dismantling and reassembling many small parts, clearances must be precisely measured and, if necessary, changed by selecting shims and spacers. Gearbox internal components are also often difficult to obtain, and in many instances, extremely expensive. Because of this, if the gearbox develops a fault or becomes noisy, the best course of action is to have the unit overhauled by a specialist repairer, or to obtain an exchange reconditioned unit.

Nevertheless, it is not impossible for the more experienced mechanic to overhaul a gearbox, provided the special tools are available, and the job is done in a deliberate step-by-step manner so that nothing is overlooked.

The tools necessary for an overhaul include internal and external circlip pliers, bearing pullers, a slide-hammer, a set of pin punches, a dial test indicator, and possibly a hydraulic press. In addition, a large, sturdy workbench and a vice will be required. Certain Land Rover special tools will be required for work on the differential assembly.

During dismantling of the gearbox, make careful notes of how each component is fitted, to make reassembly easier and more accurate.

Before dismantling the gearbox, it will help if you have some idea of which area is malfunctioning. Certain problems can be closely related to specific areas in the gearbox, which can make component examination and renewal easier. Refer to the *Fault finding* Section at the end of this manual for more information.

4 Range selector cable – removal, refitting and adjustment

Removal

1 Working underneath the vehicle, undo the locknut securing the outer cable to the support bracket on the gearbox, then remove the clevis pin securing the inner cable to the transfer box lever **(see illustration)**.

2 At the other end of the cable, prise out the C-clip securing the outer cable, and remove the clevis pin securing the inner cable to the high/low lever **(see illustration)**.

3 Undo the bolt securing the outer cable clamp to the cross-shaft housing and remove the cable.

Refitting

4 Refitting is a reversal of removal, but apply some moly grease to the inner cable end fittings, and adjust the cable as follows:

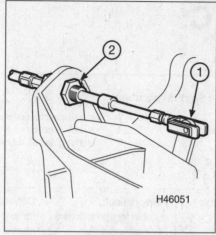

H46051

4.1 Slacken the lock nut (2) and remove the inner cable clevis pin (1)

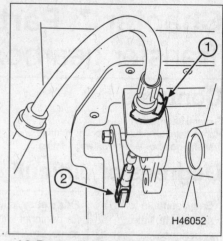

H46052

4.2 Remove the C-clip (1) and the clevis pin (2)

Adjustment

5 Slacken the locknut securing the outer cable to the bracket on the gearbox.

6 Select high range by move the lever on the transfer gearbox fully forward.

7 If the selector lever is in the correct position, Land Rover special tool LRT-41-016 can be inserted through the hole in the selector lever and housing **(see illustration)**. If it cannot, further slacken the cable locknuts until the inner cable can be moved to a position where the tool can be inserted. With the tool inserted, tighten the locknuts, then remove the tool.

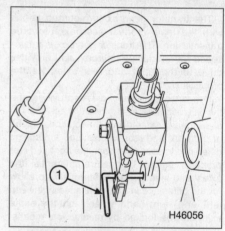

H46056

4.7 With the lever in the High range position, the special tool (1) should fit through the hole in the lever, and into the housing

Chapter 8
Propeller shafts

Contents

	Section number		Section number
General information	1	Propeller shaft securing bolt check	See Chapter 1
Propeller shaft – inspection and overhaul	3	Propeller shaft joint lubrication	See Chapter 1
Propeller shaft – removal and refitting	2	Rear propeller shaft rubber coupling – inspection and renewal	4

Degrees of difficulty

Easy, suitable for novice with little experience	**Fairly easy,** suitable for beginner with some experience	**Fairly difficult,** suitable for competent DIY mechanic	**Difficult,** suitable for experienced DIY mechanic	**Very difficult,** suitable for expert DIY or professional

Specifications

General

Propeller shaft type	Tubular, splined joint
End joints:	
Front shaft	Hookes joint with needle-roller bearings at the rear end. Universal joint and sliding spline joint at the front end
Rear shaft	Universal joint with sliding spline joint at the front end. Flexible rubber coupling at the rear end

Torque wrench settings

	Nm	lbf ft
Propeller shaft securing nuts and bolts:		
Front shaft	47	35
Rear shaft to transfer gearbox flange	47	35
Rear shaft to coupling	76	56
Rear flexible rubber coupling securing nuts and bolts	76	56

1 General information

The drive is transmitted from the transfer gearbox to the front and rear axle differentials by two tubular propeller shafts.

The front propeller shaft is fitted with a Hookes joint and a universal joint. The joints cater for the varying angle between the axle and the transmission, caused by suspension movement **(see illustration).**

The rear propeller shaft is fitted with a universal joint at the front end, and a flexible rubber coupling at the rear end **(see illustration).**

To allow for the fore-and-aft movement between the axles and transmission, a sliding, splined joint is incorporated in each propeller shaft.

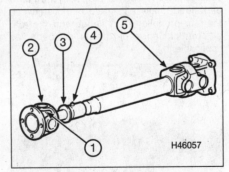

1.1 Front propeller shaft

1 Grease nipple
2 Universal joint
3 Rubber gaiter/sliding spline joint
4 Lubrication point (blanking plug for grease nipple)
5 Hookes joint

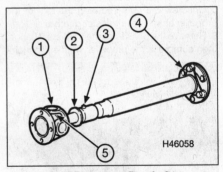

1.2 Rear propeller shaft

1 Universal joint
2 Rubber gaiter/sliding joint
3 Grease nipple
4 Flexible coupling
5 Grease nipple

2.4 Make alignment marks between the propeller shaft flange and the transfer box flange

Grease nipples are fitted to the universal joints, and the universal joints and sliding joints should periodically be lubricated in accordance with the maintenance schedule given in the relevant part of Chapter 1. The Hookes joint is a sealed unit and required no maintenance.

2 Propeller shaft – removal and refitting

Front propeller shaft

Removal

1 Jack up the vehicle, and support securely on axle stands positioned under the axles, as described in *Jacking and vehicle support*.
2 If the original propeller shaft is to be refitted, make alignment marks between the front propeller shaft flange and the differential flange.
3 Counterhold the bolts, and unscrew the nuts securing the front of the propeller shaft to the differential flange.
4 Again, if the original propeller shaft is to be refitted, make alignment marks between the rear propeller shaft flange and the transfer gearbox flange **(see illustration)**.
5 Unscrew the nuts securing the rear of the propeller shaft to the transfer gearbox flange.
6 Remove the bolts from the front shaft flange, then compress the propeller shaft sliding joint

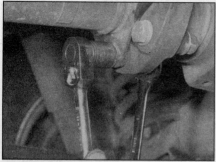

2.13 Unscrew the nuts and bolts securing the flexible coupling to the propeller shaft flange

2.10 Make alignment marks between the propeller shaft flange and the handbrake drum

until the rear of the shaft can be withdrawn from the studs on the transfer gearbox flange.
7 Withdraw the propeller shaft from under the vehicle.

Refitting

8 Refitting is a reversal of removal, bearing in mind the following points:
  a) *Ensure that the propeller shaft is refitted with the sliding joint at the front axle end.*
  b) *If the original propeller shaft is being refitted, align the marks made on the differential flange, transfer gearbox flange, and the propeller shaft flanges before removal.*
  c) *Tighten the securing nuts and bolts to the specified torque.*

Rear propeller shaft

Removal

9 Jack up the vehicle, and support securely on axle stands positioned under the axles, as described in *Jacking and vehicle support*.
10 If the original propeller shaft is to be refitted, make alignment marks between the front propeller shaft flange and the handbrake drum at the transfer gearbox **(see illustration)**.
11 Unscrew the nuts securing the front of the propeller shaft to the handbrake drum.
12 Again, if the original propeller shaft is to be refitted, make alignment marks between the rear propeller shaft flange and the rear differential flange or rubber coupling, as applicable.

2.14 Withdraw the front of the propeller shaft from the studs on the brake drum

13 Counterhold the bolts, and unscrew the nuts securing the rear of the propeller shaft to the flexible rubber coupling, as applicable **(see illustration)**.
14 Withdraw the flange bolts, then compress the propeller shaft sliding joint until the front of the propeller shaft can be withdrawn from the studs on the brake drum **(see illustration)**. Note that the rear of the propeller shaft fits over a spigot on the differential flange – it is therefore necessary to pull the shaft forwards before it can be lowered.
15 Withdraw the propeller shaft from under the vehicle.

Refitting

16 Refitting is a reversal of removal, bearing in mind the following points:
  a) *Ensure that the propeller shaft is refitted with the sliding joint towards the front of the vehicle (nearest the transfer gearbox).*
  b) *If the original propeller shaft is being refitted, align the marks made on the handbrake drum, rubber coupling, and the propeller shaft flanges before removal.*
  c) *Tighten the securing nuts and bolts to the specified torque.*

3 Propeller shaft – inspection and overhaul

Inspection

1 Wear in the universal joint needle roller bearings is characterised by vibration in the transmission, clonks on taking up the drive, and in extreme cases (lack of lubrication) unpleasant metallic noises as the bearings break up.
2 To test the universal/Hookes joints for wear with the propeller shaft in place, apply the handbrake, and chock the wheels.
3 Working under the vehicle, apply leverage between the yokes using a large screwdriver or a flat metal bar. Wear is indicated by movement between the shaft yoke and the coupling flange yoke. Check all the universal joints in this way.
4 To check the splined sleeve on the front of both shafts, try to push the shafts from side-to-side, and look for any excessive movement between the sleeve and the shaft. A further check can be made by gripping the shaft and sleeve, and turning them in opposite directions, again looking for excessive movement. As a rough guide, if *any* movement can be seen, the splines are worn, and the shaft assembly should be renewed.
5 If a universal/Hookes joint is worn, a new joint must be obtained and fitted as described later in this Section.
6 If the sliding joint is excessively worn, the complete shaft assembly must be renewed.
7 Check the condition of the rear propeller shaft flexible rubber coupling, with reference to Section 4.

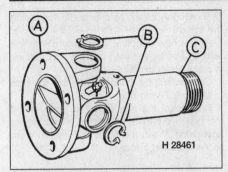

3.12 Propeller shaft universal joint

A *Coupling flange*
B *Circlips*
C *Shaft*

Overhaul

Note: *The following procedure applies to the universal joints of the front and rear propshafts – this includes the Hookes (double universal joint) joint on the front shaft.*

Dismantling

8 With the propeller shaft removed as described in Section 2, proceed as follows.

9 Working on one of the universal joints, note the position of the grease nipple on the spider in relation to the adjacent shaft yoke, and coupling flange yoke (make alignment marks on the yokes). This is vital to ensure correct reassembly, and to ensure that the shaft balance is maintained.

10 Clean away all traces of dirt and grease from the circlips located on the ends of the joint spiders, and from the grease nipple.

11 Unscrew the grease nipple.

12 Using a suitable pair of circlip pliers, remove the four joint circlips **(see illustration)**. If a circlip proves difficult to remove, as a last resort, place a drift on the bearing cup, in the centre of the circlip, and tap the top of the bearing cup to ease the pressure on the circlip.

13 Support the end of the shaft in a vice, with the yoke in a vertical plane. Using a hammer and a suitable drift (a socket of appropriate size, for example), tap the uppermost bearing cup until the bottom bearing cup protrudes from the yoke.

14 Remove the shaft from the vice, then securely grip the protruding bearing cup in the vice jaws. Turn the shaft from side-to-side, at the same time lifting the shaft until the bearing cup comes free.

15 Refit the shaft to the vice, with the exposed spider uppermost. Tap the spider with the hammer and drift until the lower bearing cup protrudes, then remove the cup as described previously.

16 The coupling flange and the spider can now be removed from the shaft, and the remaining bearing cups can be removed as described previously.

17 Where applicable, repeat the operations described in paragraphs 9 to 16 to remove the remaining joint from the shaft.

Inspection

18 With the universal joint dismantled, carefully examine the needle rollers, bearing cups and spider for wear, scoring and pitting of the surface finish. If any wear is detected, the joint must be renewed **(see illustration)**.

19 Where applicable, unscrew the sliding joint grease nipple, and thoroughly clean the nipple and its hole.

20 If working on the front propeller shaft, examine the condition of the sliding joint rubber gaiter, and renew if necessary.

21 Temporarily fit the front section of the shaft to the rear section, ensuring that the alignment marks are correctly positioned. Grip the front section of the shaft in a vice, and check for wear in the sliding joint splines, as described in paragraph 4.

Reassembly

22 If a new joint is being fitted, remove the bearing cups from the new spider. Check that all the needle rollers are present, and correctly positioned in the bearing cups.

23 Ensure that the bearing cups are one-third full of fresh multi-purpose lithium-based grease.

24 Fit the new spider, complete with seals, into the coupling flange yoke. Make sure that the grease nipple hole is aligned with the mark on the yoke made during dismantling, and note that the grease nipple hole must face away from the coupling flange.

25 Partially insert one of the bearing cups into the yoke, and enter the spider trunnion into

the bearing cup, taking care not to dislodge the needle rollers.

26 Similarly, insert a bearing cup into the opposite yoke.

27 Using the vice, carefully press both bearing cups into place, ensuring that the spider trunnions do not dislodge any of the needle rollers **(see illustration)**.

28 Using a suitable tube or socket of a slightly smaller diameter than the bearing cups, press each cup into its respective yoke, until the top of the cup just reaches the lower land of the circlip groove. **Do not** press the cups below this point, as damage may be caused to the cups and seals.

29 Fit the new circlips to retain the bearing cups **(see illustration)**.

30 Engage the spider with the yokes on the relevant propeller shaft section, then partially fit both bearing cups to the yokes, taking care not to dislodge any of the needle rollers.

31 Press the bearing cups into position, and fit the new circlips, as described in paragraphs 27 to 29.

32 Screw the grease nipple into position in the joint spider.

33 Where applicable, repeat the operations described in paragraphs 22 to 32 to fit the remaining joint to the shaft.

34 Where applicable, screw the sliding joint grease nipple into position.

35 Smear the sliding joint splines on the end of the rear section of the shaft with grease, then slide the rear section of the shaft into the front section, ensuring that the marks made during dismantling are aligned. **Note:** *Do not pack grease into the open end of the shaft front section, as this may prevent the shaft from being pushed fully home.*

36 Screw the sliding joint dust cap into position.

37 If working on the front propeller shaft, slide the rubber gaiter over the sliding joint, and secure in position with the two clips. If screw-type clips are used, fit the clips with the screws 180°, apart to help maintain the balance of the shaft.

38 Refit the propeller shaft as described in Section 2, then lubricate the joints using a grease gun applied to the grease nipples (see Chapter 1).

3.18 Universal joint bearing components

3.27 Press the cups into place using a vice and socket

3.29 Fit new circlips to retain the bearing cups

4 Rear propeller shaft rubber coupling – inspection and renewal

Inspection

1 Later models use a flexible rubber coupling to connect the rear of the propeller shaft to the rear differential flange, instead of the universal joint used on earlier models.

2 Deterioration of the rubber coupling will be self-evident on inspection. Look particularly for cracks around the bolt holes.

Renewal

3 Remove the 3 bolts/nuts and pull the rear propeller shaft forward **(see illustration 2.13)**. If the coupling is to be refitted, make alignment marks before detaching the propeller shaft.

4 Counterhold the bolts, and unscrew the nuts securing the coupling to the rear differential flange, then withdraw the coupling. Recover the washers.

5 Thoroughly clean the differential flange and the spigot.

6 Fit the new coupling, and secure with the nuts and bolts, ensuring that the washers are in place under the nuts.

7 Counterhold the bolts, and tighten the nuts to the specified torque.

8 Reconnect the rear propeller shaft, using the previously-made alignment marks where applicable. Insert the bolts and tighten them to the specified torque.

Chapter 9
Front and rear axles

Contents

Section number

Axle differential overhaul – general information 10
Front axle driveshaft – removal, gaiter renewal and refitting 2
Front axle oil level check . . . . See Chapter 1
Front axle oil renewal . . . . See Chapter 1
Front axle oil seals – renewal 5
Front axle hub carrier – removal and refitting. 4
Front hub and bearing assembly – removal and refitting 3

Section number

Front hub carrier balljoints – renewal 6
General information 1
Rear axle driveshaft – removal and refitting. 7
Rear axle oil level check. . . . . See Chapter 1
Rear axle oil renewal . . . . See Chapter 1
Rear axle pinion oil seal – renewal 9
Rear hub and bearing assembly – removal and refitting 8

Degrees of difficulty

Easy, suitable for novice with little experience	Fairly easy, suitable for beginner with some experience	Fairly difficult, suitable for competent DIY mechanic	Difficult, suitable for experienced DIY mechanic	Very difficult, suitable for expert DIY or professional

Specifications

Type
Front. . . . . Spiral bevel differential with steel driveshafts incorporating CV joints
Rear . . . . Solid axle, spiral bevel differential with fixed driveshafts
Differential ratio (front and rear) 3.538:1

Torque wrench settings	Nm	lbf ft
ABS sensor Allen bolt.	18	13
Front axle pinion flange bolt.	100	74
Front drag link balljoint nut.	80	59
Front driveshaft nut*.	490	362
Front hub assembly retaining bolts	100	74
Front hub carrier balljoint nuts:		
Upper	110	81
Lower	135	100
Front hub carrier tension collet	5	4
Front track rod balljoint nut.	80	59
Rear axle pinion flange bolt.	76	55
Rear driveshaft nut*	490	362
Rear hub-to-hub carrier bolts.	100	74
Roadwheel nuts	140	103

* Do not re-use

1 General information

The front axle comprises a one-piece steel casing which houses the differential assembly, and two driveshafts incorporating constant velocity (CV) joints at their outer ends. A hub carrier is mounted on balljoints at the outer ends of the axle. The ends of the driveshafts pass though wheel bearing/hub assemblies fitted to the hub carriers.

The rear axle is also a one-piece steel casing which houses the rear differential assembly. Solid steel driveshafts are fitted, the inner ends of which are splined into the differential assembly, while the outer ends are attached to the hubs.

2 Front axle driveshaft
– removal, gaiter renewal and refitting

Removal

1 Apply the handbrake, and loosen the nuts on the relevant front roadwheel. Jack up the front of the vehicle and support it on axle stands positioned underneath the chassis (see *Jacking and vehicle support*). Remove the relevant front roadwheel.

2 Using a chisel or punch, unstake the driveshaft nut, then unscrew it from the driveshaft **(see illustrations)**. Assistance

2.2a Unstake the driveshaft nut

2.2b Prise out the centre of the roadwheel, refit it, lower the vehicle to the ground, then undo the driveshaft nut

may be required, the nut is very tight. Discard the nut, a new one must be fitted. **Note:** *The driveshaft nut is very tight. It may be prudent to prise out the centre of the roadwheel, refit it, and lower the vehicle to the ground. Then insert the socket through the centre of the wheel and undo the nut.*

3 Remove the front brake disc as described in Chapter 10.

4 Undo the Allen bolt, and pull the ABS sensor from the front hub. Discard the O-ring seal, a new one must be fitted.

5 Undo the 3 bolts and remove the brake mudshield **(see illustration)**.

6 Undo the 4 retaining bolts and pull the hub and driveshaft assembly from the hub carrier **(see illustrations)**.

7 If required, press the driveshaft from the hub. If a press is not available, it may be possible to carefully tap the shaft from the hub using a hammer and a soft-metal drift.

Take great care not to damage the end of the shaft.

8 It is recommended that the driveshaft oil seal in the axle is renewed as described in Section 5.

Gaiter renewal

9 With the driveshaft removed, clamp the driveshaft securely in a bench vice, and release both gaiter securing clips **(see illustrations)**. Discard the clips, new ones must be fitted (normally supplied with the gaiter kit).

10 Pull the gaiter from the outer joint and, using a soft-metal drift and hammer, drive the inner part of the joint from the shaft **(see illustration)**. Note that to improve access, cut the remains of the gaiter from the joint using a sharp knife.

11 Remove the circlip from the end of the inner shaft, and slide off the spacer. Discard the circlip; a new one must be used on refitting.

2.5 Undo the bolts and remove the mudshield

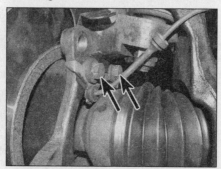

2.6a Hub-to-hub carrier upper bolts (arrowed)

2.6b Pull the hub and driveshaft from the hub carrier

2.9a Release the gaiter inner clip . . .

2.9b . . . if necessary, cut the gaiter outer clip to remove it

2.10 Note that the drift must only bear on the inner part of the joint

2.13 Fit the new clip to the gaiter, then fit them over the shaft

2.14a Fit the space to the shaft . . .

2.14b . . . and the new circlip

12 Pull the gaiter from the shaft (if it's not already been removed).

13 Clean the end of the driveshaft, fit the new clip loosely to the inner end of the gaiter, then slide the gaiter into place on the shaft (see illustration).

14 Refit the spacer to the shaft, then fit the new circlip (see illustrations).

15 Clean the old grease from the CV joint, and inspect it for wear or damage. If the CV joint is worn or damaged, the complete driveshaft must be renewed. Check with a Land Rover dealer or specialist.

16 Carefully refit the inner end of the joint to the shaft. Use a small screwdriver to ease the circlip into its groove, and ensure the joint is fully 'pushed home' onto the shaft (see illustration).

17 Empty the contents of the grease sachets (supplied with the gaiter kit) into the joint, and work it into all parts of the joint.

18 Fit the large diameter end of the gaiter to the outer CV joint, then secure the clips at both ends of the gaiter (see illustrations).

Refitting

19 Ensure the hub carrier, driveshaft splines, ABS sensor recess and hub mating faces are clean and free from debris.

20 Refit the driveshaft into the axle casing, then apply anti-seize compound to the hub carrier and hub mating faces (see illustration).

21 Ensure the ABS sensor wiring harness is correctly located in the cut-out in the hub carrier (see illustration).

22 Apply a 3.0 mm wide bead of sealant (Land Rover No STC 50554 or equivalent) to the circumference of the driveshaft spline (see illustration).

23 Refit the hub assembly to the driveshaft. The sealant will be smeared along the

2.16 Use a small screwdriver to ease the circlip into its groove as the joint is refitted

driveshaft splines as the hub is fitted. Apply a little thread-locking compound, and tighten the hub retaining bolts to the specified torque (see illustration).

24 Fit a new driveshaft nut. Only finger tighten it at this stage.

2.18a Fit the new clip to the outer end of the gaiter . . .

2.18b . . . and the inner end of the gaiter

2.20 Apply anti-seize compound (copper slip) to the hub carrier face

2.21 The ABS sensor wiring must be located in the cut-out in the hub carrier

2.22 Apply a 3 mm wide band of sealant/ locking compound to the driveshaft splines

2.23 Refit the hub over the end of the driveshaft

2.28 Use a punch to stake the nut to the driveshaft

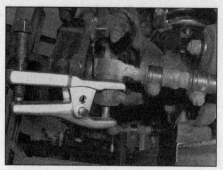

4.3a Use a separator tool to detach the steering track rod end ...

4.3b ... and drag link balljoints from the hub carrier

25 Position a new O-ring seal on the ABS sensor, then refit it and tighten the retaining Allen bolt to the specified torque.

26 Refit the brake mudshield and tighten the bolt securely.

27 Refit the brake disc as described in Chapter 10.

28 Tighten the driveshaft nut to the specified torque, then 'stake' the nut to the shaft **(see illustration)**. Assistance may be required – the torque for the nut is very high. If necessary refit the roadwheel, then lower the vehicle to the ground and tighten the nut. It will then be necessary to raise the vehicle, remove the roadwheel and stake the nut.

29 Refit the roadwheel, tighten the nuts to the specified torque, and lower the vehicle to the ground.

3 Front hub and bearing assembly – removal and refitting

Removal

1 Remove the relevant front driveshaft as described in Section 2.

2 Press the driveshaft from the hub. If a press is not available, it may be possible to carefully tap the shaft from the hub using a hammer and a soft-metal drift. Take great care not to damage the end of the shaft.

3 Examine the bearing assembly for any signs of wear or damage. Spin the races by hand to check for any roughness. If the bearing is in any way worn or damaged, the bearing and hub assembly must be renewed as a unit.

4 It is recommended that the driveshaft oil seal in the axle renewed as described in Section 5.

Refitting

5 Ensure the hub carrier, driveshaft splines, ABS sensor recess and hub mating faces are clean and free from debris.

6 With the new oil seal fitted (Section 5), refit the driveshaft into the axle casing, then apply anti-seize compound to the hub carrier and hub mating faces **(see illustration 2.20)**.

7 Ensure the ABS sensor wiring harness is correctly located in the cut-out in the hub carrier **(see illustration 2.21)**.

8 Apply a 3.0 mm wide bead of sealant (Land Rover No STC 50554 or equivalent) to the circumference of the driveshaft spline **(see illustration 2.22)**.

9 Refit the hub assembly to the driveshaft. The sealant will be smeared along the driveshaft splines as the hub is fitted. Apply a little locking compound to their threads, then tighten the hub retaining bolts to the specified torque **(see illustration 2.23)**.

10 Fit a new driveshaft nut. Only finger tighten it at this stage.

11 Refit the mudshield and tighten the bolts securely.

12 Position a new O-ring seal on the ABS sensor, then refit it and tighten the retaining Allen bolt to the specified torque.

13 Refit the brake disc as described in Chapter 10.

14 Tighten the driveshaft nut to the specified torque, then use a punch to stake the nut to the driveshaft **(see illustration 2.28)**.

Assistance may be required – the torque for the nut is very high.

15 Refit the roadwheel, tighten the nuts to the specified torque, and lower the vehicle to the ground.

4 Front axle hub carrier – removal and refitting

Note: *Two different hub carriers are fitted depending on the VIN number. On vehicles from VIN 2A 754808 the camber angle was changed using a revised hub carrier. It is permissible to fit the later hub carriers to earlier models, but they must be fitted in pairs. Never mix old and new parts on the same axle.*

Removal

1 Remove the hub assembly as described in Section 3.

2 Undo the 3 retaining bolts and remove the mudshield from the hub carrier **(see illustration 2.5)**.

3 Undo the retaining nuts, then use a universal balljoint separator tool to detach the steering track rod end and drag link balljoints from the hub carrier **(see illustrations)**.

4 Undo the nuts securing the upper and lower balljoints to the hub carrier **(see illustration)**.

5 Using a large universal balljoint separator tool, detach the upper and lower balljoints from the hub carrier **(see illustration)**. Note that a special balljoint separator is available from Land Rover designed for this task (LRT-54-027).

6 Unscrew the tension collet from the base of the hub carrier **(see illustration)**.

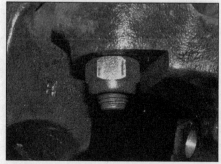

4.4 Axle-to-hub carrier upper balljoint nut

4.5 A large balljoint separator tool is needed for the hub carrier balljoint

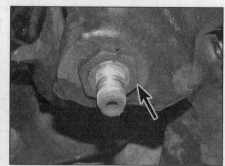

4.6 The tension collet is screwed into the lower part of the hub carrier (arrowed)

7 It is recommended that the driveshaft oil seal be renewed, as described in Section 5.

8 Thoroughly clean the hub carrier, removing all traces of dirt and grease. Polish away any burrs or raised edges which might hinder reassembly. Check for cracks or any other signs of wear or damage, and renew if necessary.

Refitting

9 Refit the tension collet to the base of the hub carrier, and tighten it to the specified torque.

10 Position the hub carrier to the balljoint tapers, then refit the nuts and tighten them to the specified torques.

11 Re-attach the steering track rod end and drag link balljoints to the hub carrier and tighten them to the specified torque (refer to Chapter 11 if necessary).

12 Refit the mudshield to the hub carrier and tighten the bolts securely.

13 Install the hub assembly as described in Section 3.

5 Front axle oil seals – renewal

Differential pinion oil seal

1 Detach the front propeller shaft from the pinion flange as described in Chapter 8. Tie the propeller shaft to one side.

2 Make alignment marks between the flange and the pinion to aid refitting.

3 Undo the flange retaining bolt, and recover the washer. In order to counterhold the flange, use two strips of steel bolted to the flange **(see illustration)**.

4 Pull the flange from position **(see illustration)**.

5 Note its fitted depth, then using a large screwdriver (or similar) carefully prise the oil seal from position **(see illustration)**. Take great care not to damage the bore in the differential housing. Be prepared for oil spillage.

6 Clean the pinion flange and the oil seal recess in the casing.

7 Lubricate the oil seal lip with clean axle oil then fit it to the casing. Drive it into

5.3 Use 2 strips of metal bolted together, and bolted to the flange to counterhold the bolt

5.5 Use a screwdriver to prise the seal from place

position using a suitable tubular spacer **(see illustration)**.

8 Refit the flange to the pinion, ensuring the previously-made marks align. Refit the washer, apply a little thread-locking compound then tighten the retaining bolt to the specified torque. Use the steel strip previously described to counterhold the flange.

9 Reconnect the front propeller shaft to the flange and tighten the retaining bolts/nuts to the specified torque as described in Chapter 8.

10 Top-up the front axle oil level as describe in Chapter 1.

Driveshaft oil seal

11 Remove the relevant driveshaft as described in Section 2.

12 Note its fitted depth, then using a large screwdriver, carefully prise the oil seal from

5.4 Pull the flange from the pinion

5.7 Use a socket (or similar) to drive the new seal into place

the casing **(see illustration)**. Take great care not to damage the bore in the casing.

13 Clean the oil seal bore in the casing.

14 Position the new seal with the metal part of the seal facing inwards, then drive it into position with a suitably-sized tubular spacer **(see illustrations)**. Note that the seal must be fitted dry.

15 Refit the hub assembly as described in Section 3.

6 Front hub carrier balljoints – renewal

Renewal of the balljoints can only be carrier out using Land Rover special tools (LRT-54-021, LTR-54-008, LRT-54-008/5, LRT-54-008/4, LRT-54-008/22 and LRT-54-008/7). The tools

5.12 Lever the old driveshaft oil seal from place

5.14a Position the metal face of the seal toward the centre of the axle . . .

5.14b . . . then use a tubular spacer to drive the seal into position

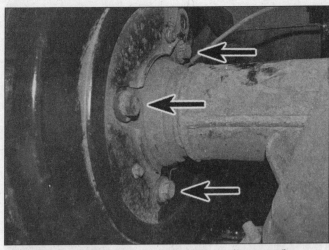

7.7 Undo the rear hub retaining bolts (3 arrowed)

7.10 Renew the hub O-ring seal (arrowed)

required incorporate a hydraulic puller to generate the large forces required to remove the balljoints from the hub carrier, and force the new one(s) into place. Due to the expense in purchasing these tools, and the unlikelihood of them being available for rental, it is recommended that renewal of the balljoints is entrusted to a Land Rover dealer or suitably-equipped specialist.

Note that the balljoints can only be renewed 3 times before the bore in the axle yoke becomes oversize. Before starting work, clean the area around the balljoints, and check for yellow paint marks approximately 12 mm wide. If 3 yellow marks are already present, Land Rover state that the axle casing must be renewed.

7 Rear axle driveshaft – removal and refitting

Removal

1 Loosen the rear roadwheel nuts, and chock the front wheels. Jack up the rear of the vehicle, and support it securely on axle stands (see *Jacking and vehicle support*). Remove the relevant rear roadwheel.
2 Drain the axle oil as described in Chapter 1, or be prepared for some oil spillage as the shaft is removed.
3 Using a chisel or punch, unstake the driveshaft nut **(see illustration 2.2a)**.
4 Have an assistant depress the brake pedal, then undo and discard the driveshaft nut. A new one must be fitted.
5 Remove the relevant rear brake disc as described in Chapter 10.
6 Undo the Allen bolt and withdraw the ABS sensor from the hub. Discard the O-ring seal, a new one must be fitted.
7 Undo the 4 retaining bolts and pull the driveshaft and hub assembly from the axle **(see illustration)**. Discard the hub O-ring seal, a new one must be fitted.

8 If required, press the driveshaft from the hub. If a press is not available, it may be possible to carefully tap the shaft from the hub using a hammer and a soft-metal drift. Take great care not to damage the end of the shaft.

Refitting

9 Ensure the hub carrier and hub mating faces are clean, then refit the driveshaft into the axle.
10 Lubricate the new O-ring seal with clean axle oil, then fit it to the hub **(see illustration)**.
11 Apply a 3.0 mm wide bead of sealant (Land Rover No STC 50554 or equivalent) to the circumference of the driveshaft spline **(see illustration 2.22)**.
12 Refit the hub assembly to the driveshaft. The sealant will be smeared along the driveshaft splines as the hub is fitted. Apply a little locking compound to the threads, then tighten the hub retaining bolts to the specified torque.
13 Fit a new driveshaft nut. Only finger tighten it at this stage.
14 Position a new O-ring seal on the ABS sensor, then refit it and tighten the retaining Allen bolt to the specified torque.
15 Refit the brake disc as described in Chapter 10.
16 Tighten the driveshaft nut to the specified torque, then stake the nut to the shaft **(see illustration 2.28)**. Assistance may be required – the torque for the nut is very high.
17 Refit the roadwheel, tighten the nuts to the specified torque, and lower the vehicle to the ground.

8 Rear hub and bearing assembly – removal and refitting

Removal

1 Remove the driveshaft as described in Section 7.
2 Press the driveshaft from the hub. If a press

is not available, it may be possible to carefully tap the shaft from the hub using a hammer and a soft-metal drift. Take great care not to damage the end of the shaft.
3 Examine the bearing assembly for any signs of wear or damage. Spin the races by hand to check for any roughness. If the bearing is in any way worn or damaged, the bearing and hub assembly must be renewed as a unit.

Refitting

4 Ensure the hub carrier and hub mating faces are clean, then refit the driveshaft into the axle.
5 Lubricate the new O-ring seal with clean axle oil, then fit it to the hub **(see illustration 7.10)**.
6 Apply a 3.0 mm wide bead of sealant (Land Rover No STC 50554 or equivalent) to the circumference of the driveshaft spline **(see illustration 2.22)**.
7 Refit the hub assembly to the driveshaft. The sealant will be smeared along the driveshaft splines as the hub is fitted. Tighten the hub retaining bolts to the specified torque.
8 Fit a new driveshaft nut. Only finger tighten it at this stage.
9 Position a new O-ring seal on the ABS sensor, then refit it and tighten the retaining Allen bolt to the specified torque.
10 Refit the brake disc as described in Chapter 10.
11 Tighten the driveshaft nut to the specified torque, then stake the nut to the shaft **(see illustration 2.28)**. Assistance may be required – the torque for the nut is very high.
12 Refit the roadwheel, tighten the nuts to the specified torque, and lower the vehicle to the ground.

9 Rear axle pinion oil seal – renewal

1 Remove the rear propeller shaft flexible coupling as described in Chapter 8.

9.2 We used a slide-hammer, with an 8 mm thread, to pull the centralising peg from the pinion flange

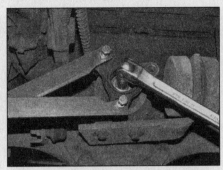

9.3 Use 2 strips of steel bolted together to counterhold the pinion flange whilst slackening the nut

9.4 On our vehicle the flange was removed from the pinion by hand – others may require a puller

9.5 Use a screwdriver to prise the oil seal from place

9.7 Fit the new seal using a socket (or similar) which bears only on the hard outer edge of the seal

9.8 The large diameter part of the centralising peg must be below the flange mounting face

2 Attach Land Rover special tool (LRT-51-009) to the pinion flange, and extract the centralising peg from the flange (see illustration).

3 Make alignment marks between the flange and the pinion, then undo the flange retaining bolt and recover the washer. In order to counterhold the flange, use two strips of steel bolted together and to the flange (see illustration).

4 Remove the flange from the pinion (see illustration). A three-legged puller may be required.

5 Note its fitted depth then, using a large screwdriver (or similar) carefully prise the oil seal from position (see illustration). Take great care not to damage the bore in the differential housing. Be prepared for oil spillage.

6 Clean the pinion flange and the oil seal recess in the casing.

7 Lubricate the oil seal lip with clean axle oil then fit it to the casing. Drive it into position using a suitable tubular spacer (see illustration).

8 Refit the flange to the pinion, ensuring the previously-made marks align. Apply a little thread-locking compound, then refit the washer and tighten the retaining bolt to the specified torque. Use the steel strips previously described to counterhold the flange.

9 Refit the centralising peg to the pinion flange using a suitable tubular spacer. Ensure the large diameter part of the peg is below the flange mounting face (see illustration).

10 Refit the flexible coupling as describe in Chapter 8.

11 Top-up the axle oil as described in Chapter 1.

10 Axle differential overhaul – general information

Overhauling a differential unit is a difficult and involved job for the DIY home mechanic. In addition to dismantling and reassembling many small parts, clearances must be precisely measured and, if necessary, changed by selecting shims and spacers.

Components are also often difficult to obtain and in many instances, extremely expensive. Because of this, if the differential develops a fault or becomes noisy, the best course of action is to have the unit overhauled by a specialist repairer, or to obtain an exchange reconditioned unit.

Nevertheless, it is not impossible for the more experienced mechanic to overhaul the differential, if the special tools are available and the job is done in a deliberate step-by-step manner so that nothing is overlooked.

The tools necessary for an overhaul include internal and external circlip pliers, bearing pullers, a slide hammer, a set of pin punches, a dial test indicator, and possibly a hydraulic press. In addition, a large, sturdy workbench and a vice will be required.

During dismantling, make careful notes of how each component is fitted, to make reassembly easier and more accurate.

Before dismantling, it will help if you have some idea what area is malfunctioning. Refer to *Fault finding* at the end of this manual for more information.

Notes

Chapter 10
Braking system

Contents

Section number

Anti lock braking system (ABS) components – removal and refitting 20
Anti-lock braking system (ABS) – general information 19
Brake pedal – removal and refitting 11
Front brake caliper – removal, overhaul and refitting 8
Front brake disc – inspection, removal and refitting 6
Front brake pad wear check . . . . See Chapter 1
Front brake pads – renewal 4
General information 1
Handbrake cable – removal and refitting 16
Handbrake lever – removal and refitting. 15
Handbrake shoes – renewal. 14
Hydraulic fluid level check . . . . See Weekly checks

Section number

Hydraulic fluid renewal . . . . See Chapter 1
Hydraulic pipes and hoses – renewal 3
Hydraulic system – bleeding 2
Master cylinder – removal, overhaul and refitting 10
Rear brake caliper – removal, overhaul and refitting 9
Rear brake disc – inspection, removal and refitting 7
Rear brake pad wear check . . . . See Chapter 1
Rear brake pads – renewal. 5
Stop-light switch – removal, refitting and adjustment 17
Vacuum pump – removal and refitting 18
Vacuum servo unit – testing, removal and refitting 12
Vacuum servo unit check valve – removal, testing and refitting 13

Degrees of difficulty

| **Easy,** suitable for novice with little experience | | **Fairly easy,** suitable for beginner with some experience | **Fairly difficult,** suitable for competent DIY mechanic | **Difficult,** suitable for experienced DIY mechanic | **Very difficult,** suitable for expert DIY or professional | |

Specifications

Front brakes

Type	Ventilated disc, with twin-piston caliper
Disc diameter	297 mm
Disc thickness:	
New	24.9 to 25.1 mm
Service limit	22.0 mm
Maximum disc run-out	0.15 mm
Brake pad friction material minimum thickness	2.0 mm

Rear brakes

Type	Solid disc, with single-piston caliper
Disc diameter	304 mm
Disc thickness:	
New	12.5 to 12.7 mm
Service limit	11.7 mm
Maximum disc run-out	0.15 mm
Brake pad friction material minimum thickness	2.0 mm

Torque wrench settings

	Nm	lbf ft
ABS wheel speed sensor Allen bolt	18	13
Brake caliper guide pin bolts (front and rear)	30	22
Brake disc retaining screw (front and rear)	13	10
Brake hose union bolts	25	18
Brake pipe union nuts	25	18
Front caliper bracket mounting bolts	175	129
Front hub-to carrier bolts	100	74
Master cylinder mounting nuts	26	19
Rear caliper bracket mounting bolts	95	70
Roadwheel nuts	140	103
Vacuum pump-to-alternator bolts	10	7
Vacuum servo unit mounting nuts	26	19

1 General information

The braking system is of the servo-assisted, dual-circuit hydraulic type, operating from a tandem master cylinder. On all models the hydraulic system is split diagonally. Under normal circumstances, both circuits operate in unison. However, in the event of hydraulic failure in one circuit, braking force will still be available at least at two wheels.

Since there is insufficient vacuum in the inlet manifold to operate the braking system servo unit, a vacuum pump is fitted to the alternator to provide the required vacuum.

All models have disc brakes all round and ABS (anti-lock braking system) as standard. The ABS system also incorporates the following features:

Electronic Brake Distribution (EBD), which replaces the pressure limiting valve on older models, and controls the distribution of hydraulic pressure between the front and rear brakes.

Electronic traction control (ETC), to maintain even torque/power distribution to the roadwheels.

Hill Descent Control (HDC), to provide a controlled descent ability in off-road conditions.

The front brakes are fitted with ventilated discs, and twin-piston calipers, whilst the rear are fitted with solid discs, and single-piston calipers.

On all models, the handbrake is in the form of a drum brake assembly mounted onto the rear of the transfer box. When the handbrake is applied, it locks the rear axle by preventing propeller shaft rotation.

When servicing any part of the system, work carefully and methodically; also observe scrupulous cleanliness when overhauling any part of the hydraulic system. Always renew components (in axle sets, where applicable) if in doubt about their condition, and use only genuine Land Rover parts, or at least those of known good quality. Note the warnings given in *Safety first!* and at relevant points in this Chapter concerning the dangers of asbestos dust and hydraulic fluid.

2 Hydraulic system – bleeding

⚠ *Warning: Hydraulic fluid is poisonous; wash off immediately and thoroughly in the case of skin contact, and seek immediate medical advice if any fluid is swallowed or gets into the eyes. Certain types of hydraulic fluid are inflammable, and may ignite when allowed into contact with hot components. When servicing any hydraulic system, it is safest to assume that the fluid IS inflammable, and to take precautions against the risk of fire as though it is petrol that is being handled. Finally, it is hygroscopic (it absorbs moisture from the air) – old fluid may be contaminated and unfit for further use. When topping-up or renewing the fluid, always use the recommended type, and ensure that it comes from a freshly-opened sealed container.*

Note: *If any brake hydraulic components upstream of the ABS modulator (including the modulator itself), Land Rover insist that the system must be bleed using their Testbook dedicated test equipment. Have this task carried out be a Land Rover dealer or suitably-equipped specialist.*

General

1 The correct operation of any hydraulic system is only possible after removing all air from the components and circuit; this is achieved by bleeding the system.

2 During the bleeding procedure, add only clean, unused hydraulic fluid of the recommended type; never re-use fluid that has already been bled from the system. Ensure that sufficient fluid is available before starting work.

3 If there is any possibility of incorrect fluid being already in the system, the brake components and circuit must be flushed completely with uncontaminated, correct fluid, and new seals should be fitted to the various components.

4 If hydraulic fluid has been lost from the system (or air has entered) because of a leak, ensure that the fault is cured before proceeding further.

5 Park the vehicle on level ground, switch off the engine and select first or reverse gear, then chock the wheels and release the handbrake.

6 Check that all pipes and hoses are secure, unions tight and bleed screws closed. Clean any dirt from around the bleed screws.

7 Unscrew the master cylinder reservoir cap, and top the master cylinder reservoir up to the MAX level line; refit the cap loosely. Remember to maintain the fluid level at least above the MIN level line throughout the procedure, or there is a risk of further air entering the system.

8 There is a number of one-man, do-it-yourself brake bleeding kits currently available from motor accessory shops. It is recommended that one of these kits is used whenever possible, as they greatly simplify the bleeding operation, and also reduce the risk of expelled air and fluid being drawn back into the system. If such a kit is not available, use the basic (two-man) method which is described in detail below.

9 If a kit is to be used, prepare the vehicle as described previously, and follow the kit manufacturer's instructions as the procedure may vary slightly according to the type being used; generally, they are as outlined below in the relevant sub-section.

10 Whichever method is used, the same sequence must be followed (paragraphs 11 and 12) to ensure the removal of all air from the system.

Bleeding

Sequence

11 If the system has been only partially disconnected, and suitable precautions

were taken to minimise fluid loss, it should be necessary only to bleed that part of the system (ie, the primary or secondary circuit).

12 If the complete system is to be bled, then it should be done working in the following sequence:

  a) *Passenger's side front brake.*
  b) *Driver's side front brake.*
  c) *Passenger's side rear brake.*
  d) *Driver's side rear brake.*

Basic (two-man) method

13 Collect a clean glass jar, a suitable length of plastic or rubber tubing which is a tight fit over the bleed screw, and a ring spanner to fit the screw. The help of an assistant will also be required.

14 Remove the dust cap from the bleed screw on the passenger's side front brake. Fit the spanner and tube to the screw, place the other end of the tube in the jar, and pour in sufficient fluid to cover the end of the tube **(see illustration)**.

15 Ensure that the master cylinder reservoir fluid level is maintained at least above the MIN level line throughout the procedure.

16 Have the assistant fully depress the brake pedal several times to build-up pressure, then maintain it on the final stroke.

17 While pedal pressure is maintained, unscrew the bleed screw (approximately one turn) and allow the compressed fluid and air to flow into the jar. The assistant should maintain pedal pressure, following it down to the floor if necessary, and should not release it until instructed to do so. When the flow stops, tighten the bleed screw again, release the pedal slowly and recheck the reservoir fluid level.

18 Repeat the steps given in paragraphs 16 and 17 until the fluid emerging from the bleed screw is free from air bubbles. If the master cylinder has been drained and refilled, and air is being bled from the first screw in the sequence, allow approximately five seconds between cycles for the master cylinder passages to refill.

19 When no more air bubbles appear, tighten the bleed screw securely, remove the tube and spanner, and refit the dust cap. Do not overtighten the bleed screw.

20 Repeat the procedure on the remaining rear brake.

Using a one-way valve kit

21 As their name implies, these kits consist of a length of tubing with a one-way valve fitted, to prevent expelled air and fluid being drawn back into the system; some kits include a translucent container, which can be positioned so that the air bubbles can be more easily seen flowing from the end of the tube.

22 The kit is connected to the bleed screw, which is then opened. The user returns to the driver's seat and depresses the brake pedal with a smooth, steady stroke and slowly releases it; this is repeated until the expelled fluid is clear of air bubbles.

23 Note that these kits simplify work so much that it is easy to forget the master cylinder reservoir fluid level; ensure that this is maintained at least above the MIN level line at all times.

Using a pressure-bleeding kit

Note: *Ensure that the pressure in the reservoir does not exceed 4.5 bar.*

24 These kits are usually operated by the reservoir of pressurised air contained in the spare tyre, although note that it will probably be necessary to reduce the tyre pressure to a lower level than normal; refer to the instructions supplied with the kit.

25 By connecting a pressurised, fluid-filled container to the master cylinder reservoir, bleeding can be carried out simply by opening each screw in turn (in the specified sequence) and allowing the fluid to flow out until no more air bubbles can be seen in the expelled fluid.

26 This method has the advantage that the large reservoir of fluid provides an additional safeguard against air being drawn into the system during bleeding.

27 Pressure bleeding is particularly effective when bleeding difficult systems, or when bleeding the complete system at the time of routine fluid renewal.

All methods

28 When bleeding is complete and firm pedal feel is restored, wash off any spilt fluid, tighten the bleed screws securely and refit their dust caps.

29 Check the hydraulic fluid level, and top-up if necessary (see *Weekly checks*).

30 Discard any hydraulic fluid that has been bled from the system; it will not be fit for re-use.

31 Check the feel of the brake pedal. If it feels at all spongy, air must still be present in the system, and further bleeding is required. Failure to bleed satisfactorily after a reasonable repetition of the bleeding procedure may be due to worn master cylinder seals.

3 Hydraulic pipes and hoses – renewal

Note: *Before starting work, refer to the warning at the beginning of Section 2 concerning the dangers of hydraulic fluid.*

1 If any pipe or hose is to be renewed, minimise fluid loss as follows. Remove the master cylinder reservoir cap, then tighten it down onto a piece of polythene to obtain an airtight seal. Alternatively, flexible hoses can be sealed, if required, using a proprietary brake hose clamp, while metal brake pipe unions can be plugged (if care is taken not to allow dirt into the system) or capped immediately they are disconnected. Place a wad of rag under any union that is to be disconnected, to catch any spilt fluid.

2 If a flexible hose is to be disconnected, unscrew the brake pipe union nut before removing the spring clip which secures the hose to its mounting bracket (where fitted).

3 To unscrew the union nuts, it is preferable to obtain a brake pipe spanner of the correct size; these are available from most large motor accessory shops **(see illustration)**. Failing this, a close-fitting open-ended spanner will be required, though if the nuts are tight or corroded, their flats may be rounded-off if the spanner slips. In such a case, a self-locking wrench is often the only way to unscrew a stubborn union, but it follows that the pipe and the damaged nuts must be renewed on reassembly. Always clean a union and surrounding area before disconnecting it.

4 If a brake pipe is to be renewed, it can be obtained, cut to length and with the union nuts and end flares in place, from Land Rover dealers. All that is then necessary is to bend it to shape, following the line of the original, before fitting it to the car. Alternatively, most motor accessory shops can make-up brake pipes from kits, but this requires very careful measurement of the original to ensure that the new one is of the correct length. The safest answer is usually to take the original to the shop as a pattern.

5 On refitting, do not overtighten the union nuts. It is not necessary to exercise brute force to obtain a sound joint.

6 Ensure that the pipes and hoses are correctly routed with no kinks, and that they are secured in the clips or brackets provided. After fitting, remove the polythene from the reservoir, and bleed the hydraulic system as described in Section 2. Wash off any spilt fluid, and check carefully for fluid leaks.

2.14 Attach the tube and spanner to the brake caliper bleed screw

3.3 Use a brake pipe spanner to slacken the unions

4.2a Slacken . . .

4.2b . . . and remove the caliper guide pin bolt

4.2c Then swing the caliper upwards . . .

4.2d . . . and secure it to the suspension coil with wire (or string, etc)

4.2e Remove the outer brake pad . . .

4.2f . . . followed by the inner pad

4 Front brake pads – renewal

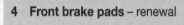

⚠ **Warning: Renew BOTH sets of front brake pads at the same time – NEVER renew the pads on only one wheel, as uneven braking may result. Note that the dust created by wear of the pads may contain asbestos, which is a health hazard. Never blow it out with compressed air, and don't inhale any of it. An approved filtering mask should be worn when working on the brakes. DO NOT use petroleum-based solvents to clean brake parts – use brake cleaner or methylated spirit only.**

4.2g Fit the inner pad, ensuring the friction material is against the disc face . . .

1 Apply the handbrake, then loosen the front roadwheel nuts. Jack up the front of the vehicle and support it securely on axle stands (see *Jacking and vehicle support*). Remove both front roadwheels.

4.2h . . . followed by the outer pad. Check that the pad is the correct way round – friction material against the disc

2 Follow the accompanying photos **(illustrations 4.2a to 4.2k)** for the actual pad renewal procedure. Be sure to stay in order and read the caption under each illustration.

4.2i If new pads have been fitted, the caliper pistons must be pushed back – shown here with a pad retraction tool. Keep an eye on the fluid level in the master cylinder reservoir – it may overflow!

4.2j Lower the caliper back down over the pads . . .

4.2k . . . then refit and tighten the caliper guide pin bolt to the specified torque

3 Depress the brake pedal repeatedly, until the pads are pressed into firm contact with the brake disc, and normal (non-assisted) pedal pressure is restored.

4 Repeat the above procedure on the remaining front brake caliper.

5 Refit the roadwheels, then lower the vehicle to the ground and tighten the roadwheel bolts to the specified torque.

6 Check the hydraulic fluid level as described in *Weekly checks*.

Caution: New pads will not give full braking efficiency until they have bedded-in. Be prepared for this, and avoid hard braking as far as possible for the first hundred miles or so after pad renewal.

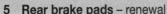

5 Rear brake pads – renewal

⚠ *Warning: Renew BOTH sets of rear brake pads at the same time – NEVER renew the pads on only one wheel, as uneven braking may result. Note that the dust created by wear of the pads may contain asbestos, which is a health hazard. Never blow it out with compressed air, and don't inhale any of it. An approved filtering mask should be worn when working on the brakes. DO NOT use petroleum-based solvents to clean brake parts – use brake cleaner or methylated spirit only.*

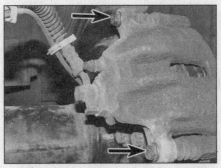

5.2a Undo the caliper guide pin bolts (arrowed) . . .

1 Apply the handbrake, then loosen the rear roadwheel nuts. Jack up the rear of the vehicle and support it securely on axle stands (see *Jacking and vehicle support*). Remove both rear roadwheels.

2 Follow the accompanying photos (illustrations 5.2a to 5.2g) for the actual pad renewal procedure. Be sure to stay in order and read the caption under each illustration.

3 Depress the brake pedal repeatedly, until the pads are pressed into firm contact with the brake disc, and normal (non-assisted) pedal pressure is restored.

4 Repeat the above procedure on the remaining rear brake caliper.

5 Refit the roadwheels, then lower the vehicle to the ground and tighten the roadwheel bolts to the specified torque.

5.2b . . . and slide the caliper from position. Support the caliper with wire or string from the vehicle body. Don't strain the rubber hose

6 Check the hydraulic fluid level as described in *Weekly checks*.

Caution: New pads will not give full braking efficiency until they have bedded-in. Be prepared for this, and avoid hard braking as far as possible for the first hundred miles or so after pad renewal.

6 Front brake disc – inspection, removal and refitting

Note: *Before starting work, refer to the warning and note at the beginning of Section 4.*

Inspection

Note: *If either disc requires renewal, BOTH should be renewed at the same time, to ensure even and consistent braking.*

1 Firmly apply the handbrake, then loosen the roadwheel nuts. Jack up the car and support it securely on axle stands (see *Jacking and vehicle support*). Remove the appropriate roadwheel.

2 Slowly rotate the brake disc, so that the full area of both sides can be checked; remove the brake pads if better access is required to the inner surface. Light scoring is normal in the area swept by the brake pads, but if heavy scoring is found, the disc must be renewed.

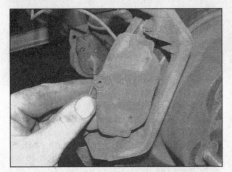

5.2c Remove the outer pad . . .

5.2d . . . followed by the inner pad

5.2e If new pads are to be fitted, the pistons must be pushed back into the caliper. Shown here with a pad retraction tool. Check the fluid level in the reservoir – it may overflow!

5.2f Fit the new pads to the caliper mounting bracket, ensuring the friction material of each pad is against the disc face

5.2g Slide the caliper over the pads, then refit and tighten the caliper guide pin bolts to the specified torque

6.3 Use a micrometer to check the thickness of the disc

6.6 Undo the caliper mounting bracket bolts (arrowed)

3 It is normal to find a lip of rust and brake dust around the disc's perimeter; this can be scraped off if required. If, however, a lip has formed due to excessive wear of the brake pad swept area, then the disc's thickness must be measured using a micrometer **(see illustration)**. Take measurements at several places around the disc, at the inside and outside of the pad swept area. If the measured thickness is below that specified, both front discs must be replaced.

4 If the disc is thought to be warped, it can be checked for run-out as follows. Either use a dial gauge mounted on any convenient fixed point, while the disc is slowly rotated, or use feeler blades to measure (at several points all around the disc) the clearance between the disc and a fixed point such as the brake caliper. If the measurements obtained are at the specified maximum or beyond, the disc is excessively warped and must be renewed; however, it is worth checking first that the axle hub bearing is in good condition (Chapter 9).

5 Check the disc for cracks, especially around the wheel studs, and any other wear or damage.

Removal

6 Undo the two bolts securing the brake caliper mounting bracket to the hub carrier, and slide it from the disc. Suspend the caliper from the suspension spring using string or wire **(see illustration)**. Do not let the caliper hang by the hose. **Note:** *If the disc has a wear*

lip at the outer edge, it may be necessary to remove the pads as described in Section 4.

7 Slacken and remove the screw securing the brake disc to the hub assembly, and remove the disc **(see illustrations)**.

Refitting

8 Refitting is the reverse of the removal procedure, noting the following points:

a) *Ensure that the mating surfaces of the disc and hub are clean and flat.*

b) *If a new disc has been fitted, use a suitable solvent to wipe any preservative coating from the disc before refitting the caliper.*

c) *Apply a little locking compound to the threads, then tighten the caliper mounting bracket bolts to the specified torque.*

d) *Refit the roadwheel, lower the vehicle to the ground, and tighten the roadwheel nuts to the specified torque. On completion, repeatedly depress the brake pedal, until normal (non-assisted) pedal pressure returns.*

7 Rear brake disc – inspection, removal and refitting

Removal and refitting

This procedure is identical to that described in Section 6 for the front brake disc.

Inspection

Refer to Section 6.

8 Front brake caliper – removal, overhaul and refitting

Note: *Before starting work, refer to the note at the beginning of Section 2 concerning the dangers of hydraulic fluid, and to the warning and note at the beginning of Section 4.*

Removal

1 Apply the handbrake, then loosen the relevant front roadwheel nuts. Jack up the front of the vehicle and support it securely on axle stands (see *Jacking and vehicle support*). Remove the appropriate roadwheel.

2 To minimise fluid loss, remove the master cylinder reservoir cap, then tighten it down onto a piece of polythene to obtain an airtight seal. Alternatively, use a brake hose clamp, a G-clamp, or a similar tool to clamp the flexible hose at the nearest convenient point to the caliper.

3 Clean the area around the caliper brake hose union bolt. Undo the union bolt, and disconnect the brake hose from the caliper. Discard the copper sealing washers, new ones must be fitted. Plug the hose end and caliper hole to minimise fluid loss and to prevent the ingress of dirt into the hydraulic system.

4 Undo the two caliper guide pin bolts, and slide the caliper from the mounting bracket, leaving the brake pads in position **(see illustration)**.

Overhaul

Note: *Prior to dismantling the caliper, check the availability of spares from your Land Rover dealer.*

5 With the caliper on the bench, wipe away all traces of dust and dirt, but *avoid inhaling the dust, as it is a health hazard.*

6 Withdraw both the partially-ejected pistons from the caliper body. The pistons can be withdrawn by hand, if loose. If one or both of the pistons are not loose enough to be withdrawn by hand, they can be pushed out by applying compressed air to the brake hose union hole. Only low pressure should be required, such as is generated by a foot

6.7a Undo the disc retaining screw (arrowed) . . .

6.7b . . . then remove the disc

8.4 Undo the caliper guide pin bolts (arrowed)

8.6 Use a foot pump to force the pistons from the caliper body. The wood is there to stop one of the pistons fully ejecting before the other

8.8 Remove the piston dust boots . . .

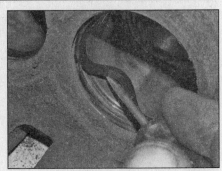

8.9 . . . and the caliper seals

pump. Try to ensure both pistons are ejected at the same time **(see illustration)**.

7 Extract both pistons from the caliper. Make identification marks between the caliper and pistons to use on refitting, to ensure each piston is refitted to its original bore.

8 Carefully prise out and remove the rubber dust boots fitted between the top of the pistons and the caliper body **(see illustration)**.

9 Using a small screwdriver, carefully remove the seals from the caliper, taking great care not to mark the bore **(see illustration)**.

10 This is the limit of caliper dismantling.

11 Pull the guide pins from the caliper mounting bracket, and examine them for wear or damage. They should be a good sliding fit in the bores, without excessive play or roughness **(see illustration)**. Discard the guide pin gaiters, new ones should be supplied in the overhaul kit.

12 Thoroughly clean all components, using only methylated spirit, isopropyl alcohol or clean hydraulic fluid as a cleaning medium. Never use mineral-based solvents such as petrol or paraffin, which will attack the hydraulic system's rubber components. Dry the components immediately, using compressed air or a clean, lint-free cloth. Use compressed air to blow clear the fluid passages.

13 Check all components, and renew any that are worn or damaged. Check particularly

the cylinder bores and pistons; these should be renewed if they are scratched, worn or corroded in any way.

14 If the assembly is fit for further use, obtain the necessary components from your Land Rover dealer.

15 On reassembly, ensure that all components are absolutely clean and dry.

16 Soak the pistons and the new piston (fluid) seals in clean hydraulic fluid. Smear clean fluid on the cylinder bore surface.

17 Fit the new piston seals, using only your fingers to manipulate them into the cylinder bore grooves **(see illustration)**.

18 Ensure that the piston seals are correctly located, then fit the new dust boots to the base of the piston **(see illustration)**.

19 Engage the lip of the dust seal with the

groove in the caliper body, and fit each piston using a twisting motion, ensuring that they enter the caliper bore squarely. If the original pistons are being re-used, use the marks made on removal to ensure that they are refitted to the correct bores.

20 As the pistons are fitted, ensure the dust boots fit correctly in the piston recesses **(see illustration)**.

21 Apply a little lithium-based grease to the caliper guide pins, then fit them, with the new gaiters, to the caliper mounting brackets **(see illustration)**.

Refitting

22 Check that the brake pads are still correctly fitted, then fit the caliper in place on the mounting bracket, ensuring the flats

8.11 Check the guide pins fit in the caliper

8.17 Fit the seal into the groove in the caliper bore

8.18 Fit the new dust boot to the base of the piston

8.20 As the piston is fitted, ensure the dust boot lip engages with the groove in the piston (arrowed)

8.21 Apply a little lithium-based grease, then fit the guide pins, with new gaiters, to the caliper mounting bracket

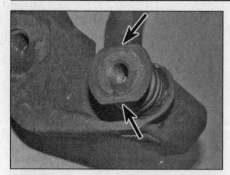

8.22 The flats on the guide pins (arrowed) must align with the caliper body

on the guide pins align with the caliper **(see illustration)**. Insert the guide pin bolts and tighten them to the specified torque.

23 Refit the hose to the caliper using new sealing washers, and tighten the union bolt to the specified torque.

24 Remove the brake hose clamp or polythene, as applicable, and bleed the hydraulic system as described in Section 2. Note that, providing the precautions described were taken to minimise brake fluid loss, it should only be necessary to bleed the relevant front brake.

25 Refit the roadwheel, then lower the vehicle to the ground and tighten the roadwheel nuts to the specified torque.

9 Rear brake caliper – removal, overhaul and refitting

Note: *Before starting work, refer to the warning at the beginning of Section 2 concerning the dangers of hydraulic fluid, and to the warning at the beginning of Section 5 concerning the dangers of asbestos dust.*

Removal

1 Apply the handbrake, then loosen the relevant rear roadwheel nuts. Jack up the rear of the vehicle and support it securely on axle stands (see *Jacking and vehicle support*). Remove the appropriate roadwheel.

2 To minimise fluid loss, remove the master cylinder reservoir cap, then tighten it down onto a piece of polythene to obtain an airtight seal. Alternatively, use a brake hose clamp, a G-clamp, or a similar tool to clamp the flexible hose at the nearest convenient point to the caliper.

3 Clean the area around the caliper brake hose union bolt. Undo the union bolt, and disconnect the brake hose from the caliper. Discard the copper sealing washers, new ones must be fitted. Plug the hose end and caliper hole to minimise fluid loss and to prevent the ingress of dirt into the hydraulic system.

4 Undo the two caliper guide pin bolts, and slide the caliper from the mounting bracket, leaving the brake pads in position **(see illustration 5.2a)**.

Overhaul

Note: *Prior to dismantling the caliper, check the availability of spares from your Land Rover dealer; on some models, it may prove difficult to obtain caliper components.*

5 Overhaul of the rear caliper is identical to the procedure described for the front caliper in Section 8.

Refitting

6 Check that the brake pads are still correctly fitted, then fit the caliper in place on the mounting bracket, ensuring the flats on the guide pins align with the caliper **(see illustration 8.22)**. Insert the guide pin bolts and tighten them to the specified torque.

7 Refit the hose to the caliper using new sealing washers, and tighten the union bolt to the specified torque.

8 Remove the brake hose clamp or polythene, as applicable, and bleed the hydraulic system as described in Section 2. Note that, providing the precautions described were taken to minimise brake fluid loss, it should only be necessary to bleed the relevant rear brake.

9 Refit the roadwheel, then lower the vehicle to the ground and tighten the roadwheel nuts to the specified torque.

10 Master cylinder – removal, overhaul and refitting

Note: *Before starting work, refer to the warning at the beginning of Section 2 concerning the dangers of hydraulic fluid.*

Removal

1 Disconnect the wiring connector from the brake fluid level sender unit, then remove the master cylinder reservoir cap and syphon the hydraulic fluid from the reservoir. **Note:** *Do not syphon the fluid by mouth, as it is poisonous; use a syringe or an old poultry baster.* Alternatively, open any convenient bleed screw in the system, and gently pump the brake pedal to expel the fluid through a plastic tube connected to the screw (see Section 2).

2 Wipe clean the area around the brake pipe unions on the side of the master cylinder, and place absorbent rags beneath the pipe unions to catch any surplus fluid. Make a note of the correct fitted positions of the unions, then unscrew the union nuts and carefully withdraw the pipes. Wash off any spilt fluid immediately with cold water.

3 On models with manual transmission, release the clip and disconnect the clutch master cylinder fluid supply pipe from the brake reservoir **(see illustration)**. Plug the pipe openings to prevent dirt ingress and fluid loss.

4 Slacken and remove the two nuts and washers securing the master cylinder to the vacuum servo unit. Withdraw the master cylinder assembly from the engine compartment **(see illustration)**.

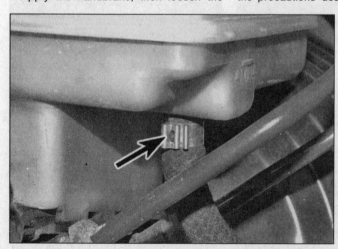

10.3 Release the clip (arrowed) and disconnect the clutch fluid supply pipe from the master cylinder reservoir – manual transmission models only

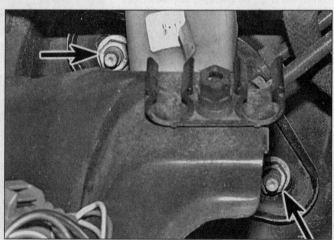

10.4 Master cylinder retaining nuts (arrowed)

10.7 Slide out the reservoir retaining clip (arrowed)

10.8 Release the clips and slide off the yellow chamber

10.10 Renew the O-ring on the master cylinder (arrowed)

Overhaul

5 At the time of writing, master cylinder overhaul was not possible, since spares are not available. If the cylinder is thought to be faulty, it must be renewed. Check with your Land Rover dealer or specialist.

6 The only parts available individually are the fluid reservoir and its mounting seals – these can be renewed as described below.

7 Pull out the retaining clip and carefully ease the reservoir out from the master cylinder body **(see illustration)**.

8 Release the clips and pull the yellow plastic chamber from the end of the cylinder **(see illustration)**.

9 Prise the two mounting seals from the master cylinder ports, noting each seal's correct fitted location.

10 Pull the seal and O-ring seal from the end of the cylinder **(see illustration)**.

11 Thoroughly clean the master cylinder, then fit the new O-ring to the end of the cylinder.

12 Fit the new seal into the yellow plastic chamber, with the smaller diameter end of the seal at the servo end **(see illustration)**.

13 Press the new seals into place on the base of the reservoir **(see illustration)**.

14 Fit the new reservoir, securing it with the retaining clip, ensuring the seals enter the master cylinder ports correctly. Note that on manual transmission models, it's necessary to cut the end off the plastic clutch fluid supply port of the reservoir **(see illustration)**.

15 Fit the yellow plastic chamber to the end of the cylinder, ensuring the tube enters the rearmost reservoir seal, and the retaining clips fully engage. Fit the new O-ring seal to the outside of the chamber **(see illustrations)**.

Refitting

16 Remove all traces of dirt from the master cylinder and servo unit mating surfaces, then fit the master cylinder, ensuring that the servo unit pushrod enters the master cylinder bore centrally. Refit the master cylinder washers and mounting nuts, and tighten them to the specified torque.

17 Wipe clean the brake pipe unions, then refit them to the master cylinder ports and tighten them to the specified torque setting.

18 Fit the new filler filter, then refill the master cylinder reservoir with new fluid.

19 Slowly depress the brake pedal to the floor, and then slowly release it – repeat this

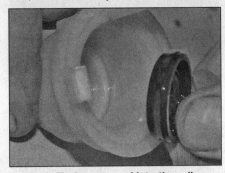

10.12 Fit the new seal into the yellow chamber, with the smaller diameter of the seal at the servo end

five times. Wait for 10 seconds, then repeat this process. As this is done, air bubbles will rise into the reservoir, effectively bleeding the master cylinder.

20 Repeat the operations described in paragraph 19 until resistance is felt at the brake pedal, then bleed the complete hydraulic system as described in Section 2.

11 Brake pedal –
removal and refitting

Removal

1 Prise out the fasteners and remove the lower facia panel from above the pedals.

2 Prise off the clip and remove the pin

10.13 Fit the new seals to the base of the reservoir

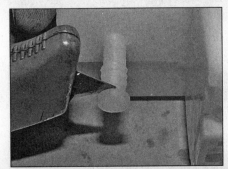

10.14 On manual transmission models, cut the end off the clutch fluid supply port with a sharp knife

10.15a The tube (arrowed) must enter the rearmost reservoir seal

10.15b Fit a new O-ring seal to the yellow chamber (arrowed)

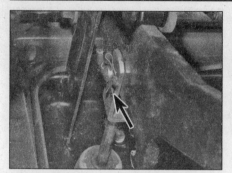

11.2 Prise off the clip (arrowed) and pull out the clutch pushrod clevis pin

11.3 Lever out the edges of the clips (arrowed) securing the servo pushrod pin to the pedal

11.4 Note the fitted positions of the pedal return springs

securing the clutch master cylinder pushrod to the pedal **(see illustration)**.

3 Lever out the clips securing the servo pushrod to the pedal **(see illustration)**.

4 Undo the bolt at each end of the pedal pivot shaft, and carefully lower the pedal assembly. Note the fitted positions of the pedal return springs **(see illustration)**.

5 Slide the pedal(s) from the shaft, noting the positions of any spacers, roll pins, etc.

Refitting

6 Lightly grease the pedal pivot bushes.

7 Refit the pedal(s) to the shaft, ensuring all bushes, spacers, etc, are in their original positions.

8 Manoeuvre the assembly into place, ensure the pedal return springs are correctly located.

9 Tighten the pivot shaft bolts securely.

10 Reconnect the pushrods to the clutch and brake pedals, and secure them with the clevis pins and clips.

11 Refit the lower facia panel.

---

12 Vacuum servo unit –
testing, removal and refitting

Testing

1 To test the operation of the servo unit, with the engine switched off, depress the footbrake several times to exhaust the vacuum. Keeping the pedal depressed, start the engine. As the engine starts, there should be a noticeable

12.8 Servo retaining nuts (arrowed)

give in the brake pedal as the vacuum builds-up. Allow the engine to run for at least two minutes, then switch it off. If the brake pedal is now depressed it should feel normal, but further applications should result in the pedal feeling firmer, with the pedal stroke decreasing with each application.

2 If the servo does not operate as described, first inspect the servo unit check valve as described in Section 13.

3 If the servo unit still fails to operate satisfactorily, the fault lies within the unit itself. Repairs to the unit are not possible, and if faulty, the servo unit must be renewed.

Removal

4 Remove the master cylinder as described in Section 10.

5 Release the retaining clip (where fitted), and disconnect the vacuum hose from the servo unit check valve.

6 From inside the vehicle, release the fasteners and release the driver's side lower facia panel.

7 Lever out the spring clip securing the servo pushrod clevis pin to the pedal **(see illustration 11.3)**.

8 Undo the two retaining nuts securing the servo unit **(see illustration)**.

9 Return to the engine compartment, and lift the servo unit out of position. Recover the spacer which is fitted between the servo unit and bulkhead.

10 Whilst the servo unit is removed, peel back the rubber gaiter from the rear of the unit, and inspect the servo unit filter. If the filter

13.2 Servo unit check valve

is clogged or dirty, renew it. Carefully prise the old filter out of position, and ease the new one into place. Fit the rubber gaiter, making sure that it is correctly seated on the servo.

Refitting

11 Apply a smear of grease to the pushrod fork, then refit the spacer to the rear of the servo unit, and manoeuvre the assembly into position.

12 From inside the vehicle, ensure that the servo unit pushrod is correctly engaged with the brake pedal. Refit the mounting nuts, and tighten them to the specified torque setting.

13 Refit the servo unit pushrod-to-brake pedal clevis pin, and secure it in position with the spring clip.

14 Refit the facia panel.

15 Return to the engine compartment, and reconnect the vacuum hose to the servo unit check valve.

16 Refit the master cylinder as described in Section 10.

---

13 Vacuum servo unit check valve – removal, testing and refitting

Removal

1 Slacken the retaining clip (where fitted), and disconnect the vacuum hose from the servo unit check valve.

2 Withdraw the valve from its rubber sealing grommet, using a pulling and twisting motion. Remove the grommet from the servo **(see illustration)**.

Testing

3 Examine the check valve for signs of damage, and renew if necessary. The valve may be tested by blowing through it in both directions, air should flow through the valve in one direction only – when blown through from the servo unit end of the valve. Renew the valve if this is not the case.

4 Examine the rubber sealing grommet and flexible vacuum hose for signs of damage or deterioration, and renew as necessary.

Refitting

5 Fit the sealing grommet into position in the servo unit.

6 Carefully ease the check valve into position, taking great care not to displace or damage the grommet. Reconnect the vacuum hose to the valve and, where necessary, securely tighten its retaining clip.

7 On completion, start the engine, and check the check valve-to-servo unit connection for signs of air leaks.

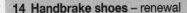

14 Handbrake shoes – renewal

1 Chock the front wheels, then jack up the rear of the vehicle and support it securely on axle stands (see *Jacking and vehicle support*).

2 Working as described in Chapter 8, disconnect the propeller shaft from the rear of the transfer box, and position the shaft clear of the handbrake assembly.

3 Apply the handbrake, then slacken and remove the handbrake drum retaining screw **(see illustration)**.

4 Release the handbrake, and remove the brake drum from the rear of the transfer box. It may be difficult to remove the drum, due to the brake shoes binding on the inner circumference of the drum. If the brake shoes are binding, first check that the handbrake is fully released, then rotate the adjuster bolt anti-clockwise so the shoes are retracted clear of the drum **(see illustration)**. The brake drum should then slide easily off the transfer box.

5 With the drum removed, inspect the shoes for signs of wear or damage. If the friction material of either shoe has worn down to, or close to, the rivets, the shoes must be renewed.

6 The shoes should also be renewed if any are fouled with oil; there is no satisfactory way of degreasing friction material, once contaminated. If there are traces of oil on the shoes, the transfer box output shaft seal should be renewed before new handbrake shoes are fitted by first draining the oil (see Chapter 1), then remove the rear propshaft

14.3 Undo the handbrake drum retaining screw (arrowed)

and output flange. Lever out the old seal and fit a new one.

7 To remove the handbrake shoes, proceed as described.

8 Note the correct fitted locations of all components then, using a suitable pair of pliers, unhook the return springs and remove them from the brake shoes **(see illustration)**.

9 Using a pair of pliers, remove the left-hand shoe retainer spring cup by depressing and turning it through 90°. With the cup removed, lift off the spring, and withdraw the retainer pin from the rear of the backplate **(see illustration)**.

10 Remove the left-hand shoe, then remove the strut which is fitted between the shoe upper ends, noting which way around it is fitted **(see illustration)**.

11 Remove the right-hand shoe spring cup, spring and retainer pin as described in paragraph 9, then detach the shoe from

14.8 Remove the brake shoe return springs

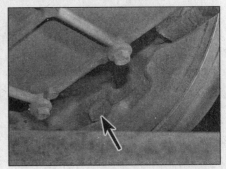

14.4 Handbrake adjuster bolt (arrowed)

the handbrake cable and remove it from the vehicle.

12 It will be necessary to transfer the cable lever from the old right-hand brake shoe to the new one. Remove the spring clip, then withdraw the pivot pin and recover the spring washers **(see illustration)**, noting their correct fitted positions. Inspect the pivot pin and spring clip for signs of wear or damage, and renew if necessary. Apply a smear of high-melting-point grease to the pin, then fit the operating lever to the new shoe; insert the pin and spring washers, securing them in position with the spring clip.

13 Whilst the shoes are removed, rotate the adjuster bolt, and check that both the adjuster plungers are free to move easily. If necessary, withdraw both the plungers from the adjuster, and unscrew the adjuster bolt and tapered nut **(see illustration)**. Remove all traces of

14.9 Depress the spring cup (arrowed), rotate it 90°, and withdraw it along with the spring

14.10 Remove the strut from between the shoe upper ends

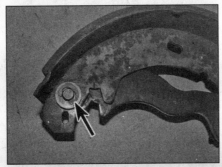

14.12 Prise off the spring clip (arrowed) and recover the washers

14.13 Unscrew the adjuster bolt, and remove the tapered nut (arrowed)

14.14 Apply high-melting point grease to the backplate contact points (arrowed)

14.19 Check all the components are correctly fitted, then refit the brake drum

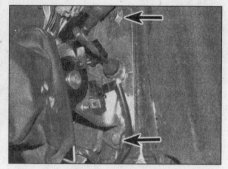

15.4 Handbrake lever assembly retaining bolts (arrowed)

corrosion from them, and apply a smear of high-temperature grease to both the plungers and adjuster bolt threads. Screw the adjuster bolt and tapered nut into position, and refit the plungers. If this does not cure the problem, renew the adjuster assembly components.

14 With the adjuster assembly operating correctly, apply a smear of high-melting-point grease to the contact areas of the new shoes and backplate **(see illustration)**. Take care to ensure that the grease does not contaminate the friction material.

15 Engage the right-hand shoe with the handbrake cable, and locate the shoe on the backplate. Install the shoe retainer pin and spring, and secure it in position with the spring cup.

16 Refit the strut to the upper end of the right-hand shoe, making sure it is the correct way up.

17 Hook the lower return spring onto the right-hand shoe, then engage the left-hand shoe with the return spring. Locate the left-hand shoe on the backplate, engaging it with the adjuster plunger slot and strut, and secure it in position with its retainer pin, spring and spring cup.

18 Check that all components are correctly positioned, then refit the upper return spring.

19 Refit the brake drum to the transfer box, tightening its retaining screw securely **(see illustration)**.

20 Adjust the handbrake as described in

Chapter 1 then, if all is well, reconnect the propeller shaft to the transfer box as described in Chapter 8.

15 Handbrake lever – removal and refitting

Removal

1 Remove the centre console as described in Chapter 12.

2 Disconnect the wiring connector from the handbrake warning light switch.

3 On earlier models, remove the circlip securing the outer cable to the lever assembly, and lift off the adjustment nut.

4 Undo the two mounting bolts and washers, then free the lever assembly from the outer cable, and lift it out of the vehicle **(see illustration)**.

Refitting

5 Refit the handbrake lever assembly, making sure that it is correctly engaged with the handbrake outer cable. Refit the handbrake lever mounting bolts, and tighten them securely.

6 Reconnect the wiring connector to the handbrake warning light switch.

7 Refit the centre console as described in Chapter 12, and adjust the handbrake cable as described in Chapter 1.

16 Handbrake cable – removal and refitting

Removal

1 Chock the front wheels, then jack up the rear of the vehicle and support it securely on axle stands (see *Jacking and vehicle support*).

2 Remove the centre console as described in Chapter 12.

3 Remove the clip, then withdraw the clevis pin securing the handbrake inner cable to the lever.

Vehicles up to VIN XA222819

4 Remove the circlip, and lift off the handbrake cable adjustment nut **(see illustration)**.

All vehicles

5 From underneath the vehicle, work back along the cable, freeing it from any relevant retaining clips and ties whilst noting its correct routing. Pull the cable from the floorpan.

6 Referring to Section 14, remove the upper and lower return springs, then remove the spring cup, spring and retainer pin, and remove the right-hand handbrake shoe. Note that the left-hand shoe and strut can be left in position on the backplate.

7 Free the handbrake cable from the rear of the backplate, and withdraw it from underneath the vehicle **(see illustrations)**.

16.4 Prise out the circlip and lift off the cable adjusting nut (arrowed)

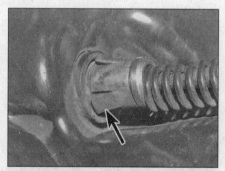

16.7a Squeeze together the sides of the clip (arrowed) and pull the cable from the backplate

16.7b Pull the cable from the transmission tunnel

Refitting

8 Apply a smear of high-melting-point grease to the cable lower end fitting, then insert the cable through the rear of the backplate.

9 Refit the right-hand brake shoe as described in Section 14, and refit the brake drum.

10 Work along the cable, routing it correctly and securing it in position with all the relevant clips and ties, and feed it up through the base of the floorpan.

Vehicles up to VIN XA222819

11 From inside the vehicle, refit the adjustment nut to the cable, and secure it in position with the circlip.

All vehicles

12 Apply a smear of grease to the clevis pin, then align the inner cable with the lever, and insert the pin. Refit the washer, and secure the clevis pin in position with the spring clip.

13 Refit the centre console as described in Chapter 12, and adjust the handbrake as described in Chapter 1.

17 Stop-light switch – removal, refitting and adjustment

Removal

1 The stop-light switch is located on the pedal bracket behind the facia. To remove the switch, release the fasteners and detach the driver's side lower facia panel from the facia.

2 Disconnect the wiring connector plug(s) from the stop-light switch **(see illustration)**.

3 Twist the switch anti-clockwise and pull it from the pedal bracket.

Refitting and adjustment

4 Depress the brake pedal, then push the switch fully into the mounting bracket and twist is clockwise to lock it in position.

5 Reconnect the switch wiring connector. If the setting of the brake switch is disturbed, it can be reset by depressing the brake pedal and pull the plunger out from the switch body, until it contacts the pedal.

6 On completion, refit the facia panel.

17.2 Disconnect the stop-light switch wiring plug (arrowed)

18 Vacuum pump – removal and refitting

Note: *At the time of writing, it was unclear whether the vacuum pump is available separately from the alternator – check with a Land Rover dealer or specialist.*

Removal

1 Remove the alternator as described in Chapter 5.

2 Undo the 4 bolts and detach the vacuum pump from the alternator **(see illustration)**.

Refitting

3 Ensure that the alternator and vacuum pump mating faces are clean and dry.

4 Refit the pump to the alternator, and tighten the bolts to the specified torque.

5 Refit the alternator as described in Chapter 5.

19 Anti-lock braking system (ABS) – general information

ABS is fitted as standard to all models. The system consists of the electronic control unit (ECU), a modulator block (which contains the hydraulic solenoid valves and accumulators, and the electrically-driven return pump), and four roadwheel sensors; one fitted to each hub. The brake pedal stop-light switch is used to indicate to the ECU that the brakes are applied. The purpose of the system is to prevent wheel(s) locking during heavy braking. This is achieved by automatic release of the brake on the relevant wheel, followed by reapplication of the brake.

The solenoid valves are controlled by the ECU, which itself receives signals from the four wheel sensors (one fitted on each hub), which monitor the speed of rotation of each wheel. By comparing these speed signals from the four wheels, the ECU can determine the speed at which the vehicle is travelling. It can then use this speed to determine when a wheel is decelerating at an abnormal rate compared to the speed of the vehicle, and

18.2 Undo the 4 bolts (arrowed), and pull the vacuum pump from the alternator

therefore predicts when a wheel is about to lock. During normal operation, the system functions in the same way as a non-ABS braking system does.

During normal operation, the solenoid valves in the modulator assembly are closed, and the governor valves are in the at-rest position. The system then functions in the same way as a non-ABS braking system does.

If the ECU senses that a wheel is about to lock, the ABS operates the relevant solenoid valve in the modulator assembly, which then isolates the brake caliper on the wheel which is about to lock from the master cylinder, effectively sealing-in the hydraulic pressure.

If the speed of rotation of the wheel continues to decrease at an abnormal rate, the electrically-driven return pump operates, and pumps the hydraulic fluid back into the master cylinder, releasing pressure on the brake caliper so that the brake is released. Once the speed of rotation of the wheel returns to an acceptable rate, the pump stops and the solenoid valve opens, allowing the hydraulic master cylinder pressure to return to the caliper, which then reapplies the brake. This cycle can be carried out at many times a second.

The action of the solenoid valves and return pump creates pulses in the hydraulic circuit. When the ABS is functioning, these pulses can be felt through the brake pedal.

Other functions are built-into the ABS system. Using the same sensors and actuators (solenoids), the system is able to regulate the fluid pressure to the rear brakes to compensate for heavy loads etc – electronic brake force distribution (EBD). The system also provides electronic traction control by using the brakes to control the spinning of any wheel that has lost traction, thus diverting the drive to the wheels that still have traction – electronic traction control (ETC). In addition the system also provides hill descent control (HDC), where the vehicle's brakes are used by the ECU to maintain vehicle stability during sharp descents off-road. The ECU that controls the ABS system, also controls the self-levelling suspension system (SLS) – where fitted.

The operation of the ABS is entirely dependent on electrical signals. To prevent the system responding to any inaccurate signals, a built-in safety circuit monitors all signals received by the ECU. The first time the vehicle exceeds 5 mph after the ignition has been switched on, the ECU tests the readings from each wheel sensor, and the operation of the modulator solenoid valves. If a fault is present, the ABS is automatically shut down by the ECU, and the warning light on the instrument panel is illuminated to inform the driver that the ABS is not operational.

Every time the ignition is switched on, the ECU performs a self-test and checks its memory for faults. This takes approximately 1 to 2 seconds, during which time the ABS warning light in the instrument panel will illuminate. The warning light should then go out, indicating the end of the self-test. If the warning light fails to go out, or illuminates whilst the vehicle is being driven, then a fault is present in the ABS.

If a fault does develop in the ABS, the vehicle must be taken to a Land Rover dealer or specialist for fault diagnosis and repair.

20 Anti lock braking system (ABS) components – removal and refitting

Modulator assembly

Note: *Before starting work, refer to the warning at the beginning of Section 2 concerning the dangers of hydraulic fluid.*

Note: *After refitting the modulator, Land Rover insist that the system must be bleed using their Testbook dedicated test equipment. Have this task carried out be a Land Rover dealer or suitably-equipped specialist.*

Removal

1 Disconnect the battery negative terminal as described in Chapter 5.

2 Disconnect the three wiring connectors from the ABS modulator assembly, located on the left-hand side of the engine compartment.

3 Unscrew the master cylinder reservoir filler cap, and top-up the reservoir to the MAX mark (see *Weekly checks*).

4 Wipe clean the area around the modulator brake pipe unions, then make a note of how the pipes are arranged, to use as a reference on refitting. Unscrew the union nuts, and carefully withdraw the pipes. Plug or tape over the pipe ends and modulator orifices, to minimise the loss of brake fluid and to prevent the entry of dirt into the system. Wash off any spilt fluid immediately with cold water.

5 Slacken and remove the mounting nuts, and release the modulator assembly from its mounting bracket. If necessary, unscrew the modulator rubber mounting bushes, and remove them. **Note:** *Do not attempt to dismantle the modulator block hydraulic assembly; overhaul of the unit is not possible.*

Refitting

6 Refitting is the reverse of the removal procedure, noting the following points:

20.9 Disconnect the ABS ECU wiring plugs

a) *Examine the rubber mounting bushes for signs of wear or damage, and renew if necessary.*
b) *Refit the brake pipes to their respective unions, and tighten the union nuts to the specified torque.*
c) *Ensure that the wiring is correctly routed, and that the connector is firmly pressed into position.*
d) *On completion, prior to refitting the battery, bleed the complete braking system using Land Rover dedicated test equipment (Testbook) – entrust this task to a Land Rover dealer or specialist.*

Electronic control unit (ECU)

Removal

7 The ABS electronic control unit (ECU) is mounted behind the glovebox. Prior to removing the ECU, disconnect the battery negative terminal as described in Chapter 5.

8 Remove the body control unit (BCU) as described in Chapter 12.

9 Disconnect the 5 multiplugs from the ABS ECU, and the multiplug from the Active Corning Enhancement (ACE) ECU – where fitted **(see illustration)**.

10 Slacken the upper nut, then remove the lower nut and remove the ECU(s) and bracket from position **(see illustration)**.

11 Undo the 4 nuts securing the ABS ECU to the bracket **(see illustration)**.

Refitting

12 Refitting is a reversal of the removal procedure. If a new ABS ECU has been fitted,

20.10 Slacken the upper nut, and undo the lower nut (arrowed)

it must be reprogrammed using Land Rover dedicated test equipment (Testbook). Entrust this task to a Land Rover dealer or specialist.

Front wheel sensor

Removal

13 Firmly apply the handbrake, then loosen the relevant front roadwheel nuts. Jack up the front of the vehicle and support it securely on axle stands (see *Jacking and vehicle support*). Remove the appropriate front roadwheel.

14 Trace the wheel sensor wiring back to its wiring connector in the engine compartment, and release it from its retaining clip. Disconnect the connector, and work back along the sensor wiring, freeing it from all the relevant retaining clips, grommets and ties.

15 Remove the brake disc as described in Section 6.

16 Clean the area around the sensor, then undo the Allen bolt and pull the sensor from the hub **(see illustration)**. Discard the O-ring seal, a new one must be fitted.

17 Slacken the 4 bolts securing the hub to the hub carrier sufficiently to enable the sensor and harness to be removed.

Refitting

18 Ensure the sensor and hub mating faces are clean and free from debris. Apply a little high-temperature anti-seize grease to the sensor body.

19 Fit a new O-ring seal to the sensor, then feed the harness through the gap between the hub and hub carrier, and position the sensor in the hub **(see illustration)**.

20.11 ABS ECU retaining nuts (arrowed)

20.16 Undo the front ABS wheel speed sensor Allen bolt (arrowed)

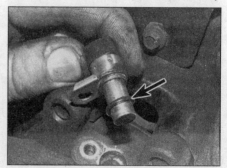

20.19 Renew the sensor O-ring seal (arrowed)

20.26a Undo the Allen screw (arrowed) and pull the rear ABS wheel speed sensor from the hub

20.26b Feed the sensor harness connector through the hole in the hub

20.28 Renew the sensor O-ring seal (arrowed)

Tighten the sensor retaining bolt to the specified torque.

20 Tighten the bolts securing the hub to the hub carrier to the specified torque.

21 Ensure that the sensor wiring is correctly routed and retained by all the necessary clips. Reconnect it to its wiring connector, and clip the connector into the retaining clip.

22 Refit the brake disc as described in Section 6.

23 Refit the roadwheel, then lower the vehicle to the ground and tighten the roadwheel nuts to the specified torque.

Rear wheel sensor

Removal

24 Remove the rear brake disc as described in Section 7.

25 Trace the wiring back from the sensor to its wiring connector. Free the connector from its retaining clip, disconnect it from the main wiring loom, then work back along the sensor wiring and free it from any relevant retaining clips.

26 Undo the Allen bolt and pull the sensor from the hub, and feed the wiring harness through the hole in the hub **(see illustrations)**.

Discard the O-ring seal, a new one must be fitted.

Refitting

27 Ensure the sensor and hub mating faces are clean, then apply a little high-temperature anti-seize grease to the sensor body.

28 With a new O-ring seal, fit the sensor to the hub and tighten the retaining bolt to the specified torque **(see illustration)**.

29 Refit the brake disc as described in Section 7.

30 Refit the roadwheel, then lower the vehicle to the ground and tighten the roadwheel nuts to the specified torque

Chapter 11
Suspension and steering

Contents

Section number

ACE fluid pump – removal and refitting 20
ACE system electronic components – removal and refitting 21
Drag link – removal, refitting and adjustment. 32
Drag link balljoint/end fitting – removal and refitting 33
Front ACE actuator – removal and refitting 8
Front ACE 'long arm' – removal, inspection and refitting 9
Front anti-roll bar – removal and refitting 6
Front anti-roll bar connecting link – removal, inspection and refitting 7
Front coil spring – removal and refitting. 3
Front shock absorber – removal, testing and refitting 2
Front suspension and steering check . . . . See Chapter 1
Front suspension Panhard rod – removal, inspection and refitting . . 4
Front suspension radius arm – removal, inspection and refitting. . . . 5
General information 1
Ignition switch/steering column lock – removal and refitting 23
Power steering fluid level check. . . . . See Weekly checks
Power steering pump – removal and refitting 29
Power steering pump drivebelt check, adjustment
 and renewal . . . . See Chapter 1
Power steering system – bleeding. 30
Rear ACE actuator – removal and refitting 18
Rear ACE 'long arm' – removal, inspection and refitting 19

Section number

Rear anti-roll bar – removal and refitting 17
Rear coil spring – removal and refitting 11
Rear shock absorber – removal, testing and refitting 10
Rear suspension air compressor unit – removal and refitting 15
Rear suspension air spring – removal and refitting 14
Rear suspension radius arm – removal, inspection and refitting 12
Rear suspension ride height sensor – removal and refitting 16
Rear suspension Watts linkage – removal, inspection and refitting. . 13
Steering box – removal, inspection and refitting 27
Steering box backlash adjustment. . . . . See Chapter 1
Steering box drop arm – removal and refitting. 28
Steering column – removal, inspection and refitting 24
Steering column intermediate shaft – removal, inspection
 and refitting. 25
Steering column universal joint – removal, inspection and refitting. . 26
Steering damper – removal and refitting 31
Steering wheel – removal and refitting. 22
Track rod – removal and refitting 34
Track rod balljoint – removal and refitting 35
Wheel alignment and steering angles – general information 36
Wheel and tyre maintenance and tyre pressure
 checks . . . . See Weekly checks

Degrees of difficulty

Easy, suitable for novice with little experience | **Fairly easy,** suitable for beginner with some experience | **Fairly difficult,** suitable for competent DIY mechanic | **Difficult,** suitable for experienced DIY mechanic | **Very difficult,** suitable for expert DIY or professional

Specifications

Front suspension
Type . . . . Axle with coil springs and shock absorbers. Axle movement controlled by radius arms and Panhard rod. Anti-roll bar or ACE (Active Cornering Enhancement) torsion bar fitted

Rear suspension
Type . . . . Axle with coil springs and shock absorbers. Axle movement controlled by trailing arms and Watts linkage. Anti-roll bar or ACE (Active Cornering Enhancement) torsion bar fitted. Self-levelling air suspension available as an option

Steering
Type . . . . Power-assisted steering box with drag link and track rod arrangement. Steering damper fitted to track rod
Power steering pump type. . . . . Hobourn Eaton 500 series

Front wheel alignment and steering angles
Note: *All measurements should be taken with the vehicle unladen, with approximately five gallons of fuel in the tank.*
Camber angle:
  Vehicles up to VIN 2A 754807 . . . . -10' ± 30'
  Vehicles from VIN 2A 754808. . . . . +20' ± 30'
Castor angle. . . . . 3°45' ± 45'
Swivel pin inclination . . . . 13°11'
Toe setting . . . . -0°10' ± 10' (total)

Roadwheels
Type . . . . Pressed-steel or aluminium alloy (depending on model)

Tyres

Size . . . . 235/70 R16, 255/65 R16 or 255/55 R18 (depending on model)
Pressures . . . . See end of *Weekly checks*

Torque wrench settings

	Nm	lbf ft
Front suspension		
ACE actuator pipe union nuts	29	21
ACE actuator to 'long arm'	48	35
ACE actuator to 'short arm'	180	133
ACE control valve solenoid cap	11	8
ACE 'long arm' to anti-roll bar link	50	37
ACE 'long arm' to anti-roll bar	180	133
ACE pressure transducer	20	15
ACE valve block bolts	18	13
Anti-roll bar:		
Connecting link balljoint nuts*:		
Lower	100	74
Upper	50	37
Mounting clamp bolts	45	33
Panhard rod bolts/nuts	230	170
Radius arm bolts/nuts	230	170
Shock absorber:		
Upper mounting bolt	125	92
Lower mounting bolts	45	33
Suspension turret to chassis	23	17
Rear suspension		
ACE actuator to 'long arm'	48	35
ACE actuator to 'short arm'	180	133
ACE 'long arm' to anti-roll bar link	50	37
ACE 'long arm' to anti-roll bar	180	133
Air compressor to casing	7	5
Air compressor to chassis	25	18
Anti-roll bar:		
Connecting link nuts	50	37
Mounting clamp bolts	45	33
Height sensor arm to radius arm	25	18
Height sensor to chassis	6	4
Radius arm nuts/bolts	230	170
Shock absorber mounting bolts	125	92
Watts linkage:		
Transverse links to pivot housing	155	114
Pivot housing to axle	230	170
Transverse links to chassis	140	103
Roadwheels		
Roadwheel nuts	140	103
Steering		
Damper bolts/nuts	125	92
Drag link:		
Balljoint nuts	80	59
Clamp bolts:		
M8 bolts	22	16
M10 bolts	33	24
Drop arm retaining nut	240	177
Intermediate shaft/universal joint clamp bolt	25	18
Power steering pump:		
Feed pipe union nut	25	18
Mounting bolts	25	18
Pulley retaining bolts	10	7
Steering box bolts	90	66
Steering column nuts	22	16
Steering pipes-to-box bolt	22	16
Steering wheel nut*	42	31
Track rod:		
Balljoint nuts*	80	59
Clamp bolts:		
M8 bolts	22	16
M10 bolts	33	24

* Do not re-use

1 General information

Both front and rear suspension is of live beam axle type, with coil springs and shock absorbers, although, self-levelling rear air suspension is available as an option.

On the front suspension, axle movement is controlled by two radius arms and a Panhard rod. On all models, an anti-roll bar is fitted. The anti-roll bar is rubber-mounted onto the vehicle body, and is connected to the axle at each end by a balljointed connecting link. On models with ACE (Active Cornering Enhancement), the anti-roll bar is partially replaced by a hydraulic actuator which lengthens or shortens in response to the first signs of body roll. The ACE ECU monitors lateral acceleration via two accelerometers, and controls the actuator using solenoids/valves and fluid pressure generated by an engine driven hydraulic pump.

On the rear suspension, axle movement is controlled by two radius arms and a Watts linkage at the centre of the axle. As with the front suspension, an anti-roll bar is fitted to all models and, on models with ACE, the bar is partially replaced by a hydraulic actuator. The actuator is controlled and powered by the same system as the front suspension. Where air suspension is fitted, the system is self-levelling to compensate for loads, towing, etc. The ride height is monitored by sensors attached between the rear axle and the vehicle chassis, and an ECU controls the flow and release of compressed air to two air 'springs' fitted between the axle and chassis. The compressed air is supplied by an on-board compressor unit. the ECU is combined with the ABS ECU to form one unit, known as the SLABS ECU (Self Levelling Anti-lock Braking System) – refer to Chapter 10 for details of the ECU removal and refitting procedure.

The steering column is linked to the steering box by an intermediate shaft and universal joint. The intermediate shaft has an integral universal joint fitted to its upper end, and is secured to the column by a clamp bolt. The lower end of the intermediate shaft is attached to the universal joint, which in turn is secured to the steering box pinion, both joints being retained with a clamp bolt.

The steering box is mounted onto the chassis. The steering box is connected to one of the hub carrier assemblies by a drag link, which has a balljoint at each end, and the hub carrier assemblies are linked by means of a track rod, which also has a balljoint at each end.

Power-assisted steering is standard on all models. The hydraulic steering system is powered by a belt-driven pump, which is driven off the crankshaft pulley.

Note: *Many of the suspension and steering components are secured in position with self-locking nuts. Whenever a self-locking nut is disturbed, it must be discarded and a new nut fitted.*

2 Front shock absorber – removal, testing and refitting

Note: *Shock absorbers must ALWAYS be renewed in pairs, even if only one appears to be defective, in order to preserve safe handling.*

Removal

1 Raise the front of the vehicle and support it securely on axle stands (see *Jacking and vehicle support*). Remove the front roadwheels.
2 On the right-hand side, release the coolant expansion tank from its mountings and position it to one side (see illustration).
3 On the left-hand side, slacken the clip and disconnect the intercooler hose from the turbocharger.
4 Place a trolley jack under the front axle on the relevant side.
5 Remove the 4 nuts securing the suspension turret to the vehicle chassis (see illustration).
6 On models with ACE (Active Cornering Enhancement) undo the nut securing the ACE pipe bracket to the suspension turret, then move the bracket to one side (see illustration).
7 Release the clip securing the wiring harness to the suspension turret (where applicable).
8 Undo and remove the shock absorber lower mounting bolts (see illustration).
9 Manoeuvre the suspension turret and shock absorber from the engine compartment. Take care not to strain the ACE/brake pipes – where applicable.
10 Undo and remove the through-bolt at the top of the shock absorbers, and separate the turret from the shock absorber (see illustration).

Testing

11 Examine the shock absorber for signs of fluid leakage or damage.
12 Test the operation of the shock absorber, while holding it in an upright position, by moving the piston through a full stroke, and then through short strokes of 50 to 100 mm. In both cases, the resistance felt should be smooth and continuous. If the resistance is

2.2 Pull the rear of the coolant expansion tank upwards to release it from the mountings

2.5 Undo the suspension turret retaining nuts

2.6 ACE pipes bracket (arrowed)

2.8 Undo the shock absorber lower mounting bolts (arrowed)

2.10 Shock absorber upper mounting bolt (arrowed)

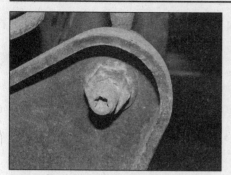

3.3 Use a Torx bit to counterhold the balljoint shank whilst undoing the anti-roll bar link nut

3.6a Compress the shock absorber upwards . . .

3.6b . . . and remove the spring

jerky, or uneven, or if there is any visible sign of wear or damage, renewal is necessary.

13 Renew the shock absorber complete if any damage or excessive wear is evident. Shock absorbers must always be renewed in axle sets, even if only one of the pair is damaged or leaking.

14 Inspect the mounting rubber for signs of damage or deterioration, and renew if necessary.

Refitting

15 Refitting is a reversal of the removal procedure, tightening all fasteners to their specified torque where given.

3 Front coil spring – removal and refitting

Removal

1 Jack up the front of the vehicle and support it securely with axle stands positioned under the chassis rails. Position a workshop trolley jack under the front axle at the relevant side.

2 Remove both front roadwheels.

3 Undo the nut each side and detach the anti-roll bar links from the axle **(see illustration)**. Recover the washer from the balljoint shanks.

4 Undo the two bolts securing the base of the shock absorber to the axle **(see illustration 2.8)**. Compress the shock absorber upwards.

5 Carefully lower the axle until it is possible to withdraw the coil spring. Whilst lowering the axle, keep a careful watch on the brake pipes

and wires, to ensure that no excess strain is being placed on them. We found it necessary to release them from the support bracket.

6 Remove the coil spring and lower seat, noting which way around it is fitted **(see illustrations)**.

7 Inspect the spring closely for signs of damage, such as cracking, and check the spring seats for signs of wear or damage. Renew worn components as necessary.

Refitting

8 Install the coil spring with the close coils uppermost (flattened coil at the top), and align the base of the spring with the cut-out in the spring seat **(see illustration)**.

9 Carefully raise the axle into position, then refit the shock absorber lower mounting bolts. Tighten the bolts to the specified torque.

10 Ensure the washers are in place on the balljoint shanks, then reconnect the anti-roll bar links, and tighten the nuts to the specified torque.

11 Refit the brake pipe/wire to the support bracket where applicable.

12 Refit the wheels and lower the vehicle to the ground.

4 Front suspension Panhard rod – removal, inspection and refitting

Removal

1 To improve access, apply the handbrake, then jack up the front of the vehicle and support

it on axle stands positioned underneath the chassis (see *Jacking and vehicle support*).

2 Slacken and remove the nuts and pivot bolts securing the Panhard rod to the chassis and axle, and remove the rod from underneath the vehicle **(see illustrations)**.

3 If necessary, slacken and remove the retaining nuts and bolts, and remove the Panhard rod mounting bracket from the chassis.

Inspection

4 Inspect the rod and mounting bracket for signs of damage, paying particular attention to the areas around the mounting bushes. Check the pivot bolt shanks for signs of wear, and renew if necessary.

5 Examine the Panhard rod mounting bushes for signs of wear and damage. If renewal is necessary, a hydraulic press and suitable spacers will be required to press the bush out of position and install the new one. Press the old bush out, and install the new bush using a suitable tubular spacer which bears only on the hard outer edge of the bush, not the bush rubber.

Refitting

6 Where removed, refit the mounting bracket to the chassis. Insert its retaining bolts and nuts, tightening them to the specified torque setting.

7 Offer up the Panhard rod, and insert both pivot bolts. Fit the new nuts to the pivot bolts, tightening them loosely only.

8 Lower the vehicle to the ground then, with it resting on its wheels, tighten both pivot bolt nuts to the specified torque setting.

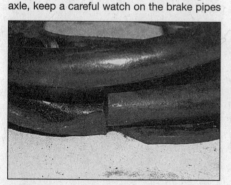

3.8 Ensure the base of the spring aligns correctly with the cut-out in the spring seat

4.2a Undo the bolt and detach the Panhard rod from the axle . . .

4.2b . . . and from the chassis

5 Front suspension radius arm – removal, inspection and refitting

Removal

1 Apply the handbrake, then loosen the relevant front roadwheel nuts. Jack up the front of the vehicle and support it on axle stands positioned underneath the chassis (see *Jacking and vehicle support*). Remove the relevant front roadwheel.
2 Position a trolley jack beneath the front axle assembly, then raise the jack until it is supporting the axle weight.
3 Slacken and remove the nut and washer securing the steering gear track rod balljoint to the hub carrier. Release the balljoint tapered shank using a universal balljoint separator. Discard the nut, a new one must be fitted.
4 Release the axle breather tube from the clips on the arms.
5 Unscrew the nut and bolt securing the radius arm to the chassis (see illustration).
6 Slacken and remove the nuts and bolts securing the radius arm to the axle, and remove the arm from underneath the vehicle (see illustration).

Inspection

7 Inspect the arm for signs of damage, paying particular attention to the areas around the mounting bushes.
8 Examine the radius arm mounting bushes for signs of wear and damage. If renewal is necessary, a hydraulic press and suitable spacers will be required to press the bush out of position and install the new one. Press the old bush out, and install the new bush using a suitable tubular spacer which bears only on the hard outer edge of the bush, not the bush rubber.

Refitting

9 Manoeuvre the arm assembly into position, and insert the pivot bolts. Fit the new nuts to the pivot bolts, tightening them loosely only at this stage.
10 Reconnect the track rod balljoint to the swivel pin housing assembly, tightening its

5.5 Undo the nut and bolt securing the radius arm to the chassis (arrowed)

new retaining nut to the specified torque setting.
11 Refit the wheel, then lower the vehicle to the ground and tighten the wheel nuts to the specified torque.
12 With the vehicle resting on its wheels, tighten the radius arm bolt/nuts to the specified torque setting.

6 Front anti-roll bar – removal and refitting

Removal

1 Apply the handbrake, then jack up the front of the vehicle and support it on axle stands positioned underneath the chassis (see *Jacking and vehicle support*).
2 Position a trolley jack beneath the front axle assembly, then raise the jack until it is supporting the axle weight.
3 Prior to removal, mark the position of each mounting clamp rubber on the anti-roll bar.

Models without ACE

4 Slacken and remove the nuts securing each end of the anti-roll bar to the connecting links.

Models with ACE

5 Remove the ACE 'long arm' as described in Section 9.
6 Slacken and remove the nut securing the left-hand end of the bar to the connecting link (see illustration).

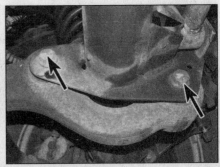

5.6 Radius arm-to-axle bolts (arrowed)

All models

7 Unscrew the bolts securing the mounting clamps to the vehicle body, then lower the anti-roll bar out from underneath the vehicle (see illustration).
8 Remove the mounting rubbers from the anti-roll bar, and inspect them for signs of damage. Renew both rubbers if they are damaged or show signs of deterioration.

Refitting

9 Fit the mounting rubbers to the anti-roll bar. Fit the rubbers so that its split will be facing forwards (see illustration).
10 Align both rubbers with the marks made prior to removal, and manoeuvre the anti-roll bar into position.
11 Ensure that the flat side of each rubber is against the vehicle body, then refit the mounting clamps. Insert the bolts, tightening them loosely only at this stage.
12 The remainder of refitting is a reversal of removal. Tighten all fasteners to the specified torque.

7 Front anti-roll bar connecting link – removal, inspection and refitting

Removal

1 Apply the handbrake, then jack up the front of the vehicle and support it on axle stands positioned underneath the chassis (see

6.6 Undo the nut (arrowed) securing the anti-roll bar to the link

6.7 Remove the bolt each side and detach the anti-roll bar clamps from the vehicle body (left-hand clamp bolt arrowed)

6.9 Fit the anti-roll bar bushes with the horizontal split facing forwards

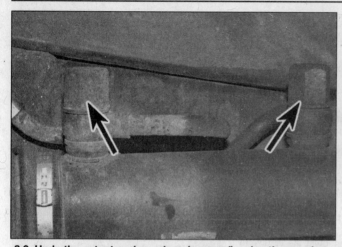

8.3 Undo the actuator pipe unions (arrowed) – plug the openings to prevent contamination

8.4 Use a second spanner to counterhold the anti-roll bar link balljoint shank

Jacking and vehicle support). Remove the relevant front roadwheel.

2 Position a trolley jack beneath the front axle assembly, then raise the jack until it is supporting the axle weight.

3 Slacken and remove the nut securing the connecting link to the anti-roll bar **(see illustration 6.6)**.

4 Remove the nut and washer securing the connecting link balljoint to the axle assembly. Remove the connecting link from the vehicle **(see illustration 3.3)**.

Inspection

5 Check that the link balljoint moves freely, without any sign of roughness. Check also that the balljoint gaiter shows no sign of deterioration, and is free from cracks and splits. If any sign of wear or damage is found, the complete link must be renewed.

Refitting

6 Locate the upper end of the link in the end of the anti-roll bar, then fit a new nut and tighten it to the specified torque.

7 Locate the balljoint shank in the axle, and refit its washer and nut. Tighten the nut to the specified torque setting.

8 Refit the roadwheel and lower the vehicle to ground. Tighten the roadwheel bolts to the specified torque.

8.6 Undo the actuator-to-short arm nut and bolt (arrowed)

---

8 Front ACE actuator – removal and refitting

⚠️ **Warning: When working on the ACE hydraulic system, it's essential no dirt be allowed to enter the system. Even the smallest amount of dirt could cause extensive damage. Always cover/plug all pipe/hose/port openings, and clean the areas around the unions before slackening them.**

Note: *In order to complete this procedure, once the actuator has been refitted, it will be necessary to bleed the ACE hydraulic system. This task necessitates the use of Land Rover dedicated test equipment (Testbook). We suggest that with the parts fitted, it should be possible to carefully drive the vehicle to a Land Rover dealer or specialist to have this task carried out.*

Removal

1 Raise the front of the vehicle and support it securely on axle stands (see *Jacking and vehicle support*). Remove the right-hand front roadwheel.

2 Undo the screws and remove the right-hand front wheel arch liner extension.

3 Clean the area around the actuator pipes,

8.7 Counterhold the actuator rod, and unto the nut

position a container underneath them, then slacken the union nuts and disconnect the pipes **(see illustration)**. Discard the sealing washers, new ones must be fitted. Plug the pipe openings to prevent dirt ingress.

4 Undo the nut and disconnect the anti-roll bar link from the end of the ACE 'long arm' **(see illustration)**.

5 Undo the bolt and remove the right-hand anti-roll bar clamp, then slacken the left-hand clamp bolt enough to allow the anti-roll bar to be lowered **(see illustration 6.7)**.

6 Undo the nut and remove the bolt securing the lower end of the actuator to the ACE 'short arm' **(see illustration)**.

7 Counterhold the end of the actuator rod and undo the nut securing the upper end of the actuator to the ACE 'long arm' and manoeuvre it from under the vehicle **(see illustration)**. Note that if the nut is difficult to undo, use Land Rover tool LRT-60-009.

8 Dismantling of the actuator is not recommended. If faulty the unit must be renewed – consult a Land Rover dealer or specialist.

Refitting

9 Refitting is a reversal of removal, noting the following points:
a) *Reconnect the pipe unions to the actuator using new sealing washers.*
b) *Tighten all fasteners to their specified torque where given.*
c) *Upon completion, have the ACE front system bled by a Land Rover dealer or specialist.*

---

9 Front ACE 'long arm' – removal, inspection and refitting

Removal

1 Slacken the long arm-to-anti-roll bar bolt (see paragraph 4) before removing the ACE actuator (paragraph 2).

2 Remove the ACE actuator as described in Section 8.
3 Undo the nut and detach the long arm from the anti-roll bar link **(see illustration 8.4)**.
4 Undo the retaining bolt, recover the washer, then pull the long arm from the anti-roll bar **(see illustrations)**. **Note:** *Do not attempt to remove the 'short arm' from the anti-roll bar – they are supplied as a complete unit.*

Inspection

5 Examine the long arm for evidence of damage or wear. If any is found, new the long arm.
6 Check the bushes at each end of the long arm for signs of damage or wear. If necessary have the bushes renewed by a Land Rover dealer or specialist, as to remove and refit the bushes requires the use of a hydraulic press.

Refitting

7 Ensure the mating faces of the long arm and anti-roll bar are clean.
8 Position the long arm on the anti-roll bar, apply a little thread-locking compound, then fit the retaining bolt and washer, and tighten it to the specified torque.
9 Fit the end of the long arm over the end of the anti-roll bar link, then refit the nut and tighten it to the specified torque.
10 Refit the ACE actuator as described in Section 8.

10 Rear shock absorber – removal, testing and refitting

Note: *Shock absorbers must ALWAYS be renewed in pairs, even if only one appears to be defective, in order to preserve safe handling.*

Removal

1 Chock the front wheels, then loosen the relevant rear roadwheel nuts. Jack up the rear of the vehicle and support it on axle stands positioned underneath the chassis (see *Jacking and vehicle support*). Remove the relevant rear roadwheel.
2 Position a trolley jack beneath the rear axle assembly, then raise the jack until it is supporting the axle weight.
3 Remove the mounting bolt at each end of the shock absorber, then compress it and remove it from the vehicle **(see illustrations)**.

Testing

4 Examine the shock absorber for signs of fluid leakage or damage.
5 Test the operation of the shock absorber, while holding it in an upright position, by moving the piston through a full stroke, and then through short strokes of 50 to 100 mm. In both cases, the resistance felt should be smooth and continuous. If the resistance is jerky, or uneven, or if there is any visible sign of wear or damage, renewal is necessary.
6 Renew the shock absorber complete if any

9.4a Undo the 'long arm' retaining bolt . . .

9.4b . . . and pull the arm from the anti-roll bar

10.3a Remove the lower shock absorber mounting bolt . . .

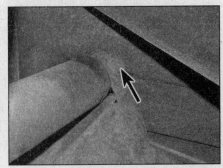
10.3b . . . and the upper mounting bolt (arrowed)

damage or excessive wear is evident. Shock absorbers must always be renewed in axle sets, even if only one of the pair is damaged or leaking.

Refitting

7 Locate the shock absorber in the upper and lower mountings, then fit the bolts and tighten them to the specified torque.
8 Refit the roadwheel, then lower the vehicle to the ground, and tighten the roadwheel nuts to the specified torque.

11 Rear coil spring – removal and refitting

Note: *Rear coil springs are not fitted to vehicles with air suspension.*

Removal

1 Remove the relevant rear shock absorber as described in Section 10.
2 Remove the brake caliper from the hub as described in Chapter 10, then disconnect the ABS sensor wiring plug **(see illustration)**. Suspend the caliper from the vehicle body using wire or string – there's no need to disconnect the brake hose.
3 Carefully lower the axle, and remove the spring.
4 Inspect the spring closely for signs of damage, such as cracking, and check the spring seats for signs of wear or damage. Renew worn components as necessary.

Refitting

5 Ensure the spring seats are clean, then install the spring with the close coils uppermost **(see illustration)**.

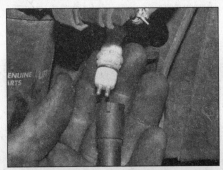
11.2 Disconnect the rear ABS wheel speed sensor wiring plug

11.5 Fit the coil springs with the close-coils uppermost

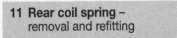

12.3 Undo the nut (arrowed) and disconnect the ride height sensor arm – models with air suspension only

12.4 Remove the nut (arrowed) and extract the radius arm-to-chassis bolt

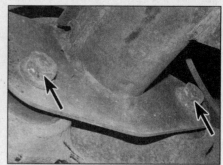

12.5 Radius arm to axle bolts (arrowed)

6 With the spring ends correctly located on the spring seats, raise the axle and refit the shock absorber as described in Section 10.

7 Refit the brake pipe clip and ABS sensor lead to the bracket.

8 Remove the jack from underneath the axle, refit the roadwheel and lower the vehicle to the ground. Tighten the roadwheel bolts to the specified torque.

12 Rear suspension radius arm – removal, inspection and refitting

Removal

1 On models with air suspension, disconnect the battery negative lead as described in Chapter 5. This is to prevent the system attempting to level the suspension when the vehicle is raised or lowered.

2 Chock the front wheels, then jack up the rear of the vehicle and support it on axle stands positioned underneath the rear axle (see *Jacking and vehicle support*). Remove the relevant rear roadwheel.

3 On models with air suspension, undo the nut/bolt and disconnect the ride height sensor arm from the radius arm **(see illustration)**.

4 Slacken and remove the nut and bolt securing the radius arm to the chassis **(see illustration)**.

5 Undo the nuts, remove the bolts, and detach the rear of the radius arm from the rear axle **(see illustration)**.

Inspection

6 Inspect the arm for signs of damage, paying particular attention to the areas around the mounting bushes.

7 Examine the radius arm mounting bushes for signs of wear and damage. If renewal is necessary, a hydraulic press and suitable spacers will be required to press the bush out of position and install the new one. Press the old bush out, and install the new bush using a suitable tubular spacer which bears only on the hard outer edge of the bush, not the bush rubber.

Refitting

8 Manoeuvre the radius arm into position, and insert the mounting bolts. Only loosely tighten the nuts at this stage.

9 On models with air suspension, refit the ride height sensor and the securing nut and bolt. Tighten them to the specified torque.

10 Refit the roadwheel and lower the vehicle to the ground.

11 Tighten the radius arm front and rear mounting bolts/nuts to the specified torque, then tighten the wheel nuts to the specified torque.

12 Where applicable, reconnect the battery negative lead as described in Chapter 5.

13 Rear suspension Watts linkage – removal, inspection and refitting

Removal

1 On models with air suspension, disconnect the battery negative lead as described in Chapter 5. This is to prevent the system attempting to level the suspension when the vehicle is raised or lowered.

2 Chock the front wheels, then jack up the rear of the vehicle and support it on axle stands positioned underneath the rear axle (see *Jacking and vehicle support*).

3 Undo the 3 nuts/bolts and remove the Watts linkage, complete with transverse links from the vehicle **(see illustrations)**.

4 Remove the 2 nuts/bolts and detach the transverse links from the pivot housing **(see illustration)**.

13.3a Remove the Watts linkage left-hand mounting bolt (arrowed) . . .

13.3b . . . central mounting bolt (arrowed) . . .

13.3c . . . and right-hand mounting bolt (arrowed)

13.4 Undo the two bolts and detach the transverse links

13.5 The transverse links are attached to the pivot housing with balljoints, not bushes

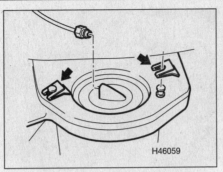

14.3 Remove the retaining clips from the top of the air spring (arrowed)

14.6 Sometimes, a pin-sized puncture will show up as a dark circle (arrowed)

Inspection

5 Inspect the pivot housing and transverse links for signs of damage, paying particular attention to the areas around the mounting bushes **(see illustration)**.

6 Examine the pivot housing and transverse links mounting bushes/balljoints for signs of wear and damage. If renewal is necessary, a hydraulic press and suitable spacers will be required to press the bush(es)/balljoints out of position and install the new one(s). Press the old bush/balljoint out, and install the new bush/balljoint using a suitable tubular spacer, which bears only on the hard outer edge of the bush/balljoint, not the bush/balljoint rubber.

Refitting

7 Refit the transverse links to the pivot housing. insert the bolts/nuts, and tighten them to the specified torque.

8 Manoeuvre the Watts linkage into position, and insert the mounting bolts. Only loosely tighten the nuts at this stage.

9 Lower the vehicle to the ground, then tighten the linkage mounting bolts to the specified torque.

10 Where applicable, reconnect the battery negative lead as described in Chapter 5.

14 Rear suspension air spring – removal and refitting

Note: *Before any part of the pressurised air circuit can be worked on, it's essential to depressurise the system. Land Rover recommend that this must be carrier out using Land Rover dedicated test equipment (Testbook). It is possible to depressurise the system without Testbook by very slowly undoing the air pipe unions on the air supply unit (see illustration 15.1) to allow the pressure within to slowly escape. If in any doubt at all, entrust any work involving the pressurised air circuit to a Land Rover dealer or suitably-equipped specialist.*

 Warning: Do not attempt to drive the vehicle with the air suspension system depressurised.

Removal

1 Depressurise the air suspension system as described above.

2 Chock the front wheels, then jack up the rear of the vehicle and support it on axle stands positioned underneath the chassis (see *Jacking and vehicle support*). Remove the relevant rear roadwheel.

3 Remove the 2 clips securing the top of the air spring to the chassis member, and allow the spring to collapse to access the air supply pipe and union **(see illustration)**.

4 Working at the top of the springs, gradually slacken the air supply pipe union and allow any residual pressure to dissipate, then fully undo the union and pull the pipe from the spring. Plug the openings to prevent dirt ingress.

5 Rotate the spring 90° to unlock it from the axle, and remove it.

Inspection

6 Inspect the fabric of the spring for any signs of damage or wear. If any is evident, the spring must be renewed **(see illustration)**.

7 Should you notice the vehicle listing (leaning) to one side, or is slow to achieve full ride height, check the springs for leaks before the air supply unit suffers irreparable damage from trying to continually re-inflate the springs.

Refitting

8 Clean the mating faces of the spring, chassis and axle.

9 Manoeuvre the spring into position, located it on the axle, then rotate it 90° to lock it in position **(see illustration)**.

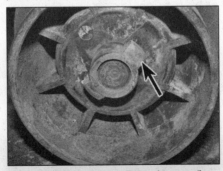

14.9 Align the bayonet fitting (arrowed) on the base of the air spring with the slot in the axle, then rotate it 90°

10 Refit the air supply pipe to the top of the spring and tighten the union securely.

11 Ensure the locating pins on the top of the spring engage correctly with the chassis, then refit the retaining clips.

12 Refit the roadwheel, lower the vehicle to the ground and tighten the wheel nuts to the specified torque setting.

15 Rear suspension air compressor unit – removal and refitting

Note: *Before any part of the pressurised air circuit can be worked on, it's essential to depressurise the system. Land Rover recommend that this must be carrier out using Land Rover dedicated test equipment (Testbook). It is possible to depressurise the system by very slowly undoing the air pipe unions a little to allow the pressure within to slowly escape. If in any doubt at all, entrust any work involving the pressurised air circuit to a Land Rover dealer or suitably-equipped specialist.*

 Warning: Do not attempt to drive the vehicle with the air suspension system depressurised.

Removal

1 If available, use Land Rover's Testbook to depressurise the air suspension system as described above, or gradually undo the pipe unions on the compressor unit, and allow any residual pressure to escape **(see illustration)**.

15.1 Slacken the unions (arrowed) and allow the system to depressurise

15.2 Undo the fasteners (arrowed) and remove the compressor unit cover

15.3 Undo the 2 bolts (arrowed) and lower the compressor unit

16.5 Undo the two bolts (arrowed) and detach the height sensor

2 The compressor unit is located midway along the vehicle, on the outside of the left-hand chassis rail. Undo the fasteners and remove the cover over the unit **(see illustration)**.

3 Position a trolley jack and block under the unit, then undo the 2 bolts securing the unit to chassis **(see illustration)**.

4 Note their fitted positions, then slowly undo the unions and disconnect the air pipes and wiring plugs from the unit. Remove the unit from the vehicle. **Note:** *to release the low pressure pipes unions, press in the collar, then push and pull the pipe from position.*

5 If required, undo the 3 bolts and remove the compressor unit from the mounting casing. Recover the mounting washers.

Refitting

6 Refitting is a reversal of removal, noting the following points:

a) *Apply a little thread-locking compound to the compressor mounting bolts before tightening them to the specified torque.*

b) *Ensure all pipes and wiring plugs are refitted to their original locations.*

c) *Tighten the unit casing-to-chassis bolts to the specified torque.*

16 Rear suspension ride height sensor – removal and refitting

Note: *If a new sensor is to be fitted, Land Rover's dedicated test equipment (Testbook) must be used to recalibrate the sensor. Entrust this task to a Land Rover dealer or specialist.*

Removal

1 Disconnect the battery negative lead as described in Chapter 5.

2 Chock the front wheels, then raise the rear of the vehicle and support it securely on axle stands (see *Jacking and vehicle support*).

3 Working underneath the vehicle, disconnect the height sensor wiring plug.

4 Undo the nut/bolt securing the sensor arm to the lower radius arm **(see illustration 12.3)**.

5 Undo the 2 mounting bolts and detach the sensor from the chassis **(see illustration)**.

Refitting

6 Refitting is a reversal of removal, noting the following points:

a) *Tighten all fasteners to the specified torque, where given.*

b) *Reconnect the battery lead as described in Chapter 5.*

c) *If a new sensor has been fitted, have the sensor recalibrated using Land Rover's Testbook equipment.*

17 Rear anti-roll bar – removal and refitting

⚠️ **Warning: When working on the ACE hydraulic system, it's essential no dirt be allowed to enter the system. Even the smallest amount of dirt could cause extensive damage. Always cover/plug all pipe/hose/port openings, and clean the areas around the unions before slackening them.**

Note: *On models with Active Cornering Enhancement (ACE), in order to complete this procedure once the actuator has been refitted, it may be necessary to bleed the ACE hydraulic system. This task necessitates the use of Land Rover dedicated test equipment (Testbook). We suggest that with the parts refitted, it should be possible to carefully drive the vehicle to a Land Rover dealer or specialist to have this task carried out. However, in the majority of cases, we have found that the system will self-bleed, providing the hydraulic system is not 'dry' (completely empty).*

17.5 Use a Torx bit to counterhold the anti-roll bar balljoint shank

Removal

1 On models with air suspension, disconnect the battery negative lead as described in Chapter 5. This is to prevent the system attempting to level the suspension when the vehicle is raised or lowered.

2 Chock the front wheels, then jack up the rear of the vehicle and support it on axle stands positioned underneath the chassis (see *Jacking and vehicle support*).

3 Position a trolley jack beneath the rear axle assembly, then raise the jack until it is supporting the axle weight.

4 Prior to removal, mark the position of each mounting clamp rubber on the anti-roll bar.

Models without ACE

5 Slacken and remove the nuts securing each end of the anti-roll links to the axle **(see illustration)**.

Models with ACE

6 Clean the area around the pipe unions, then undo the nuts and disconnect the pipes from the ACE actuator. Discard the sealing washers, new ones must be fitted. Plug the openings to prevent dirt ingress. Be prepared for fluid spillage.

7 Slacken and remove the nut securing the anti-roll bar links to the axle.

All models

8 Unscrew the bolts securing the mounting clamps to the vehicle body, then lower the anti-roll bar out from underneath the vehicle **(see illustration)**.

9 Remove the mounting rubbers from the anti-

17.8 Undo the bolt (arrowed) securing the anti-roll bar clamp – right-hand clamp shown

roll bar, and inspect them for signs of damage. Renew both rubbers if they are damaged or show signs of deterioration.

Refitting

10 Fit the mounting rubbers to the anti-roll bar. Fit the rubbers so that its split will be facing forwards.

11 Align both rubbers with the marks made prior to removal, and manoeuvre the anti-roll bar into position.

12 Ensure that the flat side of each rubber is against the vehicle body, then refit the mounting clamps. Insert the bolts, tightening them loosely only at this stage.

13 The remainder of refitting is a reversal of removal, noting the following points:

a) *Tighten all fasteners to the specified torque.*

b) *When refitting the fluid pipes to the ACE actuator (where applicable), always renew the sealing washers.*

c) *On models with ACE, if the system doesn't self-bleed, have the rear system bled by a Land Rover dealer or specialist. See the note at the start of this Section.*

18 Rear ACE actuator – removal and refitting

⚠️ **Warning: When working on the ACE hydraulic system, it's essential no dirt be allowed to enter the system. Even the smallest amount of dirt could cause extensive damage. Always cover/plug all pipe/hose/port openings, and clean the areas around the unions before slackening them.**

Note: *In order to complete this procedure once the actuator has been refitted, it may be necessary to bleed the ACE hydraulic system. This task necessitates the use of Land Rover dedicated test equipment (Testbook). We suggest that with the parts refitted, it should be possible to carefully drive the vehicle to a Land Rover dealer or specialist to have this task carried out. However, in the majority of cases, we have found that the system will self-bleed, providing the hydraulic system is not 'dry' (completely empty).*

Removal

1 Remove the rear anti-roll bar as described in Section 17.

2 Undo the retaining bolts/nuts and detach the actuator from the 'long arm' and the 'short arm' **(see illustrations 8.6 and 8.7)**.

3 No further dismantling of the unit is recommended. If faulty, it must be renewed as a complete unit.

Refitting

4 Ensure the actuator and 'long arm' mating faces are clean.

5 Position the actuator, refit the mounting bolt/nuts and tighten them to the specified torque.

6 The remainder of refitting is a reversal of removal, noting the following points:

a) *Tighten all fasteners to the specified torque where given.*

b) *Change the ACE fluid filter as described in Chapter 1.*

c) *Have the rear ACE hydraulic system bled by a Land Rover dealer or specialist.*

19 Rear ACE 'long arm' – removal, inspection and refitting

Removal

1 Remove the ACE actuator as described in Section 18.

2 Undo the nut and detach the long arm from the anti-roll bar link **(see illustration 8.4)**.

3 Undo the retaining bolt, recover the washer, then pull the long arm from the anti-roll bar **(see illustrations 9.4a and 9.4b)**. Note: *Do not attempt to remove the 'short arm' from the anti-roll bar – they are supplied as a complete unit.*

Inspection

4 Examine the long arm for evidence of damage or wear. If any is found, new the long arm.

5 Check the bushes at each end of the long arm for signs of damage or wear. If necessary have the bushes renewed by a Land Rover dealer or specialist, as to remove and refit the bushes requires the use of a hydraulic press.

Refitting

6 Ensure the mating faces of the long arm and anti-roll bar are clean.

7 Position the long arm on the anti-roll bar, fit the retaining bolt and washer, then tighten it to the specified torque.

8 Fit the end of the long arm over the end of the anti-roll bar link, then refit the nut and tighten it to the specified torque.

9 Refit the ACE actuator as described in Section 18.

20 ACE fluid pump – removal and refitting

Removal

1 Disconnect the battery negative lead as described in Chapter 5.

2 Remove the coolant fan upper cowling as described in Chapter 3.

3 Disconnect the ambient air pressure sensor and mass airflow meter wiring plug – refer to Chapter 4 if necessary.

4 Release the clips and disconnect the mass airflow sensor from the air filter.

5 Slacken the clip and disconnect the intake hose from the turbocharger. Move the hose to one side.

6 Release the clip and disconnect the pressure-sensing hose from the turbocharger outlet pipe.

7 Slacken the clips securing the turbocharger outlet pipes/hoses and remove them as an assembly to gain access to the pump.

8 Slacken the 3 bolts securing the pump drive pulley, then remove the auxiliary drivebelt as described in Chapter 1.

9 Detach the coolant reservoir from the mounting bracket, and move it to one side.

10 Undo the union bolt and detach the pressure pipe from the pump **(see illustration)**. Discard the sealing washers, new ones must be fitted. Be prepared for fluid spillage. Plug all openings to prevent dirt ingress.

11 Clamp the fluid supply hose to the pump, then slacken the clip and disconnect the hose from the pump **(see illustration)**.

12 Undo the 3 bolts and detach the pump from its mounting **(see illustration)**.

20.10 Undo the ACE pump pressure union bolt (arrowed)

20.11 Apply a clamp to the pump fluid supply hose

20.12 Undo the ACE pump mounting bolts (upper bolts shown)

21.4 Depress the clip and disconnect the ACE ECU wiring plug (arrowed)

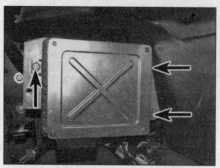

21.5 Undo the 3 nuts (arrowed) and remove the ACE ECU

21.9 Unclip the upper accelerometer

Refitting

13 Refitting is a reversal of removal, noting the following points:

a) *Tighten all fasteners to the specified torque where given.*

b) *Refit the auxiliary drivebelt as described in Chapter 1.*

c) *Renew the ACE fluid filter as described in Chapter 1.*

21 ACE system electronic components – removal and refitting

ECU

Note: *If a new ECU is fitted, it will need to be programmed using Land Rover's dedicated test equipment (Testbook). Entrust this task to a Land Rover dealer or specialist.*

1 Disconnect the battery negative lead as described in Chapter 5.

2 Remove the passenger's glovebox as described in Chapter 11, Section 26.

3 Remove the clips and remove the lower facia panel on the passenger's side.

4 Disconnect the wiring plug from the ACE ECU **(see illustration)**.

5 Undo the 3 nuts and manoeuvre the ECU from position **(see illustration)**.

6 Refitting is a reversal of removal.

Accelerometer

⚠ **Warning: The accelerometer is extremely delicate and is easily broken. Do no re-use an accelerometer that has been dropped or damaged.**

Upper

7 Remove the front upper storage compartment as described in Chapter 12, Section 26.

8 Disconnect the wiring plug from the accelerometer.

9 Unclip the accelerometer from position **(see illustration)**.

10 Refitting is a reversal of removal. Note that if a new accelerometer has been fitted, it will need to be calibrated using Land Rover's dedicated test equipment (Testbook). Entrust this task to a Land Rover dealer or specialist.

21.13 Lever the clip away from the sill to unclip the lower accelerometer

Lower

11 The lower accelerometer is located under the right-hand side of the vehicle, fitted to the inner sill under the driver's door.

12 Disconnect the wiring plug from the accelerometer.

13 Unclip the accelerometer from position **(see illustration)**.

14 Refitting is a reversal of removal. Note that if a new accelerometer has been fitted, it will need to be calibrated using Land Rover's dedicated test equipment (Testbook). Entrust this task to a Land Rover dealer or specialist.

Pressure transducer

15 The pressure transducer is located on the ACE valve block fitted to the right-hand chassis rail, midway along the length of the vehicle. Disconnect the transducer wiring plug **(see illustration)**.

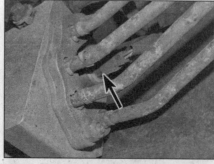

21.15 The pressure transducer is located at the front edge of the ACE valve block (arrowed)

16 Clean the area around the transducer, then unscrew it from the valve block. Be prepared for fluid spillage. Plug all openings to prevent dirt ingress. Discard the O-ring seal, a new one must be fitted.

17 Refitting is a reversal of removal, noting the following points:

a) *Renew the transducer O-ring seal.*

b) *Tighten the transducer to the specified torque.*

c) *Renew the ACE fluid filter as described in Chapter 1.*

Directional control valve solenoid

18 The direction control valve solenoids are located on the top of the ACE valve block fitted to the right-hand chassis rail, midway along the length of the vehicle. Disconnect the solenoid wiring plug **(see illustration)**.

19 Slacken the cap securing the solenoid to the control valve.

20 Undo the 3 bolts securing the valve block to the chassis rail, and lower the block a sufficiently to be able to remove the solenoid.

21 Fully unscrew the cap. Discard the O-ring seal, a new one must be fitted.

22 Separate the solenoid from the valve. Discard the O-ring seal at the base of the valve, a new one must be fitted.

23 Refitting is a reversal of removal, noting the following points:

a) *Fit new O-ring seals to the control valve and solenoid.*

b) *Fit the solenoid to the control valve with*

21.18 The directional control valve solenoids are located at the top of the ACE valve block

the arrow pointing upwards, and the connector in the correct position.

c) *Tighten the solenoid cap and valve block mounting bolts to the specified torque.*

Pressure control valve solenoid

24 The pressure control valve solenoid is located at the rear of the ACE valve block fitted to the right-hand chassis rail, midway along the length of the vehicle. Disconnect the solenoid wiring plug **(see illustration)**.

25 Fully unscrew the solenoid. Discard the O-ring seal, a new one must be fitted.

26 Separate the solenoid from the valve. Discard the O-ring seal from the base of the valve, a new one must be fitted.

27 Refitting is a reversal of removal, noting the following points:

a) *Fit new O-ring seals to the control valve and solenoid.*

b) *Fit the solenoid to the control valve with the arrow pointing away from the valve block, and the connector in the correct position.*

c) *Tighten the solenoid cap to the specified torque.*

22 Steering wheel – removal and refitting

Removal

1 Remove the driver's airbag as described in Chapter 13.

2 Disconnect the wiring plug from the horn button **(see illustration)**.

3 Centralise the steering wheel with the roadwheels straight-ahead, then slacken the steering wheel nut. Do not fully unscrew the nut at this stage.

4 Pull the wheel from the steering column shaft – it may be tight. Seek assistance if necessary.

5 Remove the steering wheel nut, and make alignment marks between the centre of the wheel and the steering column shaft **(see illustration)**. Remove the wheel. Discard the wheel retaining nut, a new one must be fitted.

21.24 The pressure control valve solenoid is located at the rear edge of the ACE valve block

22.5 Make alignment marks between the steering column shaft and the wheel

6 Attach a strip of self-adhesive tape across the airbag rotary contact unit to immobilise it **(see illustration)**.

Refitting

7 Remove the tape from the contact unit, then ensure the wheels are still in the straight-ahead position, and the directional indicator cancelling cam is aligned horizontally **(see illustration)**.

8 Locate the steering wheel on the column splines, aligning the marks made on removal, whilst making sure that the wheel is correctly engaged with the contact unit tabs **(see illustration)**.

9 Reconnect the horn button's wiring plug.

22.2 Disconnect the horn button's wiring plug

22.6 Immobilise the contact unit with self-adhesive tape (arrowed)

10 Refit the retaining nut, and tighten it to the specified torque setting.

11 Refit the driver's airbag as described in Chapter 13.

23 Ignition switch/steering column lock – removal and refitting

Ignition switch

Removal

1 Disconnect the battery negative lead as described in Chapter 5.

2 Undo the fasteners, and open the driver's side lower facia panel **(see illustration)**.

22.7 Align the indictor self-cancelling cam horizontally (arrowed)

22.8 Ensure the tabs on the contact unit engage correctly in the back of the steering wheel (arrowed)

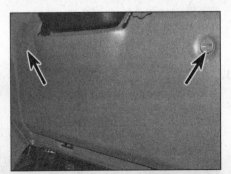

23.2 Undo the fasteners (arrowed) and open the facia access panel

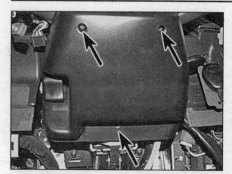

23.3a Undo the 3 retaining screws (arrowed) and unclip the lower shroud . . .

23.3b . . . recover the rubber grommet . . .

23.3c . . . and unclip the upper shroud

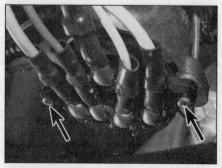

23.5 Undo the 2 screws (arrowed) and remove the ignition switch

23.9 Steering column lock shear bolts (arrowed)

14 Refit the steering column as described in Section 24.

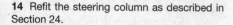

24 Steering column – removal, inspection and refitting

3 Undo the 3 steering column shroud retaining screws, unclip the shroud halves, and remove both the upper and lower shrouds from the steering column **(see illustrations)**.
4 Disconnect the ignition switch multiplug.
5 Undo the 2 retaining screws, and remove the ignition switch **(see illustration)**.

Refitting

6 Refitting is a reversal of removal.

Lock assembly

Removal

7 Remove the steering column assembly as described in Section 24.
8 Undo the two screws and remove the ignition switch assembly from the lock **(see illustration 23.5)**.

9 With the steering column held in a bench vice, using a hammer and suitable chisel, tap the head of each shear-bolt around anti-clockwise until each bolt is loose enough to be unscrewed by hand **(see illustration)**.
10 Unscrew both shear-bolts, and remove the lock assembly from the steering column.

Refitting

11 Position the lock assembly against the steering column, and fit the new shear bolts. Do not tighten them at this stage.
12 Insert the ignition key, and check that the lock functions correctly. If it does, tighten the shear bolts until their heads shear off.
13 Refit the ignition switch and tighten the retaining screws.

Removal

1 Remove the steering wheel as described in Section 22.
2 Working in the engine compartment, make alignment marks between the universal joint and the steering column, then slacken and remove the intermediate shaft-to-column universal joint pinch-bolt, and pull the joint from the column **(see illustration)**.
3 Remove the airbag rotary contact unit from the top of the column as described in Chapter 13.
4 Unclip the immobiliser passive coil from the ignition switch **(see illustration)**. Disconnect the wiring plugs as the coil is withdrawn.
5 Note their fitted positions, then disconnect the wiring plugs from the wiper and lighting switch assembly.
6 Slacken the clamp screw and remove the steering column switch assembly **(see illustration)**.
7 Disconnect the ignition switch wiring plug.
8 Release the wiring harness from any clips on the steering column.

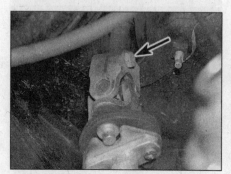

24.2 Intermediate shaft-to-steering column pinch-bolt (arrowed)

24.4 Unclip the immobiliser coil from the ignition switch barrel

24.6 Undo the column switch clamp screw (arrowed)

24.9 Steering column retaining nuts (arrowed)

9 Remove the 4 retaining nuts and remove the steering column from the cabin (**see illustration**).

Inspection

10 Examine steering column and mountings for signs of damage and deformation, and check the steering shaft for signs of free play in the column bushes. If there are signs of damage or play, the column must be renewed. Overhaul of the column is not possible.

Refitting

11 Manoeuvre the steering column into position; engage it with the universal joint, aligning the marks made on removal.
12 The remainder of refitting is a reversal of removal. Tighten all fasteners to the specified torque where given.

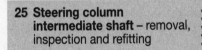

25 Steering column intermediate shaft – removal, inspection and refitting

Removal

1 Set the front wheels in the straight-ahead position, then insert an 8 mm bolt through the slot in drop arm into the steering box casing to lock the steering in the straight-ahead position (**see illustration**).
Caution: Do not turn the steering wheel with the intermediate shaft removed, of damage to the rotary contact unit may occur.
2 Using paint or a marker pen, make alignment marks between the intermediate shaft universal joint and steering column, and the shaft and lower universal joint.
3 Slacken and remove the clamp bolts securing the intermediate shaft to the steering column and universal joint (**see illustration 24.2**).
4 Disengage the shaft from the steering column and joint, and remove it from the vehicle.

Inspection

5 Inspect the intermediate shaft universal joints for signs of roughness in its bearings and ease of movement, and check the shaft coupling for signs of damage or deterioration.

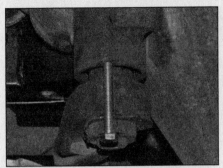

25.1 Insert an 8 mm bolt through the drop arm into the steering box

If either joint or the coupling is damaged in any way, the complete shaft assembly must be renewed.

Refitting

6 Aligning the marks made on removal, engage the shaft with the universal joint, then engage the upper end of the shaft with the steering column.
7 Make sure that the shaft is correctly seated, then insert both its clamp bolts, and tighten them to the specified torque.
8 Remove the centralising bolt from the steering box drop arm.

26 Steering column universal joint – removal, inspection and refitting

Removal

1 Remove the steering column intermediate shaft as described in Section 25.
2 Using paint or a marker pen, make alignment marks between the universal joint and steering box pinion.
3 Slacken and remove the clamp bolt securing the universal joint in position, then disengage it from the pinion, and remove it from the vehicle.

Inspection

4 Inspect the universal joint for signs of roughness in its bearings, and check it for ease of movement. If it is damaged in any way, the joint must be renewed.

27.9 Use a Torx bit to counterhold the drag link balljoint

Refitting

5 Aligning the marks made on removal, engage the universal joint with the steering box pinion.
6 Make sure that the joint is correctly seated, then insert the clamp bolt. Tighten the bolt to the specified torque setting.
7 Refit the intermediate shaft as described in Section 25

27 Steering box – removal, inspection and refitting

Removal

1 Apply the handbrake, then jack up the front of the vehicle and support it on axle stands positioned underneath the chassis (see *Jacking and vehicle support*).
2 Position the front wheels in the straight-ahead position, then engage the steering column lock and remove the ignition key.
3 Remove the front right-hand roadwheel.
4 Undo the fasteners and remove the engine undershield. To completely remove the undershield, disconnect the front propeller shaft from the axle as described in Chapter 8.
5 Undo the 2 universal joint clamp bolts, and slide the joint upwards from steering box pinion.
6 Clean the area around the steering box connection, then make identification marks on each pipe to ensure that they are correctly positioned on reassembly. Unscrew the retaining bolt and disconnect the pipes from the box; be prepared for fluid spillage, and position a suitable container beneath the pipes whilst unscrewing the union nuts. Plug the pipe ends and steering box orifices, to prevent excessive fluid leakage and the entry of dirt into the hydraulic system. Discard the O-ring seals, new ones must be fitted.
7 Undo the bolt securing the coolant rail to the chassis member, then release the clips and move the coolant rail to one side.
8 Undo the nut/bolt at each end and remove the Panhard rod – refer to Section 4.
9 Unscrew the nut securing the drag link to the steering box drop arm (**see illustration**).
10 Using a universal balljoint separator, free the drag link from the drop arm (**see illustration**).

27.10 Use a universal balljoint separator to detach the drag link from the drop arm

28.7 Use a puller to draw the drop arm from the steering box

11 Unscrew the mounting bolts, and remove the steering box assembly from the vehicle.

Inspection

12 Inspect the steering box assembly for signs of wear or damage. If overhaul of the steering box assembly is necessary, the task must be entrusted to a Land Rover dealer or specialist. Reconditioned steering boxes are available.

Refitting

13 If a new steering box is being fitted, position the drop arm so an 8 mm bolt can be inserted through the slot in the drop arm into the hole in the steering box casing **(see illustration 25.1)**.

14 Manoeuvre the steering box into position, and engage it with the universal joint splines, aligning the marks made prior to removal.

15 Position the steering box assembly on the chassis, making sure its locating lug is correctly engaged, then fit the mounting bolts and tighten them to the specified torque setting.

16 Insert the clamp bolts securing the universal joint to the steering box pinion and intermediate shaft. Tighten the clamp bolts to the specified torque.

17 Connect the drag link to the drop arm, and refit its retaining nut. Tighten the nut to the specified torque setting.

18 Refit the Panhard rod, and tighten the bolts to the specified torque.

19 Wipe clean the pipe unions, and refit them to their respective ports on the steering box using new O-ring seals. Tighten the union bolt

to the specified torque setting, and ensure that the pipes are securely retained by all the necessary retaining clips.

20 The remainder of refitting is a reversal of removal, noting the following points:
a) *Remove the centralising bolt from the steering box drop arm.*
b) *Tighten all fasteners to their specified torque where given.*
c) *Bleed the hydraulic system as described in Section 30.*

28 Steering box drop arm – removal and refitting

Note: *A new retaining nut lockwasher will be required on refitting.*

Removal

1 Apply the handbrake, then jack up the front of the vehicle and support it on axle stands positioned underneath the chassis (see *Jacking and vehicle support*).

2 Position the front wheels in the straight-ahead position, then engage the steering lock and remove the ignition key.

3 Unscrew the nut securing the drag link to the steering box drop arm.

4 Using a universal balljoint separator, free the drag link from the drop arm.

5 Bend down the lockwasher tab, then slacken and remove the drop arm retaining nut and lockwasher.

6 Make alignment marks between the drop arm and steering box shaft.

7 A suitable puller will now be required to draw the arm off the box shaft. Locate the legs of the puller behind the arm, and carefully draw it off the steering box shaft **(see illustration)**.

8 Once the arm is loose, remove the puller, then lower the drop arm away from the steering box.

Refitting

9 Align the marks made prior to removal, and locate the drop arm on the steering box shaft splines.

10 Fit a new lockwasher to the shaft, and refit the retaining nut. Tighten the nut to the specified torque setting, then secure it in position by bending down the tab of the

lockwasher so that it contacts one of the nut flats.

11 Connect the drag link to the drop arm, and refit its retaining nut. Tighten the nut to the specified torque setting.

12 Lower the vehicle to the ground, and reconnect the battery.

29 Power steering pump – removal and refitting

Removal

1 Apply the handbrake, then jack up the front of the vehicle and support it on axle stands positioned underneath the chassis (see *Jacking and vehicle support*).

2 Remove the cooling fan and viscous coupling as described in Chapter 3.

3 Slacken the bolts securing the drivebelt pulley to the power steering pump **(see illustration)**.

4 Remove the auxiliary drivebelt as described in Chapter 1, then remove the retaining bolts and withdraw the power steering pump pulley, noting which way around it is fitted.

5 Using brake hose clamps, clamp both the supply and return hoses near the power steering fluid reservoir. This will minimise fluid loss during subsequent operations.

6 Slacken the retaining clip, and disconnect the fluid supply hose from the pump. Slacken the union nut, and disconnect the feed pipe from the pump; be prepared for some fluid spillage as the pipe and hose are disconnected. Plug the hose/pipe end and pump unions, to minimise fluid loss and to prevent the entry of dirt into the system.

7 Slacken and remove the power steering pump mounting bolts, and remove the pump from the engine **(see illustration)**.

8 Overhaul of the pump is not possible; if the pump is worn or damaged, it must be renewed.

Refitting

9 Manoeuvre the pump into position, then refit its mounting bolts and tighten them to the specified torque setting where given. Ensure the drive lugs on the rear of the pump engage correctly with the coolant pump drive lugs **(see illustration)**.

29.3 Undo the 3 bolts securing the power steering pump pulley

29.7 Undo the bolts and pull the power steering pump from place

29.9 Ensure the drive lugs (arrowed) engage correctly with the coolant pump lugs

10 Reconnect the feed pipe to the pump, and tighten its union nut to the specified torque.

11 Reconnect the supply hose, and securely tighten its retaining clip.

12 Refit the pulley to the pump, making sure it is the correct way around, and install the mounting bolts.

13 Refit and tension the auxiliary drivebelt as described in Chapter 1, then tighten the pulley retaining bolts to the specified torque setting.

14 Refit the viscous coupling and cooling fan as described in Chapter 3.

15 Bleed the hydraulic system as described in Section 30.

30 Power steering system – bleeding

1 With the engine stopped, top-up the fluid reservoir up to the maximum mark with the specified type of fluid.

2 Have an assistant start the engine, while you keep watch on the fluid level. Be prepared to add more fluid as the engine starts – the fluid level is likely to drop quickly.

3 Once the fluid level has stabilised, warm the engine up to normal operating temperature. Ensure that the front wheels are positioned in the straight-ahead position, then turn the engine off.

4 Check that the power steering fluid level is still up to the maximum mark, topping-up if necessary.

5 Start the engine and allow it idle. During the following procedure, the engine speed must not be raised above idle, and the steering must not be turned.

6 Whilst an assistant turns the steering from lock-to-lock, slowly slacken the bleed screw which is situated on the top of the power steering box assembly. Ensuring that the fluid level in the reservoir remains at the maximum level, allow fluid to seep from the screw, until a steady flow of fluid which is free from air bubbles is seen to be emerging. Once this is so, securely tighten the bleed screw, and mop up all traces of fluid from the top of the steering box.

7 Turn the steering onto full left-hand lock, holding it there for a few seconds, and then onto full right-hand lock; check all steering hose/pipe unions for signs of leakage. **Note:** *Do not hold the steering at full lock for more than 10 seconds at a time, otherwise the hydraulic system may be damaged.*

8 Once all air is removed from the system, stop the engine, and check the fluid level as described in *Weekly checks*.

31 Steering damper – removal and refitting

Removal

1 Apply the handbrake, then jack up the front of the vehicle and support it on axle stands positioned underneath the chassis (see *Jacking and vehicle support*).

2 Slacken and unscrew the retaining nut/bolt securing the damper to the drag link. Free the damper from the drag link **(see illustration)**.

3 Slacken and remove the retaining nut/bolt securing the damper to the chassis **(see illustration)**. Remove the damper from the vehicle.

4 Inspect the damper assembly for signs of wear or damage, and renew if necessary. Inspect the rubber mountings for signs of damage and deterioration, and renew if necessary.

Refitting

5 Refitting is the reverse of removal. Tighten the retaining nuts to the specified torque.

32 Drag link – removal, refitting and adjustment

Removal

1 Apply the handbrake, then jack up the front of the vehicle and support it on axle stands positioned underneath the chassis (see *Jacking and vehicle support*). Remove the right-hand front roadwheel.

2 Position the front wheels in the straight-ahead position, then set the steering lock and remove the ignition key.

3 Undo the nut and bolt, then detach the steering damper from the drag link.

4 Unscrew the nut securing the drag link to the steering box drop arm. If necessary, use a Torx bit in the end of the balljoint shank to counterhold the nut.

5 Using a universal balljoint separator, free the drag link from the drop arm **(see illustration 27.10)**.

6 Repeat paragraphs 4 and 5, and free the drag link from the hub carrier assembly. If necessary, remove the roadwheel to improve access to the balljoint nut. Remove the drag link from underneath the vehicle.

7 Check that the link balljoint(s) move freely, without any sign of roughness. Check also that the balljoint gaiter(s) show no sign of deterioration, and are free from cracks and splits. If any sign of wear or damage is found, the balljoint(s) must be renewed (see Section 33). If the drag link itself is damaged, it must be renewed – do not attempt to straighten it.

Refitting

8 Offer up the drag link, and engage it with the hub carrier and steering box drop arm. Refit the retaining nuts, and tighten them to the specified torque setting.

9 Refit the damper to the drag link, and tighten the nut/bolt to the specified torque.

10 Refit the roadwheel, then lower the vehicle to the ground. Tighten the wheel nuts to the specified torque setting

11 Road test the vehicle, and check that the steering wheel is centralised when the vehicle is driven straight-ahead. If the steering wheel is more than 5° out of position, adjustment should be made by removing the wheel and repositioning it on the column splines. If the wheel is less than 5° out of alignment, adjustment can be made by altering the drag link length as follows.

Adjustment

12 Slacken the threaded adjustment rod clamp bolts on the drag link **(see illustration)**.

13 Adjust the drag link length by screwing the threaded adjustment rod in or out (as applicable):

a) *On right-hand drive models, if the steering wheel was found to be slightly right of centre, shorten the drag link length, and if it was found to be slightly left of centre, extend the drag link length.*

31.2 Remove the nut/bolt (arrowed) securing the damper to the drag link . . .

31.3 . . . and the nut/bolt securing it to the chassis

32.12 Slacken the clamp bolts, and rotate the adjuster rod (arrowed)

b) On left-hand drive models, if the steering
   wheel was found to be slightly right of
   centre, extend the drag link length, and if
   it was found to be slightly left of centre,
   shorten the drag link length.

14 Once the drag link length is correct, tighten
the clamp bolts to their specified torque.

15 Road test the vehicle and, if necessary,
repeat the adjustment procedure.

33 Drag link balljoint/end fitting – removal and refitting

Removal

1 Remove the drag link as described in
Section 32.

2 If the balljoint/end fitting is to be re-used,
use a straight-edge and a scriber, or similar, to
mark its relationship to the drag link.

3 Slacken the clamp bolt, then counting
the **exact** number of turns necessary to do
so, unscrew the balljoint/end fitting from the
threaded adjuster rod.

4 Carefully clean the balljoint/end fitting and
the threaded adjuster rod. Renew the balljoint
if its movement is sloppy or if it is too stiff, if it
is excessively worn, or if it is damaged in any
way; carefully check the stud taper and threads.
If the balljoint gaiter is damaged, the complete
balljoint assembly must be renewed; it is not
possible to obtain the gaiter separately.

Refitting

5 If the original balljoint/end fitting is being
refitted, screw it onto the threaded adjuster
rod by the number of turns noted on removal,
and tighten the clamp bolt to the specified
torque. This should line up the alignment
marks that were made on removal.

6 Refit the drag link as described in
Section 32, and check that the steering wheel
is centralised.

**34.3 Slacken the track rod adjuster clamp
bolts/nuts (arrowed)**

34 Track rod – removal and refitting

Removal

1 Apply the handbrake, then jack up the front
of the vehicle and support it on axle stands
positioned underneath the chassis (see
Jacking and vehicle support). Remove the
front roadwheels.

2 Position the front wheels in the straight-
ahead position, engage the steering lock and
remove the ignition key.

3 Slacken the threaded adjuster rod clamp
bolts/nuts **(see illustration)**.

4 Unscrew the nut securing the track rod to
the left-hand hub carrier.

5 Using a universal balljoint separator, free
the track rod from the hub carrier.

6 Repeat paragraphs 4 and 5, and free the
track rod from the right-hand hub carrier
assembly. Remove the track rod from
underneath the vehicle.

7 Check that the track rod balljoints move
freely, without any sign of roughness. Check
also that the balljoint gaiters show no sign of

deterioration, and are free from cracks and
splits. If any sign of wear or damage is found,
the balljoint(s) must be renewed (see Section
35). If the track rod itself is damaged, it must
be renewed – do not attempt to straighten it.

Refitting

8 Offer up the track rod, and engage it with
the hub carriers. Refit the retaining nuts, and
tighten them to the specified torque setting.

9 Refit the roadwheels, then lower the vehicle
to the ground and tighten the wheel nuts to
the specified torque.

10 Check the front wheel alignment as
described in Section 36.

35 Track rod balljoint – removal and refitting

Removal

1 Jack up the front of the vehicle, and support
it securely on axle stands (see Jacking and
vehicle support). Remove the left-hand front
roadwheel.

2 If the balljoint is to be re-used, use a
straight-edge and a scriber, or similar, to
mark its relationship to the track rod and threaded
adjuster rod.

3 Slacken the threaded adjuster rod clamp
bolts **(see illustration 34.3)**.

4 Unscrew the nut securing the track rod to
the left-hand hub carrier **(see illustration)**.

5 Using a universal balljoint separator,
free the track rod from the hub carrier **(see
illustration)**.

6 Unscrew the balljoint from the threaded
adjuster rod, counting the exact number of
threads to aid refitment.

7 Carefully clean the balljoint and the threaded
adjuster rod threads. Renew the balljoint if
its movement is sloppy or if it is too stiff, if

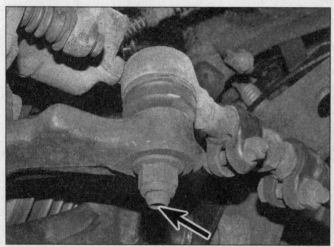

**35.4 Use a Torx bit in the end of the balljoint shank (arrowed) to
counterhold the nut**

**35.5 Use a universal separator tool to detach the track rod end
from the hub carrier**

it is excessively worn, or if it is damaged in any way; carefully check the stud taper and threads. If the balljoint gaiter is damaged, the complete balljoint assembly must be renewed; it is not possible to obtain the gaiter separately.

Refitting

8 If the original balljoint is being refitted, screw it into the threaded adjuster rod by the number of turns noted on removal. This should line up the alignment marks that were made on removal.

9 If a new balljoint is being installed, transfer the clamp from the old balljoint to the new one, then screw the new balljoint onto the threaded adjuster rod so that the balljoint taper is centralised in the hub carrier hole. Ideally, the threaded adjuster rod would be positioned midway in its adjustment range.

10 Refit the balljoint retaining nut and tighten it to the specified torque.

11 Refit the roadwheel, lower the vehicle to the ground, and tighten the roadwheel nuts to the specified torque.

12 Prior to using the vehicle, check the front wheel alignment as described in Section 36. Tighten the track rod clamp bolts to the specified torque.

36 Wheel alignment and steering angles – general information

1 Accurate front wheel alignment is essential for precise steering and handling, and for even tyre wear. Before carrying out any checking or adjusting operations, make sure that the tyres are correctly inflated, that all steering and suspension joints and linkages are in sound condition, and that the wheels are not buckled or distorted, particularly around the rims. It will also be necessary to have the vehicle positioned on flat, level ground, with enough space to push the car backwards and forwards through about half its length.

2 Front wheel alignment consists of four factors **(see illustration)**:

Camber is the angle at which the roadwheels are set from the vertical, when viewed from the front or rear of the vehicle. Positive camber is the angle (in degrees) that the wheels are tilted outwards at the top from the vertical.

Castor is the angle between the steering axis and a vertical line when viewed from each side of the vehicle. Positive castor is indicated when the steering axis is inclined towards the rear of the vehicle at its upper end.

Steering axis inclination is the angle, when viewed from the front or rear of the vehicle, between the vertical and an imaginary line drawn between the upper and lower front suspension strut mountings.

Toe setting is the amount by which the distance between the front inside edges of the roadwheels differs from that between the rear inside edges, when measured at hub height. If the distance between the front edges is less than at the rear, the wheels are said to toe-in. If it is greater than at the rear, the wheels are said to toe-out. These days, the toe setting dimensions are given as degrees deviation from the central axis of the vehicle.

3 Camber, castor and steering axis inclination are set during manufacture, and are not adjustable. Unless the vehicle has suffered accident damage, or there is gross wear in the suspension mountings or joints, it can be assumed that these settings are correct. If for any reason it is believed that they are not correct, the task of checking them should be left to a Land Rover dealer, who will have the necessary special equipment needed to measure the small angles involved.

4 It is, however, within the scope of the home mechanic to check and adjust the front wheel toe setting. To do this, a tracking gauge must first be obtained, usually from motoring accessory/parts centres. The type of gauge needed is known as a scuff plate, and measures the actual position of the contact surface of the tyre, in relation to the road surface, with the vehicle in motion. This is achieved by pushing or driving the front tyre over a plate, which then moves slightly according to the scuff of the tyre, and shows this movement on a scale.

5 Many tyre specialists will also check toe settings free, or for a nominal charge.

6 Make sure that the steering is in the straight-ahead position when making measurements. The measurement will only be accurate if the vehicle is unladen.

7 If adjustment is necessary, apply the handbrake, then jack up the front of the vehicle and support it securely on axle stands. Slacken the track rod threaded adjuster rod clamp bolts, then rotate the adjuster rod to alter the length of the track rod (as necessary); shortening the track rod will reduce toe-in/increase toe-out.

8 When the setting is correct, tighten both the clamp bolts to the specified torque setting.

9 Recheck the toe setting and, if necessary, repeat the adjustment procedure.

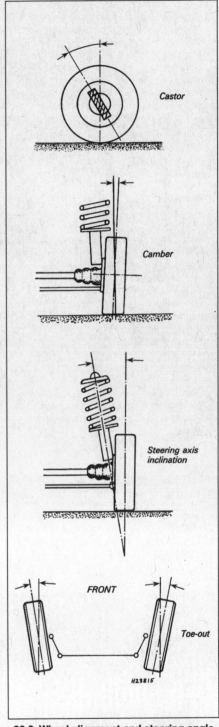

36.2 Wheel alignment and steering angle measurements

Chapter 12
Bodywork and fittings

Contents

Section number

Body control unit (BCU) – removal and refitting 17
Body exterior fittings – removal and refitting 22
Bonnet – removal, refitting and adjustment 8
Bonnet lock – removal and refitting 10
Bonnet release cable – removal and refitting 9
Central locking components – removal and refitting 17
Centre console – removal and refitting 27
Door – removal, refitting and adjustment 11
Door handle and lock components – removal, refitting and
adjustment 13
Door inner trim panel – removal and refitting 12
Door window glass and regulator – removal and refitting 14
Electric window components – removal and refitting 18
Exterior mirrors and associated components –
removal and refitting 19
Facia panel assembly – removal and refitting 28

Section number

Front bumper – removal and refitting 6
General information 1
Interior trim – removal and refitting 26
Maintenance – bodywork and underframe 2
Maintenance – upholstery and carpets 3
Major body damage – repair 5
Minor body damage – repair 4
Radiator grille – removal and refitting 29
Rear bumper – removal and refitting 7
Seat belt components – removal and refitting 25
Seat positioning motors – removal and refitting 24
Seats – removal and refitting 23
Sunroof – general information and component renewal 21
Tailgate – removal and refitting 15
Tailgate lock components – removal and refitting 16
Windscreen, tailgate and fixed windows – general information 20

Degrees of difficulty

Easy, suitable for novice with little experience	**Fairly easy,** suitable for beginner with some experience	**Fairly difficult,** suitable for competent DIY mechanic	**Difficult,** suitable for experienced DIY mechanic	**Very difficult,** suitable for expert DIY or professional

Specifications

Torque wrench settings	Nm	lbf ft
Rear bumper retaining bolts	45	33
Seat belt mounting nuts and bolts:		
Inertia reel bolt	50	37
Lower anchorage bolt	32	24
Front seat belt stalk (pretensioner)	32	24
Upper anchorage bolt	32	24
Seat mounting Torx bolts	45	33

1 General information

The bodyshell and panels are mainly zinc-coated steel, and possess excellent corrosion resistance properties. The bonnet, rear quarter panel, tailgate, roof panel and front wings are made from aluminium. Most components are welded together, but some use is made of structural adhesives.

Extensive use is made of plastic materials, mainly on the interior but also in exterior components. The front and rear bumpers are injection-moulded from a synthetic material, which is very strong and yet light. Plastic components such as wheel arch liners are fitted to the underside of the vehicle, to improve the body's resistance to corrosion.

2 Maintenance – bodywork and underframe

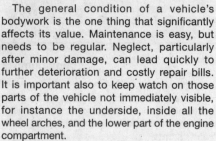

The general condition of a vehicle's bodywork is the one thing that significantly affects its value. Maintenance is easy, but needs to be regular. Neglect, particularly after minor damage, can lead quickly to further deterioration and costly repair bills. It is important also to keep watch on those parts of the vehicle not immediately visible, for instance the underside, inside all the wheel arches, and the lower part of the engine compartment.

The basic maintenance routine for the bodywork is washing – preferably with a lot of water, from a hose. This will remove all the loose solids which may have stuck to the vehicle. It is important to flush these off in such a way as to prevent grit from scratching the finish. The wheel arches and underframe need washing in the same way, to remove any accumulated mud, which will retain moisture and tend to encourage rust. Paradoxically enough, the best time to clean the underframe and wheel arches is in wet weather, when the mud is thoroughly wet and soft. In very wet weather, the underframe is usually cleaned of large accumulations automatically, and this is a good time for inspection.

Periodically, except on vehicles with a wax-based underbody protective coating, it is a good idea to have the whole of the underframe of the vehicle steam-cleaned, engine compartment included, so that a thorough inspection can be carried out to see what minor repairs and renovations are necessary. Steam-cleaning is available at many garages, and is necessary for the removal of the accumulation of oily grime, which sometimes is allowed to become thick in certain areas. If steam-cleaning facilities are not available, there are some excellent grease solvents available which can be brush-applied; the dirt can then be simply hosed off. Note that these methods should not be used on vehicles with wax-based underbody protective coating, or the coating will be removed. Such vehicles should be inspected annually, preferably just prior to Winter, when the underbody should be washed down, and any damage to the wax coating repaired. Ideally, a completely fresh coat should be applied. It would also be worth considering the use of such wax-based protection for injection into door panels, sills, box sections, etc, as an additional safeguard against rust damage, where such protection is not provided by the vehicle manufacturer.

After washing paintwork, wipe off with a chamois leather to give an unspotted clear finish. A coat of clear protective wax polish will give added protection against chemical pollutants in the air. If the paintwork sheen has dulled or oxidised, use a cleaner/polisher combination to restore the brilliance of the shine. This requires a little effort, but such dulling is usually caused because regular washing has been neglected. Care needs to be taken with metallic paintwork, as special non-abrasive cleaner/polisher is required to avoid damage to the finish. Always check that the door and ventilator opening drain holes and pipes are completely clear, so that water can be drained out. Brightwork should be treated in the same way as paintwork. Windscreens and windows can be kept clear of the smeary film which often appears, by the use of proprietary glass cleaner. Never use any form of wax or other body or chromium polish on glass.

3 Maintenance – upholstery and carpets

Mats and carpets should be brushed or vacuum-cleaned regularly, to keep them free of grit. If they are badly stained, remove them from the vehicle for scrubbing or sponging, and make quite sure they are dry before refitting. Seats and interior trim panels can be kept clean by wiping with a damp cloth. If they do become stained (which can be more apparent on light-coloured upholstery), use a little liquid detergent and a soft nail brush to scour the grime out of the grain of the material. Do not forget to keep the headlining clean in the same way as the upholstery. When using liquid cleaners inside the vehicle, do not over-wet the surfaces being cleaned. Excessive damp could get into the seams and padded interior, causing stains, offensive odours or even rot.

4 Minor body damage – repair

Minor scratches

If the scratch is very superficial, and does not penetrate to the metal of the bodywork, repair is very simple. Lightly rub the area of the scratch with a paintwork renovator, or a very fine cutting paste, to remove loose paint from the scratch and to clear the surrounding bodywork of wax polish. Rinse the area with clean water.

In the case of metallic paint, the most commonly-found 'scratches' are not in the paint, but in the lacquer top coat, and appear white. If care is taken , these can sometimes be rendered less obvious by very careful use of paintwork renovator (which would otherwise not be used on metallic paintwork); otherwise, repair of these scratches can be achieved by applying lacquer with a fine brush.

Apply touch-up paint to the scratch using a thin paintbrush; continue to apply thin layers of paint until the surface of the paint in the scratch is level with the surrounding paintwork. Allow the new paint at least two weeks to harden, then blend it into the surrounding paintwork by rubbing the paintwork in the scratch area with a paintwork renovator or a very fine cutting paste. Finally, apply wax polish.

Where the scratch has penetrated right through to the metal of the bodywork, a different repair technique is required. Remove any loose paint, etc from the bottom of the scratch with a penknife. Using a rubber or nylon applicator, fill the scratch with bodystopper paste. If required, this paste can be mixed with cellulose thinners to provide a very thin paste which is ideal for filling narrow scratches. Before the stopper-paste in the scratch hardens, wrap a piece of smooth cotton rag around the top of a finger. Dip the finger in cellulose thinners, and then quickly sweep it across the surface of the stopper-paste in the scratch; this will ensure that the surface of the stopper-paste is lightly hollowed. The scratch can now be painted over as described earlier in this Section.

Dents

The alloy body panels on the Land Rover are easier to work on than steel, and minor dents or creases can be beaten out fairly easily. However, if the damaged area is quite large, prolonged hammering will cause the metal to harden; to avoid the possibility of cracking, it must be softened or 'annealed'. This can be done easily with a gas blowlamp, but great care is required to avoid actually melting the metal. The blowlamp must always be kept moving in a circular pattern, whilst being held a respectable distance from the metal.

One method of checking when the alloy is hot enough is to rub down the surface to be annealed, and then apply a thin film of oil over it. The blowlamp should be played over the rear side of the oiled surface, until the oil evaporates and the surface is dry. Turn off the blowlamp, and allow the metal to cool naturally; the treated areas will now be softened, and it will be possible to work it with a hammer or mallet. After panel-beating, the damaged section should be rubbed down and painted as described later in this Section.

When deep denting of the vehicle's bodywork has taken place, the first task is to pull the dent out until the affected bodywork almost attains its original shape. There is little point in trying to restore the original shape completely, as the metal in the damaged area will have stretched on impact, and cannot be reshaped to its original contour. It is better to bring the level of the dent up to a point which is about 3 mm below the level of the surrounding bodywork. In cases where the dent is very shallow anyway, it is not worth trying to pull it out at all.

If the underside of the dent is accessible, it can be hammered out gently from behind using the method described earlier.

Should the dent be in a section of the bodywork which has a double skin, or some other factor making it inaccessible from behind, a different technique is called for. Drill several small holes through the metal inside the dent area, particularly in the deeper sections. Then screw long self-tapping screws into the holes just sufficiently for them to gain a good purchase in the metal. Now the dent can be pulled out by pulling on the protruding heads of the screws with a pair of pliers.

The next stage of the repair is the removal of the paint from the damaged area, and from an inch or so of the surrounding 'sound' bodywork.

Note: *On no account should coarse abrasives be used on aluminium panels in order to remove paint. The use of a wire brush or abrasive on a power drill for example, will cause deep scoring of the metal and in extreme cases, penetrate the thickness of the relatively soft aluminium alloy.*

Removal of paint is best achieved by applying paint remover to the area, allowing it to act on the paintwork for the specified time, and then removing the softened paint with a wood or nylon scraper. This method may have to be repeated in order to remove all traces of paint. A good method of removing small stubborn traces of paint is to rub the area with a nylon scouring pad soaked in thinners or paint remover. **Note:** *If it is necessary to use this method, always wear rubber gloves to protect the hands from burns from the paint remover. It is also advisable to wear eye protection, as any paint remover that gets into the eyes will cause severe inflammation, or worse.*

Finally, remove all traces of paint and remover by washing the area with plenty of clean fresh water.

To complete the preparations for filling, score the surface of the bare metal with a screwdriver or the tang of a file, or alternatively, drill small holes in the affected area. This will provide a really good 'key' for the filler paste.

To complete the repair, see the Section on filling and respraying.

Holes or gashes

Remove all the paint from the affected area, and from an inch or so of the surrounding 'sound' bodywork, using the method described in the previous Section. With the paint removed, you will be able to gauge the severity of the damage, and therefore decide whether to renew the whole panel (if this is possible) or to repair the affected area. It is often quicker and more satisfactory to fit a new panel than to attempt to repair large areas of damage.

Remove all fittings from the affected area, except those which will act as a guide to the original shape of the damaged bodywork (eg. headlight shells, etc). Then, using tin snips or a hacksaw blade, remove all loose metal and other metal badly affected by damage. Hammer the edges of the hole inwards, in order to create a slight depression for the filler paste.

Before filling can take place, it will be necessary to block the hole in some way. This can be achieved by the use of zinc gauze or aluminium tape.

Zinc gauze is probably the best material to use for a large hole. Cut a piece to the approximate size and shape of the hole to be filled, then position it in the hole so that its edges are below the level of the surrounding bodywork. It can be retained in position by several blobs of filler paste around its periphery.

Aluminium tape should be used for small or very narrow holes. Pull a piece off the roll and trim it to the approximate size and shape required, then pull off the backing paper (if used) and stick the tape over the hole; it can be overlapped if the thickness of one piece is insufficient. Burnish down the edges of the tape with the handle of a screwdriver or similar, to ensure that the tape is securely attached to the metal underneath.

Filling and respraying

Before using this Section, see the Section on dent, deep scratch, hole and gash repairs.

Many types of bodyfiller are available, but generally speaking, those proprietary kits which contain a tin of filler paste and a tube of resin hardener are best for this type of repair. A wide, flexible plastic or nylon applicator will be found invaluable for imparting a smooth and well-contoured finish to the surface of the filler.

Mix up a little filler on a clean piece of card or board. Use the hardener sparingly (follow the maker's instructions on the packet) otherwise the filler will set rapidly.

Using the applicator, apply the filler paste to the prepared area; draw the applicator across the surface of the filler to achieve the correct contour, and to level the filler surfaces. As soon as a contour that approximates the correct one is achieved, stop working the paste; if you carry on too long, the paste will become sticky and begin to 'pick-up' on the applicator. Continue to add thin layers of filler paste at twenty-minute intervals until the level of the filler is just 'proud' of the surrounding bodywork.

Once the filler has hardened, excess can be removed using a metal plane or file. From then on, progressively finer grades of abrasive paper should be used, starting with a 40-grade production paper, and finishing with a 400-grade wet-or-dry paper. Always wrap the abrasive paper around a flat rubber, cork, or wooden block, otherwise the surface of the filler will not be completely flat. During the smoothing of the filler surface, the wet-or-dry paper should be periodically rinsed in water. This will ensure that a very fine smooth finish is imparted to the filler at the final stage.

At this stage, the 'dent' should be surrounded by a ring of bare metal, which in turn should be encircled by the finely 'feathered' edge of the good paintwork. Rinse the repair with clean water, until all the dust produced by the rubbing-down operation is gone.

Spray the whole area with a light coat of grey primer, this will show up any imperfections in the surface of the filler. If at all possible, it is recommended that an etch-primer is used on untreated alloy surfaces, otherwise the primer may not be keyed sufficiently, and may subsequently flake off. Repair imperfections with fresh filler paste or bodystopper and once more, smooth the surface with abrasive paper. Repeat the spray-and-repair procedures until you are satisfied that the surface of the filler, and the feathered edge of the paintwork, is perfect. Clean the repair area with clean water, and allow it to dry fully.

The repair area is now ready for spraying. Paint spraying must be carried out in a warm, dry, windless and dust-free atmosphere. This condition can be created artificially if you have access to a large indoor working area, but if you are forced to work in the open, you will have to pick your day very carefully. If you are working indoors, dousing the floor in the work area with water will 'lay' the dust which would otherwise be in the atmosphere. If the repair is confined to one body panel, mask off the surrounding panels; this will help to minimise the effects of a slight mis-match in paint colours. Bodywork fittings will also need to be masked off. Use genuine masking tape and several thickness of newspaper for the masking operation.

Before commencing to spray, agitate the aerosol can thoroughly, then spray a test area (an old tin, or similar) until the technique is mastered. Cover the repair area with a thick coat of primer; the thickness should be built up using several thin layers of paint, rather than one thick one. Using 400-grade wet-or-dry paper, rub down the surface of the primer until it is really smooth. Whilst doing this, the work area should be thoroughly doused with water, and the wet-or-dry paper periodically rinsed in water. Allow to dry before spraying on more paint.

Spray on the top coat, again building up the thickness by using several thin layers of paint. Start spraying at the top of the repair area and then, using a side-to-side motion, work downwards until the whole repair area and about 50 mm of the surrounding original paintwork is covered. Remove all masking material 10 to 15 minutes after spraying on the final coat of paint.

Allow the new paint at least two weeks to harden, then, using a paintwork renovator or a very fine cutting paste, blend the edges of the paint into the existing paintwork. Finally, apply wax polish.

Plastic components

With the use of more and more plastic body components by the vehicle manufacturers (eg bumpers. spoilers, and in some cases major body panels), rectification of more serious damage to such items has become a matter of either entrusting repair work to a specialist in this field, or renewing complete components. Repair of such damage by the DIY owner is not really feasible, owing to the cost of the equipment and materials required for effecting such repairs. The basic technique involves making a groove along the line of the crack in the plastic, using a rotary burr in a power drill. The damaged part is then welded back together, using a hot-air gun to heat up and fuse a plastic filler rod into the groove. Any excess plastic is then removed, and the area rubbed down to a smooth finish. It is important that a filler rod of the correct plastic is used, as body components can be made of a variety of different types (eg polycarbonate, ABS, polypropylene).

Damage of a less serious nature (abrasions, minor cracks etc) can be repaired by the DIY owner using a two-part epoxy filler repair material. Once mixed in equal proportions, or applied directly from the tube, this is used in similar fashion to the bodywork filler used on metal panels. The filler is usually cured in twenty to thirty minutes, ready for sanding and painting.

If the owner is renewing a complete component himself, or if he has repaired it with epoxy filler, he will be left with the problem of finding a suitable paint for finishing which is compatible with the type of plastic used. At one time, the use of a universal paint was not possible, owing to the complex range of plastics encountered in body component applications. Standard paints, generally speaking, will not bond to plastic or rubber satisfactorily. However, it is now possible to obtain a plastic body parts finishing kit which consists of a preprimer treatment, a primer and coloured top coat. Full instructions are normally supplied with a kit, but basically, the method of use is to first apply the preprimer to the component concerned, and allow it to dry for up to 30 minutes. Then the primer is applied, and left to dry for about an hour before finally applying the special-coloured top coat. The result is a correctly-coloured component, where the paint will flex with the plastic or rubber, a property that standard paint does not normally possess.

5 Major body damage – repair

Where serious damage has occurred, or large areas need renewal due to neglect, it means that complete new panels will need welding in, and this is best left to professionals. If the damage is due to impact, it will also be necessary to check completely the alignment of the bodyshell, and this can only be carried out accurately by a Land Rover dealer using special jigs. If the body is left misaligned, it is primarily dangerous, as the car will not handle properly. Secondly, uneven stresses will be imposed on the steering, suspension and possibly transmission, causing abnormal wear, or complete failure, particularly to such items as the tyres.

6 Front bumper – removal and refitting

Removal

1 Undo the 7 screws/nuts each side (vehicles from 2003 model year have 9 screws each side) securing the wheel arch liner extensions to the bumper valance and wheel arch liner **(see illustration)**.
2 Disconnect the front foglamps wiring plugs.
3 Slacken the nut securing each of the rubber mountings to the ends of the bumper **(see illustration)**.
4 With the aid of an assistant, support the bumper, then slacken and remove the 2 nuts each side securing bumper to its chassis 'crush cans' **(see illustration)**.
5 Undo the 3 bolts on the underside of the bumper, and manoeuvre it from the vehicle. Disconnect any hoses as the bumper is withdrawn.

Refitting

6 Refitting is a reversal of removal.

7 Rear bumper – removal and refitting

Removal

1 Remove both rear bumper-mounted tail lamps as described in Chapter 13, Section 7. Release the wiring harness from any retaining clips in the lamp recesses.
2 On models with parking distance control, remove the right-hand side trim panel from the luggage compartment floor, and disconnect the harness multiplug.
3 With the aid of an assistant, support the bumper, then slacken and remove the bolts securing bumper to its chassis mounting brackets, and recover the mounting plates **(see illustration)**. Manoeuvre the bumper assembly away from the vehicle.

Refitting

4 Refitting is the reverse of removal, tightening the retaining bolts to their specified torque.

6.1 Wheel arch liner extension upper screws (arrowed)

6.3 Undo the nut (arrowed) securing the bumper rubber mounting

6.4 Undo the two nuts each side securing the bumper to the 'crush cans'

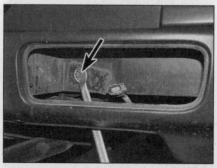

7.3 Undo the bolt (arrowed) in the bumper light aperture each side

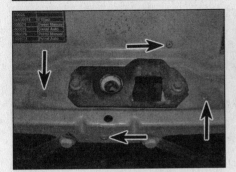

9.3 Drill out the rivets (arrowed) securing the lock shield

9.6 Undo the release handle nuts (arrowed)

9.7 Release the outer cable from the handle bracket

8 Bonnet – removal, refitting and adjustment

Removal

1 Open the bonnet, and have an assistant support it. Using a pencil or felt tip pen, mark the outline position of each bonnet hinge relative to the bonnet, to use as a guide on refitting.
2 Disconnect the windscreen washer tube at the elbow joint.
3 Undo the bonnet retaining bolts and, with the help of an assistant, carefully lift the bonnet clear.
4 Inspect the bonnet hinges for signs of wear or damage; the hinges are bolted in position, and can easily be renewed.

Refitting and adjustment

5 With the aid of an assistant, offer up the bonnet, and loosely fit the retaining bolts. Align the hinges with the marks made on removal, then tighten the retaining bolts securely.
6 Close the bonnet, and check for alignment with the adjacent panels. If necessary, slacken the bonnet bolts and realign the bonnet to suit. Once the bonnet is correctly aligned, securely tighten the bolts.
7 Once the bonnet is correctly aligned, check that the bonnet fastens and releases in a satisfactory manner.

9 Bonnet release cable – removal and refitting

Removal

1 Remove the front grille as described in Section 29.
2 On vehicles up to 2003 model year, pull the left-hand headlight from its mountings, and disconnect the wiring plugs (see Chapter 13, Section 7).
3 On all models, drill out the 4 rivets securing the lock shield to the bonnet slam panel, and remove the shield **(see illustration)**.

4 Disconnect the bonnet release cable inner and outer from the lock.
5 Undo the 4 fasteners and remove the lower facia panel from the passenger's side footwell.
6 Undo the 2 retaining nuts and detach the release handle from the vehicle body **(see illustration)**.
7 Disconnect the cable from the release handle **(see illustration)**.
8 Pull the sound insulation material from the engine compartment bulkhead, and prise the cable grommet from position.
9 Check along the length of the cable, and release it from any retaining clips.
10 Tie a length of string to the cable in the passenger's compartment, then pull the cable through from the bonnet lock end.
11 Once the cable end appears, untie the string and leave it in position in the vehicle; the string can then be used to draw the new cable back into position. Remove the grommet from the cable.

Refitting

12 Fit the grommet to the new cable.
13 Tie the string to the end of the cable, and use the string to draw the bonnet release cable through from engine compartment. Once the cable is through, untie the string.
14 The remainder of refitting is a reversal of removal.

10 Bonnet lock – removal and refitting

Removal

1 Remove the front radiator grille as described in Section 29.
2 Drill out the rivets securing the tamperproof shield to the underside of the bonnet lock **(see illustration 9.3)**.
3 Disconnect the cable from the underside of the lock.
4 Using a suitable marker pen, draw around the outline of the bonnet lock top plate and adjusting plates. These marks can then be used as a guide on refitting.

5 Undo the two bolts securing the bonnet lock to the slam panel.

Refitting

6 Refitting is the reverse of the removal procedure, using the alignment marks made prior to removal. Prior to refitting the radiator grille, check the operation of the release mechanism. Adjustment of the cable can be made by either slackening the clamp and adjusting the inner cable or, alternately, by releasing the outer cable retaining clip and repositioning the clip on the cable.

11 Door – removal, refitting and adjustment

Removal

Front door

1 Release the fasteners and remove the A-pillar lower trim panel.
2 Disconnect the wiring connectors, then release the rubber wiring harness grommet from the door pillar. Withdraw the wiring from the pillar, so that it is free to be removed with the door assembly.
3 Using a hammer and suitable punch, carefully tap out the roll-pin securing the check link to the door pillar **(see illustration)**. Discard the roll-pin – a new one should be used on refitting.
4 Prise off the C-clips from each of the

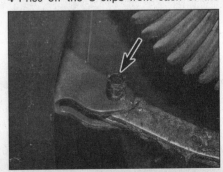

11.3 Tap out the check link roll-pin (arrowed)

11.4 Prise off the hinge C-clips (arrowed)

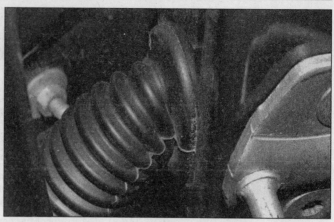

11.7 Release the rubber sleeve from the door pillar

hinge pins then, with the aid of an assistant, carefully lift the door upwards and away from the vehicle (see illustration). If the C-clips show signs of distortion, renew them.

5 Examine the hinges for signs of wear or damage. If renewal is necessary, mark the outline of the original hinge on the door/pillar, then slacken and remove the retaining bolts and remove the hinge brackets. Note the correct fitted location of the shim(s) and spacer plates which are positioned behind them. Fit the new brackets, making sure that the shim(s) and spacer plates are correctly arranged, and refit the retaining bolts. Align the brackets with the marks made prior to removal, and securely tighten the retaining bolts.

Rear door

6 Remove the B-pillar lower trim panel as described in Section 26.

7 Disconnect the wiring connectors, release the wiring harness rubber sleeve from the door pillar, then withdraw the wiring (see illustration).

8 Using a hammer and suitable punch, carefully tap out the roll-pin securing the check link to the door pillar. Discard the roll-pin – a new one must be fitted.

9 Prise off the C-clips from each of the hinge pins then, with the aid of an assistant, carefully lift the door upwards and away from the

vehicle. If the C-clips show signs of distortion, renew them.

10 Inspect the hinges as described above in paragraph 5.

Refitting

Front door

11 Apply a smear of multi-purpose grease to the hinge pivots then, with the aid of an assistant, manoeuvre the door back into position. Secure the door in position by fitting a C-clip to each of the hinge pins.

12 Align the check link with its mounting bracket, and secure it in position with a new roll-pin.

13 Feed the wiring back through the pillar, reconnect the wiring connectors, and seat the rubber grommet back in the door pillar.

14 Refit the footwell side panel, and secure it in position.

15 Adjust the door position as described below.

Rear door

16 Apply a smear of multi-purpose grease to the hinge pivots then, with the aid of an assistant, manoeuvre the door back into position. Secure the door in position by fitting a C-clip to each of the hinge pins.

17 Align the check link with its mounting bracket, and secure it in position with a new roll-pin.

18 Reconnect the wiring connectors, feed

the wiring back into the door pillar, and seat the wiring grommet in position.

19 Adjust the door position as described below.

Adjustment

20 Some vertical adjustment of the doors can be achieved by slackening the hinge retaining bolts and repositioning the hinge/door.

21 Some front-to-rear adjustment of the door position can be achieved by adding/removing shims between the door and hinge bracket. To do this, loosen (do not remove) the hinge retaining bolts, then add/remove the relevant number of shims; the shims are slotted to allow the thickness to be adjusted without removing the door. Once the door is correctly positioned, securely tighten the hinge retaining bolts.

22 Door closure may be adjusted by altering the position of the door lock striker on the body. Slacken the striker, reposition it as required, then securely retighten it. The striker can also be adjusted by adding/removing shims from behind it.

---

12 Door inner trim panel – removal and refitting

Note: It is a good idea to obtain a few trim panel retaining clips before starting, as they are often broken in the course of removal, or will be found to have broken during previous removal attempts.

Removal

Front door

1 Undo the 2 retaining screws, accessible through the pull handle (see illustration). Note that the handle is part of the trim panel.

2 Undo the retaining screw, and remove the handle surround from the door panel (see illustration).

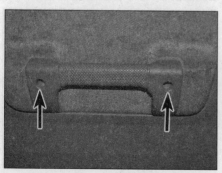

12.1 Undo the 2 screws accessible through the pull handle (arrowed)

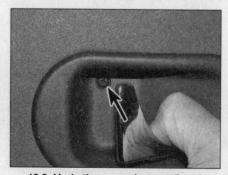

12.2 Undo the screw (arrowed) and remove the handle surround

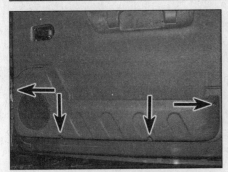

12.3 Undo the 4 screws (arrowed) through the storage pocket

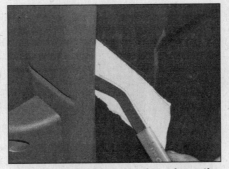

12.4a Use a flat-bladed tool to release the trim panel studs. Note the cardboard to protect the paintwork

12.4b Lift the trim panel over the lock button, and away from the door

12.5 Disconnect the electric window switch as the handle surround is withdrawn

13.2 Drill out the 3 rivets securing the interior handle (arrowed)

13.3 Detach the inner cable from the handle lever

3 Front door only: undo the 4 screws accessible through the storage pocket **(see illustration)**.
4 Release the door trim panel studs, working around the outside of the panel, carefully levering between the panel and door with a suitable flat-bladed screwdriver. When all the studs are released, slide the panel upwards and away from the door, disconnecting the speaker wiring connectors as they become accessible **(see illustrations)**.

Rear door

5 Remove the panel as described above in paragraphs 1 to 4, noting that, on models with electric rear windows, the switch wiring plug must be disconnected as the handle surround is removed **(see illustration)**.

Refitting

6 Refitting is a reverse of the removal

procedure. Prior to refitting, examine the panel retaining clips for signs of damage – renew any broken clips. On refitting, do not forget to align the inner lock button with its guide in the top of the trim panel.

13 Door handle and lock components – removal, refitting and adjustment

Removal

Front door interior handle

1 Remove the door inner trim panel as described in Section 12.
2 Drill out the pop rivets securing the door handle to the door **(see illustration)**.

3 Turn the handle assembly over and detach the operating cable from the handle **(see illustration)**.
4 Withdraw the handle assembly from the door.

Front door exterior handle

5 Remove the door inner trim panel as described in Section 12.
6 Using a sharp knife, carefully release the plastic sealing sheet from the adhesive bead and remove the sheet.
7 Pivot the clip away from the rod, then release the control rod from the exterior handle **(see illustration)**.
8 Undo the Torx screw securing the handle to the door, and open then handle, pull the rear edge of the handle outwards, then manoeuvre the front edge from the door **(see illustrations)**.

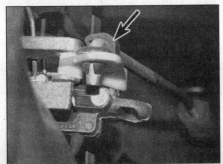

13.7 Pivot the clip (arrowed) sideways, then pull the control rod from the handle

13.8a Undo the Torx screw (arrowed) . . .

13.8b . . . then pull the rear edge of the handle from the door

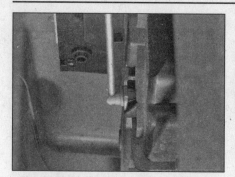

13.12 Unclip the lock button control rod

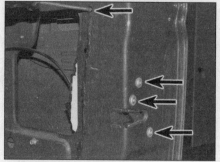

13.15 Undo the 3 Torx screws and 1 cross-head screw (arrowed)

13.16 Disconnect the release cable from the door lock

Front lock cylinder

9 It would appear that, at the time of writing, the lock cylinder is not available as a separate part. If defective, the lock cylinder and exterior handle must be renewed as a complete assembly.

Front door lock

10 Remove the front door drop glass as described in Section 14.

11 Pivot the clip away from the rod, then detach the exterior handle control rod (see illustration 13.7).

12 Pull the lock button control rod from the clip on the lock arm (see illustration).

13 Disconnect the wiring plug from the lock assembly.

14 Undo the Torx screw, open the handle, push the rear of the exterior handle forwards, and pull the rear of the exterior

handle from the door (see illustration 13.8a and 13.8b).

15 Undo the 3 Torx screws and 1 cross-head screw securing the lock assembly to the door (see illustration).

16 Manoeuvre the lock assembly downwards, and out the lower section of the door. Disconnect the release cable from the lock as it is withdrawn (see illustration).

Rear interior door handle

17 Remove the door inner trim panel as described in Section 12.

18 Drill out the pop rivets, and pull the handle from the door (see illustration).

19 Detach the operating cable from the handle assembly (see illustration).

Rear exterior door handle

20 Remove the door inner trim panel as described in Section 12.

21 Peel the plastic sealing sheet away from the door to gain access to the door lock components.

22 Release the handle operating rod from the lock assembly by pulling it from the retaining clip (see illustration).

23 Unscrew the Torx screw, push the rear of the handle forward and pull the rear edge from the door. Manoeuvre the handle from the door and disconnect the control rod (see illustrations).

Rear door lock

24 Remove the rear door drop glass as described in Section 14.

25 Release the exterior handle control rod from the lock by pressing it from the clip (see illustration 13.22).

26 Release the retaining clip, and detach

13.18 Drill out the 3 rivets securing the rear door interior handle (arrowed)

13.19 Unclip the release cable from the interior handle

13.22 Pull the exterior handle operating rod from place

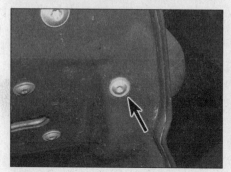

13.23a Undo the Torx screw (arrowed) . . .

13.23b . . . and pull the rear edge of the handle from the door

13.23c Note how the front edge of the handle engages with the door

13.26 Lever the lock button control rod from the clip

13.28a Undo the lock retaining Torx screws (arrowed)

13.28b Open the flap and disconnect the release cable

the interior button rod from the lock **(see illustration)**.

27 Disconnect the wiring plug from the lock assembly.

28 Undo the 3 Torx screws securing the lock assembly to the door frame, and manoeuvre the assembly downwards and out through the lower aperture in the door. Open the flap and disconnect the release cable as the assembly is withdrawn **(see illustrations)**.

Refitting

29 Refitting is the reverse of the removal sequence, noting the following points:
 a) Ensure that all link rods are securely held in position by their retaining clips.

b) Apply grease to all lock and link rod pivot points.
c) Before installing the relevant trim panel, thoroughly check the operation of all the door lock handles and the central locking system.

14 Door window glass and regulator – removal and refitting

Removal

1 Fully raise the window, and use tape to securing it in position. Remove the door inner trim panel as described in Section 12.
2 Peel the plastic sealing sheet away from

the door, to gain access to the door lock components. Proceed as described under the relevant sub-heading.

Front door drop glass
3 Remove the exterior mirror as described in Section 19.
4 Remove the inner rubber waistline sealing strip from the door **(see illustration)**.
5 Release the 2 clips and remove the outer waistline sealing strip from the door **(see illustrations)**.
6 Lower the window to access and slacken the 2 bolts securing the glass to the window regulator. Slide the regulator guide rearwards, and over the head of the bolts **(see illustrations)**. Tape the window to the door frame to prevent it falling.

14.4 Prise up the inner rubber waistline sealing strip

14.5a Release the clip at each end . . .

14.5b . . . and prise up the outer waistline sealing strip

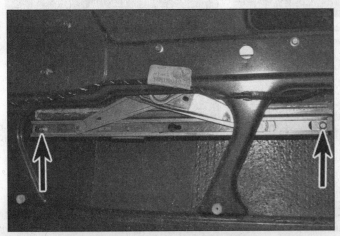

14.6a Slacken the 2 bolts (arrowed) . . .

14.6b . . . and slide the regulator guide over the heads of the bolts

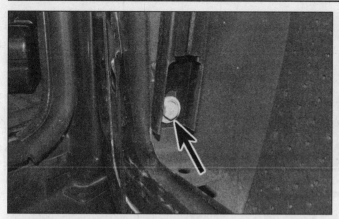

14.7a The window frame is secured by a bolt in the front lower corner (arrowed) . . .

14.7b . . . one in the rear lower corner (arrowed) . . .

14.7c . . . a Torx screw at the rear edge (arrowed) . . .

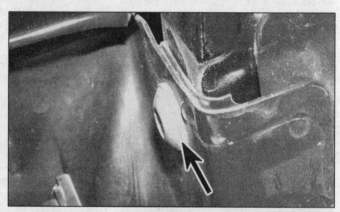

14.7d . . . a Torx screw at the front edge (arrowed) . . .

14.7e . . . and a bolt below the mirror mounting

14.7f Lift the frame, complete with glass, from the door

14.9 Prise up the inner rubber waistline sealing strip

14.10a Release the clip at each end . . .

14.10b . . . and prise up the outer waistline sealing strip

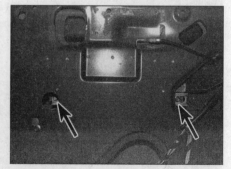

14.11 Lower the window to access the regulator guide bolts (arrowed)

7 Remove the 5 retaining bolts, and remove the window frame from the door, complete with glass **(see illustrations)**.
8 With the assembly on a bench, remove the tape, and separate the glass and frame.

Rear door drop glass

9 Remove the inner rubber waistline sealing strip from the door **(see illustration)**.
10 Release the 2 clips and remove the outer waistline sealing strip from the door **(see illustrations)**.
11 Temporarily reconnect the window switch, or refit the regulator handle, and lower the window to gain access, then slacken the 2 bolts securing the glass to the window regulator, and slide the regulator guide to one side and over the head of the bolts **(see illustration)**. Tape the glass to the frame to prevent the window dropping.
12 Remove the 6 retaining bolts, and remove the window frame from the door, complete with glass **(see illustrations)**.
13 With the assembly on a bench, remove the tape, and separate the glass and frame.

Front door window regulator

14 Ensure that the window is fully lowered, then securely tape the window glass to its frame, to prevent the window dropping when the regulator is removed.
15 Slacken the 2 bolts securing the glass to the regulator, and lift the regulator guide over

14.12a The window frame is secured by 2 Torx bolts at the rear, upper edge of the door (arrowed) . . .

14.12c . . . 1 bolt at the base of the quarter-light pillar (arrowed) . . .

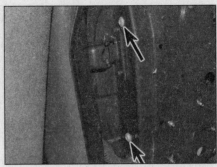

14.12b . . . 2 Torx bolts at the front edge (arrowed) . . .

14.12d . . . and 1 Torx bolt at the rear lower edge of the door

the heads of the bolts **(see illustrations 14.6a and 14.6b)**.
16 Remove the tape, raise the glass, and resecure it in position with tape.
17 Disconnect the window lift motor wiring plug.
18 Undo the 6 bolts and remove the regulator/motor assembly, manoeuvring it through the door lower aperture **(see illustrations)**.
19 If required, undo the 3 Torx screws and detach the motor from the regulator **(see illustration)**.

Rear door window regulator

20 Ensure that the window is lowered to access the regulator clamp bolts, then securely tape the window glass to its frame, to prevent the window dropping when the regulator is removed.

21 Slacken the 2 bolts securing the glass to the regulator, then slide the regulator guide to one side and over the heads of the bolts **(see illustration 14.11)**.
22 Remove the tape, raise the glass, and resecure it in position with tape.
23 Disconnect the window lift motor wiring plug.
24 Undo the 4 bolts and remove the regulator/motor assembly, manoeuvring it through the door lower aperture **(see illustration)**.
25 If required, undo the 3 Torx screws and detach the motor from the regulator.

Rear door quarter-light

26 Remove the rear door drop glass as described in this Section.
27 Undo the two bolts securing the quarter-

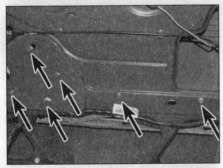

14.18a Undo the regulator retaining bolts (arrowed) . . .

14.18b . . . and manoeuvre the regulator from the door

14.19 Undo the 3 screws (arrowed) and detach the motor from the regulator

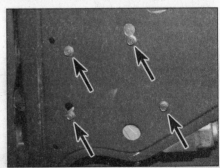

14.24 Rear window regulator bolts (arrowed)

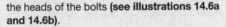

14.27 The quarter-light is secured by 2 bolts (arrowed)

15.3 Undo the screws (arrowed) securing the grab handle

15.5 Release the studs and remove the tailgate trim panel

light to the frame, and remove it **(see illustration)**.

Refitting

28 Refitting is the reverse of the removal procedure, noting the following points:
  a) *Prior to tightening the window frame retaining bolts and screws, close the door, and check that the frame is correctly aligned with the surrounding body panels. Adjust as necessary, then securely tighten all bolts.*
  b) *Refit the plastic sealing sheet, making sure it is securely stuck to the door, then install the trim panel as described in Section 12.*

15 Tailgate – removal and refitting

Note: *It is a good idea to obtain a few trim panel retaining clips before starting, as they are often broken in the course of removal, or will be found to have broken during previous removal attempts.*

Removal

1 Remove the spare wheel from the tailgate – where applicable.
2 On models fitted with speaker(s) fitted into the tailgate, undo the 6 screws and remove the speaker grille, then undo the 4 screws and remove the speaker trim casing, followed by the 8 screws and the speaker itself (see Chapter 13).

15.11 Release the rubber sleeve from the edge of the tailgate

3 Undo the two retaining screws, and remove the grab handle from the inside of the tailgate (where fitted) **(see illustration)**.
4 Undo the retaining screw, and remove the handle surround from the trim panel.
5 Release the trim panel studs, working around the outside of the panel, carefully levering between the panel and tailgate with a suitable flat-bladed screwdriver. When all the studs are released, pull the panel away from the tailgate **(see illustration)**.
6 Carefully peel away the plastic sealing sheet from the tailgate.
7 Disconnect the wiring plugs from the door lock, wiper motor, heated rear window, and number plate light.
8 Undo the 2 screws and remove the high-level brake light cover, then disconnect the wiring plugs.
9 Tie a length of string to the end of the high-level brake light wiring harness, and pull the harness through the door. When the end of the harness appears, untie the string and tape it in position to aid refitting.
10 Disconnect the washer tube from the rear of the wiper arm, and release it from the clips securing it to the tailgate frame.
11 Release the rubber sleeve from the outer edge of the tailgate, and pull the harness through **(see illustration)**.
12 Remove the circlip and washer securing the check link to the body, and free it from its bracket.
13 Using a suitable marker pen, make alignment marks between the tailgate and hinges.
14 Have an assistant support the tailgate.

16.4 Drill out the rivets and remove the interior handle (arrowed)

Undo the 6 bolts and washers securing the tailgate to its hinges, and remove the tailgate assembly from the vehicle.
15 Examine the tailgate hinges for signs of wear or damage. If renewal is necessary, first mark the outline of the hinge on the pillar. Undo the retaining bolts and remove the hinge, along with any relevant shims which are fitted behind it. Fit the new hinges, along with all the necessary shims, then align them with the marks made prior to removal before securely tightening their retaining bolts.

Refitting

16 Refitting is the reverse of removal, noting the following points:
  a) *Locate the tailgate on its hinges, and refit the retaining bolts and washers, tightening them by hand only. Align the marks made prior to removal, then securely tighten the hinge retaining bolts. Reconnect the check link, then close the tailgate and check for alignment with the surrounding body panels. Slight adjustments can be made by loosening the hinge bolts and repositioning the tailgate.*
  b) *Check the trim panel retaining clips for signs of damage – renew any broken ones before installing the panel.*

16 Tailgate lock components – removal and refitting

Removal

1 Remove the tailgate trim panel as described in paragraphs 1 to 6 of Section 15.
2 Peel the plastic sealing sheet away from the tailgate, to gain access to the lock components.
3 Proceed as described under the relevant sub-heading.

Interior lock handle

4 Drill out the two pop rivets and pull the handle from the tailgate panel **(see illustration)**.
5 Turn the assembly over, and disconnect

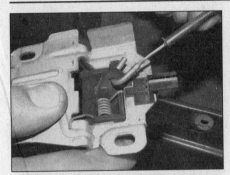

16.5 Disconnect the release cable from the interior handle

16.6 Disconnect the lock button link rod

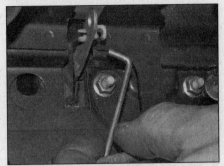

16.7 Disconnect the exterior handle control rod

16.9a Undo the 3 Torx bolts securing the tailgate lock

16.9b Disconnect the release cable from the lock

16.11 Exterior handle retaining nuts (arrowed)

the operating cable from the handle (see illustration).

Lock assembly

6 Release the lock button link rod by pushing the link rod from clip **(see illustration)**.

7 Release the retaining clip, and detach the control rod from the exterior handle **(see illustration)**.

8 Disconnect the lock wiring plug.

9 Undo the 3 retaining Torx screws and manoeuvre the lock assembly from the tailgate, disconnect the release cable as the lock is withdrawn **(see illustrations)**.

Exterior lock handle

10 Disconnect the control rod from the handle to the lock assembly, and remove the plastic clip from the control arm of the handle.

11 Undo the 2 retaining nuts and remove the exterior handle **(see illustration)**.

Refitting

12 Refitting is the reverse of the relevant removal procedure, noting the following:

a) *Ensure that all link rods are securely held in position by their retaining clips.*

b) *Apply grease to all lock and link rod pivot points.*

c) *Before installing the relevant trim panel, thoroughly check the operation of all the door lock handles and, where necessary, the central locking system.*

17 Central locking components
– removal and refitting

Lock solenoids and switches

1 The solenoids and switches are integral with

the lock assemblies, and if faulty, the complete units must be renewed – see Sections 13 and 16.

Electronic control unit

2 The central locking control function is incorporated into the Body Control Unit (BCU), which also controls operation of the anti-theft/immobiliser system, directional indicators, hazard warning lights, courtesy lights, wipers and washers, electric windows, electric sunroof, and the heated screens. The BCU is networked to the other control units in the vehicle via low speed (14 000 bps) databus. Should a fault occur in any of these systems, a fault code should be stored by the control unit. Using a generic fault code reader connected to the vehicles 16-pin diagnostic plug, located above the driver's pedal in the lower facia panel, the BCU can be interrogated and the fault code retrieved.

3 To remove the BCU, disconnect the battery negative lead as described in Chapter 5.

4 Remove the passenger's side glovebox as described in Section 26.

5 Undo the 4 fasteners and remove the passenger's side lower facia panel.

6 Note their fitted positions, and disconnect the 5 wiring plugs from the BCU **(see illustration)**.

7 Undo the nut and bolt, then manoeuvre the BCU from position **(see illustration)**.

8 Refitting is the reverse of removal. **Note:** *If a new BCU has been fitted, it will need to be reprogrammed using Land Rover dedicated test equipment (Testbook). Entrust this task to a Land Rover dealer or suitably-equipped specialist.*

17.6 Disconnect the wiring plugs (arrowed) from the Body Control Unit (BCU)

17.7 Undo the BCU retaining nut (arrowed)

18 Electric window components – removal and refitting

Window switches

1 Refer to Chapter 13, Section 4.

Window lift motor

2 Remove the door glass regulator assembly as described in Section 14.
3 Undo the screws and detach the motor from the regulator **(see illustration 14.19)**.
4 Refitting is the reverse of removal, ensuring that the motor gear is correctly engaged with the regulator mechanism. Check the operation of the motor before refitting the trim panel to the door.

Electronic control unit

5 Refer to Section 17.

19 Exterior mirrors and associated components – removal and refitting

Door mirror assembly

1 Carefully unclip the mirror inner trim panel from the door, and remove the anti-rattle pad **(see illustrations)**.
2 Disconnect the mirror wiring connector(s).
3 Support the mirror assembly, then undo the three retaining screws and washers **(see illustration)**. Remove the mounting plate from

the inner edge of the door, and recover its retaining clips.
4 Remove the mirror assembly from the door.
5 Refitting is the reverse of removal, using a new mirror seal if the original shows signs of damage or deterioration. Take care to ensure that the wiring is not trapped as the interior trim panel is refitted.

Mirror glass

Caution: If the glass is broken, wear sturdy gloves. Even if the glass is not broken, wearing gloves is a sensible precaution, should the glass break as it is being removed or refitted.

6 Position the glass so its inner edge is fully forward, then carefully ease your fingers in behind the outer edge of the glass, and gently pull the glass outwards until it is released from its retaining clips **(see illustration)**. Take great care when removing the glass; do not use excessive force, as the glass is easily broken.
7 On models with electric mirrors, disconnect the wiring connectors from the mirror heating element as they become accessible **(see illustration)**.
8 On refitting, reconnect the wiring connectors (where necessary). Carefully, engage the metal locating strip in the slot, then clip the glass back into position, ensuring that it is securely retained by each of the clips.

Mirror motor

9 Remove the mirror glass as described above.
10 Undo the retaining screws and remove the motor assembly, disconnecting its wiring

connectors as they become accessible **(see illustration)**.
11 Refitting is the reverse of removal.

Mirror switch

12 Refer to Chapter 13, Section 4.

20 Windscreen, tailgate and fixed windows – general information

These areas of glass are secured by the tight fit of the weatherstrip in the body aperture, and are bonded in position with a special adhesive. The removal and refitting of these areas of fixed glass is difficult, messy and time-consuming task, which is considered beyond the scope of the home mechanic. It is difficult, unless one has plenty of practice, to obtain a secure, waterproof fit. Furthermore, the task carries a high risk of breakage; this applies especially to the laminated glass windscreen. In view of this, owners are strongly advised to have this sort of work carried out by one of the many specialist windscreen fitters.

21 Sunroof – general information and component renewal

General information

Twin tilt/sliding sunroofs were fitted as standard to some models, and offered as an optional extra on others. The sunroof(s) is/are either manually or electrically-operated.

19.1a Unclip the mirror trim panel . . .

19.1b . . . and remove the anti-rattle pad

19.3 Undo the mirror retaining screws (arrowed)

19.6 Ease the outer edge of the mirror from the retaining clips

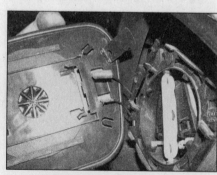

19.7 Disconnect the mirror heating element wiring plugs

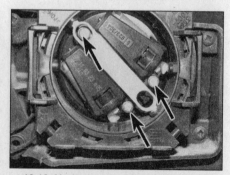

19.10 Undo the screws (arrowed) and remove the motor assembly

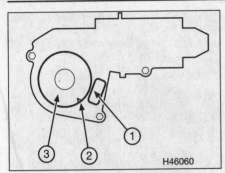

21.4 The notch (2) must align with the microswitch (1). If not, turn the 'counting' wheel (3) with an Allen key

Due to the complexity of the tilt/slide sunroof mechanism, considerable expertise is needed to repair, renew or adjust the sunroof components successfully. Removal of the sunroof first requires the headlining to be removed, which is a complex and tedious operation in itself, and not a task to be undertaken lightly (see Section 26). Therefore, any problems with the sunroof should be referred to a Land Rover dealer or specialist.

On models with an electric sunroof, if the sunroof motor fails to operate, first check the relevant fuse. The motor incorporates an automatic cut-out facility, which cuts the motor if the sunroof encounters an obstruction – the motor may therefore cut-out if the mechanism is partially seized.

1 It is possible to remove the front sunroof motor ECU after removing the front upper storage pocket assembly as described in Section 26. Removal of the rear sunroof motor requires removal of the headlining.

Sunroof motor

Removal

2 Ensure the sunroof is in the fully closed position, then disconnect the motor wiring plug.
3 Undo the 3 Torx screws and remove the motor.

Refitting

4 Ensure the motor timing notch aligns with the edge of the microswitch (see illustration).

21.9 Undo the 2 Torx screws each side (arrowed)

If it doesn't, rotate the 'counting' wheel to the correct position using an Allen key in the wheel spindle.
5 The remainder of refitting is a reversal of removal.

Sunroof ECU

6 Remove the front upper storage pocket assembly as described in Section 26.
7 Undo the two screws and lower the ECU from the roof. Disconnect the wiring plugs as the ECU is withdrawn.
8 Refitting is a reversal of removal.

Sunroof glass panel

9 Fully tilt (open) the sunroof, then undo the 4 Torx screws. Manoeuvre the sunroof panel from place (see illustration).
10 To refit the panel, position the panel in the frame, but only finger-tighten the screws at this stage.
11 Adjust the position of the panel so that a gap of 6.5 mm exists between the sunroof frame, and the front edge of the panel. Once this is achieved, tighten the screws securely.

22 Body exterior fittings – removal and refitting

Wheel arch liners and body under-panels

1 The various plastic covers fitted to the

underside of the vehicle are secured in position by a mixture of screws, nuts and retaining clips. Removal will be fairly obvious on inspection. Work methodically around the panel, removing its retaining screws and releasing its retaining clips until the panel is free and can be removed from the underside of the vehicle. Most clips used on the vehicle, with the exception of the fasteners which are used to secure the sill finishers in position, are simply prised out of position. The sill finisher clips are release by pressing out their centre pins and then removing the outer section of the clip; new clips will be required on refitting if the centre pins are not recovered.
2 On refitting, renew any retaining clips that may have been broken on removal, and ensure that the panel is securely retained by all the relevant clips, nuts and screws.

Body trim strips and badges

3 Most of the various body trim strips and badges are held in position with a special adhesive tape. Removal requires the trim/badge to be heated, to soften the adhesive, and then cut away from the surface. Due to the high risk of damage to the vehicle's paintwork during this operation, it is recommended that this task should be entrusted to a Land Rover dealer.

23 Seats – removal and refitting

Removal

Front seat

1 Disconnect the battery negative lead as described in Chapter 5, then wait at least 10 minutes for any residual electrical energy to dissipate.
2 Undo the 3 screws, prise out the clip, and remove the lower trim casing from the base of the seat (see illustrations).
3 Prise off the cap, and undo the seat belt lower anchorage bolt.
4 Undo the 4 Torx bolts securing the seat to

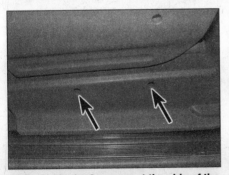

23.2a Undo the 2 screws at the side of the trim (arrowed) . . .

23.2b . . . one at the front (arrowed) . . .

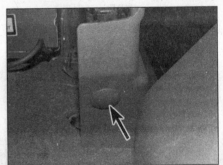

23.2c . . . and prise out the clip at the back (arrowed)

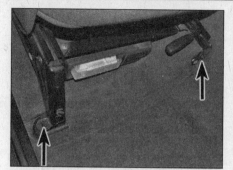

23.4 Undo the 4 Torx bolts and remove the seat (front bolts arrowed)

23.5 When refitting the seats, ensure any wiring is resecured by the appropriate clips

23.7 Undo the Torx bolts securing the seat base

23.8 Undo the Torx bolt at the rear of the seat

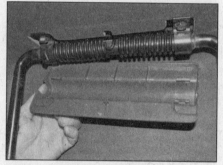

23.11 Unclip the cover from the hinge

24 Seat positioning motors
– removal and refitting

Removal

Fore-and-aft motor

1 Remove the front seat as described in Section 23.
2 Disconnect the motor wiring plug, then undo the Allen bolt securing the right-hand screw thread to the seat frame (see illustration).
3 Prise off the 2 retaining clips and remove the roll-pin. Recover the spacers.
4 Manoeuvre the right-hand thread and retainer clear of the seat frame, then remove the motor.

Rise-and-fall motor

5 Remove the front seat as described in Section 23.
6 Disconnect the motor wiring plug.
7 Prise off the 4 retaining clips, and drive out the 2 roll-pins securing the operating lever to the seat frame, then remove motor assembly.

Tilt motor

8 Remove the front seat as described in Section 23.

the vehicle (see illustration). Note that a nut on the underside of the floorpan secures the rear outer bolt.
5 Lean the seat forward, note their fitted positions and disconnect the wiring plugs from the seat base (see illustration).
6 Lift the seat assembly out of the vehicle.

Rear seat

7 Pull the carpet forwards from the rear seat base, and undo the Torx bolts securing the seat base to the vehicle body (see illustration).
8 Fold the seat forwards, then slacken and remove the seat rear retaining Torx bolts and manoeuvre the rear seat out from the vehicle (see illustration).

Third row seats

9 Fold out the seat and clip it into the floor. Do not raise the backrest.
10 Push the cup holder/tray upwards and unclip it.

11 Prise off the plastic cover from the bracket hinge (see illustration).
12 Undo the 2 bolts on the upper side of the bracket (see illustration).
13 Unclip the seat from the floor, lift it and support it in that position with a wooden block (or similar).
14 Gradually and evenly undo the 2 nuts on the underside of the mounting bracket. Note that these brackets are under some tension, and will rotate approximately 90° when released (see illustration).
Caution: Take great care not to dislodge the supporting block – the seat is heavy.
15 Remove the seat from position.

Refitting

16 Refitting is a reversal of the relevant removal procedure. Make sure that all seat mountings are tightened to the specified torque.

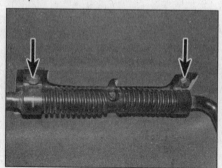

23.12 Undo the upper hinge bolts (arrowed)

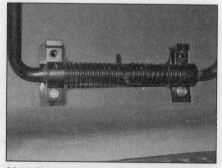

23.14 Undo the lower hinge bolts gradually – the brackets will try to rotate

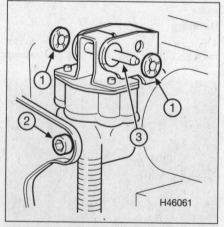

H46061

24.2 Fore-and-aft seat positioning motor

1 *Retaining clips*   3 *Roll pin*
2 *Allen bolt*

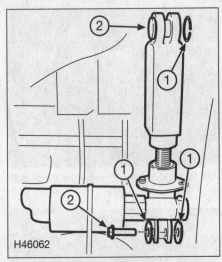

24.10 Seat tilt motor

1 Retaining clips   2 Roll pins

9 Disconnect the motor wiring plug, and release the cable tie around the motor/harness.

10 Prise off the 3 retaining clips from the motor assembly, and drive out the 2 roll-pins securing the operating lever to the seat frame (**see illustration**).

Seat recline motor

11 Removal of the recline motor requires the seat backrest cover to be removed. This is a complicated task, requiring patience and experience to successfully complete. For this

25.4 Seat belt upper anchorage nut

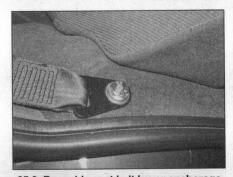

25.9 Rear side seat belt lower anchorage bolt

25.2 Front seat belt lower anchorage bolt (arrowed)

reason, we recommend the task is entrusted to an upholstery specialist.

Refitting

12 Refitting is a reversal of removal, ensuring the operating arms mounting holes are completely aligned before driving in the various roll-pins.

25 Seat belt components – removal and refitting

Removal

Front seat belt

1 Remove the B-pillar lower trim panel as described in Section 26.

2 Undo the bolt securing the seat belt

25.7 Undo the Torx bolt and remove the pretensioner

25.10 Rear side seat belt upper anchorage bolt

25.3 Undo the inertia reel retaining bolt (arrowed)

anchorage to the front seat (**see illustration**).

3 Undo the bolt securing the seat belt inertia reel to the B-pillar (**see illustration**).

4 Remove the seat belt upper anchorage nut from the B-pillar (**see illustration**).

Front seat belt stalk

5 The front seat belt stalks are equipped with pretensioners. These are pyrotechnic devices designed to quickly retract the stalk, tightening the seat belt in the event of a frontal collision. To avoid personal injury through accidental deployment, disconnect the battery negative lead as described in Chapter 5, then wait at least 10 minutes for any residual electrical energy to dissipate before commencing work.

6 Remove the front seat as described in Section 23.

7 Release the cable tie securing the pretensioner wiring harness to the seat frame, then undo the Torx bolt and remove the pretensioner (**see illustration**).

Rear seat side belt

8 Remove the C/D-pillar trim panel and the luggage compartment side trim panel as described in Section 26.

9 Prise off the cap, then undo the seat belt lower anchorage bolt (**see illustration**).

10 Unclip the cover, then undo the upper seat belt anchorage bolt (**see illustration**).

11 Undo the bolt securing the inertia seat belt to the vehicle body and remove it from position (**see illustration**).

Rear seat belt centre belt

12 Remove the rear right-hand seat as described in Section 23.

25.11 Inertia reel retaining bolt (arrowed)

25.13 Unclip the seat back trim

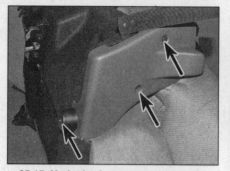

25.15 Undo the 2 screws securing the trim, and the screw retaining the plastic seat base rest (arrowed)

25.16 Seat belt anchorage bolt (arrowed)

13 Prise out the 11 retaining clips and remove the right-hand seat back trim (see illustration).
14 Prise out the retaining clips at the rear edge of the right-hand seat base trim.
15 Undo the 2 screws and remove the seat outer cover, followed by the screw securing the plastic seat base rest (see illustration).
16 Undo the bolt securing the seat belt lower anchorage to the seat frame (see illustration).
17 Undo the retaining bolt, and remove the inertia reel from the vehicle (see illustration).
18 Undo the two screws, release the 2 clips at the rear, and remove the upper seat belt cover (see illustration).

Third row seat belts

19 Remove the luggage compartment side trim panel as described in Section 26.

20 Unclip the plastic cap, and undo the upper seat belt anchorage bolt (see illustration).
21 Undo the inertia reel retaining bolt, and remove the seat belt from the vehicle (see illustration).

Refitting

22 Refitting is a reversal of the removal procedure, ensuring that all the mounting bolts are tightened to the specified torque (where given) and all disturbed trim panels are securely retained by all the relevant retaining clips.

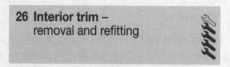

26 Interior trim –
removal and refitting

Interior trim panels

1 The interior trim panels are secured using either screws or various types of trim fasteners, usually studs or clips.
2 Check that there are no other panels overlapping the one to be removed; usually there is a sequence to be followed that will become obvious on close inspection.
3 Remove all obvious fasteners, such as screws. If the panel will not come free, it is held by hidden clips or fasteners. These are usually situated around the edge of the panel, and can be prised up to release them. Note, however, that they can break quite easily, so new ones should be available. The best way of releasing such clips in the absence of

25.17 Inertia reel retaining bolt (arrowed)

the correct type of tool is to use a large flat-bladed screwdriver. Note in many cases that an adjacent sealing strip (such as the rubber door seal) must be prised back to release a panel.
4 When removing a panel, **never** use excessive force, or the panel may be damaged. Always check carefully that all fasteners have been removed or released before attempting to withdraw a panel.
5 Refitting is the reverse of the removal procedure; secure the fasteners by pressing them firmly into place, and ensure that all disturbed components are correctly secured, to prevent rattles.

Glovebox

6 Open up the glovebox.
7 Slacken and remove the hinge retaining screws, and pull the glovebox from the facia (see illustration).

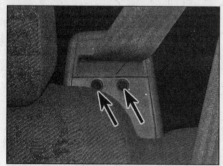

25.18 Undo the screws (arrowed), release the clips and remove the upper seat belt cover

25.20 Third row seat belt upper anchorage bolt

25.21 Third row seat belt inertia reel bolt (arrowed)

26.7 Undo the 4 bolts (arrowed) and manoeuvre the glovebox from the facia

26.9 Open the coin tray, depress the clip and pull it from the facia. The ashtray is removed in the same way

26.10a Undo the 3 screws each side (arrowed) . . .

26.10b . . . and pull the cup holder assembly from the facia

8 Refitting is the reverse of removal.

Cup holder

9 Remove the centre coin tray and ashtray (see illustration).
10 Working inside the apertures at each side, remove a total of six screws (three each side) securing the cup holder. Carefully slide the holder out from its location (see illustrations).
11 Further dismantling the cup holder is not advisable. Refitting is a reversal of removal.

Carpets

12 The passenger compartment floor carpet is in one piece, and is secured at its edges by screws or clips, usually the same fasteners used to secure the various adjoining trim panels.
13 Carpet removal and refitting is reasonably straightforward, but very time-consuming, due to the fact that all adjoining trim panels must be removed first, as must components such as the seats, the centre console and seat belt lower anchorages.

Headlining

14 The headlining is clipped to the roof, and can only be withdrawn once all fittings such as the grab handles, sunvisors, windscreen and rear quarter windows, and related trim panels have been removed, and the door, tailgate and sunroof aperture sealing strips have been prised clear.

15 Note that headlining removal requires considerable skill and experience if it is to be carried out without damage, and is therefore best entrusted to an expert.

A-pillar trim

16 Carefully pull the pillar trim panels from place. The panels are secured by 3 push-on clips (see illustration). If speakers are fitted, disconnect the wiring plugs as the trim panels are removed.
17 Refitting is a reversal of removal.

B-pillar trim

18 Pull the rubber weatherstrip seals from the door apertures either side of the B-pillar.
19 Prise off the cap, then undo the front seat belt lower anchorage bolt.

20 Release the clips at the sides of the trim (under the weatherstrip seals), then pull the B-pillar upper trim inwards to release it from the retaining clips (see illustrations). Feed the seat belt through the slot in the trim.
21 Release the clips at the sides of the lower trim (under the weatherstrips), then pull the trim inwards to release the clips (see illustrations).
22 Refitting is a reversal of removal, remembering to tighten the lower seat belt anchorage point bolt to the specified torque.

C/D-pillar trim

23 Fold the rear seats forwards.
24 Pull the trim panel above the tailgate

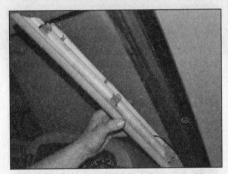

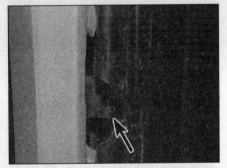

26.16 The A-pillar trims are secured by 3 push-on clips

26.20a Release the clip (arrowed) each side of the upper B-pillar trim . . .

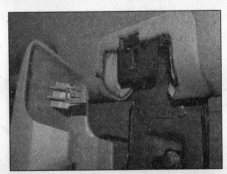

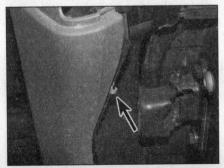

26.20b . . . and pull the trim inwards to release the clip at the top

26.21a Release the clip (arrowed) each side of the lower B-pillar trim . . .

26.21b . . . the pull it inwards to release the clips at the top of the trim

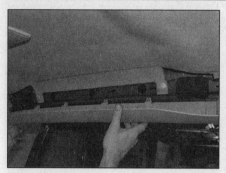

26.24 Pull the trim panel above the tailgate aperture from place

26.25 Undo the screw (arrowed) and remove the bracket

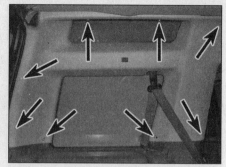

26.26 Prise out the 6 clips and undo the 2 screws (arrowed)

aperture forwards to release it from the retaining clips **(see illustration)**.

25 Prise open the end caps, undo the two bolts and remove the grab handle (where fitted) from the trim panel, or prise out the cap and remove the single screw securing the cover bracket **(see illustration)**.

26 Prise out the 6 clips securing the pillar trim to the vehicle body, then prise out the caps and undo the 2 screws **(see illustration)**.

27 On 7-seat models, undo the rear seat belt lower anchorage bolt. Recover the spacer.

28 On models with a volumetric alarm, prise the sensor from the trim panel **(see illustration)**. Disconnect the wiring plug as the sensor is withdrawn.

29 Remove the rear seat belt blanking plate **(see illustration)**.

30 Pull the trim panel from position to release the 2 remaining push-on clips.

31 Refitting is a reversal of removal.

Luggage compartment side trim panel

32 If removing the left-hand luggage compartment side trim panel, undo the retaining screw, and pull the accessory socket surround from the trim panel **(see illustration)**. Disconnect the socket wiring plug and bulb as the socket is withdrawn.

33 Remove the relevant C/D-pillar trim as described in this Section.

34 Undo the retaining screw, and lift the trim cap from place **(see illustration)**.

35 Pull away the rubber weatherstrip from the tailgate aperture adjacent to the side trim panel.

36 Remove the louvered access panel from the side trim panel, then remove the clip within the access panel recess **(see illustration)**.

7-seat models

37 Remove the relevant third row seat as described in Section 23.

38 Undo the screw in the seat stowage clip recess **(see illustration)**.

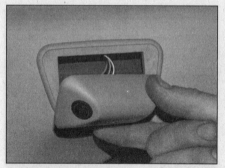

26.28 Prise the volumetric sensor from the panel

26.29 Remove the seat belt blanking plate

26.32 Undo the screw (arrowed) and remove the accessory socket surround

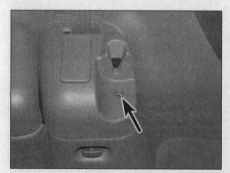

26.34 The trim cap is secured by a single screw (arrowed)

26.36 Open the louvered access panel, and prise out the clip (arrowed)

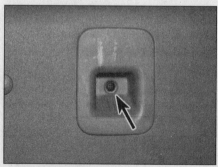

26.38 Undo the seat stowage clip recess screw (arrowed) – 7-seater models

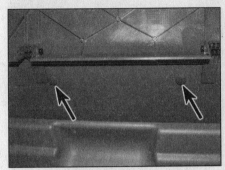

26.39 Prise out the 2 clips at the top of the storage compartment (arrowed) . . .

26.40 . . . and the one at the base (arrowed) – 5-seater models

26.41 Prise out the clip at the front of the panel

26.44 Undo the screw in the access panel recess (arrowed)

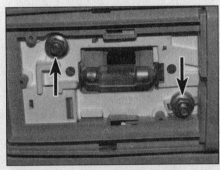

26.45 Undo the 2 nuts in the interior light recess (arrowed)

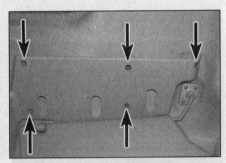

26.46 The front upper storage pocket is secured by 10 screws (5 right-hand ones arrowed)

5-seat models

39 Open the storage compartment lid, then prise out the 2 clips securing the side trim adjacent to the side window **(see illustration)**.
40 Remove the clip from the bottom rear corner of the storage compartment **(see illustration)**.

All models

41 Remove the clip at the front lower edge of the side trim panel **(see illustration)**.
42 Manoeuvre the side trim panel from position. If the panel is to be completely detached, unbolt the seat belt inertia reel (see Section 25) and feed it through the panel.
43 Refitting is a reversal of removal.

Front upper storage pocket

44 Prise open the access panel at the front edge of the storage pocket, and undo the screw in the access panel recess **(see illustration)**.
45 Prise the lens from the front interior light, and undo the 2 nuts securing the light to the headlining **(see illustration)**. Disconnect the wiring plug as the light is withdrawn.
46 Undo the 10 screws securing the storage pocket to the headlining **(see illustration)**. Note their fitted positions, and disconnect the various wiring plugs as the pocket is withdrawn. On models with manual sunroof(s), undo the screw and pull the operating handle from place.

47 Refitting is a reversal of removal.

27 Centre console – removal and refitting

Removal

Manual transmission models

1 Release the clips securing the gear lever gaiters to the centre console, then unscrew the transfer lever knob. Remove the gearchange lever knob in the same way **(see illustrations)**.

27.1a Unclip the gaiter . . .

27.1b . . . and unscrew the transfer lever knob

27.2a Pull the selector lever knob straight up . . .

27.2b . . . and recover the spacer tube

27.3 Prise up the selector lever panel

Automatic transmission models

2 Select position D (Drive), then pull the knob from the selector lever, and recover the spacer tube **(see illustrations)**.

3 Carefully prise up the selector lever panel. Disconnect the wiring plugs as the panel is withdrawn **(see illustration)**.

4 Release the transfer lever gaiter from the panel, then unscrew the transfer lever knob, and remove it along with the gaiter **(see illustration)**.

All models

5 On vehicles from 2003 model year, remove the front cup holders as described in Section 26.

6 On base trim models, remove the rubber mat from the console, prise away the cover plate from the switch pack, then undo the 4 screws and remove the switch pack. Disconnect the wiring plugs as the pack is withdrawn **(see illustrations)**.

7 On models with veneer trim, remove the cigar lighter element, then carefully prise the veneered console cover from place. Disconnect the wiring plugs as the cover is withdrawn.

8 On all models, undo the 2 bolts at the front of the console **(see illustration)**.

9 Prise the handbrake lever gaiter from the console.

10 Chock the wheels to prevent the vehicle moving, then release the handbrake.

11 Remove the spring clip, then withdraw the clevis pin securing the handbrake inner cable to the lever **(see illustrations)**. Fully raise the handbrake lever.

12 Prise the electric seat switches (where applicable) from the centre console. Disconnect the wiring plugs as the switches are withdrawn.

13 Open the storage compartment, then undo the 2 bolts at the rear of the console **(see illustration)**.

27.4 Unscrew the knob, and prise up the transfer lever gaiter

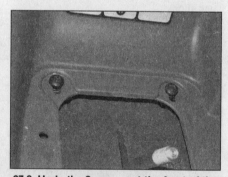

27.6a Prise away the cover plate . . .

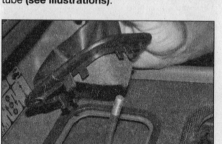

27.6b . . . and undo the 4 screws (arrowed)

27.8 Undo the 2 screws at the front of the console

27.11a Prise off the spring clip (arrowed) . . .

27.11b . . . and remove the handbrake cable clevis pin (arrowed)

27.13 Undo the 2 screws in the storage compartment at the rear of the console (arrowed)

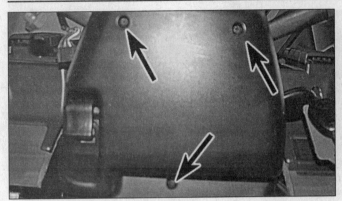

28.4 The steering column shrouds are secured by 3 screws (arrowed)

28.10 Undo the 4 screws and remove the facia access panel (arrowed)

14 Lift the console upwards and out of the vehicle. Disconnect any wiring plugs as the console is withdrawn.

Refitting

15 Refitting is a reversal of the removal procedure, noting the following:

a) *Ensure that all the wiring is correctly routed, and does not become trapped as the console is refitted.*

b) *Apply a smear of grease to the handbrake cable mechanism. Adjust the cable as described in Chapter 1.*

28 Facia panel assembly – removal and refitting

Removal

1 Disconnect the battery negative terminal, as described in Chapter 5.

2 Remove the radio/cassette/audio unit as describe in Chapter 13.

3 Remove the steering wheel as described in Chapter 11.

4 Open the lower facia access panel on the driver's side, then undo the 3 screws and remove the upper and lower steering column shrouds **(see illustration)**.

5 Remove the centre console as described in Section 27.

6 Remove the A-pillar trim panels as described in Section 26.

7 Release the clips and remove the lower facia panels from the driver's and passenger's side footwells.

8 Remove both rubber mats from the facia.

9 Remove the instrument panel as described in Chapter 13.

10 Undo the 4 retaining screws, and remove the facia access panel from the driver's side **(see illustration)**.

11 Undo the 4 small nuts securing the facia to the top of the steering column bracket **(see illustration)**.

12 Disconnect the 3 wiring plugs and earth lead connecting the main body harness to the facia harness, then disconnect the facia harness plug from the fusebox **(see illustrations)**.

13 Remove the passenger's side glovebox as described in Section 26.

14 On models with air conditioning, disconnect the heater controls wiring plug.

15 On models without air conditioning, note their fitted positions, then release the air distribution and temperature control outer cables from the clips on the heater casing, and the inner cables from the levers (see Chapter 3).

16 Locate the ICE (In-Car Entertainment) wiring plug, and separate the blue section.

17 Disconnect the passenger's airbag wiring plug **(see illustration)**.

18 Disconnect the heater blower motor wiring plug.

19 Models without a passenger's airbag have 2 bolts securing the facia to the body, whereas models with an airbag have 4 bolts accessible through the passenger's glovebox aperture **(see illustration)**.

28.11 Undo the 4 nuts – 2 either side of the steering column (right-hand screws arrowed)

28.12a Disconnect the 3 facia harness plugs (arrowed) . . .

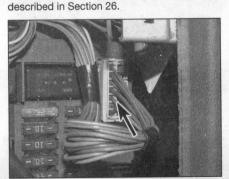

28.12b . . . and the plug from the fusebox (arrowed)

28.17 Disconnect the passenger's airbag plug – normally yellow in colour

28.19 Undo the passenger's airbag bracket bolts (arrowed)

28.20a Undo the 2 bolts either side of the transmission tunnel (left-hand bolts arrowed) . . .

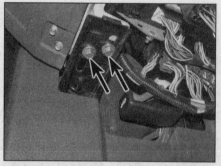

28.20b . . . and the 2 bolts at each end of the facia edge (left-hand bolts arrowed)

29.2 Release the clips and remove the headlight access covers on both sides

20 Undo the 4 bolts securing the lower edge of the facia to the transmission tunnel, and the 2 bolts each end of the lower facia edge **(see illustrations)**.
21 With assistance, manoeuvre the facia from the vehicle.

Refitting

22 Refitting is a reversal of the removal procedure, noting the following points:
  a) *Manoeuvre the facia into position, and ensure that the wiring is correctly routed and fed through the relevant facia apertures. Take great care not to trap the wiring as the facia is installed.*
  b) *Clip the facia back into position, then refit all the facia fasteners and tighten them securely.*
  c) *On completion, reconnect the battery and check that all the electrical components and switches function correctly.*

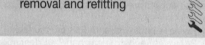

29 Radiator grille – removal and refitting

Removal

Vehicles up to 2003 model year

1 Undo the fasteners and remove the cover over the battery.
2 Release the clips and remove the headlight access covers on both sides **(see illustration)**.
3 Remove both front direction indicators as described in Chapter 13, Section 7.
4 Working through the access hole in the wheel arch liner, undo the screw securing the headlight lower trims on both sides **(see illustration)**.
5 Undo the screw in each lower corner securing the radiator grille **(see illustration)**.
6 Undo the three scrivets along the top edge and remove the grille **(see illustration)**.

Vehicle from 2003 model year

7 Undo the three scrivets along the top edge, and lift the grille from position.

Refitting

8 Refitting is the reverse of removal, ensuring that the grille locating pegs engage correctly with their mounting rubbers **(see illustration)**.

29.4 Undo the screw securing the headlight lower trims

29.5 Remove the screw in each lower corner

29.6 Slacken the screws and prise out the 3 scrivets at the top of the grille

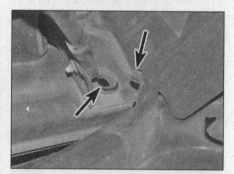

29.8 Note how the lugs on the base of the radiator grille located in the rubber mountings (arrowed)

Chapter 13
Body electrical systems

Contents

Section number

Airbag system – general information and precautions............ 19
Airbag system components – removal and refitting............. 20
Anti-theft alarm system – general information 21
Battery – removal and refitting ....See Chapter 5
Battery check and maintenance.............. See *Weekly checks*
Bulbs (exterior lights) – renewal 5
Bulbs (interior lights) – renewal............................. 6
Clock – removal and refitting 11
Electric headlight-levelling system components –
    removal and refitting...................................... 22
Electrical fault finding – general information 2
Exterior light units – removal and refitting 7
Fuses and relays – general information 3
General information and precautions......................... 1
Headlight beam alignment – general information................ 8
Headlight washer system components – removal and refitting 17
Horn – removal and refitting................................ 12
In-car entertainment systems – component removal and refitting... 18

Section number

Instrument panel – removal and refitting 9
Instrument panel components – removal and refitting............ 10
Parking distance control system – component removal and
    refitting 23
Reversing light switch (manual transmission models) –
    removal and refitting..........................See Chapter 7A
Starter inhibitor/reversing light switch (automatic transmission
    models) – removal and refitting .... See Chapter 7B
Stop-light switch – removal and refitting ....See Chapter 10
Switches – removal and refitting 4
Tailgate wiper motor – removal and refitting 15
Windscreen wiper motor and linkage – removal and refitting 14
Windscreen/tailgate washer system components –
    removal and refitting...................................... 16
Windscreen/tailgate wiper blade check and
    renewal .... See *Weekly checks*
Wiper arm – removal and refitting 13

Degrees of difficulty

Easy, suitable for novice with little experience	**Fairly easy,** suitable for beginner with some experience	**Fairly difficult,** suitable for competent DIY mechanic	**Difficult,** suitable for experienced DIY mechanic	**Very difficult,** suitable for expert DIY or professional

Specifications

System type.. 12 volt negative-earth

Relays – engine compartment fusebox

Relay number (see illustration)	Function
R1..	Fuel pump
R2..	Starter
R3..	Headlamp power wash
R4..	Cooling fan
R5..	Self levelling/ABS (SLABS)
R6..	Glow plugs
R7..	Auxiliary circuits
R8..	Heated front screen
R9..	Main relay
R10...	ABS
R11...	Air conditioning compressor clutch
R12...	Front fog lamps
R13...	Horns
R14...	ACE

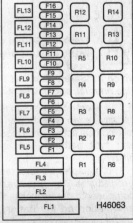

Engine compartment fusebox

Relays – passenger compartment fusebox

Relay number (see illustration)	Function
R1	Left-hand indicators
R2	Right-hand indicators
R3	Rear window lift
R4	Ignition coils (petrol only)
R5	Daytime running lamps
R6	Daytime running lamps

Bulbs

	Wattage
Automatic transmission selector illumination light	5
Direction indicator	21
Direction indicator side repeater	5
Front foglight:	
Up to 2003 model year	55 H1
From 2003 model year	55 H11
Front sidelight	5
Headlight:	
Up to 2003 model year	60/55 H4
From 2003 model year:	
Main beam	55 H7
Dipped beam	55 H7
Instrument panel lights:	
Ignition warning light	2
All other warning/illumination lights	1.2
Interior lights	5
Interior courtesy lights	10
Number plate light	5
Rear foglight	21
Reversing light	21
Stop/tail light:	
Up to 2003 model year	
Stop-light	21
Tail light	5
From 2003 model year	21/5
High-level stop-light	21
Glovebox light	5

Torque wrench settings

	Nm	lbf ft
Airbag components:		
Driver's airbag Torx screws	10	7
Control unit screws	10	7
Passenger's airbag screws	8	6

H46064

Passenger compartment fusebox

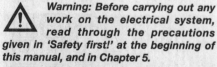

1 General information and precautions

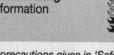 **Warning: Before carrying out any work on the electrical system, read through the precautions given in 'Safety first!' at the beginning of this manual, and in Chapter 5.**

The electrical system is of the 12 volt negative-earth type. Power for the lights and all electrical accessories is supplied by a lead-acid type battery which is charged by the alternator.

This Chapter covers repair and service procedures for the various electrical components not associated with the engine. Information on the battery, alternator and starter motor can be found in Chapter 5.

Prior to working on any component in the electrical system, the battery negative terminal should first be disconnected, to prevent the possibility of electrical short-circuits and/or fires. Refer to Chapter 5.

2 Electrical fault finding – general information

Note: *Refer to the precautions given in 'Safety first!' and in Section 1 of this Chapter before starting work. The following tests relate to testing of the main electrical circuits, and should not be used to test delicate electronic circuits (such as anti-lock braking systems), particularly where an electronic control module is used.*

General

1 A typical electrical circuit consists of an electrical component, any switches, relays, motors, fuses and fusible links or circuit breakers related to that component, and the wiring and connectors which link the component to both the battery and the chassis. To help to pinpoint a problem in an electrical circuit, wiring diagrams are included at the end of this Chapter.

2 Before attempting to diagnose an electrical fault, first study the appropriate wiring diagram to obtain a complete understanding of the components included in the particular circuit concerned. The possible sources of a fault can be narrowed down by noting if other components related to the circuit are operating properly. If several components or circuits fail at one time, the problem is likely to be related to a shared fuse or earth connection.

3 Electrical problems usually stem from simple causes, such as loose or corroded connections, a faulty earth connection, a blown fuse, a melted fusible link, or a faulty relay (refer to Section 3 for details of testing relays). Visually inspect the condition of all fuses, wires and connections in a problem circuit before testing the components. Use the wiring diagrams to determine which terminal connections will need to be checked in order to pinpoint the trouble-spot.

4 The basic tools required for electrical fault finding include a circuit tester or voltmeter (a 12 volt bulb with a set of test leads can also be used for certain tests); a self-powered test light (sometimes known as a continuity tester); an ohmmeter (to measure resistance); a battery and set of test leads; and a jumper wire, preferably with a circuit breaker or fuse incorporated, which can be used to bypass suspect wires or electrical components. Before attempting to locate a problem with test instruments, use the wiring diagram to determine where to make the connections.

 Warning: Under no circumstances may live measuring instruments such as ohmmeters, voltmeters or a bulb and test leads be used to test any of the airbag circuitry. Any testing of these components must be left to a Land Rover dealer, as there is a danger of activating the system if the correct procedures are not followed.

5 To find the source of an intermittent wiring fault (usually due to a poor or dirty connection, or damaged wiring insulation), a 'wiggle' test can be performed on the wiring. This involves wiggling the wiring by hand to see if the fault occurs as the wiring is moved. It should be possible to narrow down the source of the fault to a particular section of wiring. This method of testing can be used in conjunction with any of the tests described in the following sub-Sections.

6 Apart from problems due to poor connections, two basic types of fault can occur in an electrical circuit – open-circuit, or short-circuit.

7 Open-circuit faults are caused by a break somewhere in the circuit, which prevents current from flowing. An open-circuit fault will prevent a component from working, but will not cause the relevant circuit fuse to blow.

8 Short-circuit faults are caused by a short somewhere in the circuit, which allows the current flowing in the circuit to escape along an alternative route, usually to earth. Short-circuit faults are normally caused by a breakdown in wiring insulation, which allows a feed wire to touch either another wire, or an earthed component such as the bodyshell. A short-circuit fault will normally cause the relevant circuit fuse to blow.

Finding an open-circuit

9 To check for an open-circuit, connect one lead of a circuit tester or voltmeter to either the negative battery terminal or a known good earth.

10 Connect the other lead to a connector in the circuit being tested, preferably nearest to the battery or fuse.

11 Switch on the circuit, bearing in mind that some circuits are live only when the ignition switch is moved to a particular position.

12 If voltage is present (indicated either by the tester bulb lighting or a voltmeter reading, as applicable), this means that the section of the circuit between the relevant connector and the battery is problem-free.

13 Continue to check the remainder of the circuit in the same fashion.

14 When a point is reached at which no voltage is present, the problem must lie between that point and the previous test point with voltage. Most problems can be traced to a broken, corroded or loose connection.

Finding a short-circuit

15 To check for a short-circuit, first disconnect the load(s) from the circuit (loads are the components which draw current from a circuit, such as bulbs, motors, heating elements, etc).

16 Remove the relevant fuse from the circuit, and connect a circuit tester or voltmeter to the fuse connections.

17 Switch on the circuit, bearing in mind that some circuits are live only when the ignition switch is moved to a particular position.

18 If voltage is present (indicated either by the tester bulb lighting or a voltmeter reading, as applicable), this means that there is a short-circuit.

19 If no voltage is present, but the fuse still blows with the load(s) connected, this indicates an internal fault in the load(s).

Finding an earth fault

20 The battery negative terminal is connected to earth – the metal of the engine/transmission and the vehicle body – and most systems are wired so that they only receive a positive feed, the current returning via the metal of the vehicle body.

21 This means that the component mounting and the body form part of that circuit. Loose or corroded mountings can therefore cause a range of electrical faults, ranging from total failure of a circuit, to a puzzling partial fault. In particular, lights may shine dimly (especially when another circuit sharing the same earth point is in operation), motors (eg, wiper motors or the radiator cooling fan motor) may run slowly, and the operation of one circuit may have an apparently-unrelated effect on another.

22 Note that on many vehicles, earth straps are used between certain components, such as the engine/transmission and the body, usually where there is no metal-to-metal contact between components due to flexible rubber mountings, etc **(see illustrations)**.

23 To check whether a component is properly earthed, disconnect the battery and connect one lead of an ohmmeter to a known good earth point. Connect the other lead to the wire or earth connection being tested. The resistance reading should be zero; if not, check the connection as follows.

24 If an earth connection is thought to be faulty, dismantle the connection and clean back to bare metal both the bodyshell and the wire terminal or the component earth connection mating surface. Be careful to remove all traces of dirt and corrosion, then use a knife to trim away any paint, so that a clean metal-to-metal joint is made.

25 On reassembly, tighten the joint fasteners securely; if a wire terminal is being refitted, use serrated washers between the terminal and the bodyshell to ensure a clean and secure connection. When the connection is remade, prevent the onset of corrosion in the future by applying a coat of petroleum jelly or silicone-based grease. Alternatively, spray on (at regular intervals) a proprietary ignition sealer, or a water-dispersant lubricant.

3 Fuses and relays – general information

Fuses

1 The main fusebox is located behind the driver's side lower facia panel. An auxiliary fusebox is located in the engine compartment on the right-hand side, adjacent to the coolant expansion tank.

2 To gain access to the main fusebox, use a coin to undo the fasteners and release the panel from the driver's side of the facia. To gain access to those in the engine compartment box, unclip the lid.

3 A label identifying each fuse should be attached to the cover/lid, and a list of the circuits each fuse protects is given in the Wiring diagrams.

2.22a The earth connections in the engine compartment are just in front of the fusebox

2.22b Main earth strap (arrowed) on the bracket beneath the alternator

3.10 Relays simply pull from place

4.3 Unclip the transponder coil from the ignition switch barrel

4.4a The front wiper/washer and indicator/exterior light switches are retained by 2 screws each (arrowed)

4 To remove a fuse, first switch off the circuit concerned (or the ignition), then pull the fuse out of its terminals. The wire within the fuse is clearly visible; if the fuse is blown, it will be broken or melted.

5 To renew a fusible link (later models only), prise off its plastic cover, then undo its two retaining screws. The wire within the fuse will be broken if the fusible link has gone.

6 Always renew a fuse/fusible link with one of an identical rating; never use one with a different rating from the original, nor substitute anything else. Never renew a fuse/fusible link more than once without tracing the source of the trouble. The rating is stamped on top of the fuse/fusible link; note that are also colour-coded for easy recognition.

7 If a new fuse/fusible link blows immediately, find the cause before renewing it again – a short to earth as a result of faulty insulation is most likely. Where more than one circuit is protected, try to isolate the defect by switching on each circuit in turn (if possible) until it blows again. Always carry a supply of spare fuses/fusible links of each relevant rating on the vehicle; a spare of each fuse rating should be clipped into the base of the fusebox.

Relays

8 The relay functions are given in the Specifications at the start of this Chapter.

9 If a circuit or system controlled by a relay develops a fault and the relay is suspect, operate the system; if the relay is functioning, it should be possible to hear it click as it is

energised. If it clicks, the fault lies with the components or wiring of the system. If the relay is not being energised, then either the relay is not receiving a main supply or a switching voltage, or the relay itself is faulty. Testing is by the substitution of a known good unit, but be careful; while some relays are identical in appearance and in operation, others look similar but perform different functions.

10 To renew a relay, first ensure that the ignition switch is off. The relay can then simply be pulled out from the socket, and the new relay pressed in (see illustration).

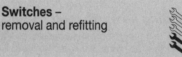

4 Switches – removal and refitting

Note: *Disconnect the battery negative lead before removing any switch, as described in Chapter 5. Refer to the precautions in Section 1 before proceeding.*

Ignition switch/ steering column lock

1 Refer to Chapter 11.

Front wiper/washer switch

2 Remove the driver's airbag rotary contact unit as described in Section 20.

3 Unclip the transponder coil from the ignition switch, and move it to one side without disconnecting the wiring plug (see illustration).

4 Disconnect the switch wiring plugs, then undo the 2 retaining screws, raise the edge of the switch bracket clear of the locating peg, and remove the switch (see illustrations).

5 Refitting is a reversal of the removal procedure.

Indicator/exterior lighting switch

6 Remove the driver's airbag rotary contact unit as described in Section 20.

7 Undo the 2 retaining screws, then carefully lift the edge of the switch bracket to clear the locating peg, and detach the switch from the bracket (see illustrations 4.4a and 4.4b).

8 Disconnect the wiring plugs as the switch is withdrawn.

9 Refitting is a reversal of removal.

Instrument panel switches

10 Carefully prise the switch from the panel (see illustration).

11 Disconnect the wiring plug as the switch is withdrawn.

12 Refitting is the reverse of removal, ensuring that the wiring connectors are securely reconnected.

Hazard warning/fuel filler flap/ heated front screen/hill descent/ off-road suspension switches

13 Carefully prise the switch from the facia (see illustration).

14 Disconnect the wiring plug as the switch is withdrawn.

15 Refitting is the reverse of removal.

4.4b Carefully lift the plastic bracket to clear the switch locating peg

4.10 Carefully pull the relevant switch from the instrument panel surround

4.13 Carefully prise the relevant switch from the facia centre panel

4.18 Disconnect the handbrake switch wiring plug . . .

4.19 . . . then undo the 2 retaining screws (arrowed)

4.21 Prise the switch cover from the console

Stop-light switch

16 Refer to Chapter 10.

Handbrake warning light switch

17 Remove the centre console as described in Chapter 12.
18 Disconnect the wiring connector from the switch (see illustration).
19 Undo the 2 retaining screws, and remove the switch from the lever (see illustration).
20 Refitting is the reverse of removal.

Electric window switches

Centre console switches

21 Carefully prise the console switch cover from place (see illustration).
22 Undo the 4 retaining screws and remove the switch panel from the console (see illustration).

23 Disconnect the wiring connector from the relevant switch, then depress the retaining clips and push the switch out of position (see illustration).
24 Refitting is the reverse of removal.

Rear door switches

25 Undo the retaining screw, and pull the interior door release handle surround far enough away from the door trim to disconnect the switch wiring plug (see illustration).
26 Push the switch from the handle surround (see illustration).
27 Refitting is a reversal of removal.

Electric mirror switch

28 Carefully prise the switch from the panel (see illustration).
29 Disconnect the wiring plug as the switch is withdrawn.
30 Refitting is a reversal of removal.

Headlight-levelling system switch

31 Undo the fasteners, and lower the driver's side lower facia panel.
32 Pull off the levelling switch knob, then unscrew the retaining nut, push the switch through the panel, and lower it through the lower facia panel recess (see illustration). Disconnect the switch wiring plug.
33 On refitting, reconnect the wiring plug, then locate the switch in the panel, tightening its retaining nut securely, and refit its control knob.

Electric sunroof switch

34 Using a suitable flat-bladed screwdriver, carefully prise the switch panel out from the overhead console, taking care not to mark either.

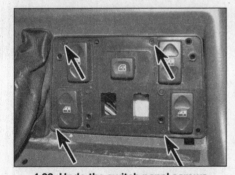

4.22 Undo the switch panel screws (arrowed)

4.23 Electric window switches – white plugs at the top

4.25 Disconnect the rear window switch wiring plug . . .

4.26 . . . then manoeuvre the surround over the handle

4.28 Carefully prise the mirror adjustment switch from the facia panel

4.32 Pull the knob from the headlight-levelling switch, then undo the retaining nut (arrowed)

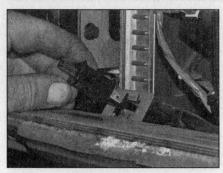

4.47 Carefully prise the glovebox light switch from the bracket

4.53a Prise the cover from the central locking switch . . .

4.53b . . . then prise the switch from the facia

35 Disconnect the wiring connector from the relevant switch, then depress the retaining clips and push the switch out from the panel.
36 On refitting, clip the switch back into the panel, reconnect the wiring connector, then clip the switch panel back into the overhead console.

Courtesy light switches

37 The function of the courtesy light switch is incorporated into the door lock assemblies. See Chapter 12 for details.

Heater control, blower motor and air recirculation switches

38 Remove the heater control panel as described in Chapter 3.
39 Pull/push the switch from the panel.
40 Refitting is the reverse of removal, ensuring that all wiring connectors are reconnected to their original positions.

Heated seat switches

41 Carefully prise the console switch cover from place **(see illustration 4.21)**.
42 Undo the 4 retaining screws and remove the switch panel from the console **(see illustration 4.22)**.
43 Disconnect the wiring connector from the relevant switch, then depress the retaining clips and push the switch out of position.
44 Refitting is the reverse of removal.

Glovebox illumination switch

45 Remove the passenger's side glovebox as described in Chapter 12, Section 26.
46 Prise out the fasteners and remove the lower facia panel from the passenger's side footwell.
47 Prise the switch from the facia, and disconnect its wiring connectors **(see illustration)**.
48 Refitting is the reverse of removal.

Electric seat switches

49 Using a small screwdriver, carefully release the two upper and lower retaining clips securing the switch panel to the side of the centre console.
50 Slide out the locking catch and disconnect the wiring plug.
51 Refitting is a reversal of removal.

Oil pressure warning light switch

52 Refer to Chapter 2A.

Central locking switch

53 Carefully prise the cover from the switch, then prise the switch from the facia panel **(see illustrations)**.
54 Disconnect the switch wiring plug.
55 Refitting is a reversal of removal.

---

5 Bulbs (exterior lights) – renewal

General

1 Whenever a bulb is renewed, note the following points:
a) *Disconnect the battery negative lead before starting work. Refer to the precautions in Section 1 before proceeding.*
b) *Remember that if the light has just been in use, the bulb may be extremely hot.*
c) *Always check the bulb contacts and holder, ensuring that there is clean metal-to-metal contact between the bulb and its live(s) and earth. Clean off any corrosion or dirt before fitting a new bulb.*
d) *Wherever bayonet-type bulbs are fitted*

5.3a Pull off the dust cover . . .

ensure that the live contact(s) bear firmly against the bulb contact.
e) *Always ensure that the new bulb is of the correct rating, and that it is completely clean before fitting it; this applies particularly to headlight bulbs (see below).*

Headlight

Vehicles up to 2003 model year

2 Remove the headlight unit as described in Section 7.
3 Remove the dust cover, then unhook and release the end of the bulb retaining clip, and release it from the rear of the light unit **(see illustrations)**.
4 Withdraw the bulb.
5 When handling the new bulb, use a tissue or clean cloth to avoid touching the glass with the fingers; moisture and grease from the skin can cause blackening and rapid failure of this type of bulb.
6 Install the new bulb, ensuring that its locating tabs are correctly located in the light cut-outs, and secure it in position with the retaining clip.
7 Refit the dust cover to the rear of the light unit, and reconnect the wiring connector.

Vehicles from 2003 model year

8 Remove the headlight unit as described in Section 7.
9 Rotate the dust cover anti-clockwise to remove it, disconnect the bulb wiring plug,

5.3b . . . then unhook the bulb retaining clip (arrowed)

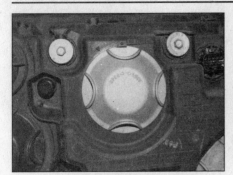

5.9a Rotate the dust cover anti-clockwise . . .

5.9b . . . then unhook the end of the retaining clip (arrowed)

5.12a Twist the sidelight bulbholder anti-clockwise and pull it from the headlight . . .

and renew the bulb as described above in paragraphs 3 to 6 (see illustrations).

10 Refit the rubber dust cover to the bulb, making sure that it is correctly seated, and fit the headlight unit as described in Section 7.

Front sidelight

Vehicles up to 2003 model year

11 Remove the headlight unit as described in Section 7.

12 Rotate the bulbholder anti-clockwise, then pull the capless bulb from the holder (see illustrations).

13 Refitting is the reverse of the removal procedure.

Vehicles from 2003 model year

14 Remove the headlight unit as described in Section 7.

15 Rotate the dust cover anti-clockwise, then pull the bulbholder from the rear of the headlight unit (see illustrations).

16 The bulb is of the capless (push-fit) type, and can be removed by simply pulling it out of the bulbholder.

17 Refitting is the reverse of removal.

Front direction indicator

Vehicles up to 2003 model year

18 Release the clips and remove the plastic cover over the top of the headlight (see illustration 7.2).

19 Undo the retaining screw, and pull the unit

from the wing (see illustration). Disconnect the wiring plugs as the unit is withdrawn.

20 Twist the main bulbholder anti-clockwise, and remove it from the rear of the unit.

21 The bulb is a bayonet fit in the holder, and can be removed by pressing it and twisting in an anti-clockwise direction.

22 To remove the unit's repeater, twist the bulbholder anti-clockwise, then pull the capless bulb from the holder (see illustration).

23 Refitting is the reverse of removal.

Vehicles from 2003 model year

24 Remove the headlight as described in Section 7.

25 Rotate the dust cover anti-clockwise and remove it (see illustration).

5.12b . . . then pull the capless bulb from the holder

5.15a Rotate the dust cover anti-clockwise . . .

5.15b . . . and pull the bulbholder from the headlight

5.19 Undo the directional indicator retaining screw (arrowed)

5.22 The front indicator has its own repeater bulb – twist the bulbholder anti-clockwise to remove it

5.25 Twist the indicator dust cover anti-clockwise

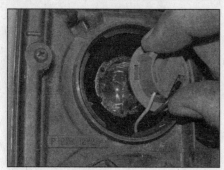

5.26 Rotate the bulbholder anti-clockwise to remove it

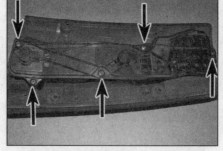

5.34 Undo the 5 screws securing the bulholder assembly (arrowed)

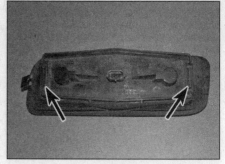

5.37a Squeeze the clips (arrowed) towards each other . . .

26 Twist the bulbholder anti-clockwise, and remove it from the rear of the light unit **(see illustration)**.
27 The bulb is a bayonet fit in the holder, and can be removed by pressing it and twisting in an anti-clockwise direction.
28 Refitting is the reverse of removal.

Direction indicator side repeater

29 Carefully push the light unit to the left, to release its retaining clip, then withdraw the unit from the wing.
30 Turn the lens unit anti-clockwise to release it, then remove it from the bulbholder.
31 The bulb is of the capless (push-fit) type, and can be removed by simply pulling it out of the bulbholder.
32 Refitting is a reverse of the removal procedure.

Rear light cluster

33 Remove the light cluster as described in Section 7.
34 Undo the 5 screws, and withdraw the bulbholder assembly from the rear of the light unit **(see illustration)**. The bulbs are a bayonet fit in the holder, and can be removed by pressing them in and twisting in an anti-clockwise direction.
35 Refitting is a reverse of the removal procedure.

Bumper-mounted rear lights

36 Reach up behind the bumper, then press the spring clip to release the light unit from the bumper **(see illustration 7.22)**.
37 Squeeze the two clips together to release the bulbholder, then remove it from the rear

of the light unit. The bulb is a bayonet fit in the holder, and can be removed by pressing it and twisting in an anti-clockwise direction **(see illustrations)**. Note that on models from 2003 model year, the reversing light bulbs are halogen type – do not touch the bulbs with bare hands.
38 Refitting is a reverse of the removal procedure.

High-level stop-light

39 Undo the two retaining screws, and detach the rear of the light unit **(see illustration)**.
40 Twist the bulbholder anti-clockwise, and withdraw it from the rear of the light unit **(see illustration)**.
41 The bulb is a bayonet fit in the holder, and can be removed by pressing it and twisting in an anti-clockwise direction.
42 Refitting is a reverse of the removal procedure.

Number plate light

43 Slacken and remove the two retaining screws, then lift out the light unit and release the bulb from its contacts **(see illustrations)**.
44 On refitting, ensure that the contacts securely grip the bulb ends (bend them carefully if necessary), then refit the light unit and tighten its retaining screws.

Front foglight

45 Lying under the front of the vehicle, reach between the wheel arch liner and the bumper.

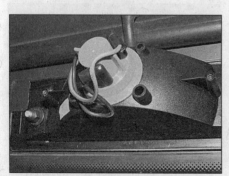

5.37b . . . then lift the bulbholder assembly from place

5.39 Undo the 2 screws (arrowed) and remove the high-level brake light cover

5.40 Rotate the bulbholder anti-clockwise and remove it

5.43a Undo the number plate light screws (arrowed)

5.43b Pull the festoon bulb from the contacts

5.46 Rotate the foglight cover anti-clockwise

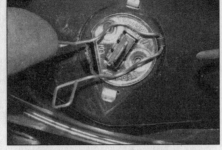

5.48 Unhook the bulb retaining clip

5.50 Twist the foglight bulb/holder anti-clockwise and pull it from place

Vehicles up to 2003 model year

46 Rotate the cover on the rear of the foglight anti-clockwise and remove it **(see illustration)**.

47 Disconnect the wiring plug from the bulb.

48 Release the clip and pull the bulb from the light **(see illustration)**.

49 Fit the new bulb ensuring the cut-out in the bulb flange aligns with the cut-out in the fitting.

Vehicles from 2003 model year

50 Twist the bulb anti-clockwise and pull it from the light unit **(see illustration)**.

51 Squeeze together the locking clips and pull the bulb from the connector. The bulb is integral with the bulbholder.

52 Refitting is a reversal of removal.

6 Bulbs (interior lights) – renewal

General

1 Refer to Section 5, paragraph 1.

Courtesy light

2 Using a suitable screwdriver, carefully prise the light unit lens out of position, and release the bulb from the light unit contacts **(see illustrations)**.

3 Install the new bulb, ensuring that it is securely held in position by the contacts (bend them carefully if necessary), then clip the lens back into position.

Instrument panel illumination/warning lights

Note: *Only the main beam warning light and illumination lights have a traditional bulb – the remaining warning lights use non-renewable light emitting diodes (LEDs).*

4 Remove the instrument panel as described in Section 9.

5 Twist the relevant bulbholder anti-clockwise, and withdraw it from the rear of the panel **(see illustration)**.

6 Most bulbs are integral with their holders, although a few are of the capless (push-fit) type **(see illustrations)**. Be very careful to ensure that the new bulbs are of the correct rating, the same as those removed; this is especially important in the case of the main beam warning light.

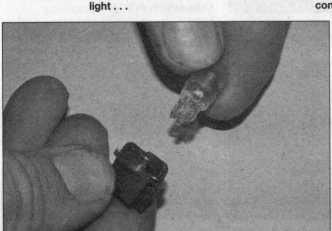

6.2a Prise the lens from the courtesy light . . .

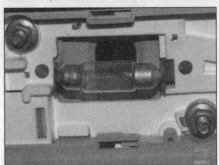

6.2b . . . and pull the bulb from the contacts

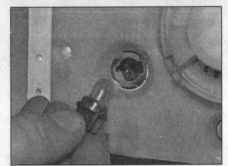

6.5 Rotate the bulbholder anti-clockwise . . .

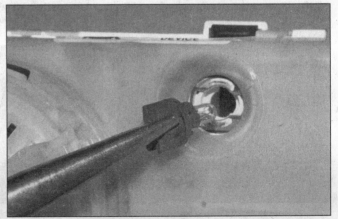

6.6a . . . and pull the capless bulb from the holder . . .   **6.6b . . . although some are integral with the bulbholder**

6.8a Carefully prise the glovebox light from place . . .

6.8b . . . then pull the festoon bulb from the contacts

7 Refit the bulbholder to the rear of the instrument panel, then refit the instrument panel as described in Section 9.

Glovebox illumination light bulb

8 Open the glovebox. Using a small flat-bladed screwdriver, carefully prise the light unit out of position, then release the bulb from its contacts **(see illustrations)**.
9 Install the new bulb, ensuring that it is securely held in position by the contacts, and clip the light unit back into position.

Heater control switch bulbs

Non-air conditioned models

10 Remove the switch as described in Section 4.

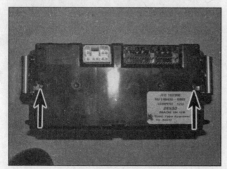

6.15a Undo the screws (arrowed) and lift off the rear cover . . .

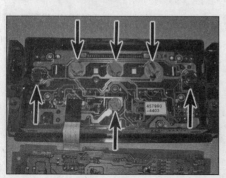

6.16 Rotate the bulbholders (arrowed) anti-clockwise and remove them

11 Twist the bulbholder anti-clockwise and pull it from the switch.
12 The bulb is of the capless (push-fit) type, and can be removed by simply pulling it out of the bulbholder.
13 Refitting is a reversal of removal.

Air conditioned models

14 Remove the control panel as described in Chapter 3.
15 Undo the 2 screws, lift off the rear cover, followed by the printed circuit board **(see illustrations)**.
16 Rotate the bulbholder anti-clockwise and pull it from the unit. The larger bulbholders contain capless bulbs, which can be pulled from the holders. The smaller bulbholders are integral with the bulbs, and must be renewed as a unit **(see illustration)**.
17 Refitting is a reversal of removal.

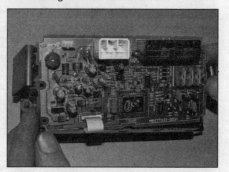

6.15b . . . then lift away the printed circuit board

6.19 The clock illumination bulb is integral with the bulbholder

Clock illumination bulb

18 Remove the clock as described in Section 11.
19 Twist the bulbholder anti-clockwise, and withdraw it from the rear of the clock. The bulb is integral with the holder **(see illustration)**.
20 Fit the new bulb to the rear of the clock, and refit the clock as described in Section 11.

Switch illumination bulbs

21 With the exception of the heater control panel switches, the switches are illuminated by non-renewable light emitting diodes (LEDs). If the illumination fails, the switch must be renewed.

Ignition transponder coil illumination bulb

22 Use a coin to twist the fasteners, then open the lower facia access panel under the steering column.
23 Undo the steering column shroud retaining screws, unclip the shroud halves, and remove both the upper and lower shrouds from the steering column.
24 Release the clip and pull the transponder coil from the ignition switch barrel **(see illustration 4.3)**.
25 Remove the bulbholder from the rear of the coil **(see illustration)**.
26 The bulb is of the capless (push-fit) type, and can be removed by simply pulling it out of the bulbholder.
27 Refitting is the reverse of removal.

Automatic transmission selector

28 There are no renewable bulbs fitted to the selector panel.

7	**Exterior light units –** removal and refitting	

Note: *Refer to the precautions in Section 1 before proceeding.*

Headlight

Vehicles up to 2003 model year

1 If working on the right-hand headlight, unclip the cover over the battery.

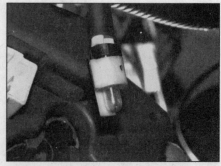

6.27 Remove the bulbholder from the rear of the transponder coil

7.2 Release the clips and remove the headlight cover

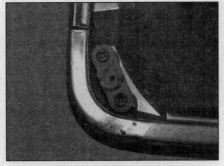

7.5 Undo the screws and remove the mounting sockets

7.8 Open the access flap, then undo the headlight retaining screw (arrowed)

2 Unclip and remove the cover over the headlight **(see illustration)**.

3 Pull the headlight unit forwards to release it from the 3 mounting studs.

4 Disconnect the headlight and sidelight wiring plugs.

5 If required, undo the 6 screws and remove the headlight mounting sockets **(see illustration)**.

6 Refitting is a direct reversal of the removal procedure. On completion, check the headlight beam alignment using the information given in Section 8.

Vehicles from 2003 model year

7 Remove the front grille as described in Chapter 12.

8 Open the access panel in the air deflector and remove the screw securing the headlight to the front panel **(see illustration)**.

9 Undo the two mounting screws at the top edge of the headlight.

10 Pull the headlight forward and disconnect the wiring plugs.

11 Refitting is a direct reversal of the removal procedure. On completion, check the headlight beam alignment using the information given in Section 8. Where necessary, check the operation of the headlight-levelling system.

Front direction indicator

Up to 2003 model year only

12 Release the clips and remove the cover over the headlight.

13 Undo the screw and pull the light unit from the wing **(see illustration 5.19)**.

14 Twist the bulbholder anti-clockwise to free it from the rear of the light unit (or, alternatively, disconnect the wiring plug from the rear of the bulbholder), and remove the light unit from the vehicle.

15 Refitting is the reverse of removal.

Direction indicator side repeater

16 Carefully push the light unit to the left, to release its retaining clip, then withdraw the unit from the wing.

17 Turn the lens unit anti-clockwise to release it, then remove the light unit from the vehicle.

18 Refitting is a reverse of the removal procedure.

Rear light cluster

19 Undo the 4 retaining screws and pull the light unit from the vehicle body **(see illustration)**.

20 Disconnect the wiring connector as the unit is removed.

21 Refitting is the reverse of removal.

Bumper-mounted rear lights

22 Reach up behind the bumper, depress the spring clip and pull/push the light unit from the bumper **(see illustration)**.

23 Squeeze together the 2 clips and detach the bulbholder assembly from the rear of the light unit.

24 Refitting is a reverse of the removal procedure.

High-level stop-light

25 Undo the two retaining screws, and detach the rear of the light unit.

26 Undo the retaining nuts, and remove the light **(see illustration)**.

27 Refitting is a reverse of the removal procedure.

Number plate light

28 Slacken and remove the two retaining screws, then lift out the light unit of position.

29 Disconnect the wiring connectors from the terminals, and remove the light unit from the vehicle.

30 Refitting is the reverse of removal.

Front foglight

Vehicles up to 2003 model year

31 To remove the right-hand foglight unit, undo the screws and remove the wheel arch liner-to-bumper panel. Disconnect the wiring plug, and the 2 condensation drain hoses.

32 To remove the left-hand foglight unit, remove the bumper as described in Chapter 12.

33 On both foglights, undo the retaining

7.19 Undo the retaining screws (arrowed) and remove the rear light cluster

7.22 Depress the spring clip (arrowed) and push the light unit from the bumper

7.26 The high-level stop-light is secured by 2 nuts (arrowed)

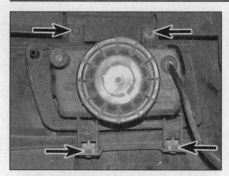

7.33 Undo the screws (arrowed) and remove the foglight

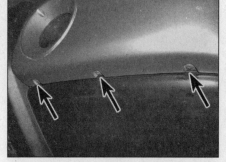

7.35a The bumper finisher trim is retained by 3 screw underneath (arrowed) . . .

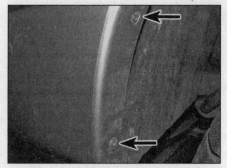

7.35b . . . and 2 screws on the rear edge (arrowed)

screws and remove foglight from the bumper **(see illustration)**.

34 Refitting is a reversal of removal.

Vehicles from 2003 model year

35 Undo the 5 screws, and remove the front bumper finisher trim **(see illustrations)**.

36 Release the retaining clip and detach the headlight washer hose from the jet.

37 Undo the 3 retaining screws and pull the foglight from the bumper. Disconnect the wiring plug as the light is withdrawn.

38 Refitting is a reversal of removal.

8 Headlight beam alignment – general information

Accurate adjustment of the headlight beam is only possible using optical beam-setting equipment, and this work should therefore be carried out by a Land Rover dealer or suitably-equipped workshop.

For reference, the headlights can be adjusted using the adjuster assemblies fitted to the rear of each light unit **(see illustrations)**.

Some models are equipped with an electrically-operated headlight beam adjustment system – the recommended settings are as follows:

0 *Front seat(s) occupied.*
1 *All seats occupied.*
2 *All seats occupied and load in luggage compartment.*

8.1a Headlight aim adjusters (arrowed) – vehicles up to 2003 model year . . .

8.1b . . . and vehicles from 2003 model year

3 *Driver's seat occupied and load in the luggage compartment.*

When adjusting the headlight aim, ensure that the switch is set in position 0.

9 Instrument panel – removal and refitting

Removal

1 Use a coin to undo the fasteners, then open the facia access panel beneath the steering column.

2 Undo the 3 retaining screws and remove the two halves of the steering column shrouds.

3 Undo the 2 screws, and pull the instrument

panel surround rearwards to release the two retaining clips **(see illustrations)**.

4 Move the surround rearwards until access can be gained to the switch wiring connectors. Disconnect each switch wiring connector, noting its correct fitted location, then remove the surround; the wiring connectors are colour-coded to aid identification.

5 Slacken and remove the four retaining screws, then carefully manoeuvre the instrument panel out of position **(see illustration)**. Disconnect the instrument panel wiring plugs as the unit is withdrawn.

Caution: Do not allow the instrument panel to rest face-down. The rotary dials are fluid damped, and storing the panel face-down may cause the fluid to leak.

Refitting

6 Refitting is a reversal of removal.

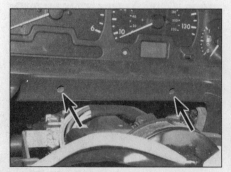

9.3a Undo the 2 screws (arrowed) . . .

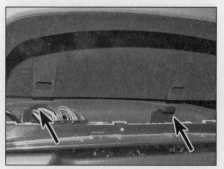

9.3b . . . and pull the surround rearwards to release the clips (arrowed)

9.5 The instrument panel is secured by 2 screws each side (left-hand ones arrowed)

11.2a Use an old feeler gauge . . .

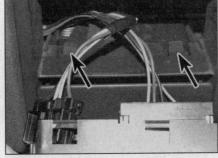

11.2b . . . to release the 4 clips (lower clips arrowed)

12.2 Disconnect the horn wiring plug (arrowed)

10 Instrument panel components – removal and refitting

Other than the main beam warning bulb and some illumination bulbs, there are no user serviceable parts within the instrument panel. Should the panel develop a fault, have the vehicles self-diagnosis system interrogated using a fault code reader by a Land Rover dealer or specialist. Any faults within the panel should generate codes which can be retrieved and interpreted using a suitable fault code reader via the vehicle's diagnostic socket, located above the driver's pedals in the lower facia panel.

11 Clock – removal and refitting

Removal

1 Remove the central locking switch from beside the clock, as described in Section 4.
2 Use a flat-bladed tool to release the 4 clips and prise the clock from the facia, taking great care not to mark either (see illustrations). Disconnect the wiring connectors.

Refitting

3 Refitting is a reversal of removal.

12 Horn – removal and refitting

Removal

1 Remove the radiator grille as described in Chapter 12.
2 Disconnect the wiring connector from the relevant horn (see illustration).
3 Slacken and remove the retaining nut and washer, then remove the horn from the vehicle.

Refitting

4 Refitting is the reverse of removal.

13 Wiper arm – removal and refitting

Removal

1 Operate the wiper motor, then switch it off so that the wiper arm returns to the 'at rest' (parked) position.
2 Stick a piece of masking tape to the windscreen along the edge of the wiper blade, to use as an alignment aid on refitting. If the tailgate wiper arm is being removed, remove the spare wheel.
3 Lift up/remove (as applicable) the wiper arm spindle nut cover, then slacken and remove the spindle nut. Lift the blade off the glass, and pull the wiper arm off its spindle. If necessary, the arm can be levered off the spindle using a suitable flat-bladed screwdriver (see illustrations).

13.3a Remove the spindle nut cover . . .

13.3b . . . then undo the spindle nut

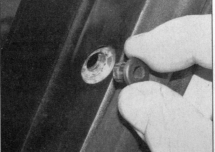

14.1 Prise out the 3 windscreen pillar trim clips . . .

14.2 . . . then pull the trim from the retaining clips (arrowed)

Refitting

4 Ensure that the wiper arm and spindle splines are clean and dry.
5 Locate the wiper arm on the spindle, aligning the wiper blade with the tape fitted on removal.
6 Refit the spindle nut, tightening it securely, and clip the nut cover back in position.

14 Windscreen wiper motor and linkage – removal and refitting

Removal

1 Prise out the centre pins, then remove the 3 clips securing the windscreen pillar trims each side (see illustration).
2 Carefully prise the pillar trims from place, releasing the 3 spring clips as the trims are withdrawn (see illustration).

14.4 Undo the large spindle nut and recover the washers

14.5a Undo the bolt in the centre of the scuttle trim panel (arrowed) . . .

14.5b . . . then slacken the screw and prise out the 2 scrivets

14.6 Wiper motor mounting plate nuts and bolt (arrowed)

14.7 Undo the wiper linkage bolt

14.11 Refit the push-on clips to the windscreen pillar trims before refitting

3 Remove both windscreen wiper arms as described in Section 13.
4 Undo the large nut from each wiper spindle, and remove the washers, noting each one's correct fitted position **(see illustration)**.

15.3 Undo the large spindle nut and recover the washers

15.6a Undo the tailgate wiper motor retaining bolts (arrowed)

15.6b Disconnect the wiper motor wiring plugs

5 Undo the central bolt, then undo the central screws and prise out the 2 plastic expanding rivets (one each side), and remove the scuttle trim panel from in front of the windscreen **(see illustrations)**.
6 Undo the 4 nuts and one bolt securing the motor mounting plate **(see illustration)**. Undo the nut securing the earth strap to the vehicle body.
7 Undo the nut and bolt securing the wiper linkage to the vehicle body **(see illustration)**.
8 Manoeuvre the motor and linkage from position, disconnecting the wiring plug as the assembly is withdrawn.
9 If necessary, mark the relative positions of the motor shaft and linkage arm, then unscrew the retaining nut from the motor spindle. Free the wiper linkage from the spindle, then remove the motor retaining bolts and separate the motor and linkage.

Refitting

10 Where necessary, assemble the motor and linkage, and securely tighten the motor retaining bolts. Locate the linkage arm on the motor spindle, aligning the marks made prior to removal, and securely tighten its retaining nut.
11 The remainder of refitting is a reversal of removal, noting that the retaining clips should be fitted to the windscreen pillar trims before attempting to refit them **(see illustration)**.

15 Tailgate wiper motor
– removal and refitting

Removal

1 Remove the spare wheel.
2 Remove the wiper arm as described in Section 13. Allow the arm to hang down, supported by the washer hose. Take care not to damage the paintwork.
3 Unscrew the large nut from the wiper spindle, and recover the washer and rubber seal **(see illustration)**.
4 Remove the tailgate inner trim panel as described in Section 15 of Chapter 12.
5 Carefully peel the plastic sheet from the tailgate frame.
6 Slacken and remove the wiper motor mounting bolts, disconnecting the wiring plugs as the motor is withdrawn **(see illustrations)**.
7 Manoeuvre the motor assembly out from the tailgate.

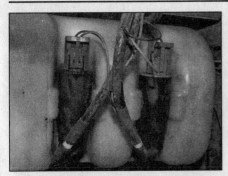

16.2 Disconnect the wiring plugs and hoses from the washer pumps

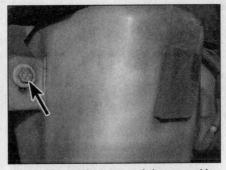

16.3a The washer reservoir is secured by 1 bolt at the rear (arrowed) . . .

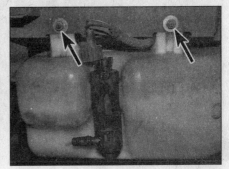

16.3b . . . and 2 nuts at the front (arrowed)

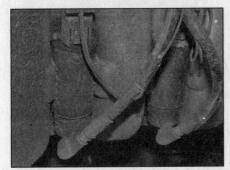

16.7 Washer pumps and hoses – vehicles from 2003 model year

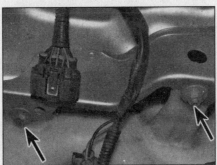

16.8 Washer reservoir front mounting nuts (arrowed) – vehicles from 2003 model year

Refitting

8 Refitting is a reversal of removal.

16 Windscreen/tailgate washer system components – removal and refitting

Washer system reservoir

Vehicles up to 2003 model year

1 Remove the front grille and bumper as described in Chapter 12.

2 Note their fitted positions, then disconnect the wiring plugs and hoses from the reservoir pumps **(see illustration)**.

3 The reservoir is retained by two nuts at the front and one bolt at the rear. Undo these fasteners, then lower the reservoir from the filler neck **(see illustrations)**.

4 If required, prise the pumps from the reservoir, and recover the fluid level indicator from the filler neck.

5 Refitting is a reversal of removal.

Vehicles from 2003 model year

6 Remove the front bumper as described in Chapter 12.

7 Note their fitted positions, then disconnect the wiring plugs and washer hoses from the reservoir pumps **(see illustration)**.

8 The reservoir is secured by 2 nuts at the front and 2 bolts at the rear. Undo the nuts/bolts and withdraw the reservoir **(see illustrations)**.

Washer pump

9 Undo the screws and remove the left-hand wheel arch-to-bumper panel.

10 Note their fitted positions, and disconnect the hoses and wiring plugs from the pump(s) **(see illustration 16.2)**.

11 Prise the pump from the reservoir.

12 Refitting is the reverse of removal, using a new sealing grommet if the original one shows signs of damage or deterioration.

Windscreen washer jets

13 Disconnect the washer hose from the base of the jet, then carefully compress the retaining clip and remove the jet **(see illustration)**. Take great care not to damage the bonnet paintwork.

14 On refitting, refit the washer, reconnect the washer hose, then check the operation of the jet. If necessary adjust the nozzle using a pin, aiming the spray to a point slightly above the centre of the wiper blade swept area.

Tailgate washer jet

15 Remove the spare wheel from the tailgate.

16 Unclip the wiper blade **(see illustration)**.

17 Release the jet and hose from the wiper arm, then pull the jet from the hose.

18 Refitting is a reversal of removal.

17 Headlight washer system components – removal and refitting

Washer system reservoir

1 Refer to Section 16.

Washer pump

2 Remove the front bumper as described in Chapter 12.

3 Disconnect the wiring plug from the pump **(see illustration)**.

16.13 Depress the clip (arrowed) and ease the washer jet from the bonnet

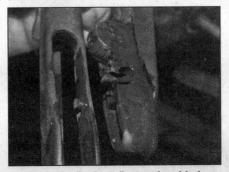

16.16 Unclip the tailgate wiper blade

17.3 Disconnect the wiring plug and hose from the headlight washer pump

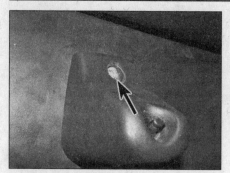

17.6 Prise out the cap and undo the washer jet retaining screw (arrowed)

17.7 Lift the jet housing and release the hose clip (arrowed)

17.11 Slide off the jet retaining clip

4 Carefully ease the pump out from the reservoir, and recover its sealing grommet.
5 Refitting is the reverse of removal, using a new sealing grommet if the old one shows signs of damage or deterioration.

Washer jet

Vehicles up to 2003 model year

6 Prise out the plastic cap and unscrew the jet housing screw (see illustration).
7 Lift up the housing a little, and release the hose clip. Disconnect the hose from the jet (see illustration).
8 Refitting is the reverse of removal.

Vehicles from 2003 model year

9 Undo the 5 retaining screws and pull the finisher trim from the bumper (see illustrations 7.35a and 7.35b).

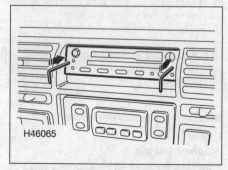

18.1a Use two 2.5 mm Allen keys and undo the screws – Low-line models

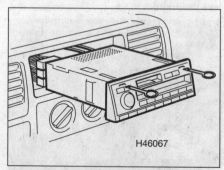

18.1c On High-line models, insert the special tools into the slots at the top of the unit to release the 2 clips

10 Release the clip and disconnect the hose from the jet.
11 Slide off the jet retaining clip (see illustration).
12 Remove the jet from the finisher trim.
13 Refitting is a reversal of removal.

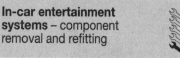

18 In-car entertainment systems – component removal and refitting

Note: *The following removal and refitting procedure is for the range of audio units which Land Rover fit as standard equipment. Removal and refitting procedures of non-standard units may differ slightly. Before removing the unit, refer to battery disconnection information in Chapter 5.*

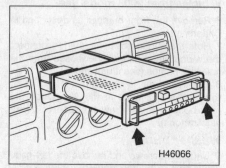

18.1b On Mid-line models, insert the special tools to release the 4 clips

18.6 The CD autochanger is secured by 2 screws each side (arrowed)

Removal

Radio/cassette player

1 On High-line and Mid-line models, two special tools, obtainable from most car accessory shops, are required for removal. On Low-line models, the unit can be removed using two 2.5 mm Allen keys (see illustrations).
2 Disconnect the battery negative lead – see Chapter 5.
3 Insert the tools into the holes, and push them until they snap into place, or insert the Allen keys and undo the screws. The radio/cassette player can then be slid out of the facia, and the aerial lead and wiring connectors disconnected.

CD autochanger

4 Remove the right-hand front seat as described in Chapter 12.
5 Disconnect the autochanger wiring plug.
6 Undo the 4 screws securing the autochanger to the vehicle body, then remove the unit (see illustration). If required, undo the screws and detach the brackets from the unit.

DVD screen player unit

7 Carefully prise the trim surrounds from each side of the DVD screen unit controls, and lower the screen.
8 Undo the 2 retaining screws in the screen recess, and the screw each side adjacent to the controls.
9 Disconnect the wiring plug as the unit is withdrawn.

CD/DVD player switch box

10 Prise out the fasteners, and remove the lower facia trim panel above the driver's pedals. Release the diagnostic socket from the panel as it is withdrawn.
11 Use a coin to undo the fasteners, and open the lower facia access panel beneath the steering column.
12 Release the cable ties securing the switch box harness to the facia.
13 Release the switch box from the support bracket, and disconnect the wiring plugs.

Power amplifier

14 Disconnect the battery negative lead as described in Chapter 5.

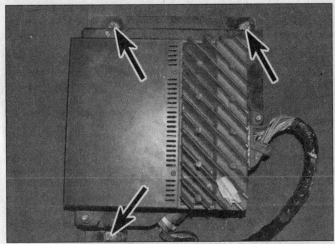

18.16 Undo the 3 nuts (arrowed) securing the mounting bracket

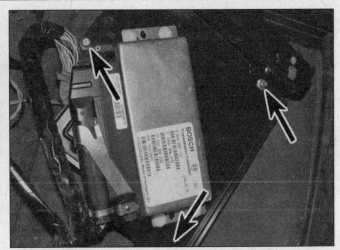

18.18 Undo the 3 screws (arrowed) and detach the amplifier from the bracket

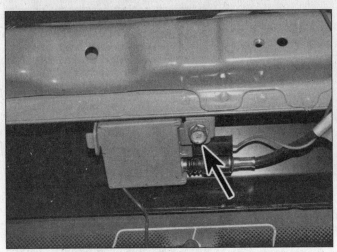

18.20 Aerial amplifier retaining bolt (arrowed)

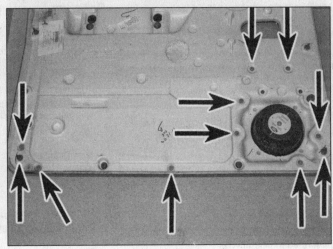

18.23 Undo the 9 Torx screws, and 2 plastic nuts securing the door pocket (arrowed)

15 Remove the passenger's front seat as described in Chapter 12.

16 Undo the 3 nuts securing the amplifier mounting bracket to the vehicle body **(see illustration)**.

17 On automatic transmission models, disconnect the multiplug from the transmission ECU located on the underside of the bracket.

18 Undo the 3 retaining screws, and detach the amplifier from the bracket **(see illustration)**.

Aerial amplifier

19 On low-spec modes, remove the right-hand C/D-pillar trim panel as described in Chapter 12, Section 26. On higher spec models, a second FM aerial is fitted behind the left-hand C/D-pillar trim panel.

20 Disconnect the wiring plugs from the amplifier, and the aerial **(see illustration)**.

21 Undo the retaining bolt and remove the amplifier.

Front door lower speaker

22 Remove the front door inner trim panel as described in Chapter 12.

23 Undo the 9 Torx screws, 2 plastic nuts, and remove the door pocket **(see illustration)**.

24 Undo the 3 screws securing the speaker to the door trim panel **(see illustration)**.

Front door upper speaker

25 Remove the front door inner trim panel as described in Chapter 12.

26 Unscrew the plastic locknut, and detach the speaker from the door trim **(see illustration)**.

Rear door lower speaker

27 Carefully prise the grille from the speaker to release the 6 retaining clips.

28 Undo the 3 retaining screws, and pull the

18.24 The door lower speaker is secured by 3 screws

18.26 The door upper speaker is secured by a plastic nut (arrowed)

18.31 Undo the 6 speaker grille retaining screws (arrowed)

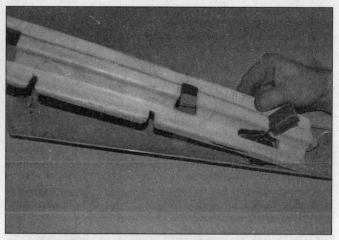

18.35a Remove the A-pillar trim insulation material . . .

speaker from the door. Disconnect the wiring plug as the speaker is withdrawn.

Rear door upper speaker

29 Remove the rear door inner trim panel, as described in Chapter 12.

30 Unscrew the plastic locknut, and detach the speaker from the door trim.

Tailgate speaker

31 Undo the 6 speaker grille retaining screws, and remove the grille **(see illustration)**.

32 Undo the 4 screws securing the speaker trim casing, and remove it.

33 Undo the 8 retaining screws, and remove the speakers. Disconnect the wiring plug as each speaker is withdrawn.

A-pillar speaker

34 Remove the A-pillar trim panel as described in Chapter 12.

35 Prise out the sound insulation material, then rotate the speaker clockwise, and detach it from the trim panel **(see illustrations)**.

ICE remote control switches

36 Remove the driver's airbag as described in Section 20.

37 Disconnect the wiring plugs from the remote control switches.

38 Undo the 2 retaining screws, and remove the switches from the steering wheel **(see illustration)**.

Refitting

39 In all cases, refitting is a reversal of removal, noting the following points:
 a) *Where necessary, reconnect the battery negative lead, and input the security code.*
 b) *Tighten all fasteners securely.*
 c) *Ensure all harnesses are correctly routed, and secured with cable ties – where applicable.*

19 Airbag system – general information and precautions

All models are equipped with a driver's airbag, with a passenger's airbag available as an option.

The driver's airbag unit is fitted to the steering wheel, and the passenger's airbag unit is fitted to the top of the facia panel. In addition to the airbag unit(s), there is a diagnostic and control unit (DCU) (which incorporates a deceleration sensor, and a safing sensor) and a warning light in the instrument panel.

The airbag system is triggered in the event of a frontal impact. The airbag(s) is/are inflated (by a built-in gas generator) within milliseconds, and forms a safety cushion between the driver and steering wheel/passenger and facia.

This prevents contact between the driver's/passenger's upper body and wheel/facia, and therefore greatly reduces the risk of injury. The airbag then deflates almost immediately.

Every time the ignition is switched on, the airbag control unit performs a self-test. The self-test takes between 5 and 8 seconds, and during this time, the airbag warning light in the instrument panel is illuminated. After the self-test has been completed, the warning light should go out. If the warning light fails to come on, remains illuminated after the initial period, or comes on at any time when the vehicle is being driven, there is a fault in the airbag system. The vehicle should be taken to a Land Rover dealer or specialist for examination at the earliest possible opportunity.

⚠ *Warning: Before carrying out any operations on the airbag system, disconnect the battery positive and negative terminals, and wait AT LEAST 10 minutes, to ensure that any residual electrical energy has been dissipated.*

⚠ *Warning: Note that the airbag must not be subjected to temperatures in excess of 90°C. When the airbag is removed, ensure that it is stored the correct way up, to prevent possible inflation.*

⚠ *Warning: Do not use electrical test equipment on the airbag system components or wiring connectors, as this could lead to the system being accidentally triggered. Testing of the airbag system can only be carried out by a Land Rover dealer or specialist with access to the special electronic test equipment (Testbook).*

⚠ *Warning: Do not allow any water, solvents or cleaning agents to contact the airbag unit(s). They must only be cleaned using a damp cloth.*

⚠ *Warning: The airbag(s) and control unit are both sensitive to impact. If either is dropped or shows signs of physical damage or deterioration, they must be renewed.*

18.35b . . . then rotate the speaker clockwise to remove it

18.38 Undo the ICE remote control switch screws (arrowed)

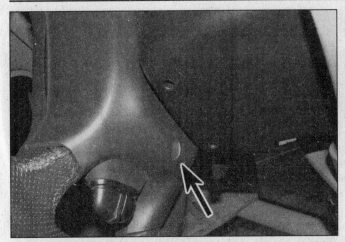

20.2 The driver's airbag is retained by 2 Torx screws accessible through the back of the steering wheel (arrowed)

20.3 Disconnect the driver's airbag wiring plug

⚠ *Warning: Disconnect the airbag(s) and control unit wiring plugs prior to using arc/mig-welding equipment on the vehicle.*

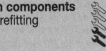

20 Airbag system components – removal and refitting

Note: *Refer to the warnings given in the previous Section before carrying out the following operations.*

1 Disconnect the battery negative then positive leads (refer to Chapter 5), and wait at least 10 minutes before proceeding as described under the relevant sub-heading.

Driver's airbag unit

Note: *New airbag retaining screws will be required on refitting.*

2 Working through the back of the steering wheel, undo the two T30 Torx bolts securing the airbag **(see illustration)**. Note that the screws will remain captive, even when completely undone.

3 Pull the airbag from the steering wheel. Disconnect the wiring plug as the airbag is withdrawn **(see illustration)**.

4 On refitting, reconnect the wiring connector, then fit the airbag unit to the centre of the steering wheel.

5 Tighten the Torx screws to the specified torque setting.

6 Reconnect the battery leads as described in Chapter 5.

Passenger's airbag unit

7 Remove the passenger's side glovebox, as described in Chapter 12, Section 26.

8 Disconnect the wiring plug from the airbag unit **(see illustration)**.

9 Undo the 4 Torx screws, and remove the airbag from the facia **(see illustration)**.

10 Refitting is a reversal of removal. Tighten the airbag Torx screws to the specified torque.

Diagnostic and control unit (DCU)

11 Remove the centre console as described in Chapter 12.

12 Disconnect the DCU wiring plug **(see illustrations)**.

13 Unscrew and remove the 3 Torx bolts, then remove the unit from the vehicle **(see illustration)**.

Caution: The DCU incorporates the safing and deceleration sensors, and is sensitive to shock. Handle with extreme care.

14 Refitting is the reverse of removal, tightening the retaining screws to the

20.8 Disconnect the passenger's airbag wiring plug

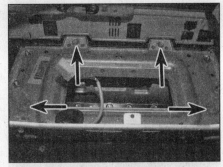

20.9 Undo the 4 Torx screws (arrowed) securing the passenger's airbag

20.12a Depress the clip . . .

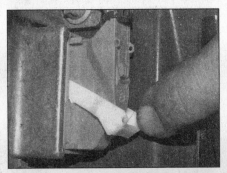

20.12b . . . then release the DCU wiring plug locking catch

20.13 Undo the 3 Torx bolts (arrowed) and remove the DCU

20.19a Release the contact unit lower clip . . .

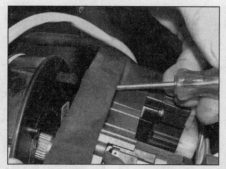

20.19b . . . and upper clip

20.19c Secure the contact unit with adhesive tape (arrowed)

specified torque setting. Ensure that the wiring connector is securely reconnected and its retaining clip is correctly seated.

Driver's airbag rotary contact unit

15 Remove the steering wheel as described in Chapter 11.

16 Use a coin to undo the fasteners, the open the lower facia access panel beneath the steering column.

17 Undo the steering column shroud retaining screws, unclip the shroud halves, and remove both the upper and lower shrouds from the steering column.

18 Trace the wiring back from the contact unit, release the connector from the bracket and disconnect it.

19 Release the two retaining clips, then free the contact unit from the top of the combination switch assembly. If the contact unit is to be re-used, wrap adhesive tape around the unit **(see illustrations)**. This will prevent unnecessary rotation of the wiring unit, and ensure that it remains correctly positioned until it is refitted.

20 If a new contact unit is being installed, ensure that the tape on the unit is unbroken. Do not install the unit if the tape has been broken.

21 Ensure that the front wheels are positioned in the straight-ahead position, then remove the tape from the contact unit.

22.2 The headlight-levelling motor is a bayonet fitting in the body

22 Clip the contact into position on the steering column combination switch assembly, and connect its wiring connector.

23 Refit the steering column shrouds, and securely tighten the retaining screws.

24 Refit the steering wheel as described in Chapter 11, making sure that it engages correctly with the contact unit.

21 Anti-theft alarm system – general information

Note: *This information is applicable only to the anti-theft alarm system fitted by Land Rover as standard equipment.*

All models in the range are fitted with an anti-theft alarm system as standard equipment. The alarm system has ultrasonic (movement) sensing, as well as sensing opening of the doors, tailgate or bonnet. If movement is detected inside the vehicle, or if the tailgate, bonnet or any of the doors are opened whilst the alarm is set, the alarm siren will sound and the hazard warning lights will flash. The alarm also has an immobiliser function, which makes the ignition and starter circuits inoperable whilst the alarm is triggered.

Should the alarm system develop a fault, the vehicle should be taken to a Land Rover dealer or specialist for examination.

22 Electric headlight-levelling system components – removal and refitting

Electric motor

1 Remove the headlight as described in Section 7.

2 The motor is a bayonet fit in the body; twist the motor to free it, and disconnect its wiring connector **(see illustration)**.

3 Refitting is the reverse of removal.

Switch

4 Refer to Section 4.

23 Parking distance control system – component removal and refitting

Electronic control unit (ECU)

1 Remove the luggage compartment left-hand side trim access panel.

2 Undo the 2 mounting bracket retaining screws, and manoeuvre the assembly from behind the side trim panel.

3 Disconnect the wiring plugs from the ECU, then undo the two retaining nuts and remove the ECU.

4 Refitting is a reversal of removal.

Ultrasonic sensors

Inner sensors

5 Remove the rear bumper as described in Chapter 12.

6 Undo the 7 bolts and 5 screws securing the panel to the bumper, and detach the panel.

7 Disconnect the wiring plug from the sensor, then rotate the external collar anti-clockwise and remove it from the sensor. Pull the sensor from the bumper.

8 When refitting the sensor, ensure the lug aligns with the cut-out in the bumper.

Outer sensors

9 Remove the light unit from the bumper as described in Section 7.

10 Working through the light aperture, disconnect the sensor wiring plug.

11 Rotate the external collar clockwise, and manoeuvre the sensor from the bumper.

12 When refitting the sensor, ensure the lug aligns with the cut-out in the bumper.

Sounder

13 Remove the ECU as described previously.

14 Undo the 2 retaining bolts and detach the sounder from the ECU mounting bracket.

15 Refitting is a reversal of removal.

LAND ROVER DISCOVERY wiring diagrams

Diagram 1

Key to symbols

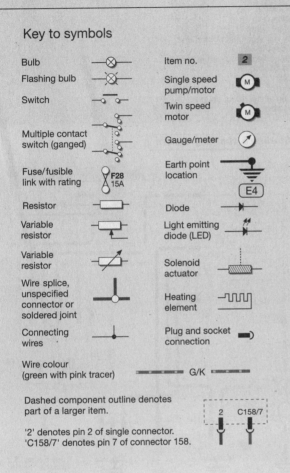

Bulb	—
Flashing bulb	—
Switch	—
Multiple contact switch (ganged)	—
Fuse/fusible link with rating	F28 15A
Resistor	—
Variable resistor	—
Variable resistor	—
Wire splice, unspecified connector or soldered joint	—
Connecting wires	—
Wire colour (green with pink tracer)	G/K

Item no.	2
Single speed pump/motor	M
Twin speed motor	M
Gauge/meter	
Earth point location	E4
Diode	—
Light emitting diode (LED)	—
Solenoid actuator	—
Heating element	—
Plug and socket connection	—

Dashed component outline denotes part of a larger item.

2 C158/7

'2' denotes pin 2 of single connector.
'C158/7' denotes pin 7 of connector 158.

Earth locations

E1	RH side of engine bay	E9	RH side of engine bay
E2	RH 'A' pillar	E10	RH side of engine bay
E3	Front LH side of engine bay	E11	At RH rear seat belt reel
E4	Under pedals	E12	At RH rear seat belt reel
E5	LH 'A' pillar	E13	At LH rear seat belt reel
E6	Behind centre console	E14	Behind centre console
E7	RH 'A' pillar	E15	Behind centre console
E8	RH side of engine bay		

Engine fusebox 6

Fuse	Rating	Circuit protected
F1	30A	Engine management
F2	15A	Engine management
F3	15A	Front fog lights
F4	20A	Headlight washers
F5	40A	Engine cooling fan
F6	10A	Air conditioning
F7	40A	LH heated front screen
F8	40A	RH heated front screen
F9	30A	Trailer lights, fuel burning heater
F10	30A	Fuel pump
F11	30A	ABS valve
F12	20A	Automatic gearbox
F13	10A	Body control unit
F14	15A	Direction indicators & hazard warning lights
F15	15A	Active cornering enhancement (ACE)
F16	10A	Horn

Passenger compartment fusebox 5

Fuse	Rating	Circuit protected
F1	25A	Central door locking
F2	10A	Fuel flap release
F3	10A	Instrument cluster, switch illumination, LH headlight main beam
F4	10A	Rear fog lights
F5	10A	LH headlight main beam
F6	25A	Air conditioning rear heater blower
F7	30A	Front heater blower
F8	30A	Heated rear window, heated mirrors
F9	10A	LH headlight dipped beam
F10	10A	RH headlight dipped beam
F11	10A	LH side & tail light, number plate light, headlight levelling, switch illumination, trailer socket, sunroof
F12	30A	Sunroof
F13	30A	Rear electric windows
F14	20A	Ignition coils (petrol models)
F15	20A	Cigar lighter, interior lights, seat heaters, vanity mirror illumination
F16	15A	Clock, radio, parking aid system, rear headphones
F17	15A	Audio system
F18	15A	Rear wiper motor
F19	15A	Front wash/wipe
F20	15A	Interior lights, clock/radio memory, immobiliser, CD player, diagnostics, key interlock
F21	15A	Transfer box, alarm, shift interlock
F22	10A	RH headlight main beam
F23	10A	Starter motor
F24	10A	Alternator, automatic transmission, engine management
F25	15A	Brake lights & reversing lights
F26	10A	Auxiliary circuits relay
F27	10A	Instruments, hill descent control
F28	10A	Self levelling suspension, anti-lock braking system (ABS)
F29	10A	Active cornering enhancement (ACE)
F30	20A	Cruise control, electric mirrors, rear screen washer, engine management control unit (Diesel)
F31	10A	Front air conditioning blower, power fold mirrors
F32	25A	Accessory socket
F33	10A	RH side & tail lights, headlight levelling switch, audio, trailer socket, switch illumination
F34	30A	Front electric windows
F35	10A	Airbag safety restraint system (SRS)

Engine fusebox 6

Passenger compartment fusebox 5

H33478

Wire colours

B	Black	P	Purple
G	Green	R	Red
K	Pink	S	Grey
Lg	Light green	U	Blue
N	Brown	W	White
O	Orange	Y	Yellow

Key to items

1 Battery
2 Ignition switch
3 Starter motor
4 Alternator
5 Passenger compartment fusebox
6 Engine fusebox
  a = glow plug relay
  b = main relay
  c = fuel pump relay
  d = starter relay
  e = cooling fan relay
  f = horn relay

7 Glow plugs
8 Inertia switch
9 Fuel tank unit
  a = fuel pump
10 Engine management control unit
11 Body control unit
12 Engine coolant temperature sensor
13 Engine cooling fan
14 LH horn
15 RH horn
16 Steering wheel rotary coupler
17 Horn switch

Diagram 2

H33479

Fuel pump & preheating system

Starting & charging system

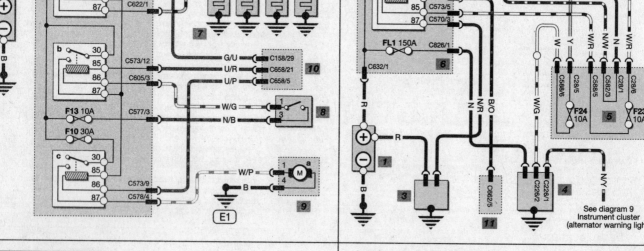

Engine cooling fan

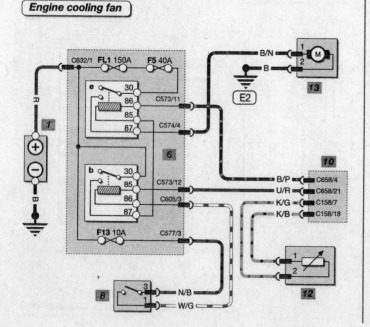

See diagram 9
Instrument cluster
(alternator warning light)

Horn

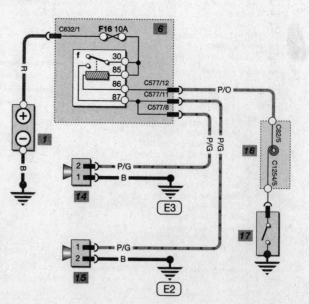

Diagram 3

Wire colours

B	Black	**P**	Purple
G	Green	**R**	Red
K	Pink	**S**	Grey
Lg	Light green	**U**	Blue
N	Brown	**W**	White
O	Orange	**Y**	Yellow

Key to items

1 Battery
2 Ignition switch
5 Passenger compartment fusebox
6 Engine fusebox
  g = auxiliary relay
16 Steering wheel rotary coupler
18 Cigar lighter
19 Accessory socket
20 Clock
21 Diagnostic connector
22 SRS control unit
23 LH seatbelt pretensioner
24 RH seatbelt pretensioner
25 Passenger''s airbag
26 Driver's airbag

H33480

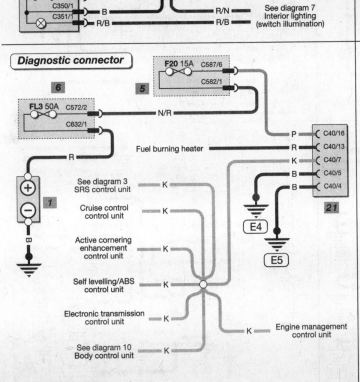

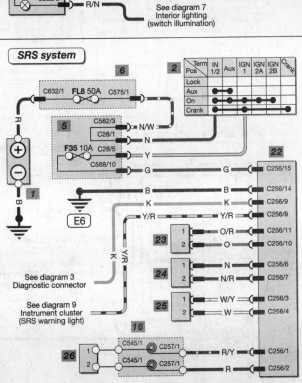

Wire colours

B	Black	**P**	Purple
G	Green	**R**	Red
K	Pink	**S**	Grey
Lg	Light green	**U**	Blue
N	Brown	**W**	White
O	Orange	**Y**	Yellow

Key to items

1 Battery
2 Ignition switch
5 Passenger compartment fusebox
6 Engine fusebox
11 Body control unit
28 Heater blower switch
29 Heater blower
30 Fresh/recirculation air switch
31 Heater blower relay
32 Diode
33 Fresh/recirculation air motor
34 Heater blower motor resistors
35 Sunroof control unit
36 Sunroof isolation switch
37 Front sunroof switch
38 Rear sunroof switch 1
39 Rear sunroof switch 2
40 Front sunroof motor
41 Rear sunroof motor
42 LH front side light
43 RH front side light
44 LH side marker light
45 RH side marker light
46 LH rear light unit
   a = tail light
47 RH rear light unit
   a = tail light
48 Number plate light
49 Light switch
   a = side light switch
50 Headlight levelling switch
51 LH headlight levelling motor
52 RH headlight levelling motor
53 Trailer socket

Diagram 4

H33481

Heater (models without A/C)

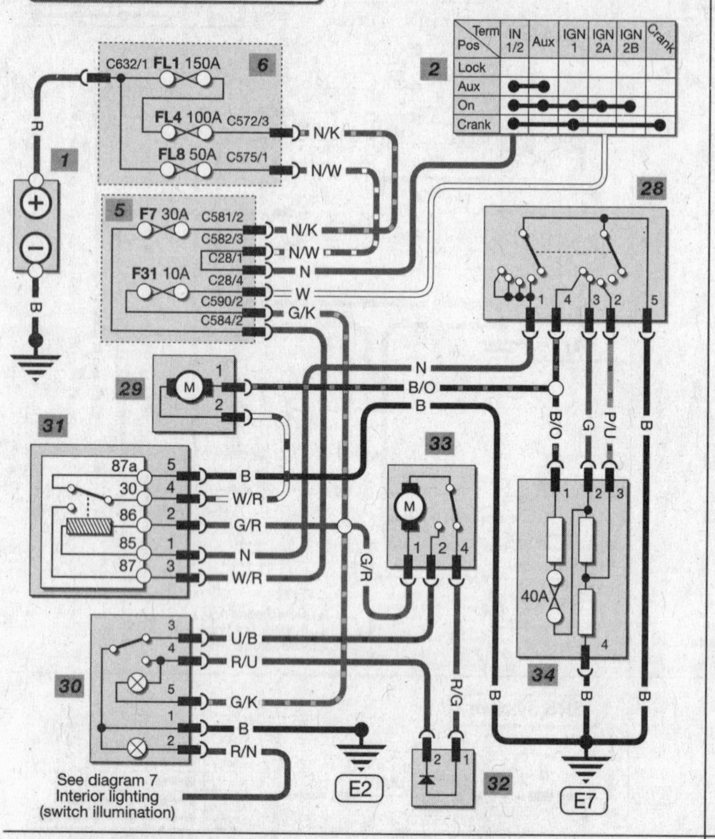

Sunroof

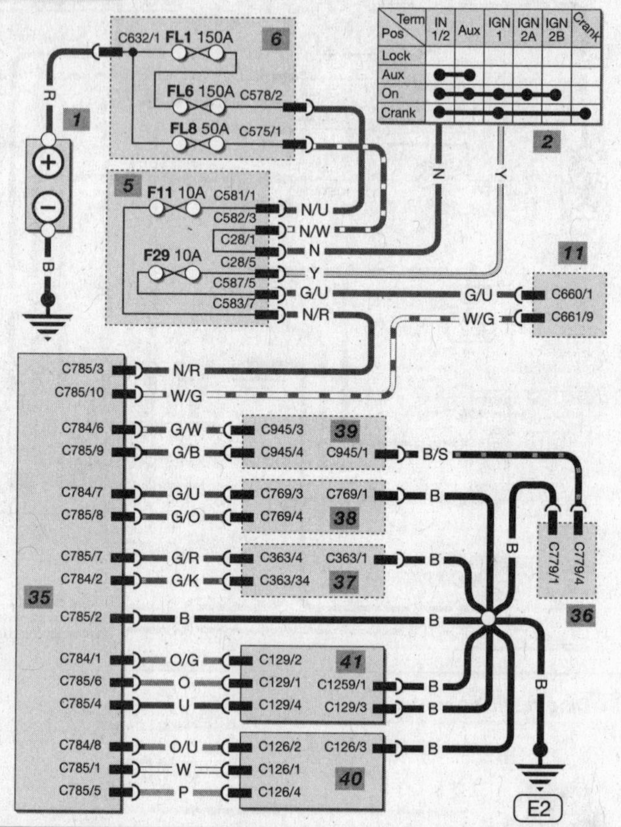

Side, tail & number plate lights

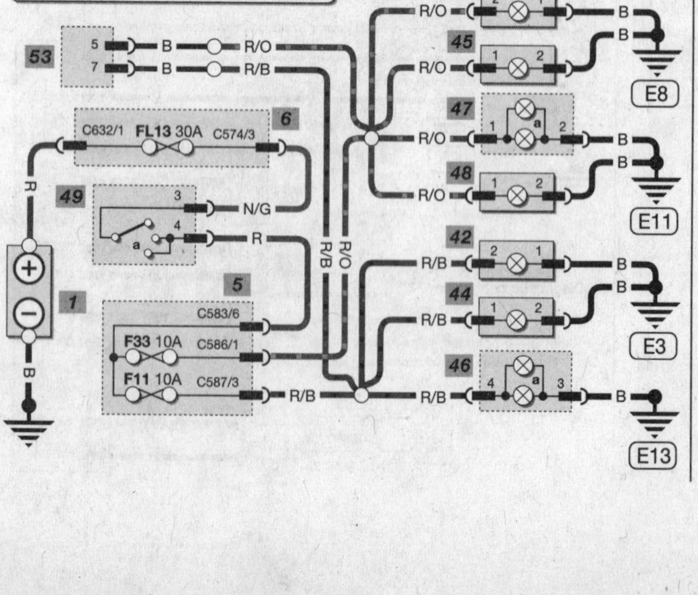

Headlight levelling

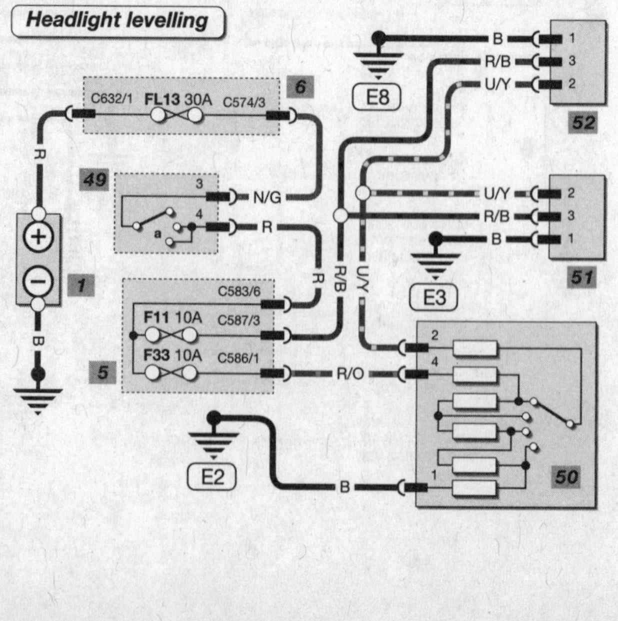

See diagram 7
Interior lighting
(switch illumination)

Wire colours

B	Black	P	Purple
G	Green	R	Red
K	Pink	S	Grey
Lg	Light green	U	Blue
N	Brown	W	White
O	Orange	Y	Yellow

Diagram 5

Key to items

1 Battery
2 Ignition switch
5 Passenger compartment fusebox
  a = driver's intelligence unit
6 Engine fusebox
  g = auxiliary relay
  h = front foglight relay
11 Body control unit
46 LH rear light unit
  b = stop light
  c = reversing light
47 RH rear light unit
  b = stop light
  c = reversing light

49 Light switch
  a = side light switch
  b = headlight switch
  c = dip main beam switch
  d = headlight flasher switch
53 Trailer socket
55 LH headlight
  a = dipped beam
  b = main beam
56 RH headlight
  a = dipped beam
  b = main beam
57 Stop light switch

58 Reversing light switch
  (manual transmission)
59 Starter inhibitor/reversing light switch
  (automatic transmission)
60 High level brake light
61 Front foglight switch
62 LH front foglight
63 RH front foglight

H33482

Headlights

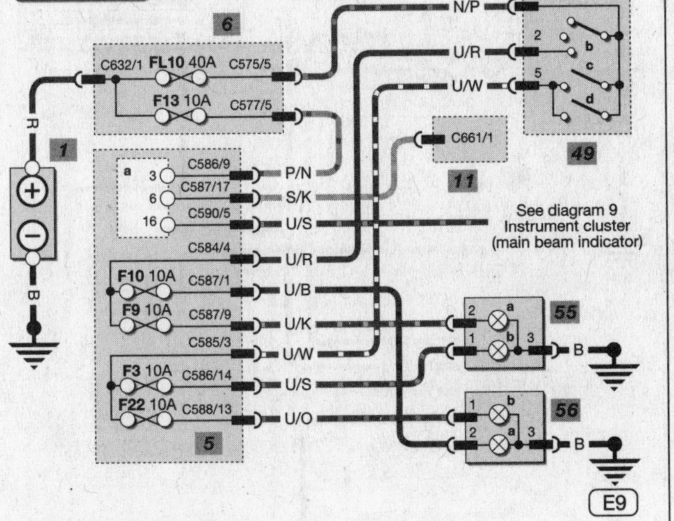

Front foglights

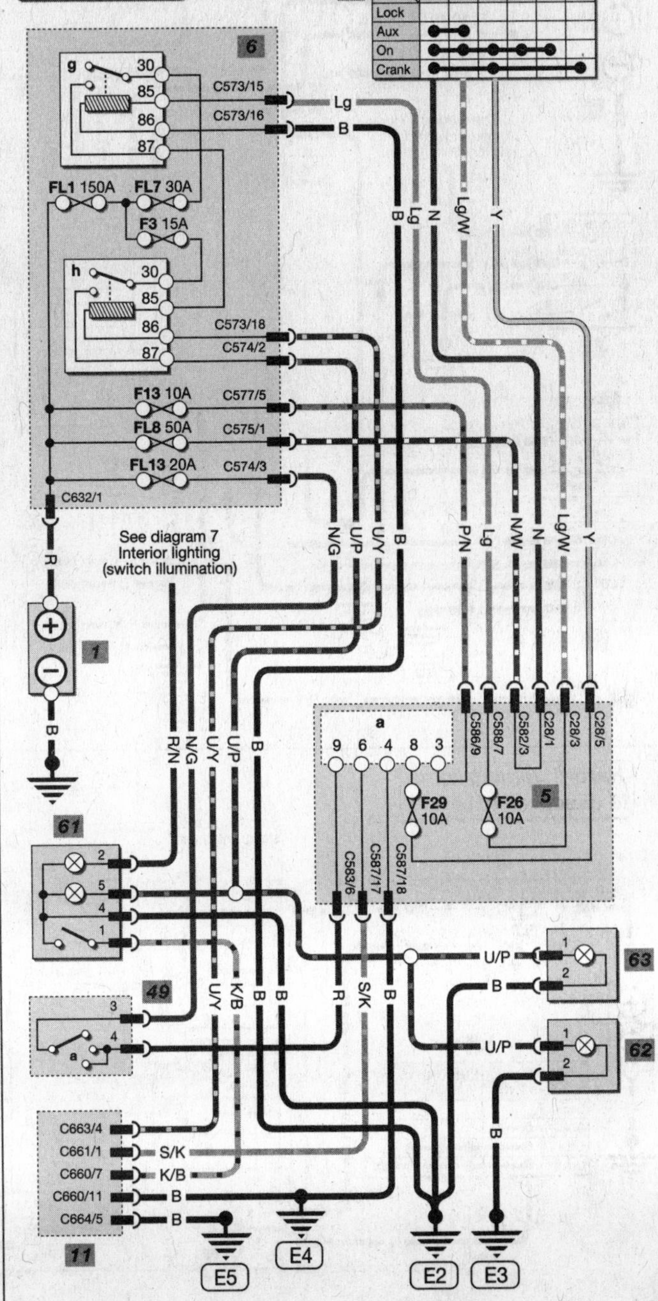

Stop & reversing lights

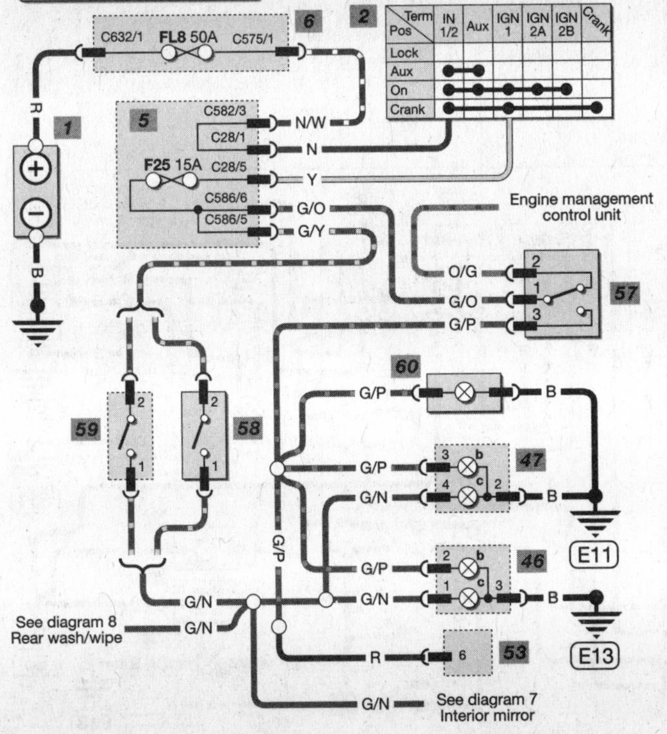

See diagram 9
Instrument cluster
(main beam indicator)

See diagram 7
Interior lighting
(switch illumination)

Engine management
control unit

See diagram 8
Rear wash/wipe

See diagram 7
Interior mirror

Wire colours

B	Black	P	Purple
G	Green	R	Red
K	Pink	S	Grey
Lg	Light green	U	Blue
N	Brown	W	White
O	Orange	Y	Yellow

Key to items

1 Battery
2 Ignition switch
5 Passenger compartment fusebox
  a = driver's intelligence unit
  b = fear foglight relay
  c = RH indicator relay
  d = LH indicator relay
6 Engine fusebox
11 Body control unit

49 Light switch
  a = side light switch
53 Trailer socket
65 LH rear light unit 2
  a = rear fog light
  b = direction indicator
66 RH rear light unit 2
  a = rear fog light
  b = direction indicator

67 Direction indicator switch
68 Hazard warning switch
69 LH front direction indicator
70 LH front indicator side repeater
71 RH front direction indicator
72 RH front indicator side repeater
73 Rear foglight switch

Diagram 6

H33483

Rear foglights

Lights on alarm

Hazard warning lights & direction indicators

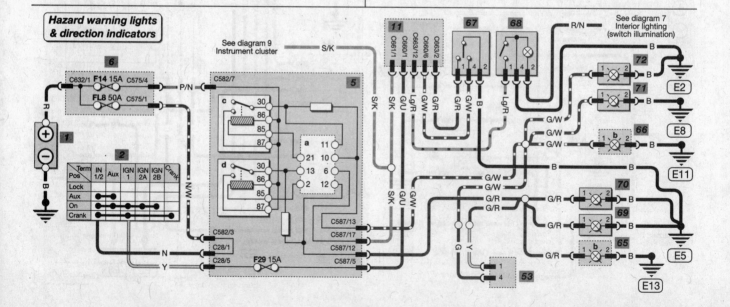

Wire colours

B	Black	P	Purple
G	Green	R	Red
K	Pink	S	Grey
Lg	Light green	U	Blue
N	Brown	W	White
O	Orange	Y	Yellow

Key to items

Diagram 7

1 Battery
2 Ignition switch
5 Passenger compartment fusebox
  a = driver's intelligence unit
  e = heated rear screen relay
6 Engine fusebox
  g = auxiliary relay
  i = heated front screen relay
11 Body control unit

49 Light switch
  a = side light switch
76 Front interior light
77 Rear interior light
78 Luggage compartment light
79 Ignition switch illumination
80 Interior mirror
81 LH vanity mirror light
82 RH vanity mirror light

83 Heated rear window switch
84 Heated rear window
85 Heated front screen relay
86 LH heated front screen element
87 RH heated front screen element
88 Glove box light
89 Glove box light switch

H33484

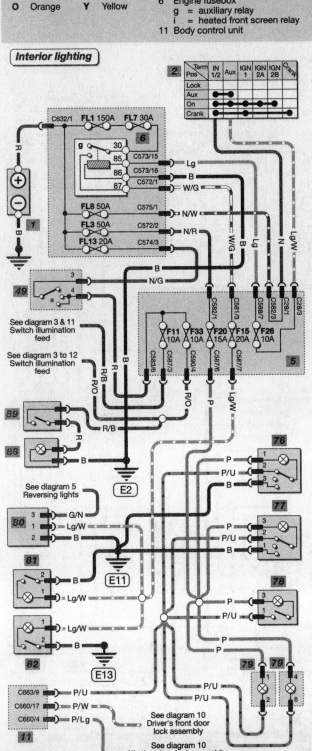

Interior lighting

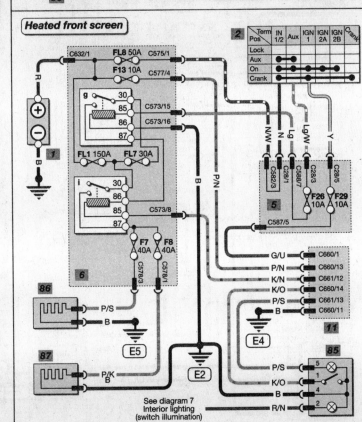

Heated rear screen

Heated front screen

Wire colours

B	Black	P	Purple
G	Green	R	Red
K	Pink	S	Grey
Lg	Light green	U	Blue
N	Brown	W	White
O	Orange	Y	Yellow

Key to items

1 Battery
2 Ignition switch
5 Passenger compartment fusebox
  a = driver's intelligence unit
  f = front wiper relay
  g = rear wiper relay
6 Engine fusebox
  g = auxiliary relay
  j = headlight washer relay
11 Body control unit

49 Light switch
  b = headlight switch
90 Windscreen wash/wipe switch
  a = variable delay
  b = washer switch
  c = intermittent wipe 1
  d = intermittent wipe 2
  e = slow wipe
  f = fast wipe
  g = flick wipe

91 Windscreen wiper motor
92 Headlight washer pump
93 Windscreen washer pump
94 Rear wiper switch
95 Rear washer switch
96 Rear washer pump
97 Rear waiper motor

Diagram 8

H33485

Front wash/wipe

Rear wash/wipe

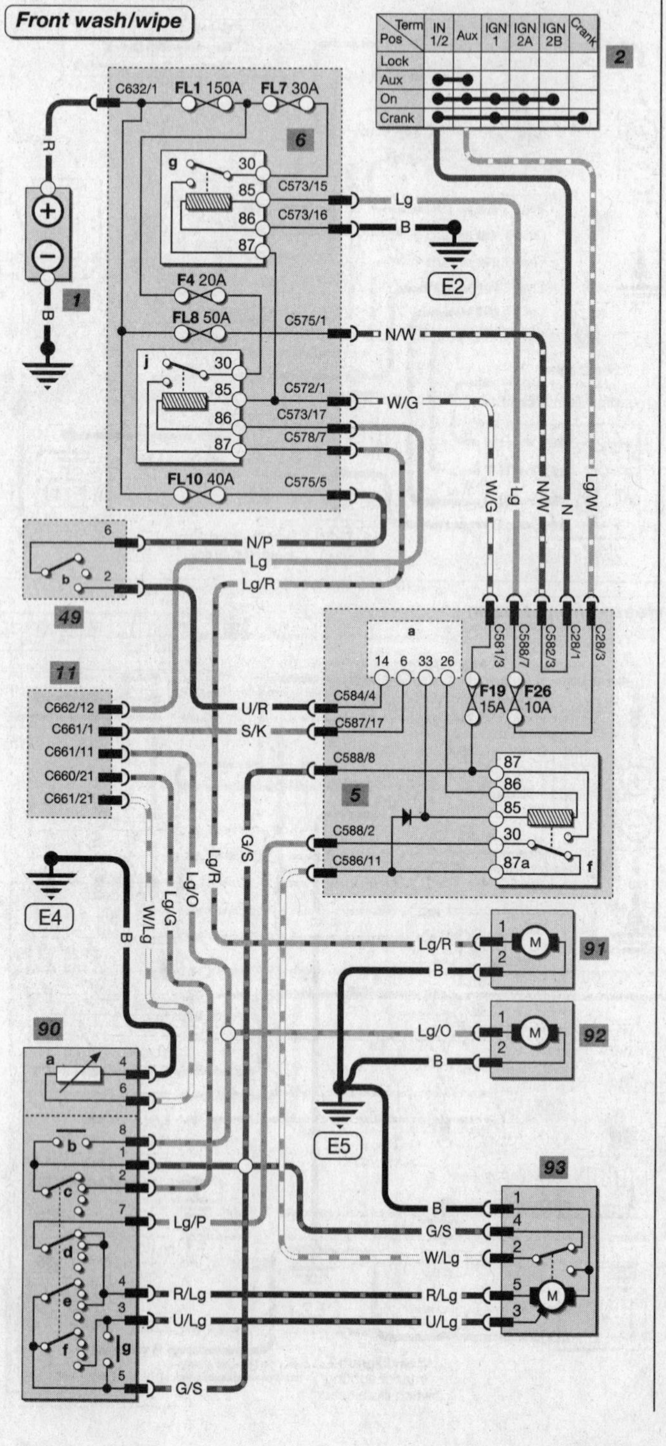

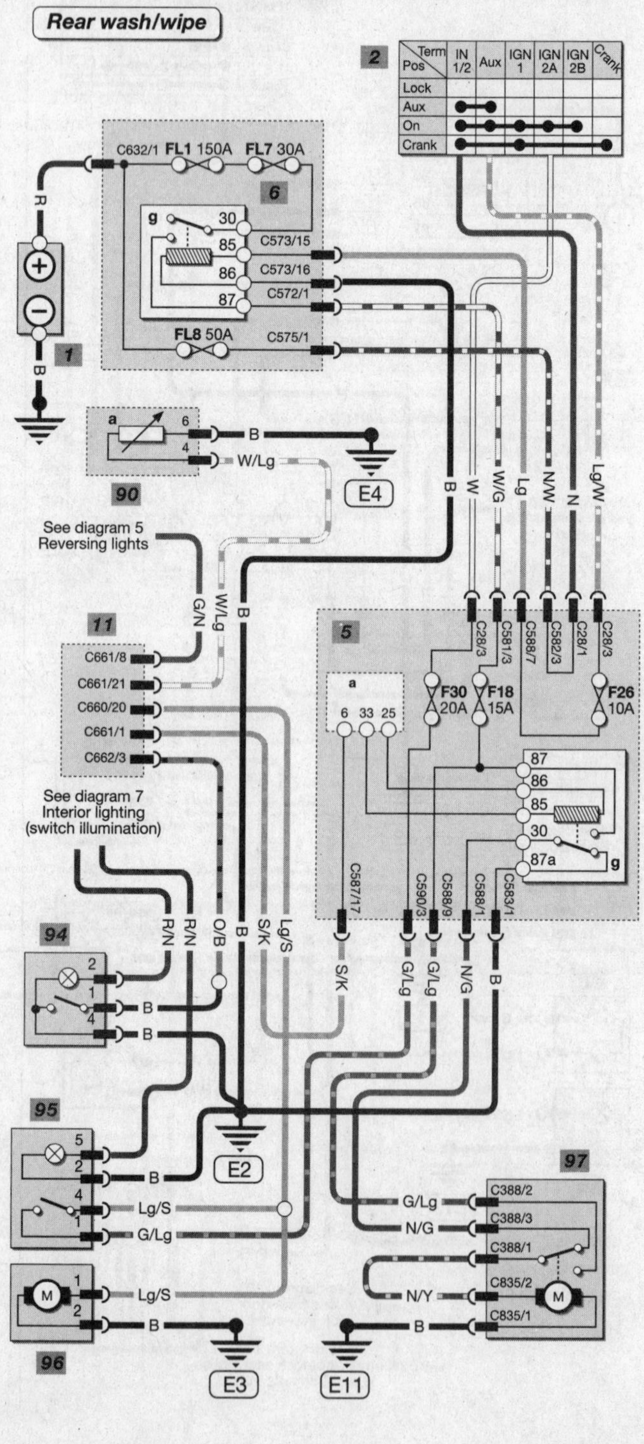

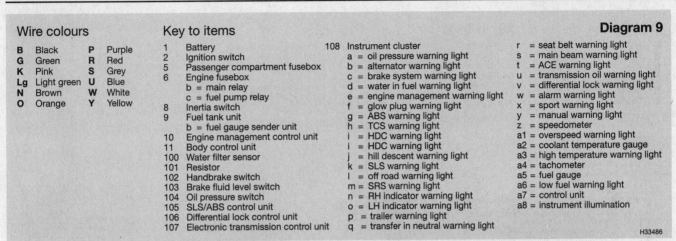

Wire colours

B	Black	**P**	Purple
G	Green	**R**	Red
K	Pink	**S**	Grey
Lg	Light green	**U**	Blue
N	Brown	**W**	White
O	Orange	**Y**	Yellow

Key to items

Diagram 9

1   Battery
2   Ignition switch
5   Passenger compartment fusebox
6   Engine fusebox
    b = main relay
    c = fuel pump relay
8   Inertia switch
9   Fuel tank unit
    b = fuel gauge sender unit
10   Engine management control unit
11   Body control unit
100   Water filter sensor
101   Resistor
102   Handbrake switch
103   Brake fluid level switch
104   Oil pressure switch
105   SLS/ABS control unit
106   Differential lock control unit
107   Electronic transmission control unit

108   Instrument cluster
   a = oil pressure warning light
   b = alternator warning light
   c = brake system warning light
   d = water in fuel warning light
   e = engine management warning light
   f = glow plug warning light
   g = ABS warning light
   h = TCS warning light
   i = HDC warning light
   i = HDC warning light
   j = hill descent warning light
   k = SLS warning light
   l = off road warning light
   m = SRS warning light
   n = RH indicator warning light
   o = LH indicator warning light
   p = trailer warning light
   q = transfer in neutral warning light

   r = seat belt warning light
   s = main beam warning light
   t = ACE warning light
   u = transmission oil warning light
   v = differential lock warning light
   w = alarm warning light
   x = sport warning light
   y = manual warning light
   z = speedometer
   a1 = overspeed warning light
   a2 = coolant temperature gauge
   a3 = high temperature warning light
   a4 = tachometer
   a5 = fuel gauge
   a6 = low fuel warning light
   a7 = control unit
   a8 = instrument illumination

H33486

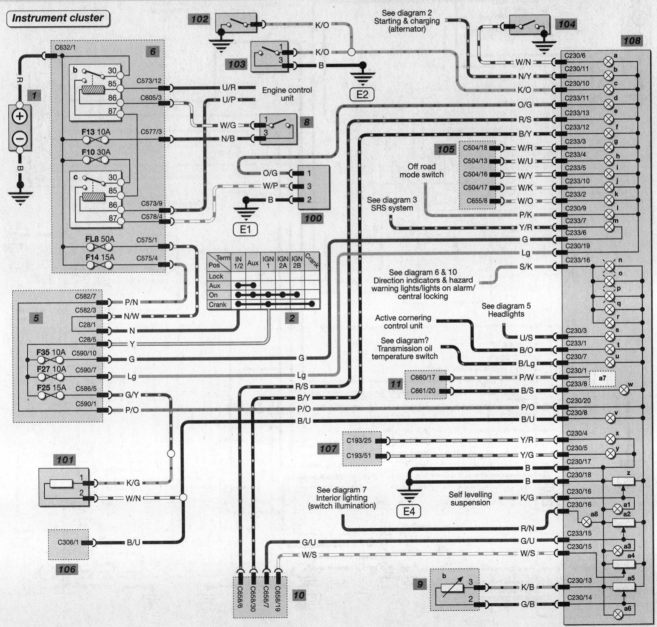

Wire colours

B	Black	**P**	Purple
G	Green	**R**	Red
K	Pink	**S**	Grey
Lg	Light green	**U**	Blue
N	Brown	**W**	White
O	Orange	**Y**	Yellow

Key to items

1 Battery
5 Passenger compartment fusebox
  a = driver's intelligence unit
6 Engine fusebox
8 Inertia switch
11 Body control unit
110 Passive coil
111 Central locking
112 Radio frequency receiver
113 LH front door lock assembly
114 RH front door lock assembly
115 LH rear door lock assembly
116 RH rear door lock assembly
117 Tailgate lock assembly

Diagram 10

H33487

Central locking

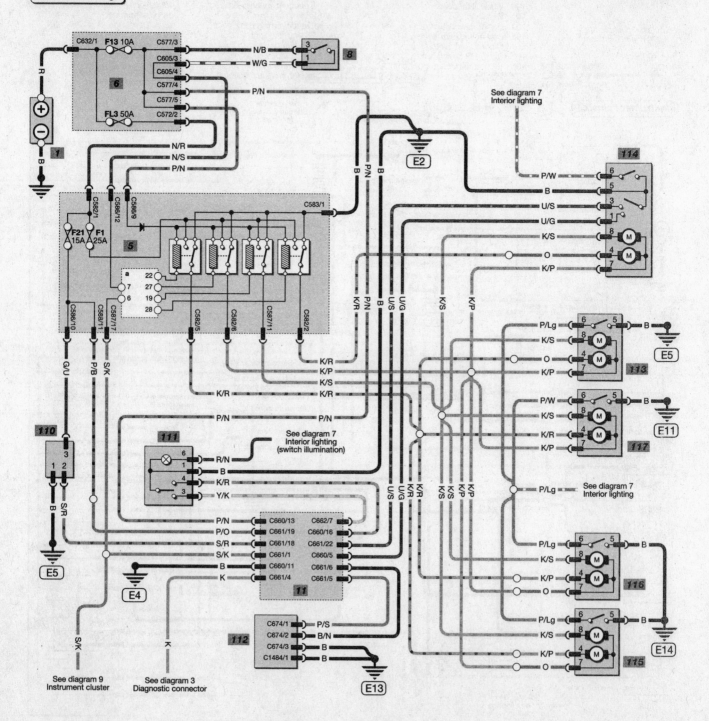

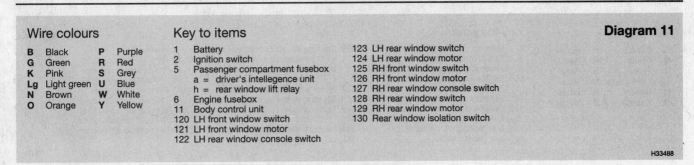

Wire colours

B	Black	P	Purple
G	Green	R	Red
K	Pink	S	Grey
Lg	Light green	U	Blue
N	Brown	W	White
O	Orange	Y	Yellow

Key to items

1   Battery
2   Ignition switch
5   Passenger compartment fusebox
   a = driver's intelligence unit
   h = rear window lift relay
6   Engine fusebox
11   Body control unit
120   LH front window switch
121   LH front window motor
122   LH rear window console switch
123   LH rear window switch
124   LH rear window motor
125   RH front window switch
126   RH front window motor
127   RH rear window console switch
128   RH rear window switch
129   RH rear window motor
130   Rear window isolation switch

Diagram 11

H33488

Electric windows

Wire colours

B	Black	P	Purple
G	Green	R	Red
K	Pink	S	Grey
Lg	Light green	U	Blue
N	Brown	W	White
O	Orange	Y	Yellow

Key to items

1   Battery
2   Ignition switch
5   Passenger compartment fusebox
6   Engine fusebox
   g = auxiliary relay
16 Steering wheel rotary coupler
135 Driver's door mirror assembly
   a = vertical adjustment
   b = horizontal adjustment
   c = mirror heater

136 Passenger's door mirror assembly
   a = vertical adjustment
   b = horizontal adjustment
   c = mirror heater
137 Mirror adjustment switch
138 Steering wheel remote controls
139 Audio unit
140 LH tweeter
141 LH front door speaker
142 LH rear door speaker

143 RH tweeter
144 RH front door speaker
145 RH rear door speaker
146 LH heated seat switch
147 RH heated seat switch
148 LH seat cushion heater
149 LH seat squab heater
150 RH seat cushion heater
151 RH seat squab heater

Diagram 12

H33489

Electric mirrors

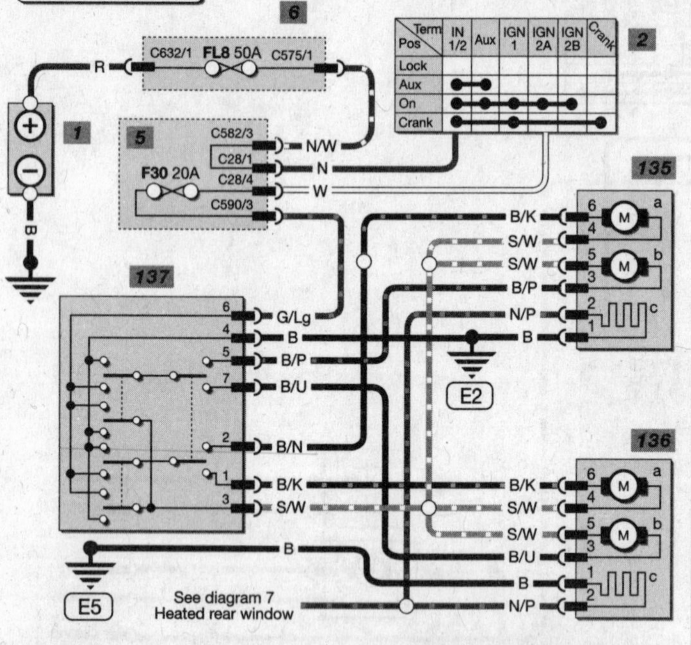

Typical audio system

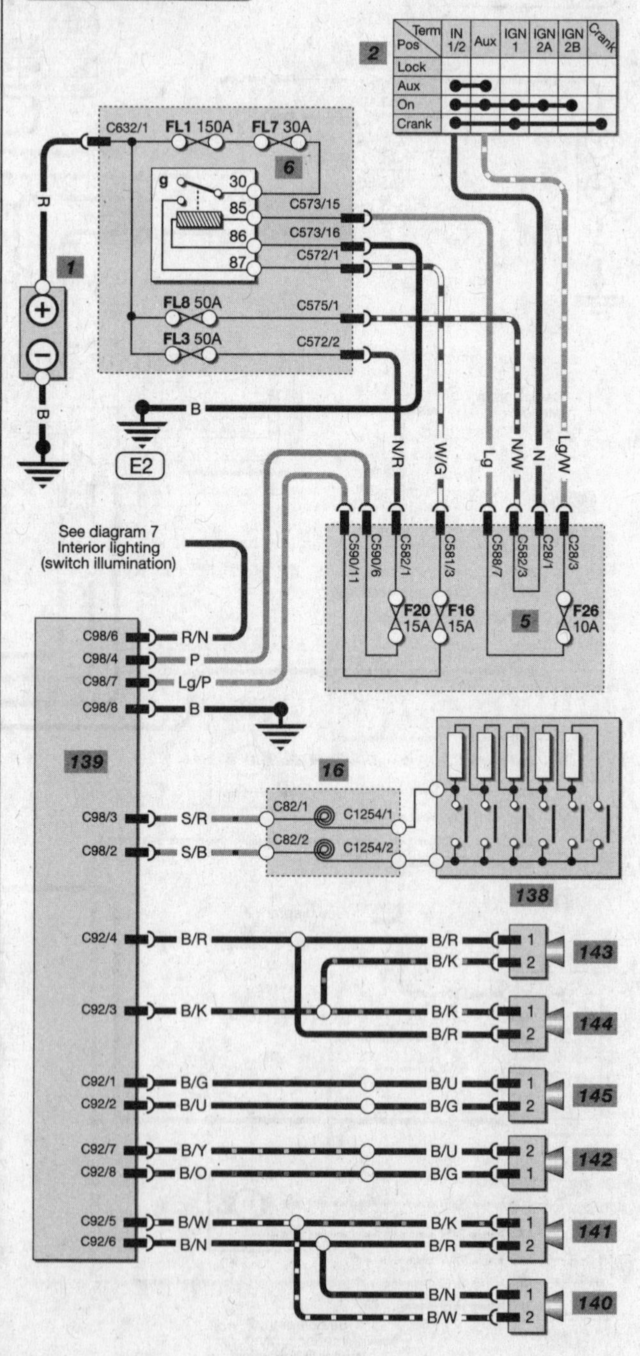

Heated seats

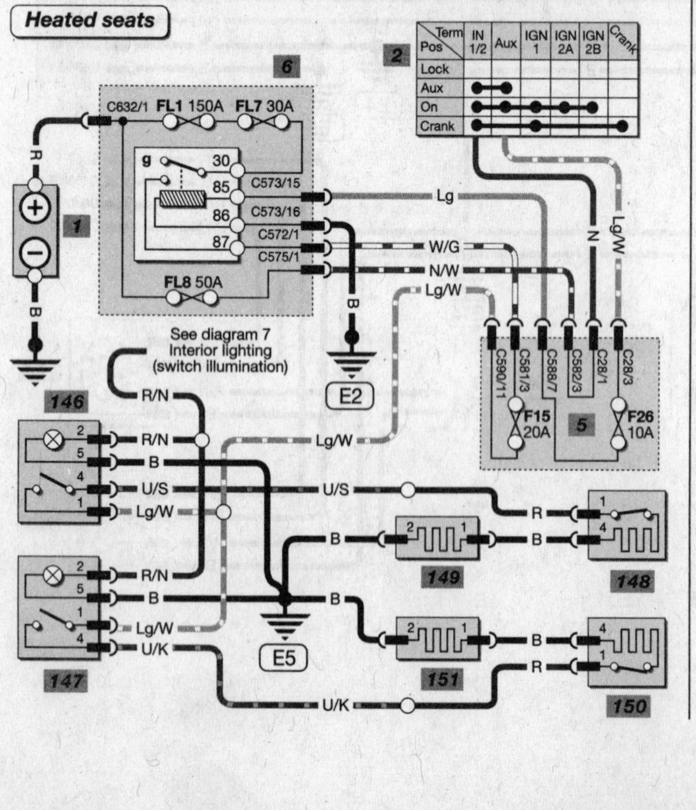

Dimensions and weights . . . . **REF•1**
Conversion factors . . . . **REF•2**
Buying spare parts . . . . **REF•3**
Vehicle identification . . . . **REF•4**
General repair procedures . . . . **REF•5**
Jacking and vehicle support . . . . **REF•6**

Radio/cassette unit anti-theft system –
  precautions . . . . **REF•6**
Tools and working facilities . . . . **REF•7**
MOT test checks . . . . **REF•9**
Fault finding . . . . **REF•13**
Glossary of technical terms . . . . **REF•24**
Index . . . . **REF•29**

Dimensions and weights

Note: *All figures are approximate, and may vary according to model. Refer to manufacturer's data for exact figures.*

Dimensions

Overall length:
  Including spare wheel . . . . 4705 mm
  Including tow hitch . . . . 4715 mm
Overall width (including mirrors) . . . . 2190 mm
Overall height:
  Excluding roof bars . . . . 1905 mm
  Including roof bars . . . . 1980 mm

Weights

Kerb weight (full fuel tank, excluding options) . . . . 2105 to 2305 kg
Maximum gross vehicle weight (all models) . . . . 2750 to 2880 kg
Maximum roof rack load:
  On-road . . . . 50 kg
  Off-road . . . . 30 kg
Maximum trailer nose weight . . . . 150 kg
Maximum towing weight:
  Unbraked trailer:
    On-road . . . . 750 kg
    Off-road . . . . 750 kg
  Trailer with overrun brakes:
    On-road . . . . 3500 kg
    Off-road . . . . 1000 kg

Length (distance)

Inches (in)	x 25.4	= Millimetres (mm)	x 0.0394	=	Inches (in)
Feet (ft)	x 0.305	= Metres (m)	x 3.281	=	Feet (ft)
Miles	x 1.609	= Kilometres (km)	x 0.621	=	Miles

Volume (capacity)

Cubic inches (cu in; in³)	x 16.387	= Cubic centimetres (cc; cm³)	x 0.061	=	Cubic inches (cu in; in³)
Imperial pints (Imp pt)	x 0.568	= Litres (l)	x 1.76	=	Imperial pints (Imp pt)
Imperial quarts (Imp qt)	x 1.137	= Litres (l)	x 0.88	=	Imperial quarts (Imp qt)
Imperial quarts (Imp qt)	x 1.201	= US quarts (US qt)	x 0.833	=	Imperial quarts (Imp qt)
US quarts (US qt)	x 0.946	= Litres (l)	x 1.057	=	US quarts (US qt)
Imperial gallons (Imp gal)	x 4.546	= Litres (l)	x 0.22	=	Imperial gallons (Imp gal)
Imperial gallons (Imp gal)	x 1.201	= US gallons (US gal)	x 0.833	=	Imperial gallons (Imp gal)
US gallons (US gal)	x 3.785	= Litres (l)	x 0.264	=	US gallons (US gal)

Mass (weight)

Ounces (oz)	x 28.35	= Grams (g)	x 0.035	=	Ounces (oz)
Pounds (lb)	x 0.454	= Kilograms (kg)	x 2.205	=	Pounds (lb)

Force

Ounces-force (ozf; oz)	x 0.278	= Newtons (N)	x 3.6	=	Ounces-force (ozf; oz)
Pounds-force (lbf; lb)	x 4.448	= Newtons (N)	x 0.225	=	Pounds-force (lbf; lb)
Newtons (N)	x 0.1	= Kilograms-force (kgf; kg)	x 9.81	=	Newtons (N)

Pressure

Pounds-force per square inch (psi; lbf/in²; lb/in²)	x 0.070	= Kilograms-force per square centimetre (kgf/cm²; kg/cm²)	x 14.223	=	Pounds-force per square inch (psi; lbf/in²; lb/in²)
Pounds-force per square inch (psi; lbf/in²; lb/in²)	x 0.068	= Atmospheres (atm)	x 14.696	=	Pounds-force per square inch (psi; lbf/in²; lb/in²)
Pounds-force per square inch (psi; lbf/in²; lb/in²)	x 0.069	= Bars	x 14.5	=	Pounds-force per square inch (psi; lbf/in²; lb/in²)
Pounds-force per square inch (psi; lbf/in²; lb/in²)	x 6.895	= Kilopascals (kPa)	x 0.145	=	Pounds-force per square inch (psi; lbf/in²; lb/in²)
Kilopascals (kPa)	x 0.01	= Kilograms-force per square centimetre (kgf/cm²; kg/cm²)	x 98.1	=	Kilopascals (kPa)
Millibar (mbar)	x 100	= Pascals (Pa)	x 0.01	=	Millibar (mbar)
Millibar (mbar)	x 0.0145	= Pounds-force per square inch (psi; lbf/in²; lb/in²)	x 68.947	=	Millibar (mbar)
Millibar (mbar)	x 0.75	= Millimetres of mercury (mmHg)	x 1.333	=	Millibar (mbar)
Millibar (mbar)	x 0.401	= Inches of water (inH₂O)	x 2.491	=	Millibar (mbar)
Millimetres of mercury (mmHg)	x 0.535	= Inches of water (inH₂O)	x 1.868	=	Millimetres of mercury (mmHg)
Inches of water (inH₂O)	x 0.036	= Pounds-force per square inch (psi; lbf/in²; lb/in²)	x 27.68	=	Inches of water (inH₂O)

Torque (moment of force)

Pounds-force inches (lbf in; lb in)	x 1.152	= Kilograms-force centimetre (kgf cm; kg cm)	x 0.868	=	Pounds-force inches (lbf in; lb in)
Pounds-force inches (lbf in; lb in)	x 0.113	= Newton metres (Nm)	x 8.85	=	Pounds-force inches (lbf in; lb in)
Pounds-force inches (lbf in; lb in)	x 0.083	= Pounds-force feet (lbf ft; lb ft)	x 12	=	Pounds-force inches (lbf in; lb in)
Pounds-force feet (lbf ft; lb ft)	x 0.138	= Kilograms-force metres (kgf m; kg m)	x 7.233	=	Pounds-force feet (lbf ft; lb ft)
Pounds-force feet (lbf ft; lb ft)	x 1.356	= Newton metres (Nm)	x 0.738	=	Pounds-force feet (lbf ft; lb ft)
Newton metres (Nm)	x 0.102	= Kilograms-force metres (kgf m; kg m)	x 9.804	=	Newton metres (Nm)

Power

Horsepower (hp)	x 745.7	= Watts (W)	x 0.0013	=	Horsepower (hp)

Velocity (speed)

Miles per hour (miles/hr; mph)	x 1.609	= Kilometres per hour (km/hr; kph)	x 0.621	=	Miles per hour (miles/hr; mph)

Fuel consumption*

Miles per gallon, Imperial (mpg)	x 0.354	= Kilometres per litre (km/l)	x 2.825	=	Miles per gallon, Imperial (mpg)
Miles per gallon, US (mpg)	x 0.425	= Kilometres per litre (km/l)	x 2.352	=	Miles per gallon, US (mpg)

Temperature

Degrees Fahrenheit = (°C x 1.8) + 32   Degrees Celsius (Degrees Centigrade; °C) = (°F - 32) x 0.56

It is common practice to convert from miles per gallon (mpg) to litres/100 kilometres (l/100km), where mpg x l/100 km = 282

Spare parts are available from many sources, including maker's appointed garages, accessory shops, and motor factors. To be sure of obtaining the correct parts, it may sometimes be necessary to quote the vehicle identification number. If possible, it can also be useful to take the old parts along for positive identification. Items such as starter motors and alternators may be available under a service exchange scheme – any parts returned should always be clean.

Our advice regarding spare part sources is as follows.

Officially-appointed garages

This is the best source of parts which are peculiar to your vehicle, and are not otherwise generally available (eg badges, interior trim, certain body panels, etc). It is also the only place at which you should buy parts if the vehicle is still under warranty.

Accessory shops

These are very good places to buy materials and components needed for the maintenance of your vehicle (oil, air and fuel filters, spark plugs, light bulbs, drivebelts, oils and greases, brake pads, touch-up paint, etc). Parts like this sold by a reputable shop are of the same standard as those used by the vehicle manufacturer.

Motor factors

Good factors will stock all the more important components which wear out comparatively quickly and can sometimes supply individual components needed for the overhaul of a larger assembly. They may also handle work such as cylinder block reboring, crankshaft regrinding and balancing, etc.

Tyre and exhaust specialists

These outlets may be independent or members of a local or national chain. They frequently offer competitive prices when compared with a main dealer or local garage, but it will pay to obtain several quotes before making a decision. Also ask what 'extras' may be added to the quote – for instance, fitting a new valve and balancing the wheel are both often charged on top of the price of a new tyre.

Other sources

Beware of parts or materials obtained from market stalls, car boot sales or similar outlets. Such items are not invariably sub-standard, but there is little chance of compensation if they do prove unsatisfactory. In the case of safety-critical components such as brake pads, there is the risk not only of financial loss, but also of an accident causing injury or death.

Second-hand components or assemblies obtained from a car breaker can be a good buy in some circumstances, but this sort of purchase is best made by the experienced DIY mechanic.

Vehicle identification

Modifications are a continuing and unpublicised process in vehicle manufacture, quite apart from major model changes. Spare parts manuals and lists are compiled upon a numerical basis, the individual vehicle identification numbers being essential to correct identification of the component concerned.

When ordering spare parts, always give as much information as possible. Quote the vehicle model, year of manufacture, body and engine numbers as appropriate.

The *Vehicle Identification Number (VIN) plate* is riveted to the top of the body front panel, and can be viewed once the bonnet is open **(see illustration)**. The plate carries the VIN number, vehicle weight information and paint and trim colour codes. The VIN number is also repeated on a plate fixed to the facia, visible through the lower left-hand corner of the windscreen **(see illustration)**.

The diesel *engine number* is stamped into the cylinder block, on the left-hand side of the engine, just below the joint with the cylinder head **(see illustration)**.

The *transmission identification number* is stamped into a flat on the bottom right-hand side of the transmission casing **(see illustration)**.

The *transfer gearbox identification number* is stamped into the lower left-hand side of the gearbox casing **(see illustration)**.

The Vehicle Identification Number is located on the front panel . . .

. . . and is also visible through the windscreen

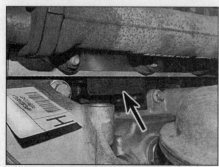

The engine number (arrowed) is located on the left-hand side of the engine block

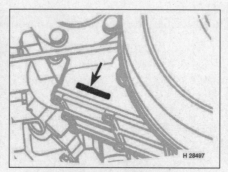

Main gearbox identification number

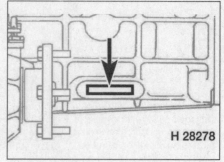

Transfer gearbox identification number

Whenever servicing, repair or overhaul work is carried out on the car or its components, observe the following procedures and instructions. This will assist in carrying out the operation efficiently and to a professional standard of workmanship.

Joint mating faces and gaskets

When separating components at their mating faces, never insert screwdrivers or similar implements into the joint between the faces in order to prise them apart. This can cause severe damage which results in oil leaks, coolant leaks, etc upon reassembly. Separation is usually achieved by tapping along the joint with a soft-faced hammer in order to break the seal. However, note that this method may not be suitable where dowels are used for component location.

Where a gasket is used between the mating faces of two components, a new one must be fitted on reassembly; fit it dry unless otherwise stated in the repair procedure. Make sure that the mating faces are clean and dry, with all traces of old gasket removed. When cleaning a joint face, use a tool which is unlikely to score or damage the face, and remove any burrs or nicks with an oilstone or fine file.

Make sure that tapped holes are cleaned with a pipe cleaner, and keep them free of jointing compound, if this is being used, unless specifically instructed otherwise.

Ensure that all orifices, channels or pipes are clear, and blow through them, preferably using compressed air.

Oil seals

Oil seals can be removed by levering them out with a wide flat-bladed screwdriver or similar implement. Alternatively, a number of self-tapping screws may be screwed into the seal, and these used as a purchase for pliers or some similar device in order to pull the seal free.

Whenever an oil seal is removed from its working location, either individually or as part of an assembly, it should be renewed.

The very fine sealing lip of the seal is easily damaged, and will not seal if the surface it contacts is not completely clean and free from scratches, nicks or grooves. If the original sealing surface of the component cannot be restored, and the manufacturer has not made provision for slight relocation of the seal relative to the sealing surface, the component should be renewed.

Protect the lips of the seal from any surface which may damage them in the course of fitting. Use tape or a conical sleeve where possible. Where indicated, lubricate the seal lips with oil before fitting and, on dual-lipped seals, fill the space between the lips with grease.

Unless otherwise stated, oil seals must be fitted with their sealing lips toward the lubricant to be sealed.

Use a tubular drift or block of wood of the appropriate size to install the seal and, if the seal housing is shouldered, drive the seal down to the shoulder. If the seal housing is unshouldered, the seal should be fitted with its face flush with the housing top face (unless otherwise instructed).

Screw threads and fastenings

Seized nuts, bolts and screws are quite a common occurrence where corrosion has set in, and the use of penetrating oil or releasing fluid will often overcome this problem if the offending item is soaked for a while before attempting to release it. The use of an impact driver may also provide a means of releasing such stubborn fastening devices, when used in conjunction with the appropriate screwdriver bit or socket. If none of these methods works, it may be necessary to resort to the careful application of heat, or the use of a hacksaw or nut splitter device. Before resorting to extreme methods, check that you are not dealing with a left-hand thread!

Studs are usually removed by locking two nuts together on the threaded part, and then using a spanner on the lower nut to unscrew the stud. Studs or bolts which have broken off below the surface of the component in which they are mounted can sometimes be removed using a stud extractor.

Always ensure that a blind tapped hole is completely free from oil, grease, water or other fluid before installing the bolt or stud. Failure to do this could cause the housing to crack due to the hydraulic action of the bolt or stud as it is screwed in.

For some screw fastenings, notably cylinder head bolts or nuts, torque wrench settings are no longer specified for the latter stages of tightening, "angle-tightening" being called up instead. Typically, a fairly low torque wrench setting will be applied to the bolts/nuts in the correct sequence, followed by one or more stages of tightening through specified angles.

When checking or retightening a nut or bolt to a specified torque setting, slacken the nut or bolt by a quarter of a turn, and then retighten to the specified setting. However, this should not be attempted where angular tightening has been used.

Locknuts, locktabs and washers

Any fastening which will rotate against a component or housing during tightening should always have a washer between it and the relevant component or housing.

Spring or split washers should always be renewed when they are used to lock a critical component such as a big-end bearing retaining bolt or nut. Locktabs which are folded over to retain a nut or bolt should always be renewed.

Self-locking nuts can be re-used in non-critical areas, providing resistance can be felt when the locking portion passes over the bolt or stud thread. However, it should be noted that self-locking stiffnuts tend to lose their effectiveness after long periods of use, and should then be renewed as a matter of course.

Split pins must always be replaced with new ones of the correct size for the hole.

When thread-locking compound is found on the threads of a fastener which is to be re-used, it should be cleaned off with a wire brush and solvent, and fresh compound applied on reassembly.

Special tools

Some repair procedures in this manual entail the use of special tools such as a press, two or three-legged pullers, spring compressors, etc. Wherever possible, suitable readily-available alternatives to the manufacturer's special tools are described, and are shown in use. In some instances, where no alternative is possible, it has been necessary to resort to the use of a manufacturer's tool, and this has been done for reasons of safety as well as the efficient completion of the repair operation. Unless you are highly-skilled and have a thorough understanding of the procedures described, never attempt to bypass the use of any special tool when the procedure described specifies its use. Not only is there a very great risk of personal injury, but expensive damage could be caused to the components involved.

Environmental considerations

When disposing of used engine oil, brake fluid, antifreeze, etc, give due consideration to any detrimental environmental effects. Do not, for instance, pour any of the above liquids down drains into the general sewage system, or onto the ground to soak away. Many local council refuse tips provide a facility for waste oil disposal, as do some garages. You can find your nearest disposal point by calling the Environment Agency on 08708 506 506 or by visiting www.oilbankline.org.uk.

Note: It is illegal and anti-social to dump oil down the drain. To find the location of your local oil recycling bank, call 08708 506 506 or visit www.oilbankline.org.uk.

⚠️ *Warning: The handbrake acts on the transmission, not the rear wheels, and may not hold the vehicle stationary when jacking. If one front wheel and one rear wheel are raised, no vehicle holding or braking effect is possible using the handbrake, therefore the wheels must always be chocked (using the chock supplied in the tool kit). If the vehicle is coupled to a trailer, disconnect the trailer from the vehicle before commencing jacking. This is to prevent the trailer pulling the vehicle off the jack and causing personal injury.*

Using the vehicle jack

The jack supplied with the vehicle tool kit should only be used for changing the roadwheels, as described in *Wheel changing* at the front of this Manual.

When jacking up a wheel, only slide the jack into position from the side of the vehicle. Position the jack head so that when raised, it will engage with the notch in the radius arm, just in front of the rear wheel, or just behind the front wheel **(see illustration)**.

Using a hydraulic (trolley) jack and axle stands

Note: *To raise the vehicle, a hydraulic jack with*

a minimum load capacity of 1500 kg must be used. **Never** work under a vehicle supported solely by a hydraulic jack, as even a hydraulic jack could fail under load – always supplement the jack with axle stands. Do not use piles of bricks or wooden blocks for supporting – the Discovery is a heavy vehicle, and makeshift methods should not be used.

When carrying out any other kind of work, raise the vehicle using a hydraulic jack, and always supplement the jack with axle stands positioned under the axles or the chassis sidemembers. **Do not** jack the vehicle, or position axle stands under any of the following components:

a) *Body structure.*
b) *Bumpers.*
c) *Underbody pipes and hoses.*
d) *Gearbox/transmission/transfer gearbox housings.*
e) *Engine sump.*
f) *Fuel tank.*

Only ever jack the vehicle up on a solid, level surface. If there is even a slight slope, take great care that the vehicle cannot move as the wheels are lifted off the ground. Jacking up on an uneven or gravelled surface is not recommended, as the weight of the vehicle will not be evenly distributed, and the jack may slip as the vehicle is raised.

As far as possible, do not leave the

Position the jack head so that when raised, it will engage with the notch in the radius arm

vehicle unattended once it has been raised, particularly if children are playing nearby.

To raise the vehicle, chock the appropriate roadwheels, then position the jack head under the front or rear radius arms, so the jack head engages with the notch. When refitting a road wheel, ensure the hub and roadwheel mating surfaces are clean and free from debris. Where alloy wheels are fitted, apply a little anti-seize compound to the mating surfaces to prevent the wheels sticking in future. If this is not practical at the time, fit the roadwheel, but remove it later to apply the compound. Take care not to allow any of the compound to come into contact with the brake friction surfaces.

Radio/cassette unit anti-theft system – precautions

The radio/cassette unit fitted as standard equipment by Land Rover may be equipped with a built-in security code, to deter thieves. If the power source to the unit is cut, the anti-theft system will activate. Even if the power source is immediately reconnected, the radio/cassette unit will not function until the correct security code has been entered. Therefore,

if you do not know the correct security code for the radio/cassette unit, **do not** disconnect the battery negative terminal of the battery, or remove the radio/cassette unit from the vehicle.

To enter the correct security code, follow the instructions provided with the radio/cassette player handbook.

If an incorrect code is entered, the unit will become locked, and cannot be operated.

If this happens or if the security code is lost or forgotten, seek the advice of your Land Rover dealer. On presentation of proof of ownership, a Land Rover dealer will be able to unlock the unit and provide you with a new security code.

Introduction

A selection of good tools is a fundamental requirement for anyone contemplating the maintenance and repair of a motor vehicle. For the owner who does not possess any, their purchase will prove a considerable expense, offsetting some of the savings made by doing-it-yourself. However, provided that the tools purchased meet the relevant national safety standards and are of good quality, they will last for many years and prove an extremely worthwhile investment.

To help the average owner to decide which tools are needed to carry out the various tasks detailed in this manual, we have compiled three lists of tools under the following headings: *Maintenance and minor repair, Repair and overhaul*, and *Special*. Newcomers to practical mechanics should start off with the *Maintenance and minor repair* tool kit, and confine themselves to the simpler jobs around the vehicle. Then, as confidence and experience grow, more difficult tasks can be undertaken, with extra tools being purchased as, and when, they are needed. In this way, a *Maintenance and minor repair* tool kit can be built up into a *Repair and overhaul* tool kit over a considerable period of time, without any major cash outlays. The experienced do-it-yourselfer will have a tool kit good enough for most repair and overhaul procedures, and will add tools from the *Special* category when it is felt that the expense is justified by the amount of use to which these tools will be put.

Maintenance and minor repair tool kit

The tools given in this list should be considered as a minimum requirement if routine maintenance, servicing and minor repair operations are to be undertaken. We recommend the purchase of combination spanners (ring one end, open-ended the other); although more expensive than open-ended ones, they do give the advantages of both types of spanner.

☐ *Combination spanners:*
  Metric - 8 to 19 mm inclusive
☐ *Adjustable spanner - 35 mm jaw (approx.)*
☐ *Spark plug spanner (with rubber insert) - petrol models*
☐ *Spark plug gap adjustment tool - petrol models*
☐ *Set of feeler gauges*
☐ *Brake bleed nipple spanner*
☐ *Screwdrivers:*
  Flat blade - 100 mm long x 6 mm dia
  Cross blade - 100 mm long x 6 mm dia
  Torx - various sizes (not all vehicles)
☐ *Combination pliers*
☐ *Hacksaw (junior)*
☐ *Tyre pump*
☐ *Tyre pressure gauge*
☐ *Oil can*
☐ *Oil filter removal tool (if applicable)*
☐ *Fine emery cloth*
☐ *Wire brush (small)*
☐ *Funnel (medium size)*
☐ *Sump drain plug key (not all vehicles)*

Repair and overhaul tool kit

These tools are virtually essential for anyone undertaking any major repairs to a motor vehicle, and are additional to those given in the *Maintenance and minor repair* list. Included in this list is a comprehensive set of sockets. Although these are expensive, they will be found invaluable as they are so versatile - particularly if various drives are included in the set. We recommend the half-inch square-drive type, as this can be used with most proprietary torque wrenches.

The tools in this list will sometimes need to be supplemented by tools from the *Special* list:

☐ *Sockets to cover range in previous list (including Torx sockets)*
☐ *Reversible ratchet drive (for use with sockets)*
☐ *Extension piece, 250 mm (for use with sockets)*
☐ *Universal joint (for use with sockets)*
☐ *Flexible handle or sliding T "breaker bar" (for use with sockets)*
☐ *Torque wrench (for use with sockets)*
☐ *Self-locking grips*
☐ *Ball pein hammer*
☐ *Soft-faced mallet (plastic or rubber)*
☐ *Screwdrivers:*
  Flat blade - long & sturdy, short (chubby), and narrow (electrician's) types
  Cross blade – long & sturdy, and short (chubby) types
☐ *Pliers:*
  Long-nosed
  Side cutters (electrician's)
  Circlip (internal and external)
☐ *Cold chisel - 25 mm*
☐ *Scriber*
☐ *Scraper*
☐ *Centre-punch*
☐ *Pin punch*
☐ *Hacksaw*
☐ *Brake hose clamp*
☐ *Brake/clutch bleeding kit*
☐ *Selection of twist drills*
☐ *Steel rule/straight-edge*
☐ *Allen keys (inc. splined/Torx type)*
☐ *Selection of files*
☐ *Wire brush*
☐ *Axle stands*
☐ *Jack (strong trolley or hydraulic type)*
☐ *Light with extension lead*
☐ *Universal electrical multi-meter*

Sockets and reversible ratchet drive

Brake bleeding kit

Torx key, socket and bit

Hose clamp

Angular-tightening gauge

Special tools

The tools in this list are those which are not used regularly, are expensive to buy, or which need to be used in accordance with their manufacturers' instructions. Unless relatively difficult mechanical jobs are undertaken frequently, it will not be economic to buy many of these tools. Where this is the case, you could consider clubbing together with friends (or joining a motorists' club) to make a joint purchase, or borrowing the tools against a deposit from a local garage or tool hire specialist.

The following list contains only those tools and instruments freely available to the public, and not those special tools produced by the vehicle manufacturer specifically for its dealer network. You will find occasional references to these manufacturers' special tools in the text of this manual. Generally, an alternative method of doing the job without the vehicle manufacturers' special tool is given. However, sometimes there is no alternative to using them. Where this is the case and the relevant tool cannot be bought or borrowed, you will have to entrust the work to a dealer.

☐ *Angular-tightening gauge*
☐ *Valve spring compressor*
☐ *Valve grinding tool*
☐ *Piston ring compressor*
☐ *Piston ring removal/installation tool*
☐ *Cylinder bore hone*
☐ *Balljoint separator*
☐ *Coil spring compressors (where applicable)*
☐ *Two/three-legged hub and bearing puller*
☐ *Impact screwdriver*
☐ *Micrometer and/or vernier calipers*
☐ *Dial gauge*
☐ *Tachometer*
☐ *Fault code reader*
☐ *Cylinder compression gauge*
☐ *Hand-operated vacuum pump and gauge*
☐ *Clutch plate alignment set*
☐ *Brake shoe steady spring cup removal tool*
☐ *Bush and bearing removal/installation set*
☐ *Stud extractors*
☐ *Tap and die set*
☐ *Lifting tackle*

Buying tools

Reputable motor accessory shops and superstores often offer excellent quality tools at discount prices, so it pays to shop around.

Remember, you don't have to buy the most expensive items on the shelf, but it is always advisable to steer clear of the very cheap tools. Beware of 'bargains' offered on market stalls, on-line or at car boot sales. There are plenty of good tools around at reasonable prices, but always aim to purchase items which meet the relevant national safety standards. If in doubt, ask the proprietor or manager of the shop for advice before making a purchase.

Care and maintenance of tools

Having purchased a reasonable tool kit, it is necessary to keep the tools in a clean and serviceable condition. After use, always wipe off any dirt, grease and metal particles using a clean, dry cloth, before putting the tools away. Never leave them lying around after they have been used. A simple tool rack on the garage or workshop wall for items such as screwdrivers and pliers is a good idea. Store all normal spanners and sockets in a metal box. Any measuring instruments, gauges, meters, etc, must be carefully stored where they cannot be damaged or become rusty.

Take a little care when tools are used. Hammer heads inevitably become marked, and screwdrivers lose the keen edge on their blades from time to time. A little timely attention with emery cloth or a file will soon restore items like this to a good finish.

Working facilities

Not to be forgotten when discussing tools is the workshop itself. If anything more than routine maintenance is to be carried out, a suitable working area becomes essential.

It is appreciated that many an owner-mechanic is forced by circumstances to remove an engine or similar item without the benefit of a garage or workshop. Having done this, any repairs should always be done under the cover of a roof.

Wherever possible, any dismantling should be done on a clean, flat workbench or table at a suitable working height.

Any workbench needs a vice; one with a jaw opening of 100 mm is suitable for most jobs. As mentioned previously, some clean dry storage space is also required for tools, as well as for any lubricants, cleaning fluids, touch-up paints etc, which become necessary.

Another item which may be required, and which has a much more general usage, is an electric drill with a chuck capacity of at least 8 mm. This, together with a good range of twist drills, is virtually essential for fitting accessories.

Last, but not least, always keep a supply of old newspapers and clean, lint-free rags available, and try to keep any working area as clean as possible.

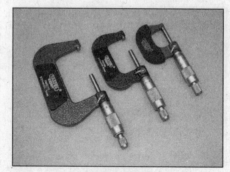

Micrometers

Dial test indicator ("dial gauge")

Oil filter removal tool (strap wrench type)

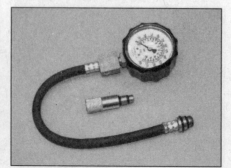

Compression tester

Bearing puller

This is a guide to getting your vehicle through the MOT test. Obviously it will not be possible to examine the vehicle to the same standard as the professional MOT tester. However, working through the following checks will enable you to identify any problem areas before submitting the vehicle for the test.

It has only been possible to summarise the test requirements here, based on the regulations in force at the time of printing. Test standards are becoming increasingly stringent, although there are some exemptions for older vehicles.

An assistant will be needed to help carry out some of these checks.

The checks have been sub-divided into four categories, as follows:

1 Checks carried out **FROM THE DRIVER'S SEAT**

2 Checks carried out **WITH THE VEHICLE ON THE GROUND**

3 Checks carried out **WITH THE VEHICLE RAISED AND THE WHEELS FREE TO TURN**

4 Checks carried out on **YOUR VEHICLE'S EXHAUST EMISSION SYSTEM**

---

1 Checks carried out **FROM THE DRIVER'S SEAT**

Handbrake (parking brake)

☐ Test the operation of the handbrake. Excessive travel (too many clicks) indicates incorrect brake or cable adjustment.
☐ Check that the handbrake cannot be released by tapping the lever sideways. Check the security of the lever mountings.

☐ If the parking brake is foot-operated, check that the pedal is secure and without excessive travel, and that the release mechanism operates correctly.
☐ Where applicable, test the operation of the electronic handbrake. The brake should engage and disengage without excessive delay. If the warning light does not extinguish when the brake is disengaged, this could indicate a fault which will need further investigation.

Footbrake

☐ Depress the brake pedal and check that it does not creep down to the floor, indicating a master cylinder fault. Release the pedal,

wait a few seconds, then depress it again. If the pedal travels nearly to the floor before firm resistance is felt, brake adjustment or repair is necessary. If the pedal feels spongy, there is air in the hydraulic system which must be removed by bleeding.

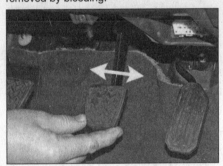

☐ Check that the brake pedal is secure and in good condition. Check also for signs of fluid leaks on the pedal, floor or carpets, which would indicate failed seals in the brake master cylinder.
☐ Check the servo unit (when applicable) by operating the brake pedal several times, then keeping the pedal depressed and starting the engine. As the engine starts, the pedal will move down slightly. If not, the vacuum hose or the servo itself may be faulty.

Steering wheel and column

☐ Examine the steering wheel for fractures or looseness of the hub, spokes or rim.
☐ Move the steering wheel from side to side and then up and down. Check that the steering wheel is not loose on the column, indicating wear or a loose retaining nut. Continue moving the steering wheel as before, but also turn it slightly from left to right.

☐ Check that the steering wheel is not loose on the column, and that there is no abnormal movement of the steering wheel, indicating wear in the column support bearings or couplings.
☐ Check that the ignition lock (where fitted) engages and disengages correctly.
☐ Steering column adjustment mechanisms (where fitted) must be able to lock the column securely in place with no play evident.

Windscreen, mirrors and sunvisor

☐ The windscreen must be free of cracks or other significant damage within the driver's field of view. (Small stone chips are acceptable.) Rear view mirrors must be secure, intact, and capable of being adjusted.

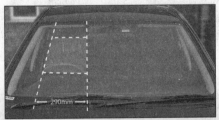

☐ The driver's sunvisor must be capable of being stored in the "up" position.

Seat belts and seats

Note: *The following checks are applicable to all seat belts, front and rear.*

□ Examine the webbing of all the belts (including rear belts if fitted) for cuts, serious fraying or deterioration. Fasten and unfasten each belt to check the buckles. If applicable, check the retracting mechanism. Check the security of all seat belt mountings accessible from inside the vehicle, ensuring any height adjustable mountings lock securely in place.

□ Seat belts with pre-tensioners, once activated, have a "flag" or similar showing on the seat belt stalk. This, in itself, is not a reason for test failure.

□ The front seats themselves must be securely attached and the backrests must lock in the upright position.

Doors

□ Both front doors must be able to be opened and closed from outside and inside, and must latch securely when closed.

Bonnet and boot/tailgate

□ The bonnet and boot/tailgate must latch securely when closed.

2 Checks carried out WITH THE VEHICLE ON THE GROUND

Vehicle identification

□ Number plates must be in good condition, secure and legible, with letters and numbers correctly spaced – spacing at (A) should be 33 mm and at (B) 11 mm. At the front, digits must be black on a white background and at the rear black on a yellow background. Other background designs (such as honeycomb) are not permitted.

□ The VIN plate and/or homologation plate must be permanently displayed and legible.

Electrical equipment

□ Switch on the ignition and check the operation of the horn.

□ Check the windscreen washers and wipers, examining the wiper blades; renew damaged or perished blades. Also check the operation of the stop-lights.

□ Check the operation of the sidelights and number plate lights. The lenses and reflectors must be secure, clean and undamaged.

□ Check the operation and alignment of the headlights. The headlight reflectors must not be tarnished and the lenses must be undamaged.

□ Switch on the ignition and check the operation of the direction indicators (including the instrument panel tell-tale) and the hazard warning lights. Operation of the sidelights and stop-lights must not affect the indicators - if it does, the cause is usually a bad earth at the rear light cluster. Indicators should flash at a rate of between 60 and 120 times per minute – faster or slower than this could indicate a fault with the flasher unit or a bad earth at one of the light units.

□ Check the operation of the rear foglight(s), including the warning light on the instrument panel or in the switch.

□ The warning lights must illuminate in accordance with the manufacturer's design. For most vehicles, the ABS and other warning lights should illuminate when the ignition is switched on, and (if the system is operating properly) extinguish after a few seconds. Refer to the owner's handbook.

Footbrake

□ Examine the master cylinder, brake pipes and servo unit for leaks, loose mountings, corrosion or other damage. If ABS is fitted, this unit should also be examined for signs of leaks or corrosion.

□ The fluid reservoir must be secure and the fluid level must be between the upper (A) and lower (B) markings.

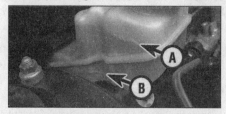

□ Inspect both front brake flexible hoses for cracks or deterioration of the rubber. Turn the steering from lock to lock, and ensure that the hoses do not contact the wheel, tyre, or any part of the steering or suspension mechanism. With the brake pedal firmly depressed, check the hoses for bulges or leaks under pressure.

Steering and suspension

□ Have your assistant turn the steering wheel from side to side slightly, up to the point where the steering gear just begins to transmit this movement to the roadwheels. Check for excessive free play between the steering wheel and the steering gear, indicating wear or insecurity of the steering column joints, the column-to-steering gear coupling, or the steering gear itself.

□ Have your assistant turn the steering wheel more vigorously in each direction, so that the roadwheels just begin to turn. As this is done, examine all the steering joints, linkages, fittings and attachments. Renew any component that shows signs of wear or damage. On vehicles with power steering, check the security and condition of the steering pump, drivebelt and hoses.

□ Check that the vehicle is standing level, and at approximately the correct ride height.

Shock absorbers

□ Depress each corner of the vehicle in turn, then release it. The vehicle should rise and then settle in its normal position. If the vehicle continues to rise and fall, the shock absorber is defective. A shock absorber which has seized will also cause the vehicle to fail.

Exhaust system

☐ Start the engine. With your assistant holding a rag over the tailpipe, check the entire system for leaks. Repair or renew leaking sections.

3 Checks carried out **WITH THE VEHICLE RAISED AND THE WHEELS FREE TO TURN**

Jack up the front and rear of the vehicle, and securely support it on axle stands. Position the stands clear of the suspension assemblies. Ensure that the wheels are clear of the ground and that the steering can be turned from lock to lock.

Steering mechanism

☐ Have your assistant turn the steering from lock to lock. Check that the steering turns smoothly, and that no part of the steering mechanism, including a wheel or tyre, fouls any brake hose or pipe or any part of the body structure.
☐ Examine the steering rack rubber gaiters for damage or insecurity of the retaining clips. If power steering is fitted, check for signs of damage or leakage of the fluid hoses, pipes or connections. Also check for excessive stiffness or binding of the steering, a missing split pin or locking device, or severe corrosion of the body structure within 30 cm of any steering component attachment point.

Front and rear suspension and wheel bearings

☐ Starting at the front right-hand side, grasp the roadwheel at the 3 o'clock and 9 o'clock positions and rock gently but firmly. Check for free play or insecurity at the wheel bearings, suspension balljoints, or suspension mount-ings, pivots and attachments.
☐ Now grasp the wheel at the 12 o'clock and 6 o'clock positions and repeat the previous inspection. Spin the wheel, and check for roughness or tightness of the front wheel bearing.

☐ If excess free play is suspected at a component pivot point, this can be confirmed by using a large screwdriver or similar tool and levering between the mounting and the component attachment. This will confirm whether the wear is in the pivot bush, its retaining bolt, or in the mounting itself (the bolt holes can often become elongated).

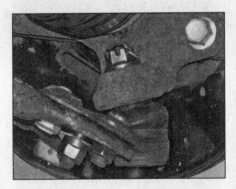

☐ Carry out all the above checks at the other front wheel, and then at both rear wheels.

Springs and shock absorbers

☐ Examine the suspension struts (when applicable) for serious fluid leakage, corrosion, or damage to the casing. Also check the security of the mounting points.
☐ If coil springs are fitted, check that the spring ends locate in their seats, and that the spring is not corroded, cracked or broken.
☐ If leaf springs are fitted, check that all leaves are intact, that the axle is securely attached to each spring, and that there is no deterioration of the spring eye mountings, bushes, and shackles.

☐ The same general checks apply to vehicles fitted with other suspension types, such as torsion bars, hydraulic displacer units, etc. Ensure that all mountings and attachments are secure, that there are no signs of excessive wear, corrosion or damage, and (on hydraulic types) that there are no fluid leaks or damaged pipes.
☐ Inspect the shock absorbers for signs of serious fluid leakage. Check for wear of the mounting bushes or attachments, or damage to the body of the unit.

Driveshafts (fwd vehicles only)

☐ Rotate each front wheel in turn and inspect the constant velocity joint gaiters for splits or damage. Also check that each driveshaft is straight and undamaged.

Braking system

☐ If possible without dismantling, check brake pad wear and disc condition. Ensure that the friction lining material has not worn excessively, (A) and that the discs are not fractured, pitted, scored or badly worn (B).

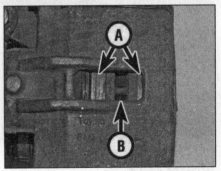

☐ Examine all the rigid brake pipes underneath the vehicle, and the flexible hose(s) at the rear. Look for corrosion, chafing or insecurity of the pipes, and for signs of bulging under pressure, chafing, splits or deterioration of the flexible hoses.
☐ Look for signs of fluid leaks at the brake calipers or on the brake backplates. Repair or renew leaking components.
☐ Slowly spin each wheel, while your assistant depresses and releases the footbrake. Ensure that each brake is operating and does not bind when the pedal is released.

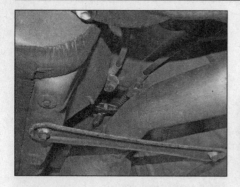

☐ Examine the handbrake mechanism, checking for frayed or broken cables, excessive corrosion, or wear or insecurity of the linkage. Check that the mechanism works on each relevant wheel, and releases fully, without binding.

☐ It is not possible to test brake efficiency without special equipment, but a road test can be carried out later to check that the vehicle pulls up in a straight line.

Fuel and exhaust systems

☐ Inspect the fuel tank (including the filler cap), fuel pipes, hoses and unions. All components must be secure and free from leaks. Locking fuel caps must lock securely and the key must be provided for the MOT test.

☐ Examine the exhaust system over its entire length, checking for any damaged, broken or missing mountings, security of the retaining clamps and rust or corrosion.

Wheels and tyres

☐ Examine the sidewalls and tread area of each tyre in turn. Check for cuts, tears, lumps, bulges, separation of the tread, and exposure of the ply or cord due to wear or damage. Check that the tyre bead is correctly seated on the wheel rim, that the valve is sound and properly seated, and that the wheel is not distorted or damaged.

☐ Check that the tyres are of the correct size for the vehicle, that they are of the same size and type on each axle, and that the pressures are correct.

☐ Check the tyre tread depth. The legal minimum at the time of writing is 1.6 mm over the central three-quarters of the tread width. Abnormal tread wear may indicate incorrect front wheel alignment or wear in steering or suspension components.

☐ If the spare wheel is fitted externally or in a separate carrier beneath the vehicle, check that mountings are secure and free of excessive corrosion.

Body corrosion

☐ Check the condition of the entire vehicle structure for signs of corrosion in load-bearing areas. (These include chassis box sections, side sills, cross-members, pillars, and all suspension, steering, braking system and seat belt mountings and anchorages.) Any corrosion which has seriously reduced the thickness of a load-bearing area (or is within 30 cm of safety-related components such as steering or suspension) is likely to cause the vehicle to fail. In this case professional repairs are likely to be needed.

☐ Damage or corrosion which causes sharp or otherwise dangerous edges to be exposed will also cause the vehicle to fail.

Towbars

☐ Check the condition of mounting points (both beneath the vehicle and within boot/hatchback areas) for signs of corrosion, ensuring that all fixings are secure and not worn or damaged. There must be no excessive play in detachable tow ball arms or quick-release mechanisms.

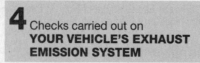

4 Checks carried out on **YOUR VEHICLE'S EXHAUST EMISSION SYSTEM**

Petrol models

☐ The engine should be warmed up, and running well (ignition system in good order, air filter element clean, etc).

☐ Before testing, run the engine at around 2500 rpm for 20 seconds. Let the engine drop to idle, and watch for smoke from the exhaust. If the idle speed is too high, or if dense blue or black smoke emerges for more than 5 seconds, the vehicle will fail. Typically, blue smoke signifies oil burning (engine wear); black smoke means unburnt fuel (dirty air cleaner element, or other fuel system fault).

☐ An exhaust gas analyser for measuring carbon monoxide (CO) and hydrocarbons (HC) is now needed. If one cannot be hired or borrowed, have a local garage perform the check.

CO emissions (mixture)

☐ The MOT tester has access to the CO limits for all vehicles. The CO level is measured at idle speed, and at 'fast idle' (2500 to 3000 rpm). The following limits are given as a general guide:

    At idle speed – Less than 0.5% CO
    At 'fast idle' – Less than 0.3% CO
    Lambda reading – 0.97 to 1.03

☐ If the CO level is too high, this may point to poor maintenance, a fuel injection system problem, faulty lambda (oxygen) sensor or catalytic converter. Try an injector cleaning treatment, and check the vehicle's ECU for fault codes.

HC emissions

☐ The MOT tester has access to HC limits for all vehicles. The HC level is measured at 'fast idle' (2500 to 3000 rpm). The following limits are given as a general guide:

    At 'fast idle' – Less then 200 ppm

☐ Excessive HC emissions are typically caused by oil being burnt (worn engine), or by a blocked crankcase ventilation system ('breather'). If the engine oil is old and thin, an oil change may help. If the engine is running badly, check the vehicle's ECU for fault codes.

Diesel models

☐ The only emission test for diesel engines is measuring exhaust smoke density, using a calibrated smoke meter. The test involves accelerating the engine at least 3 times to its maximum unloaded speed.

Note: *On engines with a timing belt, it is VITAL that the belt is in good condition before the test is carried out.*

☐ With the engine warmed up, it is first purged by running at around 2500 rpm for 20 seconds. A governor check is then carried out, by slowly accelerating the engine to its maximum speed. After this, the smoke meter is connected, and the engine is accelerated quickly to maximum speed three times. If the smoke density is less than the limits given below, the vehicle will pass:

    Non-turbo vehicles: 2.5m-1
    Turbocharged vehicles: 3.0m-1

☐ If excess smoke is produced, try fitting a new air cleaner element, or using an injector cleaning treatment. If the engine is running badly, where applicable, check the vehicle's ECU for fault codes. Also check the vehicle's EGR system, where applicable. At high mileages, the injectors may require professional attention.

Engine

- [ ] Engine fails to rotate when attempting to start
- [ ] Starter motor turns engine slowly
- [ ] Starter motor spins without turning engine
- [ ] Starter motor noisy or excessively-rough in engagement
- [ ] Engine rotates but will not start
- [ ] Engine fires but will not run
- [ ] Engine difficult to start when cold
- [ ] Engine difficult to start when hot
- [ ] Engine idles erratically
- [ ] Engine misfires at idle speed
- [ ] Engine misfires throughout the driving speed range
- [ ] Engine stalls
- [ ] Engine lacks power
- [ ] Oil pressure warning light illuminated with engine running
- [ ] Engine runs-on after switching off
- [ ] Engine noises

Cooling system

- [ ] Overheating
- [ ] Overcooling
- [ ] External coolant leakage
- [ ] Internal coolant leakage
- [ ] Corrosion

Fuel and exhaust systems

- [ ] Excessive fuel consumption
- [ ] Fuel leakage and/or fuel odour
- [ ] Excessive noise or fumes from exhaust system

Clutch

- [ ] Pedal travels to floor – no pressure or very little resistance
- [ ] Clutch fails to disengage (unable to select gears)
- [ ] Clutch slips (engine speed increases, with no increase in vehicle speed)
- [ ] Judder as clutch is engaged
- [ ] Noise when depressing or releasing clutch pedal

Manual gearbox

- [ ] Noisy in neutral with engine running
- [ ] Noisy in one particular gear
- [ ] Difficulty engaging gears
- [ ] Jumps out of gear
- [ ] Vibration
- [ ] Lubricant leaks

Automatic transmission

- [ ] Fluid leakage
- [ ] Transmission fluid brown, or has burned smell
- [ ] General gear selection problems
- [ ] Transmission will not downshift (kickdown) with accelerator fully depressed
- [ ] Engine will not start in any gear, or starts in gears other than Park or Neutral
- [ ] Transmission slips, shifts roughly, is noisy, or has no drive in forward or reverse gears

Transfer gearbox

- [ ] Noisy in neutral with engine running
- [ ] Noisy in Low or High positions
- [ ] Difficulty engaging ranges
- [ ] Jumps out of gear
- [ ] Vibration
- [ ] Lubricant leaks

Propeller shafts

- [ ] Knock or clunk when taking up drive
- [ ] Oil leak where propeller shaft enters transfer gearbox
- [ ] Oil leak where propeller shaft enters axle
- [ ] Metallic grating sound consistent with vehicle speed
- [ ] Scraping noise
- [ ] Vibration

Front and rear axles

- [ ] Vibration
- [ ] Noise on drive and overrun
- [ ] Noise consistent with roadspeed
- [ ] Knock or clunk when taking up drive
- [ ] Oil leakage

Braking system

- [ ] Vehicle pulls to one side under braking
- [ ] Noise (grinding or high-pitched squeal) when brakes applied
- [ ] Excessive brake pedal travel
- [ ] Brake pedal feels spongy when depressed
- [ ] Excessive brake pedal effort required to stop vehicle
- [ ] Judder felt through brake pedal or steering wheel when braking
- [ ] Brakes binding
- [ ] Rear wheels locking under normal braking

Suspension and steering

- [ ] Vehicle pulls to one side
- [ ] Wheel wobble and vibration
- [ ] Excessive pitching and/or rolling around corners, or during braking
- [ ] Wandering or general instability
- [ ] Excessively-stiff steering
- [ ] Excessive play in steering
- [ ] Lack of power assistance
- [ ] Tyre wear excessive

Electrical system

- [ ] Battery will not hold a charge for more than a few days
- [ ] Ignition/no-charge warning light remains illuminated with engine running
- [ ] Ignition/no-charge warning light fails to come on
- [ ] Lights inoperative
- [ ] Instrument readings inaccurate or erratic
- [ ] Horn inoperative, or unsatisfactory in operation
- [ ] Windscreen/tailgate wipers inoperative, or unsatisfactory in operation
- [ ] Windscreen/tailgate washers inoperative, or unsatisfactory in operation
- [ ] Electric windows inoperative, or unsatisfactory in operation
- [ ] Central locking system inoperative, or unsatisfactory in operation

Introduction

The vehicle owner who does his or her own maintenance according to the recommended service schedules should not have to use this section of the manual very often. Modern component reliability is such that, provided those items subject to wear or deterioration are inspected or renewed at the specified intervals, sudden failure is comparatively rare. Faults do not usually just happen as a result of sudden failure, but develop over a period of time. Major mechanical failures in particular are usually preceded by characteristic symptoms over hundreds or even thousands of miles. Those components which do occasionally fail without warning are often small and easily carried in the vehicle.

With any fault-finding, the first step is to decide where to begin investigations. Sometimes this is obvious, but on other occasions, a little detective work will be necessary. The owner who makes half a dozen haphazard adjustments or replacements may be successful in curing a fault (or its symptoms), but will be none the wiser if the fault recurs,

and ultimately may have spent more time and money than was necessary. A calm and logical approach will be found to be more satisfactory in the long run. Always take into account any warning signs or abnormalities that may have been noticed in the period preceding the fault – power loss, high or low gauge readings, unusual smells, etc – and remember that failure of components such as fuses or relays may only be pointers to some underlying fault.

The pages which follow provide an easy-reference guide to the more common problems which may occur during the operation of the vehicle. These problems and their possible causes are grouped under headings denoting various components or systems, such as Engine, Cooling system, etc. The general Chapter which deals with the problem is also shown in brackets; refer to the relevant part of that Chapter for system-specific information. Whatever the fault, certain basic principles apply. These are as follows:

Verify the fault. This is simply a matter of being sure that you know what the symptoms

are before starting work. This is particularly important if you are investigating a fault for someone else, who may not have described it very accurately.

Don't overlook the obvious. For example, if the vehicle won't start, is there fuel in the tank? (Don't take anyone else's word on this particular point, and don't trust the fuel gauge either!) If an electrical fault is indicated, look for loose or broken wires before digging out the test gear.

Cure the disease, not the symptom. Substituting a flat battery with a fully-charged one will get you off the hard shoulder, but if the underlying cause is not attended to, the new battery will go the same way.

Don't take anything for granted. Particularly, don't forget that a 'new' component may itself be defective (especially if it's been rattling around in the boot for months), and don't leave components out of a fault diagnosis sequence just because they are new or recently fitted. When you do finally diagnose a difficult fault, you'll probably realise that all the evidence was there from the start.

Engine

Engine fails to rotate when attempting to start

☐ Battery terminal connections loose or corroded (*Weekly checks*).
☐ Battery discharged or faulty (Chapter 5).
☐ Broken, loose or disconnected wiring in the starting circuit (Chapter 5).
☐ Automatic transmission not in P or N (Chapter 7B)
☐ Defective starter solenoid or switch (Chapter 5).
☐ Defective starter motor (Chapter 5).
☐ Starter pinion or flywheel ring gear teeth loose or broken (Chapters 2 and 5).
☐ Engine earth strap broken or disconnected (Chapter 5 and 12).

Engine rotates, but will not start

☐ Fuel tank empty.
☐ Battery discharged (engine rotates slowly) (Chapter 5).
☐ Battery terminal connections loose or corroded (*Weekly checks*).
☐ Immobiliser fault (Chapter 13).
☐ Preheating system faulty (Chapter 5).
☐ Air in fuel system (Chapter 4).
☐ Major mechanical failure (eg camshaft drive) (Chapter 2A).

Engine (continued)

Engine difficult to start when cold

- ☐ Battery discharged (Chapter 5).
- ☐ Battery terminal connections loose or corroded (*Weekly checks*).
- ☐ Worn, faulty or incorrectly-gapped spark plugs (Chapter 1).
- ☐ Preheating system faulty (Chapter 5).
- ☐ Wax formed in fuel (in very cold weather).
- ☐ Low cylinder compressions (Chapter 2A).

Engine difficult to start when hot

- ☐ Air filter element dirty or clogged (Chapter 1).
- ☐ Low cylinder compressions (Chapter 2A).

Starter motor noisy or excessively-rough in engagement

- ☐ Starter pinion or flywheel ring gear teeth loose or broken (Chapters 2A and 5).
- ☐ Starter motor mounting bolts loose or missing (Chapter 5).
- ☐ Starter motor internal components worn or damaged (Chapter 5).

Engine starts, but stops immediately

- ☐ Fuel pump fault – petrol models (Chapter 4A).
- ☐ Fuel lines restricted (Chapter 4).
- ☐ Air in fuel system (Chapter 4).
- ☐ Wax formed in fuel (in very cold weather).

Engine idles erratically

- ☐ Air filter element clogged (Chapter 1).
- ☐ Vacuum leak at the intake manifold or associated hoses (Chapter 4A).
- ☐ Uneven or low cylinder compressions (Chapter 2A).
- ☐ Camshaft lobes worn (Chapter 2A).
- ☐ Faulty injector(s) (Chapter 4A).
- ☐ Wax formed in fuel (in very cold weather).

Engine misfires at idle speed

- ☐ Vacuum leak at the intake manifold or associated hoses (Chapter 4A).
- ☐ Faulty injector(s) (Chapter 4A).
- ☐ Uneven or low cylinder compressions (Chapter 2A).
- ☐ Disconnected, leaking, or perished crankcase ventilation hoses (Chapter 4B).

Engine misfires throughout the driving speed range

- ☐ Fuel filter choked (Chapter 1).
- ☐ Fuel pump faulty, or delivery pressure low (Chapter 4A).
- ☐ Fuel tank vent blocked, or fuel pipes restricted (Chapter 4A).
- ☐ Vacuum leak at the intake manifold or associated hoses (Chapter 4A).
- ☐ Faulty injector(s) (Chapter 4A).
- ☐ Uneven or low cylinder compressions (Chapter 2A).

Engine hesitates on acceleration

- ☐ Vacuum leak at the intake manifold or associated hoses (Chapter 4A).
- ☐ Faulty injector(s) (Chapter 4A).

Engine stalls

- ☐ Vacuum leak at the intake manifold or associated hoses (Chapter 4A).
- ☐ Fuel filter choked (Chapter 1).
- ☐ Fuel pump faulty, or delivery pressure low (Chapter 4A).
- ☐ Fuel tank vent blocked, or fuel pipes restricted (Chapter 4A).
- ☐ Faulty injector(s) (Chapter 4A).
- ☐ Wax formed in fuel (in very cold weather).

Engine lacks power

- ☐ Timing chain or belt incorrectly fitted or tensioned (Chapter 2A).
- ☐ Fuel filter choked (Chapter 1).
- ☐ Fuel pump faulty, or delivery pressure low (Chapter 4A).
- ☐ Fuel lines leaking or restricted (Chapter 4A).
- ☐ Uneven or low cylinder compressions (Chapter 2A).
- ☐ Vacuum leak at the intake manifold or associated hoses (Chapter 4A).
- ☐ Faulty injector(s) (Chapter 4A).
- ☐ Wax formed in fuel (in very cold weather).
- ☐ Brakes binding (Chapters 1 and 10).
- ☐ Clutch slipping (Chapter 6).

Engine backfires

- ☐ Timing chain incorrectly fitted or tensioned (Chapter 2A).
- ☐ Vacuum leak at the intake manifold or associated hoses (Chapter 4A).

Oil pressure warning light illuminated with engine running

- ☐ Low oil level, or incorrect oil grade (*Weekly checks*).
- ☐ Worn engine bearings and/or oil pump (Chapter 2B).
- ☐ High engine operating température (Chapter 3).
- ☐ Oil pressure relief valve defective (Chapter 2A).
- ☐ Oil pick-up strainer clogged (Chapter 2A).

Engine runs-on after switching off

- ☐ Excessive carbon build-up in engine (Chapter 2B).
- ☐ High engine operating temperature (Chapter 3).

Engine noises

Note: *To inexperienced ears, a diesel engine can sound alarming even when there is nothing wrong with it, so it may be prudent to have an unusual noise expertly diagnosed before making renewals or repairs.*

Pre-ignition (pinking) or knocking during acceleration or under load

- ☐ Incorrect grade of fuel.
- ☐ Vacuum leak at the intake manifold or associated hoses (Chapter 4A).
- ☐ Excessive carbon build-up in engine (Chapter 2B).
- ☐ Overheating (Refer to *Cooling system* of Fault finding).

Whistling or wheezing noises

- ☐ Leaking intake manifold gasket (Chapter 4A).
- ☐ Leaking exhaust manifold gasket or pipe-to-manifold joint (Chapter 4A).
- ☐ Leaking vacuum hose (Chapters 4).
- ☐ Blowing cylinder head gasket (Chapter 2A).

Tapping or rattling noises

- ☐ Insufficient oil reaching hydraulic tappets – check oil level, or change oil (*Weekly checks* or Chapter 1).
- ☐ Worn hydraulic tappet or camshaft (Chapter 2A).
- ☐ Worn timing chain (Chapter 2A).
- ☐ Worn camshaft (Chapter 2A).
- ☐ Ancillary component fault (water pump, alternator, etc) (Chapters 3, 5, etc).

Knocking or thumping noises

- ☐ Worn big-end bearings (regular heavy knocking, perhaps less under load) (Chapter 2B).
- ☐ Worn main bearings (rumbling and knocking, perhaps worsening under load) (Chapter 2B).
- ☐ Piston slap (indicating piston and/or bore wear – most noticeable when cold) (Chapter 2B).
- ☐ Ancillary component fault (water pump, alternator, etc) (Chapters 3, 5, etc).

Cooling system

Overheating

- [ ] Insufficient coolant in system (*Weekly checks*).
- [ ] Auxiliary drivebelt broken or drivebelt tensioner faulty (Chapter 1)
- [ ] Thermostat faulty (Chapter 3).
- [ ] Radiator core blocked, or grille restricted (Chapter 3).
- [ ] Electric cooling fan or thermoswitch faulty (Chapter 3).
- [ ] Pressure cap faulty (Chapter 3).
- [ ] Inaccurate temperature gauge sender unit (Chapter 3).
- [ ] Airlock in cooling system (Chapter 1).

Overcooling

- [ ] Thermostat faulty (Chapter 3).
- [ ] Inaccurate temperature gauge sender unit (Chapter 3).

External coolant leakage

- [ ] Deteriorated or damaged hoses or hose clips (Chapter 1).
- [ ] Radiator core or heater matrix leaking (Chapter 3).
- [ ] Pressure cap faulty (Chapter 3).
- [ ] Water pump seal leaking (Chapter 3).
- [ ] Boiling due to overheating (Chapter 3).
- [ ] Core plug leaking (Chapter 2B).

Internal coolant leakage

- [ ] Leaking cylinder head gasket (Chapter 2A).
- [ ] Cracked cylinder head or cylinder bore (Chapter 2A).

Corrosion

- [ ] Infrequent draining and flushing (Chapter 1).
- [ ] Incorrect coolant mixture or inappropriate coolant type (Chapter 1).

Fuel and exhaust systems

Excessive fuel consumption

- [ ] Air filter element dirty or clogged (Chapter 1).
- [ ] Faulty injector(s) (Chapter 4A).
- [ ] Fuel tank/lines damaged or leaking, or fuel return line restricted (Chapter 4A).
- [ ] Tyres under-inflated (*Weekly checks*).
- [ ] Brakes binding (Chapter 10).

Fuel leakage and/or fuel odour

- [ ] Damaged or corroded fuel tank, pipes or connections (Chapter 4).

Excessive noise or fumes from exhaust system

- [ ] Leaking exhaust system or manifold joints (Chapters 1 and 4).
- [ ] Leaking, corroded or damaged silencers or pipe (Chapters 1 and 4).
- [ ] Broken mountings causing body or suspension contact (Chapter 1).

Clutch

Judder as clutch is engaged

- [ ] Clutch disc linings contaminated with oil or grease (Chapter 6).
- [ ] Clutch disc linings excessively worn (Chapter 6).
- [ ] Faulty or distorted pressure plate or diaphragm spring (Chapter 6).
- [ ] Worn or loose engine/transmission mountings (Chapter 2A).
- [ ] Clutch disc hub or gearbox input shaft splines worn (Chapter 6).

Clutch fails to disengage (unable to select gears)

- [ ] Leak in clutch hydraulic system (Chapter 6).
- [ ] Faulty hydraulic master or slave cylinder (Chapter 6).
- [ ] Clutch disc sticking on gearbox input shaft splines (Chapter 6).
- [ ] Clutch disc sticking to flywheel or pressure plate (Chapter 6).
- [ ] Faulty pressure plate assembly (Chapter 6).
- [ ] Clutch release mechanism worn or incorrectly assembled (Chapter 6).

Clutch slips (engine speed increases, with no increase in vehicle speed)

- [ ] Clutch disc linings excessively worn (Chapter 6).
- [ ] Clutch disc linings contaminated with oil or grease (Chapter 6).
- [ ] Faulty pressure plate or weak diaphragm spring (Chapter 6).

Pedal travels to floor – no pressure or very little resistance

- [ ] Leak in clutch hydraulic system (Chapter 6).
- [ ] Faulty hydraulic master or slave cylinder (Chapter 6).
- [ ] Broken clutch release bearing or fork (Chapter 6).
- [ ] Broken diaphragm spring in clutch pressure plate (Chapter 6).

Noise when depressing or releasing clutch pedal

- [ ] Worn clutch release bearing (Chapter 6).
- [ ] Worn or dry clutch pedal bushes (Chapter 6).
- [ ] Faulty pressure plate assembly (Chapter 6).
- [ ] Pressure plate diaphragm spring broken (Chapter 6).
- [ ] Broken clutch disc cushioning springs (Chapter 6).

Manual transmission

Difficulty engaging gears

- [ ] Clutch fault (Chapter 6).
- [ ] Worn or damaged gear linkage (Chapter 7A).
- [ ] Worn synchroniser units (Chapter 7A).*

Jumps out of gear

- [ ] Worn or damaged gear linkage (Chapter 7A).
- [ ] Incorrectly-adjusted gear linkage (Chapter 7A).
- [ ] Worn synchroniser units (Chapter 7A).*
- [ ] Worn selector forks (Chapter 7A).*

Vibration

- [ ] Lack of oil (Chapter 1).
- [ ] Worn bearings (Chapter 7A).*

Noisy in one particular gear

- [ ] Worn, damaged or chipped gear teeth (Chapter 7A).*

Noisy in neutral with engine running

- [ ] Input shaft and/or mainshaft bearings worn (noise apparent with clutch pedal released, but not when depressed) (Chapter 7A).*
- [ ] Clutch release bearing worn (noise apparent with clutch pedal depressed, possibly less when released) (Chapter 6).

Lubricant leaks

- [ ] Leaking oil seal (Chapter 7A).
- [ ] Leaking housing joint (Chapter 7A).*

Although the corrective action necessary to remedy the symptoms described is beyond the scope of the home mechanic, the above information should be helpful in isolating the cause of the condition, so that the owner can communicate clearly with a professional mechanic.

Automatic transmission

Note: *Due to the complexity of the automatic transmission, it is difficult for the home mechanic to properly diagnose and service this unit. For problems other than the following, the vehicle should be taken to a dealer service department or automatic transmission specialist.*

Fluid leakage

- [ ] Automatic transmission fluid is usually deep red in colour. Fluid leaks should not be confused with engine oil, which can easily be blown onto the transmission by air flow.
- [ ] To determine the source of a leak, first remove all built-up dirt and grime from the transmission housing and surrounding areas, using a degreasing agent or by steam-cleaning. Drive the vehicle at low speed, so that air flow will not blow the leak far from its source. Raise and support the vehicle, and determine where the leak is coming from. The following are common areas of leakage.
  - a) Fluid pan (transmission sump).
  - b) Dipstick tube (Chapter 1).
  - c) Transmission-to-fluid cooler fluid pipes/unions (Chapter 7B).

Transmission fluid brown, or has burned smell

- [ ] Transmission fluid level low, or fluid in need of renewal (Chapter 1).

Transmission will not downshift (kickdown) with accelerator pedal fully depressed

- [ ] Low transmission fluid level (Chapter 1).

General gear selection problems

- [ ] The most likely cause of gear selection problems is a faulty or poorly-adjusted gear selector mechanism. The following are common problems associated with a faulty selector mechanism:
  - a) Engine starting in gears other than Park or Neutral.
  - b) Indicator on gear selector lever pointing to a gear other than the one actually being used.
  - c) Vehicle moves when in Park or Neutral.
  - d) Poor gear shift quality, or erratic gear changes.
- [ ] Refer any problems to a Land Rover dealer, or an automatic transmission specialist.

Engine will not start in any gear, or starts in gears other than Park or Neutral

- [ ] Incorrect selector cable adjustment (Chapter 7B).

Transmission slips, shifts roughly, is noisy, or has no drive in forward or reverse gears

- [ ] There are many probable causes for the above problems, but the home mechanic should be concerned with only one possibility – fluid level. Before taking the vehicle to a dealer or transmission specialist, check the fluid level and condition of the fluid as described in Chapter 1. Correct the fluid level as necessary, or change the fluid and filter if needed. If the problem persists, professional help will be necessary.

Transfer gearbox

Noisy in neutral with engine running

☐ Worn mainshaft or output shaft bearings (Chapter 7C).*

Noisy in Low or High positions

☐ Worn, damaged or chipped gear teeth (Chapter 7C).*

Jumps out of gear

☐ Worn or damaged gear linkage (Chapter 7C).*
☐ Worn selector fork (Chapter 7C).*

Vibration

☐ Lack of oil (Chapter 1).
☐ Worn bearings (Chapter 7C).*

Difficulty engaging ranges

☐ Clutch fault (Chapter 6).
☐ ☐ain transmission fault (Chapter 7A or 7B).
☐ Worn selector fork (Chapter 7C).*

Lubricant leaks

☐ Leaking oil seal (Chapter 7C).*
☐ Leaking housing joint (Chapter 7C).*

*Although the corrective action necessary to remedy the symptoms described is beyond the scope of the home mechanic, the above information should be helpful in isolating the cause of the condition, so that the owner can communicate clearly with a professional mechanic.

Propeller shafts

Knock or clunk when taking up drive

☐ Worn universal joint bearings (Chapter 8).
☐ Worn axle drive pinion splines (Chapter 9).
☐ Loose drive flange bolts (Chapter 8).
☐ Excessive backlash in axle gears (Chapter 9).

Metallic grating sound, consistent with vehicle speed

☐ Severe wear in universal joint bearings (Chapter 8).

Vibration

☐ Wear in sliding sleeve splines (Chapter 8).
☐ Worn universal joint bearings (Chapter 8).
☐ Propeller shaft out of balance (Chapter 8).

Front and rear axles

Vibration

☐ Propeller shaft out of balance (Chapter 8).
☐ Worn hub bearings (Chapter 9).
☐ Wheels out of balance.
☐ Propeller shaft or driveshaft joints worn (Chapters 8 and 9).
☐ Suspension or steering fault (Chapter 11).

Noise on drive and overrun

☐ Worn crownwheel and pinion gears (Chapter 9).
☐ Worn differential bearings (Chapter 9).
☐ Main transmission or transfer gearbox fault (Chapter 7).

Noise consistent with road speed

☐ Worn hub bearings (Chapter 9).
☐ Worn differential bearings (Chapter 9).
☐ Main transmission or transfer gearbox fault (Chapter 7).

Knock or clunk when taking up drive

☐ Excessive crownwheel and pinion backlash (Chapter 9).
☐ Worn propeller shaft or driveshaft joints (Chapters 8 and 9).
☐ Worn driveshaft splines (Chapter 9).
☐ Driveshaft nut or roadwheel nuts loose (Chapter 9).
☐ Broken, damaged, or worn suspension components or axle mountings (Chapters 11 and 9).
☐ Main transmission or transfer gearbox fault (Chapter 7).

Oil leakage

☐ Faulty differential pinion or halfshaft oil seals (Chapter 9).
☐ Blocked axle breather valve (Chapter 9).
☐ Damaged driveshaft oil seal (Chapter 9).

Braking system

Note: *Before assuming that a brake problem exists, make sure that the tyres are in good condition and correctly inflated, the front wheel alignment is correct, and the vehicle is not loaded with weight in an unequal manner. Apart from checking the condition of all pipe and hose connections, any faults occurring on the anti-lock braking system should be referred to a Land Rover dealer for diagnosis.*

Vehicle pulls to one side under braking

☐ Worn, defective, damaged or contaminated front or rear brake pads on one side (Chapter 10).
☐ Seized or partially-seized front or rear brake caliper piston (Chapter 10).
☐ A mixture of brake pad lining materials fitted between sides (Chapter 10).
☐ Brake caliper mounting bolts loose (Chapter 10).
☐ Worn or damaged steering or suspension components (Chapter 11).

Noise (grinding or high-pitched squeal) when brakes applied

☐ Brake pad friction lining material worn down to metal backing (Chapter 10).
☐ Brake pads incorrectly fitted, or pad backing plates dry (Chapter 10).
☐ Excessive corrosion of brake disc – may be apparent after the vehicle has been standing for some time (Chapter 10).

Excessive brake pedal travel

☐ Faulty master cylinder (Chapter 10).
☐ Air in hydraulic system (Chapter 10).
☐ Faulty vacuum servo unit (Chapter 10).
☐ Faulty brake vacuum pump (Chapter 10).

Brake pedal feels spongy when depressed

☐ Air in hydraulic system (Chapter 10).
☐ Deteriorated flexible rubber brake hoses (Chapter 10).
☐ Master cylinder mountings loose (Chapter 10).
☐ Faulty master cylinder (Chapter 10).

Excessive brake pedal effort required to stop vehicle

☐ Faulty vacuum servo unit (Chapter 10).
☐ Disconnected, damaged or insecure brake servo vacuum hose (Chapters 1 and 10).
☐ Faulty brake vacuum pump (Chapter 10).
☐ Primary or secondary hydraulic circuit failure (Chapter 10).
☐ Seized brake caliper piston(s) (Chapter 10).
☐ Brake pads incorrectly fitted (Chapter 10).
☐ Incorrect grade of brake pads fitted (Chapter 10).
☐ Brake pads contaminated (Chapter 10).

Judder felt through brake pedal or steering wheel when braking

Note: *Under heavy braking, models equipped with ABS may exhibit a 'pulsing' sensation felt through the brake pedal. This is a normal feature of ABS operation, and does not necessarily indicate a fault.*

☐ Excessive run-out or distortion of brake disc(s) (Chapter 10).
☐ Brake pad linings worn (Chapter 10).
☐ Brake caliper mounting bolts loose (Chapter 10).
☐ Wear in suspension or steering components or mountings (Chapter 11).

Brakes binding

☐ Seized brake caliper piston(s) (Chapter 10).
☐ Faulty master cylinder (Chapter 10).

Suspension and steering

Note: *Before diagnosing suspension or steering faults, be sure that the trouble is not due to incorrect tyre pressures, mixtures of tyre types or binding brakes.*

Vehicle pulls to one side

☐ Defective tyre (*Weekly checks*).
☐ Excessive wear in suspension or steering components (Chapter 11).
☐ Incorrect front wheel alignment (Chapter 11).
☐ Accident damage to steering or suspension components (Chapter 11).

Wheel wobble and vibration

☐ Front roadwheels out of balance – vibration felt mainly through the steering wheel (Chapter 11).
☐ Rear roadwheels out of balance – vibration felt throughout the vehicle (Chapter 11).
☐ Roadwheels damaged or distorted (*Weekly checks*).
☐ Faulty or damaged tyre (*Weekly checks*).
☐ Worn steering or suspension joints, bushes or components (Chapter 11).
☐ Wheel nuts loose (*Wheel changing*).

Excessive pitching and/or rolling around corners or during braking

☐ Defective shock absorbers (Chapter 11).
☐ Broken or weak coil spring and/or suspension component (Chapter 11).
☐ Worn or damaged anti-roll bar or mountings (Chapter 11).
☐ ACE system fault (Chapter 11).

Wandering or general instability

☐ Incorrect front wheel alignment (Chapter 11).
☐ Worn steering or suspension joints, bushes or components (Chapter 11).
☐ Roadwheels out of balance (*Weekly checks*).
☐ Faulty or damaged tyre (*Weekly checks*).
☐ Wheel nuts loose (*Wheel changing*).
☐ Defective shock absorbers (Chapter 11).

Excessively-stiff steering

☐ Lack of steering gear lubricant (Chapter 11).
☐ Seized track-rod end balljoint (Chapter 11).

☐ Lack of power steering fluid (Chapter 1).
☐ Incorrect front wheel alignment (Chapter 11).
☐ Steering box or column damaged (Chapter 11).
☐ Power steering pump fault (Chapter 11).

Excessive play in steering

☐ Worn steering column universal joint(s) or intermediate coupling (Chapter 11).
☐ Worn steering track-rod end balljoints (Chapter 11).
☐ Worn steering box (Chapter 11).
☐ Worn steering or suspension joints, bushes or components (Chapter 11).

Lack of power assistance

☐ Broken or power steering pump drivebelt (Chapter 1).
☐ Incorrect power steering fluid level (*Weekly checks*).
☐ Restriction in power steering fluid hoses (Chapter 1).
☐ Faulty power steering pump (Chapter 11).
☐ Faulty steering box (Chapter 11).

Tyre wear excessive

Tyres worn on inside or outside edges

☐ Tyres under-inflated (wear on both edges) (*Weekly checks*).
☐ Incorrect camber or castor angles (wear on one edge only) (Chapter 11).
☐ Worn steering or suspension joints, bushes or components (Chapter 11).
☐ Excessively hard cornering.
☐ Accident damage.

Tyre treads exhibit feathered edges

☐ Incorrect toe setting (Chapter 11).

Tyres worn in centre of tread

☐ Tyres over-inflated (*Weekly checks*).

Tyres worn on inside and outside edges

☐ Tyres under-inflated (*Weekly checks*).

Tyres worn unevenly

☐ Tyres out of balance (*Weekly checks*).
☐ Faulty tyre (*Weekly checks*).
☐ Excessive wheel or tyre run-out (*Weekly checks*).
☐ Worn shock absorbers (Chapter 11).

Electrical system

Note: *For problems associated with the starting system, refer to the faults listed under Engine earlier in this Section.*

Battery will not hold a charge for more than a few days

☐ Battery defective internally (Chapter 5).
☐ Battery electrolyte level low – where applicable (Chapter 1).
☐ Battery terminal connections loose or corroded (*Weekly checks*).
☐ Alternator drivebelt worn or incorrectly adjusted (Chapter 1).
☐ Alternator not charging at correct output (Chapter 5).
☐ Alternator or voltage regulator faulty (Chapter 5).
☐ Short-circuit causing continual battery drain (Chapter 5 or 13).

Ignition/no-charge warning light remains illuminated with engine running

☐ Alternator drivebelt broken, worn, or incorrectly adjusted (Chapter 1).
☐ Alternator brushes worn, sticking, or dirty (Chapter 5).
☐ Alternator brush springs weak or broken (Chapter 5).
☐ Internal fault in alternator or voltage regulator (Chapter 5).
☐ Broken, disconnected, or loose wiring in charging circuit (Chapter 5).

Ignition/no-charge warning light fails to come on

☐ Broken, disconnected, or loose wiring in warning light circuit (Chapter 13).
☐ Alternator faulty (Chapter 5).

Electrical system (continued)

Lights inoperative

- ☐ Bulb blown (*Weekly checks* or Chapter 13).
- ☐ Corrosion of bulb or bulbholder contacts (Chapter 13).
- ☐ Blown fuse (*Weekly checks* or Chapter 13).
- ☐ Faulty relay (Chapter 13).
- ☐ Broken, loose, or disconnected wiring (Chapter 13).
- ☐ Faulty switch (Chapter 13).

Instrument readings inaccurate or erratic

Instrument readings increase with engine speed

- ☐ Faulty instrument cluster (Chapter 13).

Fuel or temperature gauge give no reading

- ☐ Faulty gauge sender unit (Chapters 3 or 4).
- ☐ Wiring open-circuit (Chapter 13).
- ☐ Faulty gauge (Chapter 13).

Fuel or temperature gauges give continuous maximum reading

- ☐ Faulty gauge sender unit (Chapters 3 or 4).
- ☐ Wiring short-circuit (Chapter 13).
- ☐ Faulty gauge (Chapter 13).

Horn inoperative, or unsatisfactory in operation

Horn operates all the time

- ☐ Horn push either earthed or stuck down (Chapter 13).
- ☐ Horn cable to horn push earthed (Chapter 13).

Horn fails to operate

- ☐ Blown fuse (*Weekly checks* or Chapter 13).
- ☐ Cable or cable connections loose, broken or disconnected (Chapter 13).
- ☐ Faulty horn (Chapter 13).

Horn emits intermittent or unsatisfactory sound

- ☐ Cable connections loose (Chapter 13).
- ☐ Horn mountings loose (Chapter 13).
- ☐ Faulty horn (Chapter 13).

Windscreen/tailgate wipers inoperative, or unsatisfactory in operation

Wipers fail to operate, or operate very slowly

- ☐ Wiper blades stuck to screen, or linkage seized or binding (Chapters 1 and 13).
- ☐ Blown fuse (*Weekly checks* or Chapter 13).
- ☐ Cable or cable connections loose, broken or disconnected (Chapter 13).
- ☐ Faulty relay (Chapter 13).
- ☐ Faulty wiper motor (Chapter 13).

Wiper blades sweep over too large or too small an area of the glass

- ☐ Wiper arms incorrectly positioned on spindles (Chapter 13).
- ☐ Excessive wear of wiper linkage (Chapter 13).
- ☐ Wiper motor or linkage mountings loose or insecure (Chapter 13).

Wiper blades fail to clean the glass effectively

- ☐ Wiper blade rubbers worn or perished (*Weekly checks*).
- ☐ Wiper arm tension springs broken, or arm pivots seized (Chapter 13).
- ☐ Insufficient windscreen washer additive to adequately remove road film (*Weekly checks*).

Windscreen/tailgate washers inoperative, or unsatisfactory in operation

One or more washer jets inoperative

- ☐ Blocked washer jet (Chapter 13).
- ☐ Disconnected, kinked or restricted fluid hose (Chapter 13).
- ☐ Insufficient fluid in washer reservoir (*Weekly checks*).

Washer pump fails to operate

- ☐ Broken or disconnected wiring or connections (Chapter 13).
- ☐ Blown fuse (*Weekly checks* or Chapter 13).
- ☐ Faulty washer switch (Chapter 13).
- ☐ Faulty washer pump (Chapter 13).

Electric windows inoperative, or unsatisfactory in operation

Window glass will only move in one direction

- ☐ Faulty switch (Chapter 12).

Window glass slow to move

- ☐ Regulator seized or damaged, or in need of lubrication (Chapter 12).
- ☐ Door internal components or trim fouling regulator (Chapter 12).
- ☐ Faulty motor (Chapter 12).

Window glass fails to move

- ☐ Blown fuse (*Weekly checks* or Chapter 13).
- ☐ Faulty relay (Chapter 13).
- ☐ Broken or disconnected wiring or connections (Chapter 13).
- ☐ Faulty motor (Chapter 12).

Central locking system inoperative, or unsatisfactory in operation

Complete system failure

- ☐ Blown fuse (*Weekly checks* or Chapter 13).
- ☐ Faulty relay (Chapter 13).
- ☐ Broken or disconnected wiring or connections (Chapter 13).

Latch locks but will not unlock, or unlocks but will not lock

- ☐ Faulty switch (Chapter 13).
- ☐ Broken or disconnected latch operating rods or levers (Chapter 12).
- ☐ Faulty relay (Chapter 13).

One solenoid/motor fails to operate

- ☐ Broken or disconnected wiring or connections (Chapter 13).
- ☐ Faulty solenoid/motor (Chapter 12).
- ☐ Broken, binding or disconnected latch operating rods or levers (Chapter 12).
- ☐ Fault in door latch (Chapter 12).

A

ABS (Anti-lock brake system) A system, usually electronically controlled, that senses incipient wheel lockup during braking and relieves hydraulic pressure at wheels that are about to skid.

Air bag An inflatable bag hidden in the steering wheel (driver's side) or the dash or glovebox (passenger side). In a head-on collision, the bags inflate, preventing the driver and front passenger from being thrown forward into the steering wheel or windscreen.

Air cleaner A metal or plastic housing, containing a filter element, which removes dust and dirt from the air being drawn into the engine.

Air filter element The actual filter in an air cleaner system, usually manufactured from pleated paper and requiring renewal at regular intervals.

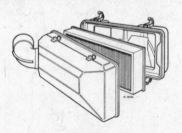

Air filter

Allen key A hexagonal wrench which fits into a recessed hexagonal hole.

Alligator clip A long-nosed spring-loaded metal clip with meshing teeth. Used to make temporary electrical connections.

Alternator A component in the electrical system which converts mechanical energy from a drivebelt into electrical energy to charge the battery and to operate the starting system, ignition system and electrical accessories.

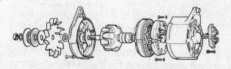

Alternator (exploded view)

Ampere (amp) A unit of measurement for the flow of electric current. One amp is the amount of current produced by one volt acting through a resistance of one ohm.

Anaerobic sealer A substance used to prevent bolts and screws from loosening. Anaerobic means that it does not require oxygen for activation. The Loctite brand is widely used.

Antifreeze A substance (usually ethylene glycol) mixed with water, and added to a vehicle's cooling system, to prevent freezing of the coolant in winter. Antifreeze also contains chemicals to inhibit corrosion and the formation of rust and other deposits that would tend to clog the radiator and coolant passages and reduce cooling efficiency.

Anti-seize compound A coating that reduces the risk of seizing on fasteners that are subjected to high temperatures, such as exhaust manifold bolts and nuts.

Anti-seize compound

Asbestos A natural fibrous mineral with great heat resistance, commonly used in the composition of brake friction materials. Asbestos is a health hazard and the dust created by brake systems should never be inhaled or ingested.

Axle A shaft on which a wheel revolves, or which revolves with a wheel. Also, a solid beam that connects the two wheels at one end of the vehicle. An axle which also transmits power to the wheels is known as a live axle.

Axle assembly

Axleshaft A single rotating shaft, on either side of the differential, which delivers power from the final drive assembly to the drive wheels. Also called a driveshaft or a halfshaft.

B

Ball bearing An anti-friction bearing consisting of a hardened inner and outer race with hardened steel balls between two races.

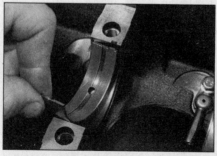

Bearing

Bearing The curved surface on a shaft or in a bore, or the part assembled into either, that permits relative motion between them with minimum wear and friction.

Big-end bearing The bearing in the end of the connecting rod that's attached to the crankshaft.

Bleed nipple A valve on a brake wheel cylinder, caliper or other hydraulic component that is opened to purge the hydraulic system of air. Also called a bleed screw.

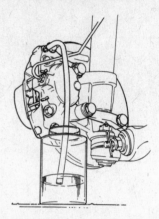

Brake bleeding

Brake bleeding Procedure for removing air from lines of a hydraulic brake system.

Brake disc The component of a disc brake that rotates with the wheels.

Brake drum The component of a drum brake that rotates with the wheels.

Brake linings The friction material which contacts the brake disc or drum to retard the vehicle's speed. The linings are bonded or riveted to the brake pads or shoes.

Brake pads The replaceable friction pads that pinch the brake disc when the brakes are applied. Brake pads consist of a friction material bonded or riveted to a rigid backing plate.

Brake shoe The crescent-shaped carrier to which the brake linings are mounted and which forces the lining against the rotating drum during braking.

Braking systems For more information on braking systems, consult the *Haynes Automotive Brake Manual*.

Breaker bar A long socket wrench handle providing greater leverage.

Bulkhead The insulated partition between the engine and the passenger compartment.

C

Caliper The non-rotating part of a disc-brake assembly that straddles the disc and carries the brake pads. The caliper also contains the hydraulic components that cause the pads to pinch the disc when the brakes are applied. A caliper is also a measuring tool that can be set to measure inside or outside dimensions of an object.

Camshaft A rotating shaft on which a series of cam lobes operate the valve mechanisms. The camshaft may be driven by gears, by sprockets and chain or by sprockets and a belt.

Canister A container in an evaporative emission control system; contains activated charcoal granules to trap vapours from the fuel system.

Canister

Carburettor A device which mixes fuel with air in the proper proportions to provide a desired power output from a spark ignition internal combustion engine.

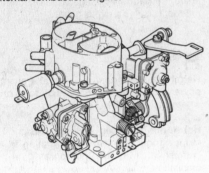

Carburettor

Castellated Resembling the parapets along the top of a castle wall. For example, a castellated balljoint stud nut.

Castellated nut

Castor In wheel alignment, the backward or forward tilt of the steering axis. Castor is positive when the steering axis is inclined rearward at the top.

Catalytic converter A silencer-like device in the exhaust system which converts certain pollutants in the exhaust gases into less harmful substances.

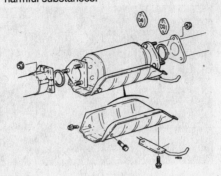

Catalytic converter

Circlip A ring-shaped clip used to prevent endwise movement of cylindrical parts and shafts. An internal circlip is installed in a groove in a housing; an external circlip fits into a groove on the outside of a cylindrical piece such as a shaft.

Clearance The amount of space between two parts. For example, between a piston and a cylinder, between a bearing and a journal, etc.

Coil spring A spiral of elastic steel found in various sizes throughout a vehicle, for example as a springing medium in the suspension and in the valve train.

Compression Reduction in volume, and increase in pressure and temperature, of a gas, caused by squeezing it into a smaller space.

Compression ratio The relationship between cylinder volume when the piston is at top dead centre and cylinder volume when the piston is at bottom dead centre.

Constant velocity (CV) joint A type of universal joint that cancels out vibrations caused by driving power being transmitted through an angle.

Core plug A disc or cup-shaped metal device inserted in a hole in a casting through which core was removed when the casting was formed. Also known as a freeze plug or expansion plug.

Crankcase The lower part of the engine block in which the crankshaft rotates.

Crankshaft The main rotating member, or shaft, running the length of the crankcase, with offset "throws" to which the connecting rods are attached.

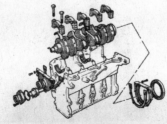

Crankshaft assembly

Crocodile clip See Alligator clip

D

Diagnostic code Code numbers obtained by accessing the diagnostic mode of an engine management computer. This code can be used to determine the area in the system where a malfunction may be located.

Disc brake A brake design incorporating a rotating disc onto which brake pads are squeezed. The resulting friction converts the energy of a moving vehicle into heat.

Double-overhead cam (DOHC) An engine that uses two overhead camshafts, usually one for the intake valves and one for the exhaust valves.

Drivebelt(s) The belt(s) used to drive accessories such as the alternator, water pump, power steering pump, air conditioning compressor, etc. off the crankshaft pulley.

Accessory drivebelts

Driveshaft Any shaft used to transmit motion. Commonly used when referring to the axleshafts on a front wheel drive vehicle.

Driveshaft

Drum brake A type of brake using a drum-shaped metal cylinder attached to the inner surface of the wheel. When the brake pedal is pressed, curved brake shoes with friction linings press against the inside of the drum to slow or stop the vehicle.

Drum brake assembly

E

EGR valve A valve used to introduce exhaust gases into the intake air stream.

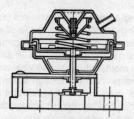

EGR valve

Electronic control unit (ECU) A computer which controls (for instance) ignition and fuel injection systems, or an anti-lock braking system. For more information refer to the *Haynes Automotive Electrical and Electronic Systems Manual*.

Electronic Fuel Injection (EFI) A computer controlled fuel system that distributes fuel through an injector located in each intake port of the engine.

Emergency brake A braking system, independent of the main hydraulic system, that can be used to slow or stop the vehicle if the primary brakes fail, or to hold the vehicle stationary even though the brake pedal isn't depressed. It usually consists of a hand lever that actuates either front or rear brakes mechanically through a series of cables and linkages. Also known as a handbrake or parking brake.

Endfloat The amount of lengthwise movement between two parts. As applied to a crankshaft, the distance that the crankshaft can move forward and back in the cylinder block.

Engine management system (EMS) A computer controlled system which manages the fuel injection and the ignition systems in an integrated fashion.

Exhaust manifold A part with several passages through which exhaust gases leave the engine combustion chambers and enter the exhaust pipe.

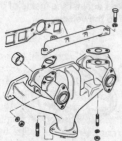

Exhaust manifold

F

Fan clutch A viscous (fluid) drive coupling device which permits variable engine fan speeds in relation to engine speeds.

Feeler blade A thin strip or blade of hardened steel, ground to an exact thickness, used to check or measure clearances between parts.

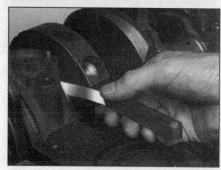

Feeler blade

Firing order The order in which the engine cylinders fire, or deliver their power strokes, beginning with the number one cylinder.

Flywheel A heavy spinning wheel in which energy is absorbed and stored by means of momentum. On cars, the flywheel is attached to the crankshaft to smooth out firing impulses.

Free play The amount of travel before any action takes place. The "looseness" in a linkage, or an assembly of parts, between the initial application of force and actual movement. For example, the distance the brake pedal moves before the pistons in the master cylinder are actuated.

Fuse An electrical device which protects a circuit against accidental overload. The typical fuse contains a soft piece of metal which is calibrated to melt at a predetermined current flow (expressed as amps) and break the circuit.

Fusible link A circuit protection device consisting of a conductor surrounded by heat-resistant insulation. The conductor is smaller than the wire it protects, so it acts as the weakest link in the circuit. Unlike a blown fuse, a failed fusible link must frequently be cut from the wire for replacement.

G

Gap The distance the spark must travel in jumping from the centre electrode to the side

Adjusting spark plug gap

electrode in a spark plug. Also refers to the spacing between the points in a contact breaker assembly in a conventional points-type ignition, or to the distance between the reluctor or rotor and the pickup coil in an electronic ignition.

Gasket Any thin, soft material - usually cork, cardboard, asbestos or soft metal - installed between two metal surfaces to ensure a good seal. For instance, the cylinder head gasket seals the joint between the block and the cylinder head.

Gasket

Gauge An instrument panel display used to monitor engine conditions. A gauge with a movable pointer on a dial or a fixed scale is an analogue gauge. A gauge with a numerical readout is called a digital gauge.

H

Halfshaft A rotating shaft that transmits power from the final drive unit to a drive wheel, usually when referring to a live rear axle.

Harmonic balancer A device designed to reduce torsion or twisting vibration in the crankshaft. May be incorporated in the crankshaft pulley. Also known as a vibration damper.

Hone An abrasive tool for correcting small irregularities or differences in diameter in an engine cylinder, brake cylinder, etc.

Hydraulic tappet A tappet that utilises hydraulic pressure from the engine's lubrication system to maintain zero clearance (constant contact with both camshaft and valve stem). Automatically adjusts to variation in valve stem length. Hydraulic tappets also reduce valve noise.

I

Ignition timing The moment at which the spark plug fires, usually expressed in the number of crankshaft degrees before the piston reaches the top of its stroke.

Inlet manifold A tube or housing with passages through which flows the air-fuel mixture (carburettor vehicles and vehicles with throttle body injection) or air only (port fuel-injected vehicles) to the port openings in the cylinder head.

J

Jump start Starting the engine of a vehicle with a discharged or weak battery by attaching jump leads from the weak battery to a charged or helper battery.

L

Load Sensing Proportioning Valve (LSPV) A brake hydraulic system control valve that works like a proportioning valve, but also takes into consideration the amount of weight carried by the rear axle.

Locknut A nut used to lock an adjustment nut, or other threaded component, in place. For example, a locknut is employed to keep the adjusting nut on the rocker arm in position.

Lockwasher A form of washer designed to prevent an attaching nut from working loose.

M

MacPherson strut A type of front suspension system devised by Earle MacPherson at Ford of England. In its original form, a simple lateral link with the anti-roll bar creates the lower control arm. A long strut - an integral coil spring and shock absorber - is mounted between the body and the steering knuckle. Many modern so-called MacPherson strut systems use a conventional lower A-arm and don't rely on the anti-roll bar for location.

Multimeter An electrical test instrument with the capability to measure voltage, current and resistance.

N

NOx Oxides of Nitrogen. A common toxic pollutant emitted by petrol and diesel engines at higher temperatures.

O

Ohm The unit of electrical resistance. One volt applied to a resistance of one ohm will produce a current of one amp.

Ohmmeter An instrument for measuring electrical resistance.

O-ring A type of sealing ring made of a special rubber-like material; in use, the O-ring is compressed into a groove to provide the sealing action.

O-ring

Overhead cam (ohc) engine An engine with the camshaft(s) located on top of the cylinder head(s).

Overhead valve (ohv) engine An engine with the valves located in the cylinder head, but with the camshaft located in the engine block.

Oxygen sensor A device installed in the engine exhaust manifold, which senses the oxygen content in the exhaust and converts this information into an electric current. Also called a Lambda sensor.

P

Phillips screw A type of screw head having a cross instead of a slot for a corresponding type of screwdriver.

Plastigage A thin strip of plastic thread, available in different sizes, used for measuring clearances. For example, a strip of Plastigage is laid across a bearing journal. The parts are assembled and dismantled; the width of the crushed strip indicates the clearance between journal and bearing.

Plastigage

Propeller shaft The long hollow tube with universal joints at both ends that carries power from the transmission to the differential on front-engined rear wheel drive vehicles.

Proportioning valve A hydraulic control valve which limits the amount of pressure to the rear brakes during panic stops to prevent wheel lock-up.

R

Rack-and-pinion steering A steering system with a pinion gear on the end of the steering shaft that mates with a rack (think of a geared wheel opened up and laid flat). When the steering wheel is turned, the pinion turns, moving the rack to the left or right. This movement is transmitted through the track rods to the steering arms at the wheels.

Radiator A liquid-to-air heat transfer device designed to reduce the temperature of the coolant in an internal combustion engine cooling system.

Refrigerant Any substance used as a heat transfer agent in an air-conditioning system. R-12 has been the principle refrigerant for many years; recently, however, manufacturers have begun using R-134a, a non-CFC substance that is considered less harmful to the ozone in the upper atmosphere.

Rocker arm A lever arm that rocks on a shaft or pivots on a stud. In an overhead valve engine, the rocker arm converts the upward movement of the pushrod into a downward movement to open a valve.

Rotor In a distributor, the rotating device inside the cap that connects the centre electrode and the outer terminals as it turns, distributing the high voltage from the coil secondary winding to the proper spark plug. Also, that part of an alternator which rotates inside the stator. Also, the rotating assembly of a turbocharger, including the compressor wheel, shaft and turbine wheel.

Runout The amount of wobble (in-and-out movement) of a gear or wheel as it's rotated. The amount a shaft rotates "out-of-true." The out-of-round condition of a rotating part.

S

Sealant A liquid or paste used to prevent leakage at a joint. Sometimes used in conjunction with a gasket.

Sealed beam lamp An older headlight design which integrates the reflector, lens and filaments into a hermetically-sealed one-piece unit. When a filament burns out or the lens cracks, the entire unit is simply replaced.

Serpentine drivebelt A single, long, wide accessory drivebelt that's used on some newer vehicles to drive all the accessories, instead of a series of smaller, shorter belts. Serpentine drivebelts are usually tensioned by an automatic tensioner.

Serpentine drivebelt

Shim Thin spacer, commonly used to adjust the clearance or relative positions between two parts. For example, shims inserted into or under bucket tappets control valve clearances. Clearance is adjusted by changing the thickness of the shim.

Slide hammer A special puller that screws into or hooks onto a component such as a shaft or bearing; a heavy sliding handle on the shaft bottoms against the end of the shaft to knock the component free.

Sprocket A tooth or projection on the periphery of a wheel, shaped to engage with a chain or drivebelt. Commonly used to refer to the sprocket wheel itself.

Starter inhibitor switch On vehicles with an automatic transmission, a switch that prevents starting if the vehicle is not in Neutral or Park.

Strut See MacPherson strut.

T

Tappet A cylindrical component which transmits motion from the cam to the valve stem, either directly or via a pushrod and rocker arm. Also called a cam follower.

Thermostat A heat-controlled valve that regulates the flow of coolant between the cylinder block and the radiator, so maintaining optimum engine operating temperature. A thermostat is also used in some air cleaners in which the temperature is regulated.

Thrust bearing The bearing in the clutch assembly that is moved in to the release levers by clutch pedal action to disengage the clutch. Also referred to as a release bearing.

Timing belt A toothed belt which drives the camshaft. Serious engine damage may result if it breaks in service.

Timing chain A chain which drives the camshaft.

Toe-in The amount the front wheels are closer together at the front than at the rear. On rear wheel drive vehicles, a slight amount of toe-in is usually specified to keep the front wheels running parallel on the road by offsetting other forces that tend to spread the wheels apart.

Toe-out The amount the front wheels are closer together at the rear than at the front. On front wheel drive vehicles, a slight amount of toe-out is usually specified.

Tools For full information on choosing and using tools, refer to the *Haynes Automotive Tools Manual*.

Tracer A stripe of a second colour applied to a wire insulator to distinguish that wire from another one with the same colour insulator.

Tune-up A process of accurate and careful adjustments and parts replacement to obtain the best possible engine performance.

Turbocharger A centrifugal device, driven by exhaust gases, that pressurises the intake air. Normally used to increase the power output from a given engine displacement, but can also be used primarily to reduce exhaust emissions (as on VW's "Umwelt" Diesel engine).

U

Universal joint or U-joint A double-pivoted connection for transmitting power from a driving to a driven shaft through an angle. A U-joint consists of two Y-shaped yokes and a cross-shaped member called the spider.

V

Valve A device through which the flow of liquid, gas, vacuum, or loose material in bulk may be started, stopped, or regulated by a movable part that opens, shuts, or partially obstructs one or more ports or passageways. A valve is also the movable part of such a device.

Valve clearance The clearance between the valve tip (the end of the valve stem) and the rocker arm or tappet. The valve clearance is measured when the valve is closed.

Vernier caliper A precision measuring instrument that measures inside and outside dimensions. Not quite as accurate as a micrometer, but more convenient.

Viscosity The thickness of a liquid or its resistance to flow.

Volt A unit for expressing electrical "pressure" in a circuit. One volt that will produce a current of one ampere through a resistance of one ohm.

W

Welding Various processes used to join metal items by heating the areas to be joined to a molten state and fusing them together. For more information refer to the *Haynes Automotive Welding Manual*.

Wiring diagram A drawing portraying the components and wires in a vehicle's electrical system, using standardised symbols. For more information refer to the *Haynes Automotive Electrical and Electronic Systems Manual*.

Note: *References throughout this index are in the form* **"Chapter number"** • **"Page number"**. *So, for example, 2A•15 refers to page 15 of Chapter 2A.*

A

A-pillar trim – 12•19
Accelerator pedal – 4A•3
  position sensor – 4A•8
Accelerometer (ACE system) – 11•12
Accessory shops – REF•3
ACE actuator – 11•6, 11•11
  gaiter – 1•11
ACE electronic components – 11•12
ACE fluid – 0•15, 0•19
  pump – 11•11
ACE long arm – 11•6, 11•11
ACE system filter – 1•16
Acknowledgements – 0•5
Aerial amplifier – 13•17
Air conditioning system – 3•7, 3•8
Air filter – 1•13, 4A•3
Air pressure sensor – 4A•8
Air recirculation switch – 13•6
Air suspension
  air spring – 11•9
  compressor unit – 11•9
  intake filter – 1•15
Air temperature sensor – 3•10, 4A•8
Airbags – 0•6, 13•18, 13•19
  rotary contact unit – 13•20
Airflow sensor – 4A•8
Alarm system – 13•20
  handset battery – 1•13
Alternator – 5•3, 5•4

Ambient air pressure sensor – 4A•8
Ambient temperature sensor – 3•10
Amplifier – 13•16
Antifreeze – 0•15, 0•19, 1•14
Anti-lock braking system
  (ABS) – 10•13, 10•14
  wheel speed sensor harness – 1•10
Anti-roll bar – 11•5, 11•10
Anti-theft alarm system – 13•20
Asbestos – 0•6
Automatic transmission – 7B•1 *et seq*
  fault finding – REF•17
  fluid – 0•19, 1•12
  fluid filter – 7B•6
  selector illumination – 13•10
Auxiliary drivebelt – 1•9
Axle hub carrier – 9•4
Axle oil – 0•19, 1•10, 1•16
  oil seals – 9•5, 9•6

B

B-pillar trim – 12•19
Badges – 12•15
Battery – 0•6, 0•17, 5•2, 5•3
  alarm handset – 1•13
Big-end bearings – 2B•9
Bleeding
  brakes – 10•2
  clutch – 6•5
  fuel system – 4A•4
  power steering system – 11•17

Blower motor – 3•6, 3•10
  switch – 13•6
Body corrosion – REF•12
Body electrical systems – 13•1 *et seq*
Body under-panels – 12•15
Bodywork and fittings – 12•1 *et seq*
Bonnet – 12•5
Braking system – 1•9, 10•1 *et seq*, REF•9,
  REF•10, REF•11
  fault finding – REF•19
  fluid – 0•14, 0•19, 1•11
  pedal – 10•9
  seal – 1•16
Bulbs – 13•6, 13•9
Bumpers – 12•4
Burning – 0•6
Buying spare parts – REF•3

C

C-pillar trim – 12•19
Cabin air temperature sensor – 3•10
Cables
  automatic transmission selector – 7B•2
  bonnet release – 12•5
  handbrake – 10•12
  heater control – 3•6
  range selector – 7C•2
Calipers – 1•7, 10•6, 10•8
Camshaft – 2A•7
  oil seal – 2A•16
Carpets – 12•2, 12•19

Note: References throughout this index are in the form "Chapter number" • "Page number". So, for example, 2A•15 refers to page 15 of Chapter 2A.

Cassette player – 13•16
  anti-theft system – precautions – REF•6
CD autochanger – 13•16
CD/DVD player switch box – 13•16
Central locking – 12•13
  switch – 13•6
Centre console – 12•21
Centrifugal rotor – 1•6
Charging – 5•2, 5•3
Clock – 13•13
  illumination bulb – 13•10
Clutch – 6•1 *et seq*
  fault finding – REF•16
  fluid – 0•14, 0•19
  pedal – 6•5
  release mechanism – 6•3
Coil spring – 11•4, 11•7
Compression – 2A•3
Compressor – 3•8
Condenser – 3•8
  cooling fan – 3•9
Connecting rods – 2B•7, 2B•8, 2B•10
Console – 12•21
Conversion factors – REF•2
Coolant – 0•15, 0•19, 1•13
  pump – 3•4
  temperature gauge sender – 3•3
Cooling fan – 3•3, 3•9
Cooling, heating and ventilation
  systems – 3•1 *et seq*
  fault finding – REF•16
  hoses – 3•2
Courtesy light – 13•9
  switches – 13•6
Crankcase – 2B•7
  breather hose – 1•8
  emission control – 4B•1, 4B•2
Crankshaft – 2B•7, 2B•9, 2B•10
  oil seals – 2A•16
  position sensor – 4A•8
  pulley – 2A•5
  speed sensor – 4A•8
  spigot bush – 2A•17
Crushing – 0•6
Cup holder – 12•19
Cut-off switch – 4A•7
Cylinder block – 2B•7
Cylinder head – 2B•5, 2B•6, 2A•10
  cover – 2A•4

D

D-pillar trim – 12•19
Dents – 12•2
Diagnostic and control unit (DCU)
  airbag system – 13•19
Diesel injection equipment – 0•6
Differential – 9•7
  pinion oil seal – 9•5
Dimensions – REF•1
Direction indicators – 13•7, 13•8, 13•11
Directional control valve solenoid
  ACE system – 11•12
Discovery manual – 0•5
Discs – 1•7, 10•5, 10•6
Doors – 12•5, 12•6, 12•7, 12•9, REF•10

Drag link – 11•17, 11•18
Drivebelt – 1•9
Driveplate – 2A•16
Driveshafts – 9•2, 9•6, REF•11
  oil seal – 9•5
Drivetrain – 1•9
Drop arm – 11•16
Dump valve – 1•13
DVD screen player unit – 13•16

E

Earth fault – 13•3
Electric headlight-levelling system – 13•20
Electric seat switches – 13•6
Electric shock – 0•6
Electric window components – 12•14
  switches – 13•5
Electrical systems – 0•18, 1•8, REF•10
  fault finding – 13•2, REF•21, REF•22
Electronic control unit
  ABS – 10•14
  ACE system – 11•12
  airbag system – 13•19
  automatic transmission – 7B•5
  central locking – 12•13
  electric windows – 12•14
  fuel system – 4A•7
  parking distance control system – 13•20
  sunroof – 12•15
Emissions control
  systems – 4B•1 *et seq*, REF•12
Engine electrical systems – 5•1 *et seq*
Engine in-car repair
  procedures – 2A•1 *et seq*
  fault finding – REF•14, REF•15
Engine management electronic
  components – 4A•7
Engine oil – 0•13, 0•19, 1•6
Environmental considerations – REF•5
Evaporator – 3•9, 3•10
Exhaust emission control – 4B•2
Exhaust gas recirculation
  system – 4B•1, 4B•2
Exhaust manifold – 4A•11
Exhaust specialists – REF•3
Exhaust system – 1•10, 4A•11, REF•11, REF•12
Expansion valve – 3•9, 3•10

F

Facia panel assembly – 12•23
Fan – 3•3, 3•9
Fault finding – REF•13 *et seq*
  automatic transmission – REF•17
  braking system – REF•19
  clutch – REF•16
  cooling system – REF•16
  electrical system – 13•2, REF•21, REF•22
  engine – REF•14, REF•15
  front and rear axles – REF•18
  fuel and exhaust systems – REF•16
  manual gearbox – REF•17
  propeller shafts – REF•18
  suspension and steering – REF•20
  transfer gearbox – REF•18

Filling – 12•3
Filters
  ACE system – 1•16
  air – 1•13, 4A•3
  air suspension intake – 1•15
  automatic transmission fluid – 7B•6
  fuel – 1•12, 4A•8
  oil – 1•6
  servo – 1•16
Fire – 0•6
Fixed windows – 12•14
Fluid leaks – 1•7
Flywheel – 2A•16
Foglight – 13•8, 13•11
Front and rear axles – 9•1 *et seq*
  fault finding – REF•18
Front screen switch – 13•4
Front upper storage pocket – 12•21
Fuel and exhaust systems – 4A•1 *et seq*
  fault finding – REF•16
Fuel Burning Heater (FBH) – 3•7
Fuel cooler – 4A•4
Fuel cut-off switch – 4A•7
Fuel filler flap switch – 13•4
Fuel filter – 1•12
  water sensor – 4A•8
Fuel gauge sender unit – 4A•4
Fuel injectors – 4A•5
Fuel pressure regulator – 4A•7
Fuel pump – 4A•4
Fuel sedimenter – 1•9
Fuel system – REF•12
Fuel tank – 4A•5
Fuel temperature sensor – 4A•7
Fume or gas intoxication – 0•6
Fuses – 13•3

G

Gaiters
  ACE actuator – 1•11
  driveshaft – 9•2
Gashes – 12•3
Gaskets – REF•5
Gear selector indicator – 7B•3
General engine overhaul
  procedures – 2B•1 *et seq*
General repair procedures – REF•5
Glossary of technical terms – REF•24 *et seq*
Glovebox – 12•18
  illumination light bulb – 13•10
  illumination switch – 13•6
Glow plugs – 5•5
Grille – 12•24

H

Handbrake – 1•7, 10•11, 10•12, REF•9
  warning light switch – 13•5
Handles (door) – 12•7
Handset battery – 1•13
Hazard warning switch – 13•4
Headlight – 13•6, 13•10
  beam alignment – 13•12
  washer system – 13•15

Note: *References throughout this index are in the form "Chapter number" • "Page number". So, for example, 2A•15 refers to page 15 of Chapter 2A.*

Headlight-levelling system – 13•20
    switch – 13•5
Headlining – 12•19
Heated front screen switch – 13•4
Heated seat switches – 13•6
Heating system – 3•4
    blower motor – 3•6, 3•10
    control panel and cables – 3•6
    switch bulbs – 13•10
    switches – 13•6
    matrix – 3•6
Height sensor – 11•10
High-level stop-light – 13•8, 13•11
Hill descent switch – 13•4
Hinge lubrication – 1•8
Holes – 12•3
Horn – 13•13
Hoses – 1•8, 1•16, 3•2, 10•3
    leaks – 1•7
Hub and bearing – 9•4, 9•6
Hub carrier – 9•4
    balljoints – 9•5
Hydraulic adjusters – 2A•7
Hydrofluoric acid – 0•6

I

Identifying leaks – 0•9
Ignition switch – 11•13
Ignition transponder coil illumination bulb
    – 13•10
In-car entertainment systems – 13•16
    remote control switches – 13•18
Indicators – 13•7, 13•8, 13•11
    switch – 13•4
Inertia fuel cut-off switch – 4A•7
Injectors – 4A•5
    rocker shaft – 2A•9
Instruments – 1•8, 13•12, 13•13
    illumination – 13•9
    switches – 13•4
Intake air temperature sensor – 4A•8
Intake manifold – 4A•10
Intercooler – 1•10, 1•15, 4A•9

J

Jacking and vehicle support – REF•6
Joint mating faces – REF•5
Jump starting – 0•8

L

Leakdown tests – 2A•3
Leaks – 0•9, 1•7
Light units – 13•10
Lighting switch – 13•4
Locknuts, locktabs and washers – REF•5
Locks
    bonnet – 12•5
    central locking – 12•13
    door – 12•7
    lubrication – 1•8
    steering column – 11•13
    tailgate – 12•12
Long arm – 11•6

Lubricants and fluids – 0•19
Luggage compartment side trim
    panel – 12•20

M

Main bearings – 2B•9
Manifold absolute pressure sensor – 4A•8
Manifolds – 4A•10
Manual transmission – 7A•1 *et seq*
    fault finding – REF•17
    oil – 0•19, 1•9, 1•11
Mass airflow sensor – 4A•8
Master cylinder
    brake – 10•8
    clutch – 6•4
Matrix – 3•6
Mirrors – 12•14, REF•9
    switch – 13•5
Modulator assembly (ABS) – 10•14
MOT test checks – REF•9 *et seq*
Motor factors – REF•3
Mountings – 2A•18

N

Number plate light – 13•8, 13•11

O

Off-road suspension switch – 13•4
Oil automatic transmission – 1•12
Oil
    axles – 0•19, 1•10, 1•16
    engine – 0•13, 0•19, 1•6
    manual gearbox – 0•19, 1•9, 1•11
    transfer gearbox – 0•19, 1•9, 1•12
Oil cooler – 2A•17, 7B•5
Oil filter – 1•6
Oil pressure switch – 2A•18
Oil pump – 2A•14
Oil seals – 2A•16, 9•5, 9•6, REF•5
    valve stem – 2B•6
Open-circuit – 13•3

P

Pads – 1•7, 10•4, 10•5
Panhard rod – 11•4
Parking distance control system – 13•20
Parts – REF•3
Passenger cabin air temperature sensor
    – 3•10
Pedals
    accelerator – 4A•3, 4A•8
    brake – 10•9
    clutch – 6•5
Pipes – 10•3
Pistons – 2B•7, 2B•8, 2B•10
Plastic components – 12•4
Poisonous or irritant substances – 0•6
Power amplifier – 13•16

Power steering fluid – 0•15, 0•19
Power steering pump – 11•16
Preheating system – 5•5
Pressure control valve solenoid
    ACE system – 11•13
Pressure transducer (ACE system) – 11•12
Priming and bleeding fuel system – 4A•4
Propeller shafts – 1•11, 8•1 *et seq*
    fault finding – REF•18
    joint – 1•10
Puncture repair – 0•10

Q

Quarter-light – 12•11

R

Radiator – 1•10, 3•2
    grille – 12•24
Radio – 13•16
    anti-theft system – precautions – REF•6
Radius arm – 11•5, 11•8
Range selector cable – 7C•2
Rear light cluster – 13•8, 13•11
Receiver/drier – 3•8
Regulator (window glass) – 12•9
Relays – 13•4
Release bearing (clutch) – 6•3
Repair procedures – REF•5
Respraying – 12•3
Reversing light switch – 7A•2
Ride height sensor – 11•10
    harness – 1•11
Road test – 1•8
Roadside repairs – 0•7 *et seq*
Rocker arms – 2A•7
Rocker shaft – 2A•9
Routine maintenance – bodywork and
    underframe – 12•2
Routine maintenance – upholstery
    and carpets – 12•2
*Routine maintenance &
    servicing* – 1•1 *et seq*

S

Safety first! – 0•6, 0•14, 0•15
Scalding – 0•6
Scratches – 12•2
Screen washer fluid – 0•14
Screw threads and fastenings – REF•5
Seat belts – 1•11, 12•17
Seats – 12•15, 12•16
    switches – 13•6
Selector – 7B•2
    illumination – 13•10
    indicator – 7B•3
Servo unit – 10•10
    filter – 1•16
Shock absorbers – 11•3, 11•7, REF•10,
    REF•11
Shoes – 10•11
Short-circuit – 13•3
Sidelight – 13•7
Slave cylinder (clutch) – 6•4

Note: *References throughout this index are in the form "**Chapter number**" • "**Page number**". So, for example, 2A•15 refers to page 15 of Chapter 2A.*

Sounder (parking distance control system) – 13•20
Spare parts – REF•3
Speakers – 13•17, 13•18
Spigot bush – 2A•17
Springs – 11•4, 11•7, REF•11
Sprockets and guides – 2A•6
Starter inhibitor switch – 7B•3
Starter motor – 5•4,5•5
Starting system – 5•4
Start-up after overhaul – 2B•11
Steering – 1•8, REF•10, REF•11
  angles – 11•19
Steering box – 1•15, 11•15
  drop arm – 11•16
Steering column – 11•14, REF•9
  intermediate shaft – 11•15
  lock – 11•13
  universal joint – 11•15
Steering damper – 11•17
Steering wheel – 11•13, REF•9
Stiffener plate – 2A•14
Stop-light – 13•8, 13•11
  switch – 10•13
Sump – 2A•13
Sunlight sensor – 3•10
Sunroof – 12•14, 12•15
  switch – 13•5
Suspension and steering – 1•8, 11•1 *et seq*, REF•10, REF•11
  fault finding – REF•20
Switches – 13•4
  central locking – 12•13
  fuel cut-off – 4A•7
  heater control – 13•10
  ICE remote control – 13•18
  ignition – 11•13
  illumination bulbs – 13•10
  oil pressure – 2A•18
  reversing light – 7A•2
  starter inhibitor – 7B•3
  stop-light – 10•13

T

Tailgate – 12•12
  washer system – 13•15
  window – 12•14
  wiper motor – 13•14
Tappets – 2A•7
Temperature gauge sender – 3•3
Temperature sensor – 3•10, 4A•7, 4A•8
Thermistor – 3•9
Thermostat – 3•3
Timing chain, sprockets and guides – 2A•6
  chain cover – 2A•6
Tools and working facilities – REF•5, REF•7 *et seq*
Top dead centre (TDC) for No 1 piston location – 2A•4
Towing – 0•11
Towing bracket – 1•11
Track rod – 11•18
Transfer gearbox – 7C•1 *et seq*
  fault finding – REF•18
  oil – 0•19
Transfer gearbox oil – 1•9, 1•12
Transponder coil illumination bulb – 13•10
Trim panels – 12•6, 12•15, 12•18
Turbocharger – 4A•8, 4A•9
Tyres – REF•12
  condition and pressure – 0•16
  pressures – 0•19
  specialists – REF•3

U

Ultrasonic sensors
  parking distance control system – 13•20
Underbonnet check points – 0•12
Underframe – 12•2
Under-panels – 12•15
Upholstery – 12•2
Upper storage pocket – 12•21

V

Vacuum pump – 10•13
Vacuum servo unit – 10•10
  filter – 1•16
Valves – 2B•5
  springs – 2B•6
  stem oil seals – 2B•6
Vehicle identification – REF•4, REF•10
Ventilation system – 3•4

W

Warning lights – 13•9
Washer fluid – 0•14
Washer jets – 13•15, 13•16
Washer pump – 13•15
Washer system reservoir – 13•15
Water sensor (fuel filter) – 4A•8
Watts linkage – 11•8
Weekly checks – 0•12 *et seq*
Weights – REF•1
Wheels – REF•12
  alignment – 11•19
  bearings – REF•11
  changing – 0•10
Wheel arch liners – 12•15
Wheel sensor (ABS) – 10•14, 10•15
  harness – 1•10
Windows – 12•14
  glass and regulator – 12•9
  lift motor – 12•14
  switches – 13•5
Windscreen – 12•14, REF•9
  washer system – 13•15
  wiper motor and linkage – 13•13
Wiper arm – 13•13
Wiper blades – 0•18
Wiper motor and linkage – 13•13, 13•14
Wiper/washer switch – 13•4
Wiring diagrams – 13•21 *et seq*
Working facilities – REF•7

Haynes Manuals – The Complete UK Car List

Title	Book No.
ALFA ROMEO Alfasud/Sprint (74 - 88) up to F *	0292
Alfa Romeo Alfetta (73 – 87) up to E *	0531
AUDI 80, 90 & Coupe Petrol (79 – Nov 88) up to F	0605
Audi 80, 90 & Coupe Petrol (Oct 86 – 90) D to H	1491
Audi 100 & A6 Petrol & Diesel (May 91 – May 97) H to P	3504
Audi A3 Petrol & Diesel (96 – May 03) P to 03	4253
Audi A3 Petrol & Diesel (June 03 – Mar 08) 03 to 08	4884
Audi A4 Petrol & Diesel (95 – 00) M to X	3575
Audi A4 Petrol & Diesel (01 – 04) X to 54	4609
Audi A4 Petrol & Diesel (Jan 05 – Feb 08) 54 to 57	4885
AUSTIN A35 & A40 (56 – 67) up to F *	0118
Mini (59 – 69) up to H *	0527
Mini (69 – 01) up to X	0646
Austin Healey 100/6 & 3000 (56 – 68) up to G *	0049
BEDFORD/Vauxhall Rascal & Suzuki Supercarry (86 – Oct 94) C to M	3015
BMW 1-Series 4-cyl Petrol & Diesel (04 – Aug 11) 54 to 11	4918
BMW 316, 320 & 320i (4-cyl)(75 – Feb 83) up to Y *	0276
BMW 3- & 5- Series Petrol (81 – 91) up to J	1948
BMW 3-Series Petrol (Apr 91 – 99) H to V	3210
BMW 3-Series Petrol (Sept 98 – 06) S to 56	4067
BMW 3-Series Petrol & Diesel (05 – Sept 08) 54 to 58	4782
BMW 5-Series 6-cyl Petrol (April 96 – Aug 03) N to 03	4151
BMW 5-Series Diesel (Sept 03 – 10) 53 to 10	4901
BMW 1500, 1502, 1600, 1602, 2000 & 2002 (59 – 77) up to S *	0240
CHRYSLER PT Cruiser Petrol (00-09) W to 09	4058
CITROEN 2CV, Ami & Dyane (67 – 90) up to H	0196
Citroen AX Petrol & Diesel (87- 97) D to P	3014
Citroen Berlingo & Peugeot Partner Petrol & Diesel (96 – 10) P to 60	4281
Citroen C1 Petrol (05 – 11) 05 to 11	4922
Citroen C2 Petrol & Diesel (03 – 10) 53 to 60	5635
Citroen C3 Petrol & Diesel (02 – 09) 51 to 59	4890
Citroen C4 Petrol & Diesel (04 – 10) 54 to 60	5576
Citroen C5 Petrol & Diesel (01 – 08) Y to 08	4745
Citroen C15 Van Petrol & Diesel (89 – Oct 98) F to S	3509
Citroen CX Petrol (75 – 88) up to F	0528
Citroen Saxo Petrol & Diesel (96 – 04) N to 54	3506
Citroen Xantia Petrol & Diesel (93 – 01) K to Y	3082
Citroen XM Petrol & Diesel (89 – 00) G to X	3451
Citroen Xsara Petrol & Diesel (97 – Sept 00) R to W	3751
Citroen Xsara Picasso Petrol & Diesel (00 – 02) W to 52	3944
Citroen Xsara Picasso (Mar 04 – 08) 04 to 58	4784
Citroen ZX Diesel (91 – 98) J to S	1922
Citroen ZX Petrol (91 – 98) H to S	1881
FIAT 126 (73 – 87) up to E *	0305
Fiat 500 (57 – 73) up to M *	0090
Fiat 500 & Panda (04 – 12) 53 to 61	5558
Fiat Bravo & Brava Petrol (95 – 00) N to W	3572
Fiat Cinquecento (93 – 98) K to R	3501
Fiat Grande Punto, Punto Evo & Punto Petrol (06 – 15) 55 to 15	5956
Fiat Panda (81 – 95) up to M	0793
Fiat Punto Petrol & Diesel (94 – Oct 99) L to V	3251
Fiat Punto Petrol (Oct 99 – July 03) V to 03	4066
Fiat Punto Petrol (03 – 07) 03 to 07	4746
Fiat Punto Petrol (Oct 99 – 07) V to 07	5634
Fiat X1/9 (74 – 89) up to G *	0273
FORD Anglia (59 – 68) up to G *	0001
Ford Capri II (& III) 1.6 & 2.0 (74 – 87) up to E *	0283
Ford Capri II (& III) 2.8 & 3.0 V6 (74 – 87) up to E	1309
Ford C-Max Petrol & Diesel (03 – 10) 53 to 60	4900
Ford Escort Mk I 1100 & 1300 (68 – 74) up to N *	0171
Ford Escort Mk I Mexico, RS 1600 & RS 2000 (70 – 74) up to N *	0139
Ford Escort Mk II Mexico, RS 1800 & RS 2000 (75 – 80) up to W *	0735
Ford Escort (75 – Aug 80) up to V *	0280
Ford Escort Petrol (Sept 80 – Sept 90) up to H	0686
Ford Escort & Orion Petrol (Sept 90 – 00) H to X	1737
Ford Escort & Orion Diesel (Sept 90 – 00) H to X	4081
Ford Fiesta Petrol (Feb 89 – Oct 95) F to N	1595
Ford Fiesta Petrol & Diesel (Oct 95 – Mar 02) N to 02	3397
Ford Fiesta Petrol & Diesel (Apr 02 – 08) 02 to 58	4170
Ford Fiesta Petrol & Diesel (08 – 11) 58 to 11	4907
Ford Focus Petrol & Diesel (98 – 01) S to Y	3759
Ford Focus Petrol & Diesel (Oct 01 – 05) 51 to 05	4167
Ford Focus Petrol (05 – 11) 54 to 61	4785
Ford Focus Diesel (05 – 11) 54 to 61	4807
Ford Focus Petrol & Diesel (11 – 14) 60 to 14	5632
Ford Fusion Petrol & Diesel (02 – 11) 02 to 61	5566
Ford Galaxy Petrol & Diesel (95 – Aug 00) M to W	3984
Ford Galaxy Petrol & Diesel (00 – 06) X to 06	5556
Ford Granada Petrol (Sept 77 – Feb 85) up to B *	0481
Ford Ka (96 – 08) P to 58	5567
Ford Ka Petrol (09 – 14) 58 to 14	5637
Ford Mondeo Petrol (93 – Sept 00) K to X	1923
Ford Mondeo Petrol & Diesel (Oct 00 – Jul 03) X to 03	3990
Ford Mondeo Petrol & Diesel (July 03 – 07) 03 to 56	4619
Ford Mondeo Petrol & Diesel (Apr 07 – 12) 07 to 61	5548
Ford Mondeo Diesel (93 – Sept 00) L to X	3465
Ford Transit Connect Diesel (02 – 11) 02 to 11	4903
Ford Transit Diesel (Feb 86 – 99) C to T	3019
Ford Transit Diesel (00 – Oct 06) X to 56	4775
Ford Transit Diesel (Nov 06 – 13) 56 to 63	5629
Ford 1.6 & 1.8 litre Diesel Engine (84 – 96) A to N	1172
HILLMAN Imp (63 – 76) up to R *	0022
HONDA Civic (Feb 84 – Oct 87) A to E	1226
Honda Civic (Nov 91 – 96) J to N	3199
Honda Civic Petrol (Mar 95 – 00) M to X	4050
Honda Civic Petrol & Diesel (01 – 05) X to 55	4611
Honda CR-V Petrol & Diesel (02 – 06) 51 to 56	4747
Honda Jazz (02 to 08) 51 to 58	4735
JAGUAR E-Type (61 – 72) up to L *	0140
Jaguar Mk I & II, 240 & 340 (55 – 69) up to H *	0098
Jaguar XJ6, XJ & Sovereign, Daimler Sovereign (68 – Oct 86) up to D	0242
Jaguar XJ6 & Sovereign (Oct 86 – Sept 94) D to M	3261
Jaguar XJ12, XJS & Sovereign, Daimler Double Six (72 – 88) up to F	0478
Jaguar X Type Petrol & Diesel (01 – 10) V to 60	5631
JEEP Cherokee Petrol (93 – 96) K to N	1943
LAND ROVER 90, 110 & Defender Diesel (83 – 07) up to 56	3017
Land Rover Discovery Petrol & Diesel (89 – 98) G to S	3016
Land Rover Discovery Diesel (Nov 98 – Jul 04) S to 04	4606
Land Rover Discovery Diesel (Aug 04 – Apr 09) 04 to 09	5562
Land Rover Freelander Petrol & Diesel (97 – Sept 03) R to 53	3929
Land Rover Freelander (97 – Oct 06) R to 56	5571
Land Rover Freelander Diesel (Nov 06 – 14) 56 to 64	5636
Land Rover Series II, IIA & III 4-cyl Petrol (58 – 85) up to C	0314
Land Rover Series II, IIA & III Petrol & Diesel (58 – 85) up to C	5568
MAZDA 323 (Mar 81 – Oct 89) up to G	1608
Mazda 323 (Oct 89 – 98) G to R	3455
Mazda B1600, B1800 & B2000 Pick-up Petrol (72 – 88) up to F	0267
Mazda MX-5 (89 – 05) G to 05	5565
Mazda RX-7 (79 – 85) up to C *	0460
MERCEDES-BENZ 190, 190E & 190D Petrol & Diesel (83 – 93) A to L	3450
Mercedes-Benz 200D, 240D, 240TD, 300D & 300TD 123 Series Diesel (Oct 76 – 85) up to C	1114
Mercedes-Benz 250 & 280 (68 – 72) up to L *	0346
Mercedes-Benz 250 & 280 123 Series Petrol (Oct 76 – 84) up to B *	0677
Mercedes-Benz 124 Series Petrol & Diesel (85 – Aug 93) C to K	3253
Mercedes-Benz A-Class Petrol & Diesel (98 – 04) S to 54	4748
Mercedes-Benz C-Class Petrol & Diesel (93 – Aug 00) L to W	3511
Mercedes-Benz C-Class (00 – 07) X to 07	4780
Mercedes-Benz E-Class Diesel (Jun 02 – Feb 10) 02 to 59	5710
Mercedes-Benz Sprinter Diesel (95 – Apr 06) M to 06	4902
MGA (55 – 62)	0475
MGB (62 – 80) up to W	0111
MGB 1962 to 1980 (special edition) *	4894
MG Midget & Austin-Healey Sprite (58 – 80) up to W *	0265
MINI Petrol (July 01 – 06) Y to 56	4273
MINI Petrol & Diesel (Nov 06 – 13) 56 to 13	4904
MITSUBISHI Shogun & L200 Pick-ups Petrol (83 – 94) up to M	1944
MORRIS Minor 1000 (56 – 71) up to K	0024
NISSAN Almera Petrol (95 – Feb 00) N to V	4053
Nissan Almera & Tino Petrol (Feb 00 – 07) V to 56	4612
Nissan Micra (83 – Jan 93) up to K	0931
Nissan Micra (93 – 02) K to 52	3254
Nissan Micra Petrol (03 – Oct 10) 52 to 60	4734
Nissan Primera Petrol (90 - Aug 99) H to T	1851
Nissan Qashqai Petrol & Diesel (07 – 12) 56 to 62	5610
OPEL Ascona & Manta (B-Series) (Sept 75 – 88) up to F *	0316
Opel Ascona Petrol (81 – 88)	3215
Opel Ascona Petrol (Oct 91 – Feb 98)	3156
Opel Corsa Petrol (83 – Mar 93)	3160
Opel Corsa Petrol (Mar 93 – 97)	3159
Opel Kadett Petrol (Oct 84 – Oct 91)	3196
Opel Omega & Senator Petrol (Nov 86 – 94)	3157
Opel Vectra Petrol (Oct 88 – Oct 95)	3158
PEUGEOT 106 Petrol & Diesel (91 – 04) J to 53)	1882
Peugeot 107 Petrol (05 – 11) 05 to 11)	4923
Peugeot 205 Petrol (83 – 97) A to P	0932

* Classic reprint

Chapter 4 Part B:
Emissions control systems

Contents

	Section number		Section number
Emissions control systems – testing and component renewal	2	General information	1

Degrees of difficulty

Easy, suitable for novice with little experience	**Fairly easy,** suitable for beginner with some experience	**Fairly difficult,** suitable for competent DIY mechanic	**Difficult,** suitable for experienced DIY mechanic	**Very difficult,** suitable for expert DIY or professional

Specifications

General

Emission standard:
Engine Serial No prefixes 10P to 14.	PEU2
Engine Serial No prefixes 15P to 19.	PEU3

Torque wrench settings	**Nm**	**lbf ft**
EGR delivery pipe bolts	10	7
EGR valve securing bolts	10	7

1 General information

In order to reduce harmful emissions from the engine, an EGR (Exhaust Gas Recirculation) system and a crankcase emission control system are fitted. The EGR system allows a controlled amount of the exhaust gases to combine with the fresh air entering the intake system. This reduces the combustion temperature by slowing the fuel-burn rate, which results in lower NO2 emissions. The flow of exhaust gases into the intake manifold is controlled by the engine management ECM via solenoid valves which control the flow of vacuum to a diaphragm attached to the EGR valve. The crankcase emission control system allows vapour and gases from the crankcase to pass through an oil separator plate in the cylinder head cover, then through a breather hose into the intake ducting to be burnt during the combustion process. A depression limiting valve is fitted to the end of the breather hose, which limits the depression in the crankcase as the engine speed increases.

 Warning: It is necessary to take certain precautions when working on the fuel system components, particularly the fuel injectors. Before carrying out any operations on the fuel system, refer to the precautions given in "Safety first!" at the beginning of this manual, and to any additional warning notes at the start of the relevant Sections. Absolute cleanliness is essential when working on the fuel system – do not allow dirt to enter when any part of the system is disconnected.

Crankcase emission control

A crankcase ventilation system is fitted to all models.

Oil fumes and piston blow-by gases (combustion gases which have passed by the piston rings) are drawn from the crankcase/cylinder head cover through an oil separator, into the air intake tract. The gases are then drawn into the engine together with fresh air/fuel mixture. Condensed oil vapour is returned from the main oil separator to the engine sump.

Exhaust gas recirculation system

The system is designed to recirculate small quantities of exhaust gas into the intake tract, and therefore into the combustion process. This process reduces the level of oxides of nitrogen present in the final exhaust gas which is released into the atmosphere, and also lowers the combustion temperature.

The volume of exhaust gas recirculated is controlled by vacuum, via a solenoid valve. The solenoid valve is controlled by the engine management ECM.

A vacuum-operated recirculation valve is fitted to the exhaust manifold, to regulate the quantity of exhaust gas recirculated. The valve is operated by the vacuum supplied via the solenoid valve.

Between idle speed and a predetermined engine load, power is supplied to the solenoid valve, which allows the recirculation valve to open. Under full-load conditions, the exhaust gas recirculation is cut off. Additional control is provided by the colant temperature sensor, which cuts off the vacuum supply until the coolant temperature reaches 40°C, preventing the recirculation valve from opening during the engine warm-up period.

2 Emissions control systems
– testing and component renewal

Crankcase emission control

Testing

1 If the system is thought to be faulty, firstly, check that the hoses are unobstructed. On high-mileage vehicles, particularly those regularly used for short journeys, a jelly-like deposit may be evident inside the system hoses and oil separator. If excessive deposits are present, the relevant component(s) should be removed and cleaned.

2 Periodically inspect the system components for security and damage, and renew them as necessary. Note that damaged or loose hoses can cause various engine running problems (erratic idle speed, stalling, etc) which can be difficult to trace.

Component renewal

3 Renewal procedures for the hoses and oil separator are self-evident.

Exhaust emission control

Testing

4 The system can only be tested accurately using a suitable exhaust gas analyser (suitable for use with diesel engines).

Component renewal

5 The catalytic converter is integral with the exhaust system front section.

2.10 EGR valve vacuum hose (arrowed)

6 Removal and refitting are described in Chapter 4A.

EGR valve

Testing

7 Testing of the EGR valve should be entrusted to a Land Rover dealer or suitably-equipped specialist.

Removal

8 Disconnect the battery negative lead, as described in Chapter 5.

9 Undo the 3 bolts and remove the plastic cover from the top of the engine.

10 Disconnect the vacuum hose from the EGR valve **(see illustration)**.

11 Slacken the clip and disconnect the air intake hose from the EGR valve.

12 Undo the 4 bolts and detach the EGR valve from the intake manifold **(see illustration)**. Discard the gasket.

2.12 Undo the 4 bolts securing the EGR valve (arrowed)

13 Remove the 2 bolts and release the EGR valve clip from the cylinder head.

14 Release the 2 Allen screws and detach the EGR pipe from the exhaust manifold.

Refitting

15 Refitting is a reversal of removal, but use new gaskets when refitting the valve and reconnecting the delivery pipe.

EGR modulator valve

16 Two different types of modulator are fitted: Type 1 has a single modulator, and Type 2 has two modulators. On both systems, the modulator valves are mounted on a plate on the right-hand side of the engine compartment **(see illustrations)**.

17 Removal and refitting of the valve(s) should be self-evident, but note the fitted locations of the vacuum hoses prior to removal.

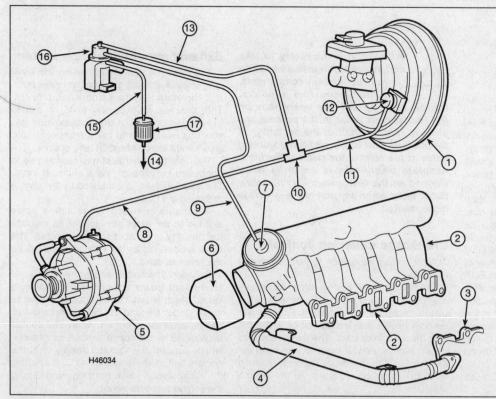

2.16a Type 1 EGR system

1 Brake servo
2 Intake manifold
3 Exhaust manifold
4 EGR pipe
5 Vacuum pump/alternator assembly
6 Intake hose from intercooler
7 EGR valve assembly
8 Hose to vacuum pump
9 Vacuum hose to EGR valve suction port (blue)
10 T-piece
11 Vacuum hose to brake servo
12 Non-return valve
13 Vacuum hose (light brown)
14 To atmosphere
15 Vent hose – EGR modulator-to-in line filter (green)
16 EGR modulator
17 In-line filter

H46034

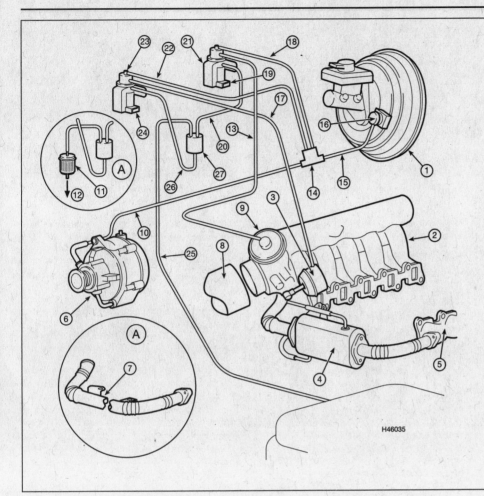

2.16b Type 2 EGR system

1   Brake servo
2   Intake manifold
3   ILT valve
4   EGR cooler – EU3 models
5   Exhaust manifold
6   Alternator/vacuum pump assembly
7   EGR pipe – EU2 models
8   Air intake hose from the intercooler
9   EGR valve
10 Vacuum hose to pump
11 In-line filter
12 To atmosphere
13 Vacuum hose to EGR valve suction
    port (blue)
14 T-piece
15 Vacuum hose to brake servo
16 Non-return valve
17 Vacuum hose to ILT valve suction
    port (blue)
18 EGR modulator vacuum hose (brown)
19 EGR modulator electrical connection
20 Vent hose – EGR modulator to in-line
    filter (green)
21 EGR valve modulator
22 ILT modulator vacuum hose (brown)
23 ILT valve modulator
24 ILT modulator wiring connector
    (green)
25 Vent hose to air cleaner
26 Vent hose – ILT valve modulator to
    in-line filter (green)
27 3-way connector
A = pre-EU3 emission standard

H46035

Notes